Planning for Rites and Rituals

A Resource for Episcopal Worship, Year A, 2019–2020

Planning for Rites and Rituals

A Resource for Episcopal Worship, Year A, 2019–2020

CHURCH
PUBLISHING
INCORPORATED

Church Publishing Incorporated
19 East 34th Street
New York, NY 10016

Cover design by: Jennifer Kopec, 2 Pug Design
Typeset by: Linda Brooks

A record of this book is available from the Library of Congress.

ISBN: 9781640652033 (pbk.)

Contents

Lent

Holy Week

Easter

Pentecost

Welcome

Welcome to Year A, 2019-2020 of *Planning for Rites and Rituals*. All of us at Church Publishing are pleased to bring you this resource for liturgical planning.

CPI's editorial team (Milton Brasher-Cunningham, Sharon Ely Pearson, and Nancy Bryan), tasked with creating this volume, worked with some amazing folks to bring you a wide range of thought-provoking, creative options for Sundays and holy days throughout the liturgical year. Looking for ways to engage a range of ages? It's here. Looking for help "seeing" the images in each week's scripture? We've got that. Want hymns keyed to the lectionary or brief introductions to the scriptures? It's all here, in a single resource.

You will find this resource offers planning suggestions grouped by liturgical season and date. Each section of the book opens with an overview of the liturgical calendar, as well as *Seasonal Rites*, which offers a number of expansive ideas for worship in and outside the primary Sunday service. Specific suggestions for every Sunday and holy day follow, offering a variety of material for the liturgy as well as ideas for formation and community engagement within and beyond your church doors.

Dozens of individuals were part of the creation of this all-in-one volume. Priests, educators, musicians, members of Altar Guilds, and many others are featured within these pages. Our intention is to provide a similar mix of established writers and new voices—those working in small parishes and those in larger ones, those in rural locales and those in cities, clergy and lay—in each successive volume of this resource over the years to come.

Here is a description of the areas to deepen themes of each Sunday and holy day, along with those who have contributed their creative ideas this year:

- *Preaching the Gospel for Year A* was written by **Micah T. J. Jackson**, president of Bexley Seabury Seminary. The *Preparing for* seasonal overviews were written by **Marcus Halley**, rector of St. Paul's Church on Lake of the Isles in Minneapolis. The *Weekday Commemorations* were written by **Martha Baker**, writer, editor, and educator in St. Louis, Missouri.

- *Engaging All Ages* offers ideas for enriching all ages in their engagement with worship (children, youth, and adults). They include thoughts for the congregation to take home and discuss, things to notice or highlight during worship (colors, senses, symbols, gestures), and ideas for action. Contributors for these portions are: **Jerusalem Jackson Greer**, Staff Officer for Evangelism for the Episcopal Church; **Sharon Ely Pearson**, a Christian educator from Norwalk, Connecticut; and **Patrick Kangrga**, associate for youth ministries at Trinity Episcopal Church in Menlo Park, California.

- *Prayers of the People* are the offerings of **Geralyn Wolf**, assistant bishop in the diocese of Long Island, and first appeared as *Intercessions for Year A*, available from Church Publishing.

- *Ideas for the Day* approach the day and its text in preaching and worship, including contemporary issues, movies, technology and social media, literature, historical events, and figures related to the Sunday lections and season. Contributing these ideas are: **Jane A. Gober**, interim rector of Grace Episcopal Church in Pemberton, New Jersey; **Victoria Garvey**, biblical scholar and educator in Chicago; **Ernesto Medina**, recently retired rector of St. Martha's Episcopal Church in Papillion, Nebraska; **Jay Fluellen**, composer, organist, and choir director of the African American Episcopal Church of St. Thomas in Philadelphia; **Anna V. Ostenso Moore**, associate priest for Family Ministry at St. Mark's Cathedral in Minneapolis; and **Sharon Ely Pearson**, Christian educator from Norwalk, Connecticut.

♦ *Making Connections* offers insights into connecting our Episcopal tradition to each Sunday. These may take the form of referencing other areas of the Book of Common Prayer, our Baptismal Covenant, or faith in daily life. Contributors here are: **Lelanda Lee,** a writer, poet, and church and community leader in Longmont, Colorado; **Molly F. James,** deputy executive officer of the General Convention; and **Heidi J. A. Carter,** lay minister associate at St. Paul's Episcopal Church in Kansas City, Missouri.

♦ *Images in the Readings* tap into the metaphors, names, history, and theology that are found in the day's lections. **Gail Ramshaw**, well-known Lutheran scholar and author, is the source of those connections. *Hymns for the Day* are drawn from **Carl Daw, Jr**. and **Thomas Pavlechko**'s *Liturgical Music for the Revised Common Lectionary, Year A* (Church Publishing Incorporated, 2009). These complement the theme and readings of the day and come from *Hymnal 1982, Lift Every Voice and Sing II*, and *Wonder, Love, and Praise*.

Your feedback and perspective, of course, are also critical to these efforts. Let us hear from you—what would you appreciate seeing? What was most helpful? Who are the writers you would recommend to us for future editions?

We are also delighted to offer a new digital resource, RitePlanning, which has been designed to work with the resources in this volume. A trial subscription is available through the Church Publishing website (**https://www.churchpublishing. org/riteplanning**).

Thank you for the trust you put in Church Publishing Incorporated to provide liturgical planning tools for your parish use. We value our partnership on the journey and are grateful for the many ways in which you care for the church's worship.

Welcome

Preaching the Gospel According to Matthew

Every Gospel portrays Jesus in a slightly different way. This is not a problem to be resolved but a gift to be enjoyed. Throughout Year A of the lectionary, preachers have the opportunity to help their hearers get to know Jesus the way Matthew saw him—a master storyteller, concerned about the way God's people should live, and a fulfillment of the Torah and ancient prophecy. Each of these themes weaves in and out of Matthew's Gospel and gives preachers a way to engage with this way of understanding Jesus and his message.

One prominent feature of Matthew's Gospel is Jesus' use of parables. Depending on the exact definition of a parable, there are about three dozen of them in the Gospels. About twenty appear in the Gospel of Matthew. Of those, thirteen are on the menu for Year A. They come together in three chunks, one in late July, one in September/October, and one in November, right before Advent begins.

These brief forays into the parables give a preacher an opportunity to show the way that narrative can illuminate the Gospel. For preachers who are comfortable using stories, these weeks are a good time to do some "updating" of the imagery. For many contemporary Christians, Jesus' reliance on agricultural metaphors or parables that assume the economic world of his time can mean that they don't deliver the "punch" they would have to their original hearers. Updating the Parable of the Sower to tell of a Silicon Valley venture capitalist who invests in all who come to her might make the point a little clearer. This work, while creative and sometimes difficult, can give the hearers more of a handle on the underlying message than simply saying how much a talent of silver is worth is today's dollars.

Matthew's Gospel is the only one to use the word "church," and it was influential in the development of the early Christian communities. It remains so today. For example, it is in Matthew's Gospel that the baptismal formula appears (28:19, Trinity Sunday). The most familiar version of the Lord's Prayer also appears in Matthew (though, surprisingly, not in Year A's Sunday lectionary).

Matthew calls this way of life the "Kingdom of Heaven" (or less commonly, the Kingdom of God). This expression is used to show how the world would look for those who live under God's rule. For Matthew and his community, the Kingdom of Heaven is not only a future hope, but a present reality, seen in the healings and miracles of Jesus and in the radical love and justice practiced by Jesus' followers.

Contemporary preachers can follow Matthew's example by showing the ways in which Jesus' healing ministry is being extended today through the work of the Church. Also, preachers can illustrate the kingdom by looking for and highlighting the ways that the Church embodies the teachings of Jesus through acts of hospitality, justice, and love. Hearers will appreciate seeing how the actions they and their neighbors are taking are bringing truth and form to the prayer of "thy Kingdom come."

A third important concern for Matthew is that Jesus is an heir to King David, the fulfillment of ancient prophecy, and the Son of God. To show this, Matthew begins with Jesus' earthly genealogy, beginning with Abraham. The genealogy itself does not appear in the Sunday lectionary, but on Advent 4, preachers will have a chance to talk about Jesus as a fulfillment of Isaiah's prophecy as shown by the angel's message to Joseph. Indeed, Matthew's Gospel portrays Jesus as fulfilling many Old Testament prophecies about the Messiah. These are often highlighted by saying "this was to fulfill what had been spoken through the prophet" and similar formulations. Throughout the year, preachers will have many chances to connect Jesus to messianic prophecy.

Preaching the Gospel

For Matthew, Jesus is also the Son of God. And it's not only a few who realize it. The Devil (Lent 1), the demons sent into the swine (8:29, not on any Sunday), the disciples (Proper 14), the High Priest, some in the crowd, and the centurion (Palm Sunday) all recognize him as God's son. Clearly this is an important theological claim for Matthew's community, and for us today. Interestingly, Jesus refers to himself some thirty times as the "Son of Man." Scholars have offered various explanations for the difference in emphasis. It's a thorny problem in the world of christology, but perhaps it's not a concern that should be addressed from the pulpit, unless your community seems to be asking about it.

All this talk about Jesus as heir to King David and fulfilling ancient prophecy, not to mention all the passages in Matthew's Gospel that address the Jewish leadership and the Jewish Law, require that I mention the dangers of supercessionism and anti-Judaism. Throughout history, Matthew's Gospel has been used to suggest that Christians have supplanted the Jewish community as God's chosen people and have blamed the Jewish community for Christ's death. This has had terrible (sometimes fatal) consequences for Jews and has damaged Jewish-Christian relations. Though it is solid Christian theology to show Jesus as the Messiah and the fulfillment of prophecy, preachers should be careful not to employ (and might consider expressly rejecting) interpretations that perpetuate these anti-semitic stereotypes. This is always a concern in Holy Week, but Matthew's emphasis on prophecy requires vigilance throughout the year.

These are some of the themes that I picked out as I read through Matthew's Gospel. As a preacher preparing to preach through Year A, it is a good idea to set aside a bit of time to read the entire Gospel yourself. Do it one sitting if you're able, but break it up if you must. As you do, ask yourself "How does Matthew understand who Jesus is?" "What does Jesus do in this Gospel, and how does he do it?" "What sort of person do you think Matthew was thinking about when he wrote this Gospel?" Scholars have various answers to these questions, but take the time to answer them for yourself before you read their ideas, or at least generate some of your own to compare with theirs.

As you do this exercise, you may encounter some of the themes I or others in this book have identified. Ideally, you will also find connections to your life and ministry and those of the community you serve. Commentary writing scholars could never find the deep connections between the Gospel and your community the way that you can, and these insights are often the source of the most effective and life-transforming preaching.

The Way of Love: What Does It Mean to Adopt a Rule of Life?[1]

What does it mean to adopt a rule of life? The term itself is simply religious language for something we all do whenever we decide to direct intentional, sustained effort toward an overarching goal that requires persistent, disciplined effort. It isn't something that can be accomplished quickly. For example, in an academic setting, while it's possible to pass an exam by furiously studying the night before, mastery of a given subject matter requires continual study over time. In the realm of physical health, it's not a rule of life to go on a starvation diet to lose weight, but rather to make small, daily changes in our eating and exercise habits. If we want to save money, we need to adopt and stick to a budget, which is nothing more than a financial rule of life.

A spiritual rule of life is comprised of specific practices that help us pay attention and respond to God. It is a conscious effort on our part to be open to the love of God in Jesus, to receive that love for ourselves, and then offer love to others as we feel called. If we adhere to a few essential spiritual practices over time, they gradually shape our character and determine the course of our lives.

The writer Brian McLaren puts it this way:

> Spiritual practices are those actions within our power that help us narrow the gap between the person we are and the person we hope to become. They help us become good and deep company for ourselves and others. They're about surviving our twenties or forties or eighties and not becoming a jerk in the process. About not letting what happens to us deform or destroy us. About realizing that what we earn or accumulate means nothing compared to what we become and who we are. Spiritual practices are about life, about training ourselves to become the kinds of people who have eyes and actually see, and who have ears and actually hear, and so experience not just survival but life that is real, worth living, and good.[2]

McLaren goes on to say that our character—the kind of people we are—determines how much of God we can experience, and maybe even which version of God we experience. Thus, there's a lot at stake here for us, for it is through spiritual practices that we learn to love God.

The primary goal of Presiding Bishop Michael Curry's *Way of Love* is for us to grow in our love for Jesus as we experience his love for us. The second is to grow in our capacity to love others as Jesus loves. The kind of love we're aiming for isn't a feeling that washes over us, as wonderful as that feeling of love can be. Rather, it is sustained and sometimes sacrificial effort. In the words of St. Paul, this is love that is patient and kind; love that is not arrogant or boastful or rude; love that believes, hopes and endures all things; love that never ends (1 Corinthians 13:1–13). Growing in our capacity to both receive and offer such love is the fruit of a life that is connected to love of Jesus, as a branch is to the vine. The practices of the Way of Love help us stay connected.

If we're honest, most of us feel inadequate when it comes to the disciplines of our faith. I know that I do. But here's something to remember about spiritual practices: they aren't meant to be chores to plough through or exercises to whip us into spiritual shape. In the words of the Benedictine nun Joan Chittister: "A relationship with God is not something to achieved." Rather, she writes, "God is a presence to which we can respond." Nor is the spiritual life separate from the rest of our lives, but rather, "a way of being in the world that is open to God and open to others." Spiritual practices help open us to God's presence.

1 Mariann Edgar Budde, *Receiving Jesus: The Way of Love* (New York: Church Publishing, forthcoming.

2 Brian McLaren, *Finding Our Way Again: The Return of the Ancient Practices* (Nashville, Thomas Nelson, 2008), 14.

The seven practices of the Way of Love are not necessarily dramatic gestures on our part. On occasion they might be, but they are mostly small steps we take every day whose impact will be felt over time. Nor is this a program explicitly designed to fix the challenges we face as a church in institutional decline. There is no guarantee that even if every Episcopalian under the sun decided to follow the Way of Love that we would reverse the trends of shrinking membership. On the other hand, if we never engage in these practices, or others like them, we may not have a church worth saving. The church isn't a building, an institution, a small community desperate to survive. It is, as the Presiding Bishop loves to remind us, a gathering of people who have heard the call to follow Jesus in his ways of love for the world, person by person, community by community.

The Seven Practices

The first practice in a Jesus-focused life is to *turn*—turn our gaze, our mind, our thoughts, our attention to Jesus. As simple as it sounds, it is the foundational practice, referring back to the first conscious decision we made, or have yet to make, to be a follower of Jesus. To turn also describes the daily decision to focus our attention on Jesus, asking for his guidance and grace.

The second practice is to *learn*, to commit each day to some form of learning, reading the Bible, or listening to devotional material focused on Jesus' teachings. Sometimes the learning process involves deep engagement through a class or study; other times, it's a small, daily encounter with sources of wisdom and inspiration. What matters most here isn't the quantity of our learning, but the steady commitment to take in a bit of insight each day.

The third practice, to *pray*, flows naturally from first and second, yet also stands alone. We pray at all times and places. I have learned that making an effort to sit down in the same place every day for even a few minutes has a quiet, yet powerful impact on my life. It's a time to sort through and settle my thoughts, as murky water settles in stillness, and allow bits of clarity to emerge. It's a time to speak my heart, often with sighs instead of words, before God. And it's a time to listen. We may not hear anything in the silence, but we might. And we never will hear anything from God if we don't take time to listen.

In terms of time, we can commit ourselves to turn, learn, and pray each day in as little as fifteen minutes

a day. We can always spend more time, but the benefit comes with the habit of setting aside time, no matter the amount. It's best to start small.

The fourth practice, to *worship*, moves us from the personal to the collective. Following Jesus is a communal endeavor, and we cannot grow in the ways of love on our own. Theologian Norman Wirzba writes, "The church at its best is like a school that trains people in the way of love, an unusual school that lasts a lifetime and from which we never really graduate.[3] We apprentice ourselves to one another in Christian community and together experience Christ's presence.

The fifth practice, to *bless*, takes us out into our lives and churches and into the world around us. To bless, that is, to speak words of kindness and affirmation, is perhaps the loveliest and understated of spiritual practices. The Celtic author and poet John O'Donohue describes blessing as a lost art form. "The world can be harsh and negative," he writes, "but if we remain generous and patient, kindness inevitably reveals itself. Something deep in the human soul seems to depend on the presence of kindness; something instinctive in us expects it, and once we sense it, we are able to trust and open ourselves."[4] Each day we are given countless opportunities to speak kindness into another person's life, to offer a word of hope in times of uncertainty.

The sixth practice, to *go*, is for many the most challenging. This is the call to cross the borders of our familiarity in order better understand the experience of another. The great criminal justice reformer of our time, Bryan Stevenson, speaks of being proximate to suffering, getting close to those who bear the brunt of our society's ills, and coming to know them as neighbors and friends.[5] Walking in the way of love requires us to show up in those places where love is needed most.

The final practice, to *rest*, is also one with which many struggle and may well be the most countercultural for our time. Yet we are mortal, and our souls and bodies are restored in rest. To rest is to remember that we are not alone and that all does not depend on us. We can lay our burdens down and make space in our lives for renewal and the things that make for joy. Scripture teaches that sabbath isn't something we earn; it is our birthright as children of God.

3 Norman Wirzba, *Way of Love: Recovering the Heart of Christianity* (New York: HarperCollins, 2016), 8.

4 John O'Donohue, *To Bless the Space Between Us: A Book of Blessings* (New York: Doubleday, 2008), 185.

5 Bryan Stevenson, *Just Mercy: A Story of Justice and Redemption* (New York: Spiegel & Grau, 2014), 14.

Seven may seem, at first, like a daunting number of spiritual practices. It would be if the goal was to check them off each day as tasks on a to-do list. I have found it helpful to ponder the seven practices over the course of a week, a month, or a season of my life. We may be drawn, for our soul's sake, to a season of learning; we may feel an internal nudge to go beyond ourselves in some small or significant way. One question to ask at the outset: which of the seven practices come easily for you? With which do you struggle? Is there one that speaks with particular urgency, as something your life needs right now?

The purpose of these intentional practices is to open ourselves to experience Jesus with us. So often we think of the Christian faith as an obligation, or as a set of beliefs that we must hold. There are obligations and beliefs, but if we get stuck there, we can lose sight of, or never experience at all, what is most important. What is most important is Jesus' invitation to experience a loving, personal relationship with God. No matter our struggles and doubts, no matter our past sins or persistent failings, our relationship with God is one we can trust. In God we can find refuge and solid ground upon which to stand.

The Way of Love is the journey of a lifetime. It's a way of knowing God, receiving and sharing Jesus' love, and being a blessing to the world. May you experience something of God's light and love for you in this coming year.

Mariann Edgar Budde
9th Bishop of Washington
From her forthcoming book
  Receiving Jesus: The Way of Love
www.churchpublishing.org/receivingjesus

The Way of Love

Advent

Preparing for Advent

The Season of Advent marks the beginning of the new Church Year (Advent I through Last Sunday after Pentecost). As the Body of Christ, we begin with hope—hope for:

- Christ's apocalyptic coming,
- Christ's historic coming remembered on the feast of his Incarnation, and
- Christ's daily visitation.

While Advent is a season of penitence (albeit to a lesser degree than the Season of Lent), it is important to note that penitence is not an opportunity for self-harm or self-abasement; rather, seasons of penitence (Advent and Lent) represent opportunities to engage more deeply in spiritual practice that allows us to see and experience the love of Christ with great clarity and devotion.

Advent begins the Incarnation cycle of the Christian Calendar, which includes Advent, Christmas, and the season after the Epiphany. These days, dependent on the central Feast of the Incarnation, all highlight the importance of the doctrine of the Incarnation to our understanding of what it means to be Christ. The Son of God took residence in colonized, brown, poor, Jewish flesh—flesh that would have been overlooked by the many in power and flesh that was repeatedly brutalized by oppressive regime of Rome. Holding this reality against the hope that colors this season, we see a wrinkle developing—it might be true that what we hope for will arrive in a form we are tempted to overlook or even to look upon with contempt.

As James Farwell has noted (*Planning for Rites and Rituals, Year C, 2018–2019*), planning for this season draws a through line that connects the hopes of those in our faith communities and surrounding geographic communities with the mystery of the Incarnation and the surprising ways that God's continuous incarnation manifests itself in and around us.

It is also true that many congregations will be planning for Advent, Christmas, and the season after the Epiphany in the middle of an increasingly frantic schedule. As the secular holiday seasons approach, ministry volunteers are likely to find time increasingly limited even as the church calendar fills up with all sorts of events. Planning liturgy during this season takes patience and forward thinking that allows for worshipers and guests to experience the depth of the season without taxing the resources of the community beyond capacity.

Theological Themes that Might Shape Liturgy, Catechesis, and Education

Hope and anticipation are themes that readily come to mind during the season of Advent. The Christian hope during Advent, hope for Christ, stands diametrically opposed to the secular hope of an increasingly secular season. Christian hope invites us to prepare for the manifestation of our hope through a season of penitence, which helps to deepen otherwise unsatisfactory expressions of hope. As the Collect for Advent IV names for us, we are to practice our faith in this season (and every season) in such a way that Jesus "at his coming, may find in us a mansion prepared for himself."

Liturgical Possibilities

Rites

Liturgy planners for the Season of Advent are at a marked advantage. Individuals and communities who normally ignore, or even hold in contempt, the message of the church are likely more open to hearing the message of the Gospel during this season. How we plan and execute our worship has the potential of modeling a different, more just, more reflective, more compassionate way of marking this season.

One of the ways that might distinguish a uniquely spiritual expression of hope is by beginning our liturgies with the Penitential Order. It has been said repeatedly, but Advent is a penitential season. Beginning by hearing God's commandments, reflecting on our need for grace in the face of failing to live up to those commandments, and then opening ourselves up to the need to daily rely on God's grace is a helpful way to reorient the season away from rampant consumerism.

In this season, and indeed all seasons, it might be a helpful practice to write prayers of the people that are unique for the context of the worshiping community. Give hope an address. What are the hopes of your community? How might our prayers function not only to voice those prayers to God, but also to remind our communities of our duty to be the bringers of hope to those who are around us?

Space

Depending on the flexibility of your physical space, you might consider using it to mark the difference in the season. Lowering overhead light and using more candlelight (if you have adjustable lighting) and rearranging chairs (if you have moveable seating) are options.

Other Rituals and Resources

Advent lends itself to a variety of additional ritual acts. One of the more popular rituals is the lighting of the Advent Wreath. Some congregations append a wreath-lighting liturgy to the beginning of the liturgy. Doing anything prior to the beginning of the actual liturgy feels like an unnecessary add-on. This is doubly problematic if you attempt to involve newer people, families, young children, and so on in the lighting because it can come across that their ministry really is not valuable enough to be included in the main liturgy. On the other hand, congregations that include an elaborate liturgy during the Entrance Rite can make the lighting of the Advent Wreath more of a spectacle than it is meant to be, "gilding the lily" of a liturgy already saturated with more meaning than the average worshiper has room to absorb.

Congregations will make decisions about color (violet or blue) with each having its particular value. Some congregations will choose to observe "Gaudete Sunday" on Advent III. They will do this by altering the color to rose for that particular Sunday. Particularly in a time when "regular attendance" is something like once month, disrupting the consistency of the season might be something worth challenging, particularly if its observance is not a long-standing or helpful practice of a particular community.

Many congregations observe a Lessons and Carols service of some kind during Advent. Some choose to alter the Liturgy of the Word in the Holy Eucharist to adopt a Lessons and Carols format while others will choose to hold an entirely separate liturgy (it should be noted that the former is not supported rubrically by the Book of Common Prayer). It might be worth exploring what it means to use a penitential seasons such as Advent to develop a culture that has the bandwidth to support an additional liturgy.

Through the Eyes of a Child

During Advent, we, along with our families and all who are the church, wait for the birth of the baby Jesus, who is a gift God gave to us and to all people because God loves us so much and has made us one big family. It is a time we prepare for when Jesus will come again to earth, and God will be in all and make all things new. During this season, we ask what we can give to others to celebrate the fact that in Jesus, God loves us so much that his promise to be with us always is complete. In Advent, we tell stories of hope and promise and wonder how the light breaks through the darkness. The Advent wreath helps us to count the days and weeks toward Christmas, a circle of evergreen shows us that God's love never ends, and we light candles (one for each Sunday of Advent) to help us remember that Jesus brings the light into the world.

Through the Eyes of Youth

In Advent we advertise that we have faith in the birth of Jesus as well as faith that Christ will come again. We in the church prepare for the birth of Christ by giving the gift of ourselves as we wait in joy. It is a time of action: hold onto the promise that Christ will come again by hosting an "alternative gift fair" such as an angel tree in which members of your community can provide gifts to those in your community who are in need. Pray, ask, and respond: Who are the people in our world who need the message of God's love? What are our hopes for how people today can receive the message of God's love? How do we help others know God's love?

Of all the Christian stories, the ones associated with Christmas seem to be the most ubiquitous. It is also true that the season leading up to Christmas is crowded with other, often mixed messages about the purpose of this season. It is important that the local church find ways to help our young people discern the spiritual reason behind this season. Preparing take-home kits to observe Advent at home by creating an Advent Wreath to help mark the days might be a great way to put Christian Formation in the hands of parents and guardians.

Through the Eyes of Daily Life

Advent is a time of preparation, of patience, of remembering what grounds and sustains us. The function of Advent is to remind us who God is and who we are meant to be as well. Advent is about the riches of emptiness. God coming as an infant without retinue or riches is the metaphor of a humility that requires us to remember how really small we are in the universe. In our secular culture, a tone of wanting more, spending more, and accumulating riches on earth surround us. As Christians, we long for our society to live up to God's vision, for the kingdom to come in its fullness outside of materialism. The cry of Advent, "Wake up! Be alert! Watch for his coming" is difficult amidst the busyness of the season. We can practice some simple, but not easy, disciplines. We can fast from the media to become more alert to the still small voice of God. We can focus on the giving of ourselves to God. Plan to spend time apart from the busyness of the season each day so you can be alert to God in the silent, the small, and the simple.

The Church suggests that Advent is a preparatory time for Christmas wherein we hope for the coming of Christ. Secular society says that the season before Christmas (inaccurately and curiously mislabeled as the "Twelve Days of Christmas") is a preparatory time for Christmas wherein we buy all the gifts and attend all the parties we can. Planning liturgy during this time should aim to bear witness to the former without creating shame on behalf of the faithful. Preaching that points out spiritual practices that can be observed with little disruption might be helpful ways to create the bandwidth for deeper spiritual engagement. Modeling practices within the liturgy (silence and reflection, for example) might also be helpful.

Through the Eyes of Those Outside of the Church

People who normally ignore the church are more inclined to pay attention to how the church recognizes and marks this season. If our observance of Advent mirrors the anxiety and frantic nature with which secular society marks the days leading up to Christmas, we might be unwittingly communicating our own irrelevance. We are a people of hope and no where is that hope modeled more clearly than when a community holds vigil for the inbreaking of love into the world. We might think about leaning into the weirdness of the Christian story—apocalypses, prophesies, weirdly clad wild-haired charismatic preachers—as opposed to making apologies for it.

Through the Eyes of the Global Community

Advent is a time of concern for God's judgment, particularly in reference to the coming kingdom. The power of this theme of judgment brings about a realization of the sinfulness of the present age. As Christians, we believe it is Jesus who bears this judgment through his life, death, and resurrection, revealing the reign of God to the church in every generation. Our Eucharistic Prayer reminds us that Christ will come again. This is the hope for Advent, and this is the hope we find in the Lord's Prayer in "thy will be done" and "thy Kingdom come." These familiar words call us into a reality of the real presence of Christ in our lives as we look at our own response to today's world. The Collects of Advent remind us how we are living in the reality of Christ's presence that allows us to approach ethical, social justice, and global issues.

Seasonal Rites for Advent

Advent Blessing

The following blessing may be used by a bishop or priest whenever a blessing is appropriate. It is a three-fold form, with an Amen at the end of each sentence, leading into a Trinitarian blessing.

May Almighty God, by whose providence our Savior Christ came among us in great humility, sanctify you with the light of his blessing and set you free from all sin. *Amen.*

May he whose second Coming in power and great glory we await, make you steadfast in faith, joyful in hope, and constant in love. *Amen.*

May you, who rejoice in the first Advent of our Redeemer, at his second Advent be rewarded with unending life. *Amen.*

And the blessing of God Almighty, the Father, the Son, and the Holy Spirit, be upon you and remain with you for ever. *Amen.*

The Advent Wreath

The Advent Wreath is a visual symbol marking the progress of the season of Advent. When it is used in the church, no special prayers or ceremonial elaboration beyond what is described in the Prayer Book is desirable. At morning services, the appropriate number of candles is lighted before the service begins. When used in private homes, the Advent Wreath provides a convenient focus for devotions at the time of the evening meal. Here we offer the Prayer for Light as well as prayers for using and Advent Wreath in the home.

Prayer for Light

Grant us, Lord, the lamp of charity which never fails, that it may burn in us and shed its light on those around us, and that by its brightness we may have a vision of that holy City, where dwells the true and never-failing Light, Jesus Christ our Lord. *Amen.*

Prayers for the Advent Wreath at Home[1]

First Week in Advent

Leader: Almighty God, give us grace to cast away the works of darkness.

And put on the armor of light,

Leader: Now in the time of this mortal life in which your Son Jesus Christ came to visit us in great humility; that in the last day, when he shall come again in his glorious majesty to judge both the living and the dead, we may rise to the life immortal; through him who lives and reigns with you and the Holy Spirit, one God, now and for ever. *Amen.*

Second Week in Advent

Leader: Merciful God, who sent your messengers the prophets to preach repentance,

And prepare the way for our salvation:

Leader: Give us grace to heed their warnings and forsake our sins, that we may greet with joy the coming of Jesus Christ our Redeemer: who lives and reigns with you and the Holy Spirit, one God, now and for ever. *Amen.*

Third Week in Advent

Leader: Stir up your power, O Lord.

And with great might come among us;

Leader: And, because we are sorely hindered by our sins, let your bountiful grace and mercy speedily help and deliver us; through Jesus Christ our Lord, to whom with you and the Holy Spirit, be honor and glory, now and for ever. *Amen.*

1 Anne E. Kitch. *The Anglican Family Prayer Book* (Harrisburg, PA: Morehouse Publishing, 2004), 115–121.

Advent

Fourth Week in Advent

Leader: Purify our conscience, Almighty God,

by your daily visitation,

Leader: That your Son Jesus Christ, at his coming, may find in us a mansion prepared for himself; who lives and reigns with you, in the unity of the Holy Spirit, one God, now and for ever. *Amen.*

Advent Festival of Lessons and Hymns

Nine lessons are customarily selected (but fewer may be used), interspersed with appropriate Advent hymns, canticles, and anthems. When possible, each lesson should be read by a different lector, preferably voices of male and female readers as well as a variety of ages. The lesson from the third chapter of Genesis is never omitted.

Genesis 2:4b–9, 15–25
Genesis 3:1–22 or 3:1–15
Isaiah 40:1–11
Jeremiah 31:31–34
Isaiah 64:1–9a
Isaiah 6:1–11
Isaiah 35:1–10
Baruch 4:36—5:9
Isaiah 7:10–15
Micah 5:2–4
Isaiah 11:1–9
Zephaniah 3:14–18
Isaiah 65:17–25
Luke 1:5–25 or Luke 1:26–38 or Luke 1:26–56

The Celebration of our Lady of Guadalupe

Thursday, December 12

The Feast of Our Lady of Guadalupe (Dia de Nuestra Señora de Guadalupe) is a celebration of the appearance of the Virgin Mary to an Aztec peasant during the first years of Spanish rule. Today it is both a national and religious holiday in Mexico. The festival begins on the eve of December 12, when concero dancers gather in the atrium of the church.

In the Roman Catholic tradition, the liturgy includes a celebration of the Eucharist followed by a festive meal.

Readings

Zechariah 2:10–13 *or* Revelation 11:19a; 12:1–6a, 10
Luke 1:26–38 *or* Luke 1:39–47

O God of power and mercy, you blessed the Americas at Tepeyac with the presence of the Virgin Mary of Guadalupe. May her prayers help all men and women to accept each other as brothers and sisters. Through Your justice present in our hearts, may your peace reign in the world. We ask this through our Lord Jesus Christ, Your Son, who lives and reigns with you and the Holy Spirit, One God, forever and ever. *Amen.*

The Angelus (English)

Leader: The Angel of the Lord declared unto Mary

And she conceived by the Holy Ghost.

Leader: Hail Mary, full of grace: The Lord is with thee. Blessed art thou among women and blessed is the fruit of thy womb, Jesus. Holy Mary, Mother of God: Pray for us sinners now and at the hour of our death. *Amen.*

Leader: Behold, the handmaid of the Lord.

Be it done unto me according to thy word.

Leader: Hail Mary . . .

Holy Mary . . .

Leader: And the Word was made flesh

And dwelt among us.

Leader: Hail Mary . . .

Holy Mary . . .

Leader: Pray for us, O holy Mother of God,

That we may be made worthy of the promises of Christ.

Leader: Let us pray.

Pour forth, we beseech thee, O Lord, thy grace unto our hearts, that we, to whom the Incarnation of Christ, thy Son, was made known by the message of an angel, may by his passion and cross be brought to the glory of his Resurrection, through the same Christ, our Lord, Amen.

El Angelus (Español)

Líder: El Angel del Señor anunció a María.

Y concibió por obra del Espíritu Santo.

Líder: Dios te salve, María. Llena eres de gracia: El Señor es contigo. Bendita tú eres entre todas las mujeres. Y bendito es el fruto de tu vientre: Jesús.

Santa María, Madre de Dios, ruega por nosotros pecadores, ahora y en la hora de nuestra muerte. Amén.

Líder: He aqui la esclava del Señor.

Hagase en mi segun Tu palabra.

Líder: Dios te salve María . . . .

Santa María . . . .

Líder: Y el Verbo se hizo carne.

Y habito entre nosotros.

Líder: Dios te salve María . . . .

Santa María . . . .

Líder: Ruega por nosotros, Santa Madre de Dios.

Para que seamos dignos de alcanzar las promesas de Jesucristo.

Todos: Derrama, Señor, Tu gracia en nuestros corazones; que habiendo conocido la Encarnación de Cristo, Tu Hijo, por la voz del Angel, por los meritos de Su Pasión y cruz seamos llevados a la gloria de la Resurrección. Por el mismo Cristo, Nuestro Señor. Amén.

Las Posadas

Las Posadas (Spanish for "the inn" or "lodgings") is a traditional Mexican festival which reenacts Joseph's search for room at the inn. Beginning on December 16 and continuing for nine days leading up to Christmas Eve worship, a procession carrying a doll representing the Christ Child and images of Joseph and Mary riding a burro walks through the community streets. The processional stops at a previously selected home and asks for lodging for the night. People are invited in to read scriptures and sing Christmas carols. Refreshments are provided by the hosts. The doll is left at the chosen home and picked up the next night when the procession begins again.

Elements for the Procession

Invite participants to sing together a beloved Christmas carol, such as "O Little Town of Bethlehem" or the traditional Mexican song "Los Peregrinos" ("The Pilgrims").

The Collect

O God, you have caused this holy night to shine with brightness of the true Light: Grant that we, who have known the mystery of that Light on earth, may also enjoy him perfectly in heaven; where with you and the Holy Spirit he lives and reigns, one God, in glory everlasting. *Amen.*

The Phos Hilaron

O gracious Light, pure brightness of the everlasting Father in heaven, O Jesus Christ, holy and blessed!

Now as we come to the setting of the sun, and our eyes behold the vesper light, we sing your praises, O God: Father, Son, and Holy Spirit.

You are worthy at all times to be praised by happy voices, O Son of God, O Giver of life,

And to be glorified through all the worlds.

The Song of Mary, the *Magnificat*, Luke 1:46–55

And Mary said, "My soul magnifies the Lord, and my spirit rejoices in God my Savior, for he has looked with favor on the lowliness of his servant. Surely, from now on all generations will call me blessed; for the Mighty One has done great things for me, and holy is his name. His mercy is for those who fear him from generation to generation. He has shown strength with his arms; he has scattered the proud in the thoughts of their hearts. He has brought down the powerful from their thrones, and lifted up the lowly; he has filled the hungry with good things, and sent the rich away empty. He has helped his servant Israel, in remembrance of his mercy, according to the promise he made to our ancestors, to Abraham and to his descendants forever."

Advent

Advent

Evening Prayer for Advent with Prayers for an End to Global Poverty[2]

The following short form of Evening Prayer may be used by families and other groups throughout Advent. If desired, the devotion may be accompanied by the lighting of an Advent Wreath.

Opening Verse and Candle Lighting

All may gather in silence. After a period of meditation, the appropriate number of candles on an Advent Wreath, or some other candle, may be lit.

Leader: Light and peace, in Jesus Christ our Lord.

Thanks be to God.

Scripture Reading

One of the following or another short passage of Scripture is read:

Sundays:

The spirit of the Lord God is upon me, because the Lord has anointed me; he has sent me to bring good news to the oppressed, to bind up the brokenhearted, to proclaim liberty to the captives, and release to the prisoners; to proclaim the year of the Lord's favor. (Isaiah 61:1–2a)

Mondays:

Drop down, O heavens, from above, and let the skies rain down righteousness; let the earth open, that salvation may spring forth, and let it cause justice to sprout up also. (Isaiah 45:8)

Tuesdays:

Watch, for you do not know when the master of the house will come, in the evening, or at midnight, or at cockcrow, or in the morning, lest he come suddenly and find you asleep. (Mark 13: 35–36)

Wednesdays:

In the wilderness prepare the way of the Lord, make straight in the desert a highway for our God. (Isaiah 40:3)

Thursdays:

The glory of the Lord shall be revealed, and all flesh shall see it together. (Isaiah 40:5)

Fridays:

Arise, O Jerusalem, stand upon the height and look toward the east, and see your children gathered from west and east at the word of the Holy One. (Baruch 5:5)

Saturdays:

Prepare the way of the Lord, make straight his paths; all nations shall see the salvation of God. (Luke 3: 4–5)

Canticle

All may say together the Magnificat, the Canticle of the Blessed Virgin Mary. The Canticle speaks to us in Advent about submission to God's patterns for our lives and reveals how radically different a human society reordered according to God's design will look from than the world in which we currently live. God has cast down the mighty from their thrones, Mary sings, and lifted up the lowly. He has filled the hungry with good things, and the rich he has sent away empty.

My soul proclaims the greatness of the Lord, my spirit rejoices in God my Savior;*
For he has looked with favor on his lowly servant.

From this day all generations will call me blessed; *
the Almighty has done great things for me, and holy is his Name.

He has mercy on those who fear him *
in every generation.

He has shown the strength of his arm; *
He has scattered the proud in their conceit.
He has cast down the mighty from their thrones, *
and has lifted up the lowly.

---

2 This litany was prepared by the Office of Government Relations **https://www.episcopalchurch.org/library/article/evening-prayer-advent-prayers-end-global-poverty**; accessed February 7, 2019.

He has filled the hungry with good things, *
and the rich he has sent away empty.
He has come to the help of his servant Israel *
for he has remembered his promise of mercy,
The promise he made to our fathers, *
to Abraham and his children for ever.

Glory be to the Father, and to the Son, and to
the Holy Spirit, *
as it was in the beginning, is now,
and will be forever. Amen.

Prayers

The following prayers—which are based on the Millennium Development Goals—are then said responsively:

Leader: As we await the coming of our Savior, let us pray for the world God so loves, particularly for those whose cries are known only to Christ, the Word Made Flesh.

Lord, hear our prayer.

Leader: That God, whose Son Jesus Christ was born not in the palace of a king but in the throes of poverty, may hear the cries of the poor, hungry, and oppressed, and may move human hearts to hear their cries as well.

Lord, hear our prayer.

Leader: For those who lack access to basic education, that the light of knowledge may blossom and shine in the lives of all God's people.

Lord, hear our prayer.

Leader: For an end to the divisions and inequalities that scar God's creation, particularly the barriers to freedom faced by God's children throughout the world because of gender; that all who have been formed in God's image might have equality in pursuit of the blessings of creation.

Lord, hear our prayer.

Leader: For the health of women, children and families around the world, that all God's people may be empowered to strengthen their communities and repair the breaches which divide nations and peoples.

Lord, hear our prayer.

Leader: For an end to pandemic disease throughout the world, that plagues of death may no longer fuel poverty, destabilize nations, and inhibit reconciliation and restoration throughout the world

Lord, hear our prayer.

Leader: For an end to the waste and desecration of God's creation, that all communities and nations may find sustenance in the fruits of the earth and the water God has given us.

Lord, hear our prayer.

Leader: For all people who already enjoy the abundance of creation and the blessings of prosperity, that their hearts may be lifted up to the needs of the poor and afflicted.

Lord, hear our prayer.

Leader: For the departed, particularly those who have died as a result of poverty, hunger, disease, violence, or hardness of the human heart.

Lord, hear our prayer.

The Leader then concludes with the Collect appointed in the Prayer Book for the appropriate week of Advent.

Advent

An Advent Litany of Darkness and Light[3]

Voice 1: We wait in the darkness, expectantly, longingly, anxiously, thoughtfully.

Voice 2: The darkness is our friend. In the darkness of the womb, we have all been nurtured and protected. In the darkness of the womb, the Christ-child was made ready for the journey into light.

> *You are with us, O God,*
> *in darkness and in light.*

Voice 1: It is only in the darkness that we can see the splendor of the universe—blankets of stars, the solitary glowings of distant planets.

Voice 2: It was the darkness that allowed the Magi to find the star that guided them to where the Christ-child lay.

> *You are with us, O God,*
> *in darkness and in light.*

Voice 1: In the darkness of the night, desert people find relief from the cruel relentless heat of the sun.

Voice 2: In the blessed darkness, Mary and Joseph were able to flee with the infant Jesus to safety in Egypt.

> *You are with us, O God,*
> *in darkness and in light.*

Voice 1: In the darkness of sleep, we are soothed and restored, healed and renewed.

Voice 2: In the darkness of sleep, dreams rise up. God spoke to Jacob and Joseph through dreams. God is speaking still.

> *You are with us, O God,*
> *in darkness and in light.*

Voice 1: In the solitude of darkness, we sometimes remember those who need God's presence in a special way—the sick, the unemployed, the bereaved, the persecuted, the homeless; those who are demoralized and discouraged, those whose fear has turned to cynicism, those whose vulnerability has become bitterness.

Voice 2: Sometimes in the darkness, we remember those who are near to our hearts—colleagues, partners, parents, children, neighbors, friends. We thank God for their presence and ask God to bless and protect them in all that they do—at home, at school, as they travel, as they work, as they play.

> *You are with us, O God,*
> *in darkness and in light.*

Voice 1: Sometimes, in the solitude of darkness, our fears and concerns, our hopes and our visions rise to the surface. We come face to face with ourselves and with the road that lies ahead of us. And in that same darkness, we find companionship for the journey.

Voice 2: In that same darkness, we sometimes allow ourselves to wonder and worry whether the human race is going to make it at all.

> *We know you are with us, O God,*
> *yet we still await your coming.*
> *In the darkness that contains*
> *both our hopelessness and our expectancy,*
> *we watch for a sign of God's Hope.*
> *Amen.*

---

3 "An Advent Litany of Darkness and Light" from *The Wideness of God's Mercy: Litanies to Enlarge Our Prayers* Jeffrey W. Rowthorn, editor (New York: Church Publishing, 2007), 65–66

The First Sunday of Advent

December 1, 2019

The day will come when God's wisdom and presence will be fully revealed. It will be a time of both tremendous hope and promise, but it will also be a time of judgment. God's people must live in readiness for that great day to come.

Color   Violet or Blue

Preface   Advent

Collect

Almighty God, give us grace to cast away the works of darkness, and put on the armor of light, now in the time of this mortal life in which your Son Jesus Christ came to visit us in great humility; that in the last day, when he shall come again in his glorious majesty to judge both the living and the dead, we may rise to the life immortal; through him who lives and reigns with you and the Holy Spirit, one God, now and forever. Amen.

Readings and Psalm

Isaiah 2:1–5

In our lesson from the Hebrew Bible **the prophet Isaiah sets forth a majestic vision of a time when people throughout the world will worship the Lord and live in peace with one another.** The mountain of the city of Jerusalem will be raised up to become a symbol of hope and justice to every nation. Many peoples will look to Jerusalem and to its holy Mount Zion as the place from which God will issue God's word and law, bringing about an end to strife and warfare.

Psalm 122

A pilgrim's song of praise and prayer for the peace of Jerusalem.

Romans 13:11–14

In this reading **Paul urges a way of life in full awareness of the nearness of salvation.** Disciples must recognize that the nighttime of sinfulness is passing. The daylight, the time for new conduct and the following of Jesus, now comes.

Matthew 24:36–44

In our gospel lesson **Jesus tells his disciples of the need for readiness because the Son of Man will come at a day and hour which no one knows.** People will continue to go about their usual affairs, when suddenly this time of judgment will happen. Disciples are to be ever watchful, imagining themselves like a householder whose alertness could prevent a robbery.

Prayers of the People

Let us offer our prayers to God, who clothes us in the armor of light and offers us the gift of immortal life, responding, *"O come, O come, Emmanuel."*

For peace throughout the world, that swords of destruction may become tools for industry, and spears of war the word that pierces every heart with the light of hope; let us pray.

O come, O come, Emmanuel.

For the grace to choose the path that leads to eternal life, generously giving toward the relief of poverty and despair, homelessness and fear, so that through our actions the saving love of Christ may be revealed; let us pray.

O come, O come, Emmanuel.

Advent

Advent

For the leaders of the nations of the world, that power be tempered by wisdom, and the quest for money be seen as a false strength; let us pray.

O come, O come, Emmanuel.

For Christians throughout the world, especially those who endure religious persecution and the prejudice of unfriendly governments, that our prayers may empower them in their time of need; let us pray.

O come, O come, Emmanuel.

That we may hunger for the teachings of the Lord, seeking opportunities for education, bible study, and fellowship with those who follow the way of Jesus; let us pray.

O come, O come, Emmanuel.

In thanksgiving for those who stay awake in the dark corners of human experience, abiding faithfully with those whose faith is shallow and whose fears are great; let us pray.

O come, O come, Emmanuel.

In thanksgiving for the life-giving gifts of those who have died, leaving us a harvest of love from which to eat for years to come; let us pray.

O come, O come, Emmanuel.

In anticipation of Jesus' dwelling amongst us, let us continue the offering of our prayers.
(*Special intentions of the congregation, the diocese, and the Anglican Communion may be added here or before the formal intercessions.*)

The Celebrant adds a concluding Collect.

Images in the Readings

The apocalyptic imagery of **the end of the world**, like the flood sweeping all things away, echoes from the Old Testament into the preaching of Jesus, and continues in contemporary disaster movies and terrorist activity. For Christians, fear about the end always comes to rest in trust in the presence of God. When all is over, at our end, is God.

Today's readings expand and challenge our society's welcome of God arriving as only baby Jesus, for God comes as **judge** and calls us into a life of justice for all, evoking in us both anticipation and

fear. Often in classical art, Justice is a towering robed woman who judges right from wrong.

Often in the Bible God meets with humankind on a **mountain**. In our language a "mountaintop experience" is one so overwhelming that it changes one's future. Sinai, Horeb, Jerusalem, the mount of Jesus' sermon, the Mount of Transfiguration, the Mount of Olives, Golgotha, Zion: all are superimposed on our church buildings, for the Christian mountain is wherever we receive the word and sacraments.

In English, the phrase **"swords into plowshares"** indicates the hope for world peace, a hope for which Christians pray to God.

Ideas for the Day

- Advent is a baffling season: beginning with an end, ending with a beginning; remembering a birth that was millennia past while looking forward to a final coming sometime in the future. It is fitting then, that we begin the season with one of the prophets—quite mystifying figures themselves—who declares "The word that Isaiah saw." That particular Hebrew verb describes a special way of seeing: a vision-of-the-future-replete-with-improbable-hope. Advent is an interrupter: it begins with a word that is seen, with visions of hope for a better future. Advent will end with a mother nurturing a child whose name is a promise: God-with-us.

- In this season of preparation and expectation, let us find active ways to express our faith, through areas of personal development, family development, and church community development. At the personal level, plant herbs, learn to notate music, write in a diary, create a Spotify playlist of twenty uplifting songs by various artists. At the family level, find ways to prepare meals together. At the church level, assist in planning an event for the community. These active ways of engaging our faith will allow us to ". . . cast off the works of darkness and put on the armor of light."

- We are offered a glimpse of God's ultimate vision for creation and humanity. We are challenged to set life goals around that vision. Advent invites the church to dream of what God's will being done fully "on earth as in heaven" might mean in light of Jesus' words and acts.

Making Connections

Advent is a time of preparation, and not just for Christmas. It is a time to prepare for the return of Jesus. Advent marks the beginning of a new year in the life of the Church, and the readings today are a collective invitation to turn over a new leaf, to live life in a new way. We can do that in two ways: by having joyful expectations and actively preparing, perhaps through prayer or other spiritual practices. Each of us can do something to prepare for Jesus, and our thing is likely different from others.

Engaging All Ages

"Swords into plowshares" is a theme often cited by groups working for peaceful solutions to the world's problems, including the Episcopal Peace Fellowship: http://www.epfnational.org/. How might their efforts and resources be used to engage children, youth, and adults in worship? How might your formation programing on this day speak about becoming voices of non-violence in daily life?

Hymns for the Day

The Hymnal 1982
Blest be the King whose coming 74
Once he came in blessing 53
The King shall come when morning dawns 73
Christ is the world's true Light 542
Glorious things of thee are spoken 522, 523
Judge eternal, throned in splendor 596
O day of God, draw nigh 600, 601
Thy kingdom come, O God 613
"Thy kingdom come!" on bended knee 615
Awake, my soul, and with the sun 11
Awake, my soul, stretch every nerve 546
Awake, thou Spirit of the watchmen 540
Eternal Ruler of the ceaseless round 617
Hark! a thrilling voice is sounding 59
Jesus came, adored by angels 454
Lo! he comes, with clouds descending 57, 58
Rejoice! rejoice, believers 68
"Sleepers, wake!" A voice astounds us 61, 62

Lift Every Voice and Sing II
We're Marching to Zion 12
Down by the riverside 210
Great day 5
Rockin' Jerusalem 17
Better be ready 4

Wonder, Love, and Praise

Weekday Commemorations

Monday, December 2
Channing Moore Williams,
Bishop and Missionary, 1910
Bishop Williams was born in Richmond, Virginia, on July 18, 1829, and brought up in straitened circumstances by his widowed mother. He attended the College of William and Mary and the Virginia Theological Seminary. Ordained deacon in 1855, he offered himself for work in China; two years later he was sent to Japan and opened work in Nagaski. Williams translated parts of the Prayer Book into Japanese; he was a close friend and warm supporter of Bishop Schereschewsky, his successor in China.

Tuesday, December 3
Francis Xavier, Priest and Missionary, 1552
The Spaniard Francis Xavier (b. 1506) met Ignatius Loyola while studying in Paris. Francis and his companions bound themselves to serve God in 1534 — thus, began the Society of Jesus (Jesuits). Xavier and Loyola were ordained together in 1537. Francis traveled to India, then on to Sri Lanka and Indonesia. In 1549, he moved to Japan and learned the language to prepare a catechism for his mission among peoples he came to respect. In 1551, he traveled to China, hoping to launch a new mission, but he died before he secured passage into China. Francis is buried in Goa, India.

Advent

Advent

Wednesday, December 4
John of Damascus, Priest and Theologian, c. 760
John succeeded his father as tax collector for the Mohammedan Caliph of Damascus. About 715, John entered St. Sabas monastery near Jerusalem, where he lived ascetically, studying the fathers. He was ordained a priest in 726, the year the Byzantine Emperor Leo the Isaurian banned Holy Images, beginning the iconoclastic controversy. About 730, John wrote three treatises against the Iconoclasts, arguing that images were not idols, representations of saints, and distinguishing between veneration and worship. True worship, he wrote, was due to God alone. John also synthesized theology in *The Fount of Knowledge*. To Anglicans, he is known for his Easter hymns, including "Come, ye faithful, raise the strain."

Thursday, December 5
Clement of Alexandria,
Priest and Theologian, c. 210
Clement's liberal approach to secular knowledge laid the foundations of Christian humanism. Born mid-second century, Clement was a cultured Greek philosopher. He sought truth widely until he met Pantaenus, founder of the Christian Catechetical School at Alexandria. In 190, Clement succeeded Pantaenus as headmaster; Origen was Clement's most eminent pupil. Clement's learning and allegorical exegeses helped commend Christianity to intellectual circles of Alexandria during an age of Gnosticism. Clement dissented from the negative Gnostic view of the world, which denied free will. In *What Rich Man Will Be Saved?*, Clement sanctioned the "right use" of wealth and goods. Among his writings is the hymn "Master of eager youth." The time and place of his death are unknown.

Friday, December 6
Nicholas of Myra, Bishop, c. 342
Nicholas is the traditional patron saint of seafarers and sailors, archers, repentant thieves, brewers, pawn brokers, and, most important, children. He bore gifts to children. His name, Sinterklaas, was brought to America by Dutch colonists in New York, and from there, Saint Nicholas became known as Santa Claus. Because of many miracles attributed to his intercessions, Nicholas is also called the Wonderworker. Born in Patara, Lycia in Asia Minor (now Turkey) in 270, he traveled to Egypt and around Palestine, and became the bishop of Myra. He was tortured and imprisoned during the persecution of Diocletian. After his release, he was possibly present at the First Ecumenical Council of Nicea in 325.

Saturday, December 7
Ambrose of Milan, Bishop and Theologian, 397
Ambrose was hastily baptized so he could become a bishop on December 7, 373, after the Milanese people demanded his election. He had been brought up in a Christian family; in 373, he succeeded his father as governor in Upper Italy. As bishop and a statesman of the Church, he soon won renown defending orthodoxy against Arianism. He was a skilled hymnodist, introducing antiphonal chanting to enrich liturgical texture; among hymns attributed to him is a series for the Little Hours. Ambrose, who was a fine educator in matters of doctrine, persuaded Augustine of Hippo to convert. He feared not to rebuke emperors, including the rageful Theodosius, made to perform public penance for slaughtering thousands of citizens.

The Second Sunday of Advent

December 8, 2019

John the Baptist proclaims the coming of Jesus and calls people into repentance through baptism.

Color   Violet or Blue

Preface   Advent

Collect

Merciful God, who sent your messengers the prophets to preach repentance and prepare the way for our salvation: Give us grace to heed their warnings and forsake our sins, that we may greet with joy the coming of Jesus Christ our Redeemer; who lives and reigns with you and the Holy Spirit, one God, now and forever. Amen.

Readings and Psalm

Isaiah 11:1–10

In our lesson from the Hebrew Bible **the prophet foresees a time when God will bring forth a righteous judge and a new spirit of peace in the world.** The wise and faithful judge will come from the stump of Jesse—that is, from the line of the great King David, whose father was Jesse. The Spirit of the Lord will be his as he defends the humble and slays the wicked. The new age of peace will extend even to the animal kingdom.

Psalm 72:1–7, 18–19

The psalm asks that God endow the king with compassionate justice and righteousness, and that his reign may extend over all nations and throughout all generations.

Romans 15:4–13

In this reading **Paul points to several passages from the Hebrew scriptures to show how God's promise that the Gentile peoples should come to praise God was being fulfilled.** The new Roman converts, whom Paul hopes soon to visit, are urged to live in harmony and to recognize the manner in which Christ's ministry has brought these prophecies to fruition. He is the root of Jesse, that is, the promised son of David, on whom their hope is to be set.

Matthew 3:1–12

Our gospel lesson tells of **the ministry of John the Baptist, his message of repentance and his prophecy of the mighty one to come.** John himself is the messenger of preparation foretold by Isaiah. He baptizes with water those who confess their sins and wish to change their ways, but he chastises those who do not show the fruits of repentance. Soon comes the one who will baptize with the Holy Spirit and with refining fire.

Prayers of the People

As we anticipate the glorious birth of the Messiah, let us gather our prayers and thanksgivings as an offering of faith, responding, "O come, O come, Emmanuel."

That we may confess our collusion with evil, turn from the wrong we have done, and recommit ourselves to a holy life; let us pray.

> *O come, O come, Emmanuel.*

That righteousness may flourish throughout the legislative bodies of our nation, so that integrity overcomes the interests of special groups, and honesty the financial influence of the affluent; let us pray.

> *O come, O come, Emmanuel.*

That we be given the faith to go into the wilderness of our time and culture, giving voice to the promises of Christ and the glory of his reign; let us pray.

> *O come, O come, Emmanuel.*

That all people everywhere may choose to be washed through the water and fire of baptism, sharing in Christ's death and united in his resurrection; let us pray.

> *O come, O come, Emmanuel.*

That we may honor our children, whose keen sense of the mystery of faith leads us to a deeper understanding of the Eucharistic Meal, and the humility to share gifts of hope across all the tables of the world; let us pray.

O come, O come, Emmanuel.

That those who care for the sick may be given the strength to endure and the patience to carry on in the midst of trials, and that those who have died may rest in peace; let us pray.

O come, O come, Emmanuel.

In thanksgiving for programs and people who assist those troubled with alcoholism, gambling, and any addiction that holds our souls in bondage; let us pray.

O come, O come, Emmanuel.

In thanksgiving for those who are generous in their giving for the mission of the Church: its ministry and witness, its temporal responsibilities and spiritual treasures; let us pray.

O come, O come, Emmanuel.

As a people ever-watchful for the coming of the Messiah, let us continue our intercessions.

(Special intentions of the congregation, the diocese, and the Anglican Communion may be added here or before the formal intercessions.)

The Celebrant adds a concluding Collect.

Images in the Readings

Ancient Near Eastern iconography often depicted the monarch as a **tree of life**, whose successful reign insured a vibrant life for the people. Both first and second readings rely on this ancient imagery when they refer to the "root of Jesse." In Israelite history, Jesse, the father of the legendary King David, is described as the root of the tree that was King David. John the Baptist warns that some trees will be cut down to make way for Christ, who is our tree of life.

The gospel reading situates John the Baptist in the **wilderness**, baptizing in the Jordan River, the **river** that the Israelites crossed on their way into the promised land. Led by Jesus, our Joshua, who entered the wilderness of our lives, Christians too cross a river in baptism and so enter into the kingdom of God.

The lion and the lamb has become a beloved symbol of peace between natural enemies. The toddler is playing with the adder. In Christ is the promise of this extraordinary hope for the world.

Ideas for the Day

+ Poet Anne Sexton claims that there are two things impossible to ignore: love and a cough. Let's add John the Baptizer, who crashes into our Christmas preparations this week and next like an irritating cough; beneath that rough exterior lies a man smitten with a passionate love for God and people. "Repent," he says. In the Bible, repentance, that turning around to take an honest look at ourselves, is something like a dance. It takes two: God and a newly aware "us." Think of John the B as the host on prom night. Our dance cards are full, and it is God in whose arms we glide, God teaching us steps we thought we knew or thought we were too gawky to try.

+ The beautiful imagery of all creation beginning at peace (Isaiah 11) has inspired poets and artists for generations. How might you share some poetry or paintings in your preaching, prayers, or focal installations during worship?

+ How do we focus our voice to have the most impact in today's culture? There are many voices that call to us throughout the Bible. They ring out truth in times of tribulation. From the prophet Isaiah to John the Baptist to Jesus Christ, the message is loud and clear. Live your life in preparation for glory to come. The way of Christianity is not easy, and we must find strength in the messages voices from the Bible have given us. These voices direct us in ways to live our lives properly. We can use these messages to empower our voice in our current age, whether it is through a blog, through activism, or through being a positive force to all of those we encounter; our voice must echo the voices of those who came before.

Advent

Making Connections

Christ is coming to fill all with the gifts of joy and peace. Christ is both Savior and Judge. We are loved and redeemed by God, no matter how many times we fall into sin. We are also held accountable for our actions. God is calling us to live out the Way of Love, to turn and to learn from our sins. God will forgive us and lift us up when we fall, but that does not mean we can give up or stop trying. We must always be seeking to follow the Way of Love more deeply.

Engaging All Ages

The story of John the Baptist, including the narrative details from the gospel of Luke (1:5–80) offer an opportunity for drama or storytelling in the liturgy. What objects can be shared (honey, locusts, camel's hair) to bring our senses to the person and message of John? What if members (invited in advance) of the congregation participated in the readings by shouting out "Repent!" at the appropriate times?

Hymns for the Day

The Hymnal 1982

Blessed be the God of Israel 444
Hail to the Lord's Anointed 616
God is working his purpose out 534
Lord, enthroned in heavenly splendor 307
O day of peace that dimly shines 597
Holy Father, great Creator 368
Redeemer of the nations, come 55
Savior of the nations, come 54
Comfort, comfort ye my people 67
Hark! a thrilling voice is sounding 59
Herald, sound the note of judgment 70
On Jordan's bank the Baptist's cry 76
Prepare the way, O Zion 65
There's a voice in the wilderness crying 75
What is the crying at Jordan? 69

Lift Every Voice and Sing II

Christ is coming 6

Wonder, Love, and Praise

Blessed be the God of Israel 889
Isaiah the prophet has written of old 723

Weekday Commemorations

Thursday, December 12
Francis de Sales, Bishop, and Jane de Chantal, Vowed Religious 1622 and 1641

Although Francis served as the Roman Catholic bishop of Geneva (1567-1622), he is better known for spiritual direction and for writing *Introduction to the Devout Life* whose influence extended from Roman to Anglo-Catholics. A melancholy man, he was convinced he was predestined for hell; however, in 1587, in Paris, he found a loving God. That vision of God's mercy and love marked his writings forevermore. In addition to writing, Francis worked with Jane de Chantal to found the Congregation of the Visitation, a new women's order whose charism began with the sick but evolved toward contemplative life.

Friday, December 13
Lucy of Syracuse, Martyr, 304

Lucy stands for "light," the meaning of her name. Born of a noble family about 283 in Syracuse, Sicily, she was denounced as Christian during the Diocletian persecution, and she died by a sword run through her throat in 303. Lucy was said to be so beautiful as to have attracted the unwanted attention of a pagan suitor. To discourage him, Lucy reportedly gouged out her eyes; therefore, in religious art, she often appears those suffering from eye diseases. Her day in Italy is celebrated with torchlight processions; in Sweden, Saint Lucy is haloed with light in a crown of lit candles.

Saturday, December 14
John of the Cross, Mystic and Monastic Reformer, 1591

Born in 1542, at Fontiveros, near Avila, Spain, John of the Cross was unknown outside the Discalced Carmelites for nearly three hundred years after his death. More recently, scholars of Christian spirituality have found in him a hidden treasure. He opened a monastery of "Discalced" (strict observance) Carmelites, in 1568, disillusioned with what he considered the laxity of the Camelites. This action led to his imprisonment by the General Chapter of the Calced Carmelites. He wrote poetry to comfort himself, composing *The Spiritual Canticle* and a number of shorter poems.

Advent

The Third Sunday of Advent

December 15, 2019

The promised day of God is dawning. John is the herald of that day. Jesus proclaimed the kingdom of God by everything he said and did.

Advent

Color   Violet or Blue

Preface   Advent

Collect

Stir up your power, O Lord, and with great might come among us; and, because we are sorely hindered by our sins, let your bountiful grace and mercy speedily help and deliver us; through Jesus Christ our Lord, to whom, with you and the Holy Spirit, be honor and glory, now and forever. Amen.

Readings and Psalm

Isaiah 35:1–10

In the reading from the Hebrew Bible **the prophet envisions a time of abundance and healing for Israel.** As when the people were led out of Egypt into the promised land, so this new return will be in the power of God. Retribution will fall upon the Lord's enemies, but there will be water in the wilderness for the redeemed. In words that are later used by Jesus to describe what is taking place in his ministry, the prophet foretells an age when the blind and deaf, the lame and dumb will be healed.

Psalm 146:5–10

A hymn of praise to the Lord, who forms the world and rules in justice, who heals and cares for the needy.

or

Luke 1:47–55 (Magnificat)

Mary offers a song of praise to God who has looked with favor on her and who has lifted up the lowly and brought down the powerful.

James 5:7–10

This lesson is **an exhortation to patient expectation in preparation for the coming of the Lord.** One may learn from the farmer, who must wait for the crop to ripen, or from the prophets who bore suffering with patience. Such endurance excludes a grumbling blaming of one another. The Lord will come soon.

Matthew 11:2–11

In our gospel passage **Jesus responds to a question from John the Baptist about his mission and then describes John's ministry.** Jesus' answer to John's question suggests that people must make up their own minds about his role while observing the healings that are taking place in accordance with ancient prophecies. Those who hear Jesus are also to recognize that John is a prophet and more: he is the one who prepares for the Lord's coming.

Prayers of the People

Be strong, do not fear! Our God is coming. Confident that our waiting is not in vain, let us offer our prayers as we respond, *"O come, O come, Emmanuel."*

O come Emmanuel, free us from the bondage of our sins, our pride and hypocrisy, our greed and self-serving interests, that we may know your redeeming love and reveal its liberating joy; let us pray.

O come, O come, Emmanuel.

O Wisdom from on high, show us the path of the Holy Way, and set our feet upon its joy; let us pray.

O come, O come, Emmanuel.

O Lord of Might, who gives sight to the blind and opens the ears of those who cannot hear, who heals the sick, raises the dead, and brings good news to the poor, give us a share of your power that we may do the works you do; let us pray.

O come, O come, Emmanuel.

O Branch of Jesse's tree, we give thanks for our spiritual ancestors, by whose faith the lamp of truth illumines the disciples of every age; let us pray.

O come, O come, Emmanuel.

O Key of David, unlock the doors of oppression and violence that imprison humankind, and set free those living in the bondage of slavery, the victims of abusive relationships, and those chained by poverty; let us pray.

O come, O come, Emmanuel.

O Dayspring from on high, may the dawn overcome every darkness, as your messengers plant the barren land with the seeds of hope; let us pray.

O come, O come, Emmanuel.

O Desire of Nations, free us from the division that separates nations and peoples, and fill the leaders of the world with a passion for peace; let us pray.

O come, O come, Emmanuel.

O Come, Emmanuel, lift up those who are lowly, and raise from the dead those who have fallen asleep; let us pray.

O come, O come, Emmanuel.

May we continue to proclaim our trust in the Lord's constant watch, as we add to these prayers and petitions.

(Special intentions of the congregation, the diocese, and the Anglican Communion may be added here or before the formal intercessions.)

The Celebrant adds a concluding Collect.

Images in the Readings

The **flowering wilderness** is the image presented in both the first reading and the gospel. Often the Bible uses imagery from nature to celebrate the presence of God. All of nature rejoices in God's continuing creation. We are called to ecological care for God's good earth, making literal the symbol of a flowering wilderness.

The **healing of the blind and lame** is a recurring image in Old Testament to describe the effect of the presence of God. The gospels say that Jesus healed the blind, the lame, the lepers, and the deaf; he raised the dead; and he preached to the poor—thus enacting all the miracles that are cited in the ancient poems.

In the ancient Near East, conquerors built massive **highway**s to allow for civic processions to display their power. The Bible cites and then transforms this image: there will be a highway on which the people will return in safety into their own city. Might is changed into right.

Ideas for the Day

♦ "Are you the one?" John had the grit to ask the question. The biblical landscape is littered with questions starting with "Where are you?" in Genesis 3. Questions are most often directed to a second person, a "you" that invites over-hearers and readers of the texts through the millennia to ponder the questions. John's query today, like Jesus' "Who do you say that I am?" of the Synoptics, bids us answer the questions for ourselves. Is the Jesus we meet in the gospels the One? Or are we looking for another Messiah, a comfier one, someone a little less disruptive and challenging?

♦ It is in living out our Baptismal Covenant call that the church responds to the question raised by John, "Are you the one who is to come, or are we to wait for another?" (Matt. 11:3). The first reading and the gospel lection lie behind the church's call to be deeply involved in the ministry of service and justice. The church continues in the role of Jesus, pointing out God's coming reign in such actions.

Advent

Advent

♦ Patience is a required virtue when we follow a Christian path. It is additionally important not to grumble against those around us. If we are constantly observing what others are not doing, then we are not devoting enough time and energy to what we are doing, working towards our own Christian walk. It has become so easy to post a negative comment on something we see online. In fact, there are some people in our society whose entire lives are consumed with cutting down others in order to build themselves up. We must reject this path. The Christian is one of constructivism. We must seek constantly to build relationships and never tear them down.

Making Connections

In the service of Evening Prayer in our Book of Common Prayer, it is notable that no matter what the reading, our tradition asserts that saying the Magnificat is always a good idea. It points to the reality of the Incarnation, the truth that God is with us, one of us. It also notes that God is not about blessing those who have with more. God is a God of those on the margins. God stands in solidarity with those who are poor, powerless—those whom—society often ignores and those who have been victims of injustice. How might we join God?

Engaging All Ages

♦ During the Liturgy of the Word, engage in storytelling. The stories of Jesus that lie behind his statement to John's disciples, such as a healing a paralyzed man (Mark 2:1–12) and restoring a girl to life (Luke 8:40–42, 49–56) offer some possibilities.

♦ We pray for God's Kingdom to come every time we pray the Lord's Prayer. How do you support families in teaching (and saying) this prayer at home in daily life?

Hymns for the Day

The Hymnal 1982

Blessed be the God of Israel 444
Watchman, tell us of the night 640
O for a thousand tongues to sing 493
Come, thou long-expected Jesus 66
O heavenly Word, eternal Light 63, 64
The Lord will come and not be slow 462
"Thy kingdom come!" on bended knee 615
Hark! the glad sound! the Savior comes 71, 72
Herald, sound the note of judgment 70
O for a thousand tongues to sing 493
On Jordan's bank the Baptist's cry 76
Prepare the way, O Zion 65
There's a voice in the wilderness crying 75
Word of God, come down on earth 633

Lift Every Voice and Sing II

Wonder, Love, and Praise
Blessed be the God of Israel 889
The desert shall rejoice 722

Weekday Commemorations

Tuesday, December 17
Dorothy L. Sayers,
Apologist and Spiritual Writer, 1957
Sayers wrote not just detective stories about Lord Peter Wimsey and Harriet Vane. She was also a theologian, linguist, translator, and advocate for Christianity. Sayers (b. 1893), daughter of the chaplain of Christ Church, graduated from Oxford in 1915; she received her degree five years later when women were finally allowed such recognition. While a successful copywriter at Benson's advertising, she wrote her first mystery, *Whose Body?* Sayers' religious writing began with the play *The Zeal for They House*; she upbraided the church for neglecting dogma and doctrine in *Creed or Chaos*, thus sealing her place as a Christian apologist.

Friday, December 20
Katharina von Bora, Church Reformer, 1552

Although drawn to religious life, Katharina shifted her interest to ecclesiastical reform after noting the church's abuses. In 1523, she and eleven Cistercian sisters sought Martin Luther's help in escaping their convent. They were smuggled out but had nowhere to go—certainly not to their families. They found husbands in the reform community. Katharina found a husband in Luther himself. She became a model pastor's wife, raising their six children, providing hospitality, and assisting in his preaching and publishing. Encouraged by Luther, she actively participated in theological dialogues at her table, drawing on her impressive knowledge of Scripture and Latin.

Saturday, December 21
Saint Thomas the Apostle

John's gospel narrates incidents in Thomas' life. He was with Jesus when he went to Judea to visit friends at Bethany. At the Last Supper, Thomas questioned our Lord: "Lord, we do not know where you are going; how can we know the way?" Thomas questioned Christ's resurrection until Jesus himself showed Thomas his wounds. Thomas, a staunch friend, was skeptical but did not deserve to be reduced to "doubting Thomas": he did not dare believe; also, a doubter was needed for contrast in the story, and Thomas became the protagonist. According to tradition, Thomas evangelized Parthians, Syrian Christians, and Indians in Kerala. The Gospel of Thomas, an apocryphal writing, is attributed to Saint Thomas the Apostle.

Advent

The Fourth Sunday of Advent

December 22, 2019

Jesus' imminent birth is proclaimed in the scriptures; his continued presence in the world is proclaimed by the Church today.

Color   Violet or Blue

Preface   Advent

Collect

Purify our conscience, Almighty God, by your daily visitation, that your Son Jesus Christ, at his coming, may find in us a mansion prepared for himself; who lives and reigns with you, in the unity of the Holy Spirit, one God, now and forever. Amen.

Readings and Psalm

Isaiah 7:10–16

In the first lesson we hear that **the prophet Isaiah insists that King Ahaz of Judah will receive a sign from God, whether he wants it or not, the sign of a young woman bearing a son to be called Emmanuel.** Ahaz was more inclined to depend on political alliances than on the Lord. Isaiah prophesied that, by the time the infant began to make his own choices, the Lord would destroy Judah's immediate enemies. Christians have seen the ultimate fulfillment of these prophetic words in the birth of Jesus.

Psalm 80:1–7, 17–19

A lament and a plea to the Lord, the shepherd of Israel, that God will turn away divine anger and restore the people.

Romans 1:1–7

Paul greets the new disciples in Rome and summarizes the gospel message. The prophecies concerning one to be descended from King David in human terms, and declared Son of God through the power of the Holy Spirit by resurrection from the dead, have been fulfilled. The Lord Jesus Christ has given grace and the commission of apostleship to bring peoples of all nations to faith and obedience.

Matthew 1:18–25

The gospel tells **the story of the birth of Jesus.** While she was betrothed to Joseph, Mary finds that she is bearing a child. But an angel tells Joseph not to fear: this is the work of the Holy Spirit. The baby is to be named Jesus, which means "The Lord saves." The evangelist perceives this birth to be the fulfillment of an ancient prophecy which told of a virgin who would bear a son. The narrative makes clear the divine origin of this child who will save the people from their sins.

Prayers of the People

From the depths of our interior mansions, and in heightened expectancy of the coming of the Messiah, let us offer our prayers, responding, *"O come, O come, Emmanuel."*

O come, Emmanuel and purify our conscience, that we may be an empty vessel prepared for the coming of your Word; let us pray.

O come, O come, Emmanuel.

O Wisdom, open our eyes to the signs of your grace in the world about us, and bind us to your will, that we may bear witness to your abundant life; let us pray.

O come, O come, Emmanuel.

O Lord of Might, strengthen us by your humility, that as we drink from the tears of the poor, and eat from their outstretched hands, we may be filled with the riches of enduring faith; let us pray.

O come, O come, Emmanuel.

O Branch of Jesse, stretch out your limbs of hope, that all the peoples of the world may come under the shade of your tree, where war shall cease and the fruits of love flourish; let us pray.

O come, O come, Emmanuel.

O Key of David, unlock our fear of those who differ from us, and remind us that the essence of our being is one, united across nations and races, cultures and time; let us pray.

O come, O come, Emmanuel.

O Dayspring from on high, fill us with thanksgiving at the beginning of the day, and when night falls place within us a heart of gratitude; let us pray.

O come, O come, Emmanuel.

O Desire of Nations, grant our leaders moral and ethical wholesomeness, that together with them we may form a just and righteous society; let us pray.

O come, O come, Emmanuel.

O come, Emmanuel, do not tarry; to the dead bring life, to the living hope, and to all creation the renewal of your first gifts; let us pray.

O come, O come, Emmanuel.

In the communion of the Blessed Virgin Mary and all your saints, let us continue our prayers.

(Special intentions of the congregation, the diocese, and the Anglican Communion may be added here or before the formal intercessions.)

The Celebrant adds a concluding Collect.

Images in the Readings

In Matthew's narratives, an **angel** figures in the stories of Jesus' birth and resurrection. In our society, many depictions of angels are unfortunately quite cutesy, not very helpful as images of the might of God. The angel is the divine messenger, the extension of the power and mercy of God, and in the Bible often the way that believers encounter the Almighty.

The **pregnant woman** can be a symbol of the life that comes from God. In the Bible, many women, from Eve in Genesis 4:1 on, conceive and bear children with the help of God. When we acclaim God as creator, we attest that God is continually creating life on this earth.

This Sunday it is **Joseph** who hears and receives the word of God. The history of art often depicted Joseph as an old man as a technique to convey that he was not instrumental in Mary's pregnancy. However, often in the Scriptures a woman's pregnancy is seen as a gift from God. We are now Mary, and God is in us. We are now Joseph, receiving from God a gift we cannot have achieved on our own.

Ideas for the Day

- Even before we reach the actual feast toward which we've been leaning these four weeks, we get the news in today's gospel that Christmas *is*. Not just *was* a couple of thousand years ago, or *will be* in a Second Coming, but *is*, and *was* and *will be*. Immanuel, that name coined by Isaiah, is actually a sentence in Hebrew's nuanced grammar: "God *was/is/will be* with us." Christmas is timeless, or as poet U. A. Fanthorpe put it in the poem "BC:AD", "This was the moment when Before Turned into After, and the future's Uninvented timekeepers presented arms."

- Do we listen to the angels in our life? We sometimes feel that our lives run at a hectic pace. The universe of the internet has fostered the illusion of the need to always be plugged in: know the latest news, watch the latest funny video, listen the best new music, find ways to respond appropriately to twenty different emails, and so on. This constant need for updating and rapid-fire engagement with technology can be a distraction. The angels in our lives still speak through personal human contact. Are we prepared to listen to their message? Would we give up an hour of screen time to go visit a congregant who is shut in? The universe of human interaction is far more fascinating than anything the internet will ever be able to create.

- The role of the Christian congregation, and the individual Christian, is to reflect the presence of God in the world today. From the fourth Sunday of Advent through the Feast of the Epiphany, the church celebrates the Incarnation; God is present "in the flesh" of human life. God meets us in the midst of our human struggle.

Advent

Making Connections

It is worth noting the angel's first words to Joseph: "Do not be afraid." God knows our fear. God understands that we are afraid to step out into an uncertain future. And so he sends his angels to remind us that God is calling us to new and wonderful possibilities. God wishes for us to trust and to let go of those fears that do not serve us. If we can rest in the beautiful truth of God's Way of Love, how might we then go more boldly into the future?

Engaging All Ages

This Sunday is often a day when churches hold pageants and "green" the church. If neither of these participatory events occur in your congregation, distribute cut out paper hearts with your worship bulletin. Invite congregants of all ages to write or draw something on the heart that they would like to give to the Christ child or a hope they have of the new possibilities that the angels proclaim. These can be placed in the alms basins during the offertory or gathered at the empty créche of your nativity.

Hymns for the Day

The Hymnal 1982

God himself is with us 475
How bright appears the Morning Star 496, 497
O come, O come, Emmanuel 56
Come, thou long-expected Jesus 66
How bright appears the Morning Star 496, 497
By the Creator, Joseph was appointed 261, 262
Come now, and praise the humble saint 260
Creator of the stars of night 60
How bright appears the Morning Star 496, 497
Redeemer of the nations, come 55
Savior of the nations, come 54

Lift Every Voice and Sing II

Wonder, Love, and Praise

Weekday Commemorations

Thursday, December 26
Saint Stephen, Deacon and Martyr
Stephen became the first deacon by his appointment to assist the apostles. He was one of the "seven men of good repute, full of the Spirit and of wisdom," chosen by the apostles to help them serve at tables and care for widows. Stephen served beyond tables, for the Acts of the Apostles describes him preaching and performing miracles. These activities pushed him to confront Jews, who accused him of blasphemy and brought him before the Sanhedrin; his powerful sermon before the council is recorded in Acts 7. Enraged, councilmen dragged him out of the city to stone him to death. In fear, the Christian community scattered and, thus, spread the Word.

Friday, December 27
Saint John, Apostle and Evangelist
John and James, sons of Zebedee, were fishers who became "fishers of men" as disciples. With Peter and James, John became one with the "inner circle" whom Jesus chose to witness his raising of Jairus' daughter, his Transfiguration, and his praying in the garden of Gethsemane. John and James were such angry males that Jesus called them "sons of thunder." Ambitious, they sought to sit next to Jesus at table; willing companions, they shared the communal cup of wine, little knowing the cost. Possibly, John held a special relationship as the "disciple whom Jesus loved," the one asked to care for his mother. It is said that John, alone of the Twelve, lived long—no martyr he.

Saturday, December 28
The Holy Innocents
The Holy Innocents were the baby boys ordered killed by Herod. Herod the Great, ruler of the Jews, was described by the historian Josephus as "a man of great barbarity towards everyone." Appointed by the Romans in 40 BCE, Herod kept peace in Palestine for thirty-seven years. Ruthless yet able, this Idumaean was married to the daughter of Hyrcanus, the last legal Hasmonean ruler, so Herod always feared losing his throne. According to the story, the Wise Ones' report of the birth of a King of the Jews scared him: He ordered the slaughter of all male children under two in Bethlehem. Although not recorded in secular history, the massacre of the innocents keeps to Herod's character.

Christmas

Preparing for Christmas

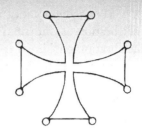

Theological Themes that Might Shape Liturgy, Catechesis, and Education

If the Season of Advent is all about hope and anticipation, then Christmastide is all about the fulfillment of that hope in the mystery of the Incarnation. It can be difficult to separate the distinctive qualities of Advent and Christmas from the franken-season of secular Christmas, but it is important to think about intentional ways to celebrate this season in ways that rise above the seasonal noise. This may mean intentionally eschewing the anxiety that accompanies performing the sacred traditions of the season that do little to convey the rich meaning of the season. As with any liturgy, but especially true during festival occasions, adding too many idiosyncratic elements to the liturgy might undermine the messages the occasion is meant to convey.

The Incarnation is the central theme of Christmas and not simply the incarnation of the Christ in the form of a newborn in a manger. It is important to draw direct connections between the physical body of Christ, expressed in the Christ-child, and the mystical body of Christ, the Church. The alternative is the liturgical fetishization of an aloof infant deity that does little to edify the assembly or equip the saints for the work of ministry.

Liturgical Possibilities

Rites

As the Holy Eucharist is "the principal act of Christian worship on the Lord's Day and other major Feasts," it is likely that, unless there are extenuating circumstances, your community will commemorate the Lord's incarnation by celebrating the Holy Eucharist. If prior planning has connected Christmas with the previous season of Advent, it might be helpful to make the changes necessary to highlight the different qualities of this season. For example, if you have chosen to use the Penitential Order through Advent, you might consider returning to a regular Entrance Rite. This also has the added benefit of appealing to those who will visit our congregations but aren't familiar with celebrations of the Eucharist that deviate from the typical form.

Depending on the worship life of your faith community, you might consider if and how you will observe the Feasts that immediately follow Christmas. J. Neil Alexander astutely observes that the Feast of the Holy Innocents (December 28) is the only one thematically associated with the Christmas season. The other two—St. Stephen (December 26) and St. John the Evangelist (December 27)—are only in the Christmas Season by coincidence. One need not perform liturgical acrobatics either to mandate their commemoration if it isn't germane to a particular community or to force homiletical connections that do not actually exist.

Space, Other Rituals, and Resources

In spaces that feature adjustable lighting or flexible seating, it might be helpful to use the resources at our disposal to further highlight the difference of the season. Christmas is also an opportunity to involve more people in the celebration than usual such as in the performance of a pageant. While creativity is to be celebrated, the warning still stands: the key portions of the liturgy should still be observed, or else the message of the Incarnation gets lost.

Christmas

Many communities will have at least one celebration of Christmas on the Eve and one celebration on Christmas Day. If possible, these services should be distinct, perhaps employing a different Entrance Rite on the Eve (taking advantage of the light in a way that is rubrically sound) and reverting to a traditional Entrance Rite for the celebration on Christmas Day. There are resources in the Book of Common Prayer and the *Book of Occasional Services* that can help with this planning. Think simple but meaningful.

Through the Eyes of a Child

At Christmas, we who are the church welcome Jesus and joyfully celebrate his birth. The church is often filled with greens and trees and lights. Something wonderful has happened, and it is time to celebrate. We give thanks for God's greatest gift of love to us, the Son, Jesus Christ. We give to others in response to the gift that has been given to us. This is the time to blend family traditions—meals, visits, and activities—with an awareness of the birth of Jesus. The traditional crèche and manger need to have a prominent place for children to touch and re-enact the story of the birth of Jesus. Child-friendly pageants and Christmas plays that invite the children into telling and being a part of the story are critical, as well as doing something as a family, such as gathering up clothes that no longer fit to give to those in need, to teach and demonstrate ways to bring the light of Christ into the darkness. Music is also important; singing the beloved Christmas carols that announce the birth of Christ will offer the child a way to proclaim how the love of God breaks into the world in the birth of Jesus.

Young people are likely to be inundated with all sorts of messages surrounding the Christmas Season, some less helpful and spiritually edifying than others. Their experience marking this season in worship can go a long way to pointing to the real meaning of this season. As with all liturgical and aesthetic differences throughout the year, it would be incredibly helpful to find ways of pointing out and explaining those differences to children (flash cards, notes in the bulletin, etc.) This has the added benefit both of explaining this meaning to adults who are often less apt to ask what they do not know and of empowering parents to bring Christian Formation into their homes.

Through the Eyes of Youth

The Church is called to demonstrate how the birth of Jesus changes the whole world. This is the time for families to talk about God, for parents to share their faith with their teens, and particularly talk about their faith in regard to family traditions, which show or "embody" Christ's presence through the way the family marks the change in seasons. To welcome all to the joy of the birth of Christ, encourage youth to invite friends to attend worship services, to sit at dinner table, and to gather for sharing of gifts at the tree. Some of the sharing of gifts could include special reflections on gifts of faith, gifts of courage, gifts of sports, or intellectual gifts. Invite youth into the question, "Where is there need for peace in our country? In our world? What can one do? Jesus came to offer peace to all people; how can each one of us make a difference?" Choose a particular project to complete during the Christmas and Epiphany seasons.

Young people are often included in the additional aspects of the Christmas liturgies (acolyting, Christmas pageants, etc.). The danger with creating too much of a fuss during this season is that we simply teach young people to mimic the anxiety of the wider, secular society. Striking a balance is key.

Through the Eyes of Daily Life

Christmas is to be celebrated for twelve days. Reflect on how we can live the joy of Jesus' birth this and every day, knowing that the Spirit of Christ dwells in us and guides us so that we may be his witnesses in all that we say and do. How do you live your life, knowing that God's Word lives among us?

Given that the mystery of the Incarnation is inexhaustible, we might think about how to give people tools to further explore the meaning of the Incarnation at home. Preparing resources for worshipers to take home with them might be a wonderful way to think about a church Christmas gift (the gift that keeps on giving—for twelve days).

Through the Eyes of Those Outside of the Church

Because many outside of the Church will be unclear about the distinction of Advent and Christmas, how we celebrate Christmas is an opportunity to proclaim the relevance of the mystery of the Incarnation for the world. This season presents a great opportunity to empower regular worshipers with resources to invite their family, friends, and others to attend worship.

Christmas should also be observed in a manner that conveys its gravity. A poorly executed liturgy might unintentionally convey a message that undermines the magnitude of the Incarnation. Consider a rehearsal that not only helps to tighten up the liturgy, but also helps to convey the message to the liturgical ministers who then, by their liturgical performance, will convey that meaning to the gathered community.

Through the Eyes of the Global Community

Christmas is the perfect time to offer opportunities for seeing the season of Christmas from the perspective of children from around the world. While the tradition of the 1979 Prayer Book centers us on the incarnation, it is vitally important that we look at the state of children from a global perspective. Holy Innocents (December 28th) is often overlooked; this is a time to learn of those places were children are persecuted and the places where children have no hope. Expand the vision of mission during Christmas to respond to those who are most vulnerable, which includes the children of our world. The United Nations and the Children's Defense Fund offer current statistics and initiatives that a congregation can learn from and discuss as a way to discern possible mission initiatives for the New Year.

Christmas

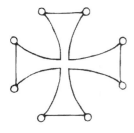

Christmas Blessing[1]

The following blessing may be used by a bishop or priest whenever a blessing is appropriate. It is a three-fold form, with an Amen at the end of each sentence, leading into a Trinitarian blessing.

May Almighty God, who sent his Son to take our nature upon him, bless you in this holy season, scatter the darkness of sin, and brighten your heart with the light of his holiness. *Amen.*

May God, who sent his angels to proclaim the glad news of the Savior's birth, fill you will joy, and make you heralds of the gospel. *Amen.*

May God, who in the Word made flesh joined heaven to earth and earth to heaven, give you his peace and favor. *Amen.*

And the blessing of God Almighty, the Father, the Son, and the Holy Spirit, be upon you and remain with you for ever. *Amen.*

The Christmas Crèche[2]

At their entry into the church for the celebration of the Holy Eucharist, the Celebrant (and other ministers) may make a station at a Christmas Crèche. The figure of the Christ Child may be carried in the procession and placed in the Crèche. Other figures may also be brought in if desired.

A versicle may be said, followed by a prayer.

V. The word was made flesh and dwelt among us.
R. And we beheld his glory.

Most merciful and loving God, you have made this day holy by the incarnation of your Son Jesus Christ, and by the child-bearing of the Blessed Virgin Mary: Grant that we your people may enter with joy into the celebration of this day, and may also rejoice for ever as your adopted sons and daughters; through Jesus Christ our Lord. *Amen.*

Blessing of a Christmas Tree

The Christmas tree stems from an ancient tradition of bringing evergreens into the home during the winter months as a hopeful reminder that spring would come. It has now become a familiar symbol of the Christian holiday in homes and in many churches.

Most Holy and Blessed One, you sent your beloved Son into the world to show us the path to true life. May the green of this tree remind us of the everlasting life you offer. May the boughs of this tree remind us that we are the living branches of your love. May the life of this tree remind us of the cross on which your Son gave his life. May the lights of this tree remind us that Christ is the light of the world. As we gather round this tree, we gather in your name, and in your light, and in your love. *Amen.*[3]

Christmas Festival of Lessons and Music

Nine Lessons are customarily selected (but fewer may be used), interspersed with appropriate carols, hymns, canticles, and anthems during this service, which can take place within the twelve days of Christmas. When possible, each Lesson should be read by a different lector, preferably voices of male and female readers as well as a variety of ages. The Lesson from the third chapter of Genesis is never omitted.

Genesis 2:4b–9, 15–25
Genesis 3:1–23 *or* 3:1–5
Isaiah 40:1–11
Isaiah 35:1–10
Isaiah 7:10–15
Luke 1:5–25
Luke 1:26–58
Luke 1:39–46 *or* 1:39–56
Luke 1:57–80
Luke 2:1–20
Luke 2:21–36
Hebrews 1:1–12
John 1:1–18

---

1 Ibid, 23.
2 *Book of Occasional Services*, 36.

3 Anne E. Kitch. *The Anglican Family Prayer Book* (Harrisburg, PA: Morehouse Publishing, 2004), 125–126.

On-the-Spot Christmas Pageant in Four Parts

Hold an impromptu Christmas pageant by inviting partici-pants to act out with silent movements the Christmas story as it is read. Makeshift costumes and props could be made available with part of the congregation assigned as the chorus, volunteers given the role as narrators/readers, and children (of all ages) being given the parts of Mary, Joseph, animals, shepherds, and angels.

Read: Luke 2:1–4

At that time Emperor Augustus ordered a census to be taken throughout the Roman Empire. When this first census took place, Quirinius was the governor of Syria. Everyone, then, went to register himself, each to his own hometown. Joseph went from the town of Nazareth in Galilee to the town of Bethlehem in Judea, the birthplace of King David. Joseph went there because he was a descendant of David.

Sing: "O, Little Town of Bethlehem"

Read: Luke 2:5–7

He went to register with Mary, who was promised in marriage to him. She was pregnant, and while they were in Bethlehem, the time came for her to have her baby. She gave birth to her first son, wrapped him in cloths and laid him in a manger—there was no room for them to stay in the inn.

Sing: "Silent Night, Holy Night"

Read: Luke 2:8–14

There were some shepherds in that part of the country who were spending the night in the fields, taking care of their flocks. An angel of the Lord appeared to them, and the glory of the Lord shone over them. They were terribly afraid, but the angel said to them, "Don't be afraid! I am here with good news for you, which will bring great joy to all the people. This very day in David's town your Savior was born—Christ the Lord! And this is what will prove it to you: you will find a baby wrapped in cloths and lying in a manger." Suddenly a great army of heaven's angels appeared with the angel, singing praises to God: "Glory to God in the highest heaven, and peace on earth to those with whom he is pleased!"

Sing: "Go, Tell It On the Mountain"

Read: Luke 2:15–20

When the angels went away from them back into heaven, the shepherds said to one another, "Let's go to Bethlehem and see this thing that has happened, which the Lord has told us." So they hurried off and found Mary and Joseph and saw the baby lying in the manger. When the shepherds saw him, they told them what the angel had said about the child. All who heard it were amazed at what the shepherds said. Mary remembered all these things and thought deeply about them. The shepherds went back, singing praises to God for all they had heard and seen; it had been just as the angel had told them.

Sing: "O Come, All Ye Faithful"

Feast of the Holy Innocents[4]

Saturday, December 28

Psalm 124 is appointed for this day. Different individuals can read each portion a refrain offered by all.

If you had not been on our side
when destructive powers rose up and barred our path,
if you had not been committed to our good,
like monsters they would have swallowed us alive.
Refrain: Praise to the God who is for us, and for all
that is being created.

Their anger was kindled against us,
like the sweep of the forest fire.
Their fury bore down upon us,
like the raging torrent in flood,
the waters of chaos that know no limits,
trespassers that are hard to forgive. *Refrain.*

Thanks be to you, our deliverer,
you have not given us as prey to their teeth.
We escaped like a bird from the snare of the fowler:
the frame snapped and we have flown free. *Refrain.*

In the joy of deliverance we praise you, O God.
Our hearts expand in a new generosity:
we embody love with which you create.
Even the powers you do not destroy:
you redeem all our failures to live,
you are strong to bring good out of evil. *Refrain.*

---

4 Jim Cotter. *Psalms for a Pilgrim People* (Harrisburg, PA: Morehouse Publishing, 1998), 282.

Service for New Year's Eve[5]

During the evening of December 31, which is the eve of the Feast of the Holy Name and also the eve of the civil New Year, this service begins with the Service of Light (BCP, 109) and continues with readings, silence, and prayer.

The Hebrew Year

Exodus 23:9–16, 20–21
Psalm 111 *or* Psalm 119:1–8

O God our Creator, you have divided our life into days and seasons, and called us to acknowledge your providence year after year: Accept your people who come to offer their praises, and, in your mercy, receive their prayers; through Jesus Christ our Lord. *Amen.*

The Promised Land

Deuteronomy 11:8–12, 26–28
Psalm 36:5–10 *or* Psalm 89, Part I

Almighty God, the source of all life, giver of all blessing, and savior of all who turn to you: Have mercy upon this nation; deliver us from falsehood, malice, and disobedience; turn our feet into your paths; and grant that we may serve you in peace; through Jesus Christ our Lord. *Amen.*

A Season for All Things

Ecclesiastes 3:1–15
Psalm 90

In your wisdom, O Lord our God, you have made all things, and have allotted to each of us the days of our life: Grant that we may live in your presence, be guided by your Holy Spirit, and offer all our works to your honor and glory; through Jesus Christ our Lord. *Amen.*

Remember your Creator

Ecclesiastes 12:1–8
Psalm 130

Immortal Lord God, you inhabit eternity, and have brought us your unworthy servants to the close of another year: Pardon, we entreat you, our transgressions of the past, and graciously abide with us all the days of our life; through Jesus Christ our Lord. *Amen.*

Marking the Times, and Winter

Ecclesiasticus 43:1–22
Psalm 19 *or* Psalm 148 *or* Psalm 74:11–22

Almighty Father, you give the sun for a light by day, and the moon and the starts by night: Graciously receive us, this night and always, into your favor and protection, defending us from all harm and governing us with your Holy Spirit, that every shadow of ignorance, every failure of faith or weakness of heart, every evil or wrong desire may be removed far from us; so that we, being justified in our Lord Jesus Christ, may be sanctified by your Spirit, and glorified by your infinite mercies in the day of the glorious appearing of our Lord and Savior Jesus Christ. *Amen.*

The Acceptable Time

2 Corinthians 5:17—6:2
Psalm 63:1–8 *or* Canticle 5 *or* Canticle 17

Most gracious and merciful God, you have reconciled us to yourself through Jesus Christ your Son, and called us to new life in him: Grant that we, who begin this year in his Name, may complete it to his honor and glory; who lives and reigns now and for ever. *Amen.*

Christmas

---

5 Ibid, 43–45.

While it is Called Today
Hebrews 3:1–15 (16—4:13)
Psalm 95

O God, through your Son you have taught us to be watchful, and to await the sudden day of judgment: Strengthen us against Satan and his forces of wickedness, the evil powers of this world, and the sinful desires within us; and grant that, having served you all the days of our life, we may finally come to the dwelling place your Son has prepared for us; who lives and reigns for ever and ever. *Amen.*

New Heavens and New Earth
Revelation 21:1–14, 22–24
Canticle 19

Almighty and merciful God, through your well beloved Son Jesus Christ, the King of kings and Lord of lords, you have willed to make all things new: Grant that we may be renewed by your Holy Spirit, and may come at last to that heavenly country where your people hunger and thirst no more, and the tears are wiped away from every eye; through Jesus Christ our Lord. *Amen.*

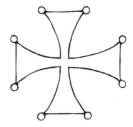

Christmas Eve

December 24, 2019

God came in Jesus of Nazareth to reveal the power of God's love and healing. In the birth of Jesus we realize that God shares life with us intimately. We meet God "in the flesh" of human struggle and most especially in the midst of human love. Christmas celebrates the incarnation of God; God "in the flesh of" human life. (Carne comes from the Latin for meat or flesh.)

Color White

Preface Of the Incarnation

Collect

O God, you have caused this holy night to shine with the brightness of the true Light: Grant that we, who have known the mystery of that Light on earth, may also enjoy him perfectly in heaven; where with you and the Holy Spirit he lives and reigns, one God, in glory everlasting. Amen.

Readings and Psalm

Isaiah 9:2–7

From the Hebrew Bible we hear **a hymn of thanksgiving and hope offered at the birth of a new king in Jerusalem.** The prophet hails the one born to be the ruler of his people. His reign will end oppression and bring justice, righteousness, and a lasting peace. Christians see these words coming to fulfillment in Jesus.

Psalm 96 (Cantate Domino)

A song of praise to the Lord in which the whole heavens and earth are invited to join.

Titus 2:11–14

This New Testament reading speaks of **the two comings of Christ: first in his sacrificial ministry for all people and then in glory.** He has enabled his disciples to free themselves from ways of evil. Disciplined and eager to do good, they look forward to the fulfillment of the hope God has given to the world in Jesus.

Luke 2:1–14 (15–20)

The gospel presents **the story of the birth of Jesus.** He is born amid very humble human circumstances. A government registration program requires Joseph and Mary to go to Bethlehem, the city of David. Because there was no other place for them to stay, Mary lays her new son in a stable manger.

An angel then appears to shepherds and announces the joyful news of the Savior's birth.

If the longer version is used, the last sentence may read:

An angel announces the joyful news of the Savior's birth to shepherds who come to Bethlehem and report the angelic vision.

Prayers of the People

The Word has been made flesh, the light of God's love has broken through our darkness, the Daystar from on high now shines in our hearts. Filled with the joy of Jesus' birth, let us pray together in the power of his Spirit, responding, "Lord, hear our prayer."

That the Prince of Peace may guide the leaders of the nations, and all men and women everywhere, into the ways of freedom and truth; let us pray.

Lord, hear our prayer.

For N., Archbishop of Canterbury, N., Presiding Bishop of our Church, and N., our Bishop, that they may guide us in our journey to Bethlehem, uniting the whole Church as we live into our spiritual kinship with one another; let us pray.

Lord, hear our prayer.

Christmas

For those for whom the darkness has suffocated hope: the lonely, the fearful, the hungry, and those who bear a private grief; that they may see the dawn of God's love, and revive the eternal hope that never fades away; let us pray.

Lord, hear our prayer.

For our families and friends, and for all our absent sisters and brothers; for those who are sick, especially _____; and for those who have died and who now feast at the heavenly banquet of God's grace; let us pray.

Lord, hear our prayer.

That we may be released from the captivity of our sins, the places of interior blindness that cause us to choose darkness over light; that we may be forgiven by the power of the Holy Spirit; let us pray.

Lord, hear our prayer.

That we who gather to share the Holy Eucharist, and those throughout the world who come to receive this sacrament of Holy Presence, may bear witness to Christ born in our hearts; let us pray.

Lord, hear our prayer.

In the wonder of this night, [or In the beauty of this morning,] let us continue to offer our petitions. *(Special intentions of the congregation, the diocese, and the Anglican Communion may be added here or before the formal intercessions.)*

The Celebrant adds a concluding Collect.

Images in the Readings

Luke writes that **angels**, messengers from heaven, a link between God and humankind, announce Christ and sing praise to God. It is a challenge to describe and, especially, to depict angels in a worthy manner. Contrary to popular notions, Christian doctrine does not teach that dead Christians become angels, but rather that angels are supernatural beings that signify and convey the power of God. In Luke, the angels proclaim the meaning of the incarnation. Recall that in Luke's telling of the annunciation to Mary, the angel is Gabriel, who Jewish tradition identified as the one who proclaims the arrival of the eschaton.

Although in some places in the Bible cities are described as evil and filled with temptations, in Isaiah 62 the city **Jerusalem** symbolizes God's protection, God's very presence on earth. Throughout history, the church has used the image of Jerusalem as a picture of itself: we are like Jerusalem, a magnificent city, protected by the arms of God, thriving on word and sacrament. This imagery might not be clear to all worshipers, who might likely think that we are referring to the actual city of the twenty-first century: sometimes in our worship "Jerusalem" identifies first-century geography, sometimes it is a metaphor for the church, and sometimes it is the name of a current city filled with international religious conflict.

On a day that we think about the **birth** of Jesus, we recall also the water of our rebirth in baptism.

Ideas for the Day

♦ One of the reasons that Luke tells his story the way he does—quietly, unpretentiously, no one but the family and a few shepherds in attendance—is to remind us that the miraculous happens in the most unexpected places to the most unlikely of people who do what they can to make room for a God who risks so much, who dares to become one of us. God came among us in diapers once upon a time in backwater Bethlehem. God continues to come among us still, wherever and however we find ourselves, because God "so loved the world" not just once, but always, even when we can't believe it, even in the mess of our world, even now. Christmas is, period.

♦ "Sing to the Lord a new song." Create a melody tree. Take a sheet of ten-staff manuscript paper. Cut it into strips so that each staff is separate, giving you ten single line staves. Using the *Hymnal 1982* and four other hymn supplement resources, (i.e., *Wonder Love and Praise, Voices Found, Lift Every Voice and Sing*, etc.) find melodies of the Christmas season. Look particularly for music by composers who are still living. On your single staff notate ten melodies. Include the words. Tape your melody strips to pipe cleaners. Affix them to a base to form a tree/plant-like pattern. You could also take the melody strips and paste them in an artful way to poster boards. Sing, sing, sing.

The kindness and grace-filled actions we experience every day from other people can give us hope. Regular practices of Prayer and Sabbath—practices that allow our bodies, our minds and our spirits time to Rest and recharge help us to keep our hope strong. All of these things point us to the source of all our hope. The actions of others inspire us and prayer and rest strengthen us because they deepen our connection to God. Our hope is found in God, in an eternal well, an eternal Way of Love and Blessing.

Making Connections

God came into the world as vulnerable infant. God chose the messiest entrance possible—to be born of a woman in a manger. In that truth God tells us that the mess of our lives is not something to hide or fear. We are invited to come to the manger just as we are, just as the shepherds did, just as Jesus did—mess and all. We are invited to Pray and Worship, to be filled with the overwhelming, unconditional love of God, so that we might Go from this place and pour out that love in the world.

Engaging All Ages

Assembling luminaria to be placed outside of a church on Christmas Eve is fun for all ages. All that is needed is a cup of sand placed in an open white paper bag, with a white votive candle resting in the sand. These can be assembled in advance and placed outside along the sidewalks, stone walls, or entrances to your sanctuary by many. Adults can then light them as darkness approaches, providing a welcoming light to all who enter (and pass by) throughout the evening.

Hymns for the Day

The Hymnal 1982

Hark! the herald angels sing 87
It came upon the midnight clear 89, 90
Sing, O sing, this blessed morn 88
The people who in darkness walked 125, 126
Unto us a boy is born! 98
Joy to the world! the Lord is come 100
A child is born in Bethlehem 103
A stable lamp is lighted 104
Angels we have heard on high 96
Away in a manger 101
From heaven above to earth I come 80
Go, tell it on the mountain 99
God rest you merry, gentlemen 105
In the bleak midwinter 112
Lo, how a Rose e'er blooming 81
O come, all ye faithful 83
O little town of Bethlehem 78, 79
Once in royal David's city 102
Silent night, holy night 111
The first Nowell the angel did say 109
The snow lay on the ground 110

Lift Every Voice and Sing II

Away in a manger 27
Go, tell it on the mountain 21
Mary borned a baby 22
Silent night, holy night 26
That boy-child of Mary was born in a stable 25

Wonder, Love, and Praise

Shengye qing, shengye jing /
    Holy night, blessed night 725

Christmas

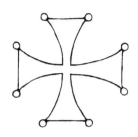

The Nativity of Our Lord Jesus Christ: Christmas Day

December 25, 2019

Christmas

God came in Jesus of Nazareth to reveal the power of God's love and healing. In the birth of Jesus, we realize that God shares life with us intimately. We meet God "in the flesh" of human struggle and most especially in the midst of human love. Christmas celebrates the incarnation of God; God "in the flesh of" human life. (Carne comes from the Latin for meat or flesh.)

Color   White

Preface   Of the Incarnation

Collect

Almighty God, you have given your only-begotten Son to take our nature upon him, and to be born this day of a pure virgin: Grant that we, who have been born again and made your children by adoption and grace, may daily be renewed by your Holy Spirit; through our Lord Jesus Christ, to whom with you and the same Spirit be honor and glory, now and forever. Amen.

Readings and Psalm

Isaiah 52:7–10

The Hebrew scripture lection heralds **a time of great joy as the Lord saves the people and brings deliverance to Jerusalem.** The long exile is at an end. The messenger proclaims the good news, "The Lord reigns." The watchmen of the city respond with shouts of triumph to see God's salvation.

Psalm 98

A song of thanksgiving and praise to the victorious Lord, who has made righteousness known and shown faithfulness to God's people.

Hebrews 1:1–4 (5–12)

In this lesson **the Letter to the Hebrews begins with a declaration of Jesus' sonship. He is far above all angels at the right hand of God.** Previously God had spoken through the prophets, but now the will of God is expressed in the Son, through whom the world was created and who bears the stamp of divine being. After making purification for sins, he has taken his seat of greatest honor.

If using Hebrews 1:1–12, this concluding sentence may be added:

A series of quotations from the Hebrew Bible is used to show the Son's superiority to the angels, who are the highest order of created beings.

John 1:1–14

The gospel opens with **a hymn to the expression of God's very being, God's Word, who has now become flesh and lived among us.** Through the Word all things have their life. The Word is the light of all humankind, and was witnessed to by John the Baptist. Although the world made by the Word did not recognize the Word, those who believe in the Word have been given the right to become children of God.

Prayers of the People

The Word has been made flesh, the light of God's love has broken through our darkness, the Daystar from on high now shines in our hearts. Filled with the joy of Jesus' birth, let us pray together in the power of his Spirit, responding, "Lord, hear our prayer."

That the Prince of Peace may guide the leaders of the nations, and all men and women everywhere, into the ways of freedom and truth; let us pray.

Lord, hear our prayer.

For N., Archbishop of Canterbury, N., Presiding Bishop of our Church, and N., our Bishop, that they may guide us in our journey to Bethlehem, uniting the whole Church as we live into our spiritual kinship with one another; let us pray.

Lord, hear our prayer.

For those for whom the darkness has suffocated hope: the lonely, the fearful, the hungry, and those who bear a private grief; that they may see the dawn of God's love, and revive the eternal hope that never fades away; let us pray.

Lord, hear our prayer.

For our families and friends, and for all our absent sisters and brothers; for those who are sick, especially _____; and for those who have died and who now feast at the heavenly banquet of God's grace; let us pray.

Lord, hear our prayer.

That we may be released from the captivity of our sins, the places of interior blindness that cause us to choose darkness over light; that we may be forgiven by the power of the Holy Spirit; let us pray.

Lord, hear our prayer.

That we who gather to share the Holy Eucharist, and those throughout the world who come to receive this sacrament of Holy Presence, may bear witness to Christ born in our hearts; let us pray.

Lord, hear our prayer.

In the wonder of this night, [*or* In the beauty of this morning,] let us continue to offer our petitions. (*Special intentions of the congregation, the diocese, and the Anglican Communion may be added here or before the formal intercessions.*)

The Celebrant adds a concluding Collect.

Images in the Readings

Luke writes that **angels**, messengers from heaven, a link between God and humankind, announce Christ and sing praise to God. It is a challenge to describe and, especially, to depict angels in a worthy manner. Contrary to popular notions, Christian doctrine does not teach that dead Christians become angels, but rather that angels are supernatural beings that signify and convey the power of God. In Luke, the angels proclaim the meaning of the incarnation. Recall that in Luke's telling of the annunciation to Mary, the angel is Gabriel, who Jewish tradition identified as the one who proclaims the arrival of the eschaton.

Although in some places in the Bible cities are described as evil and filled with temptations, in Isaiah 62 the city **Jerusalem** symbolizes God's protection, God's very presence on earth. Throughout history, the church has used the image of Jerusalem as a picture of itself: we are like Jerusalem, a magnificent city, protected by the arms of God, thriving on word and sacrament. This imagery might not be clear to all worshipers, who might likely think that we are referring to the actual city of the twenty-first century: sometimes in our worship "Jerusalem" identifies first-century geography, sometimes it is a metaphor for the church, and sometimes it is the name of a current city filled with international religious conflict.

On a day that we think about the **birth** of Jesus, we recall also the water of our rebirth in baptism.

Christmas

Ideas for the Day

♦ The celebrant said "The Lord be with you," but instead of the expected response, what came back was "And I'll sit with you" from a four-year-old congregant. The kiddo had it right. In the magnificent opening of the fourth gospel, the verse translated "the Word became flesh and dwelt among us" is really something more like "the Word . . . pitched a tent in our campsite" in the Greek. Moved into our neighborhood. Wanted to hang out with us. "The Lord be with you." "And I'll sit with you." God did. This year, let's return the favor.

♦ Luke's account of Jesus being placed in a manger at his birth because there was no room in the inn serves as a constant reminder to the Christian that God identifies with the weak, the poor, and the outcast.

♦ In this season of birth/rebirth, let us be open to wonder. Babies have a natural ability for this. Observe how they react to something new. Sheer wonder envelopes their whole face. O how jaded we have become. Yet in many ways, our Christian perspective gives us the opportunity to see old things anew. We can infuse wonder into old traditions by adding, expanding, and updating. This can best be done by connecting with traditions that are not of our own particular culture. Christians around the world bring their own voices and approaches to living their faith. What can we learn by joining with others in new ways, engaging in our innate ability to wonder?

Making Connections

The Gospel of John affirms the eternal reality of the light of Christ that shines in the darkness. Always. The darkness does not overcome it. This can be a great comfort to us in the midst of our own moments of personal darkness. Whether it be the darkness of illness or the loss of a loved one or the darkness of financial challenges or a broken dream. Or the darkness we see in the world. Wherever we find darkness, we can proclaim that the darkness will not overcome us! Not today. Not tomorrow. Not ever.

Engaging All Ages

Plan in advance to invite congregants and families to bring and display their crèches in your nave, narthex, or parish hall. Invite individuals to share stories about their crèches, such as the history of the crèche and the traditions that they observe during the Christmas season. If your church has a traditional crèche with an interesting story, invite a long-standing member or leader to also share the story.

Hymns for the Day

The Hymnal 1982
Awake, thou Spirit of the watchmen 540
Surely it is God who saves me 678, 679
Good Christian friends, rejoice 107
Love came down at Christmas 84
Angels we have heard on high 96
Christians, awake, salute the happy morn 106
Go, tell it on the mountain 99
O come, all ye faithful 83
Once in royal David's city 102
Hark! the herald angels sing 87
'Twas in the moon of wintertime 114
While shepherds watched their flocks by night 94, 95

Lift Every Voice and Sing II
Go, tell it on the mountain 21
Rise up, shepherd, and follow 24

Wonder, Love, and Praise

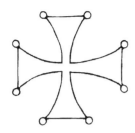

The First Sunday after Christmas

December 29, 2019

God came in Jesus fully to reveal God's love and forgiveness to all.

Color White

Preface Of the Incarnation

Collect

Almighty God, you have poured upon us the new light of your incarnate Word: Grant that this light, enkindled in our hearts, may shine forth in our lives; through Jesus Christ our Lord, who lives and reigns with you, in the unity of the Holy Spirit, one God, now and forever. Amen.

Readings and Psalm

Isaiah 61:10–62:3

In our Hebrew Bible reading **the prophet joyfully responds on behalf of all God's people to the Lord's promises for a redeemed Jerusalem.** He is a messenger to those who are poor and have suffered many troubles. Now he feels himself clothed in salvation and integrity, like a bridegroom or bride. In the sight of all people this nation shall become like a fresh garden. The prophet will not keep silence until the deliverance of Jerusalem is known throughout the world.

Psalm 147 or 147:13–21

A hymn of praise to the Lord, who rules over nature and has shown faithfulness to Jerusalem and God's people Israel.

Galatians 3:23–25; 4:4–7

In this epistle lesson **Paul explains what the role of the law has been and how, in our new relationship of faith, we have become sons and heirs of the Father.** Before the coming of Christ and justification by faith we were like small children who had to be closely watched. God's own Son was born a subject of the law. Through him we now are given the status of sons coming into their maturity. We are enabled, through the Spirit of his Son, to call upon God with the same Aramaic word for Father that Jesus is remembered to have used, *Abba.*

John 1:1–18

The gospel opens with **a hymn to God's Word, the expression of God's very being and the creative power of all life, who has now become flesh and lived among us.** The Word is the light of all humankind, and was witnessed to by John the Baptist. Although the world made by the Word did not recognize the Word, those who did believe in the Word have been given the right to become children of God. The law came through Moses, but grace and truth come through the only Son, who makes the Father known.

Prayers of the People

Let us pray to God who has given us the revelation of divine grace and truth through the birth of Jesus, the Messiah, responding, "Lord, hear our prayer."

For hearts and minds open to accepting God's gift of the Word, allowing the light of Christ to enkindle our hearts with love, and to bear its message to one another; let us pray.

Lord, hear our prayer.

For faith, that the garments of salvation and righteousness may clothe us, and bring to our outward actions the inner workings of God's joy in our lives; let us pray.

Lord, hear our prayer.

Christmas

For the leaders of our country and our state, that the light of Christ may illumine their hearts, empowering them to boldly proclaim the truth without fear or deception; let us pray.

Lord, hear our prayer.

For the victims of war, political upheaval, and economic uncertainty, that we may not forget their needs but continually seek ways to offer the assistance that Christ would have us bring; let us pray.

Lord, hear our prayer.

For those who are limited by illness, living with the uncertainty of debilitating diseases or the darkness of mental despair, that they may continue to call upon the hope of God; let us pray.

Lord, hear our prayer.

For all who have died and for all who are lonely or grieving, that they may remain close to the heart of the Risen One, whose presence knows no end; let us pray.

Lord, hear our prayer.

For the Church as we move toward the challenges of the future, that we rejoice in the faith of our ancestors and in the ever-present support of our sisters and brothers in this household; let us pray.

Lord, hear our prayer.

For each of us, that as we enjoy the material blessings of this season, the light and love of Jesus may continually transform us into a spiritual people through whom the Word of God is revealed; let us pray.

Lord, hear our prayer.

Standing in the midst of the true light that shines upon the face of the universe, let us continue our prayers.

(Special intentions of the congregation, the diocese, and the Anglican Communion may be added here or before the formal intercessions.)

The Celebrant adds a concluding Collect.

Images in the Readings

The image that recurs in the three readings is the **child**. Jesus is the child of God; the children of Bethlehem are slaughtered; God has treated Israel like beloved children; the sacrifice of Jesus makes believers into children of God. The challenge in our culture is to keep this image from shallow sentimentality.

The gospel reading contrasts the protected child with the **victim**. All three readings speak their good news against the backdrop, not of joyous Christmas celebration, but of endless human suffering. Many medieval churches displayed life-sized depictions of the slaughter of the innocents, with weeping mothers holding bleeding infants. This art hinted at what is to come: Mary weeping over the dead Jesus. Christianity is not for the squeamish.

God, like a **loving parent**, a father, a mother, is carrying the toddler to safety.

Ideas for the Day

♦ John the Baptizer, from whom we heard in Advent 2 and 3, is back in a cameo appearance. He has generally been called "the Baptizer" because of his major ministry in the Synoptics, but here in the fourth gospel, he spends much of his time pointing to another. So in this gospel he might better be described as "John the Witness" who consistently testifies to the power, authority and stature of another. For the author of this gospel then, John is the first iconic disciple, the first to recognize Jesus and recruit others to the new Way at its infancy.

♦ The wearing of vestments reflects the reading from Isaiah: "he has clothed me with the garments of salvation." In the early church, those who were baptized were given new white garments to wear as a sign of their redeemed relationship with God and the church. Later, the vesting of the priest became associated with being clothed with "the robe of righteousness."

♦ "For as the earth brings forth its sprouts, and as a garden causes what is sown in it to sprout up, so the Lord God will cause righteous and praise to sprout up before all the nations." Let us be good gardeners. To help plants grow, we must know their needs, learning how much water they need, learning how much sunlight they need, among other aspects, all geared towards helping their growth. Isn't it the same with the members of our church community. Just as an African violet has different needs than a jade plant, different members within our community needs vary as well. Let us tend our plant gardens and community member gardens with the same care.

Making Connections

Fourteenth century mystic Julian of Norwich proclaimed that we have the eternal promise from God that we will not be overcome. We may not always understand the darkness, but the light of Christ is shining in our lives, and the world will never go out. To remember this, you might keep a candle handy in your house or your personal prayer space. When you find yourself in a moment of personal darkness, you can be reminded that the light of Christ is shining, and like Eleanor Roosevelt, you can choose to light a candle rather than curse the darkness.

Engaging All Ages

Today's gospel offers an opportunity to explore the meaning of light (and darkness) in our lives and the world today. Questions to spur conversation: In what ways do you see darkness in our world today? How does that darkness not see, recognize, or understand the light of Jesus? What are the barriers that keep the light of Jesus from being seen? What difference would our understanding the light of Christ make in that area of darkness? How can Christians, as bearers of the light, take that light in areas of darkness in our world?

Hymns for the Day

The Hymnal 1982

Arise, shine, for your light has come S 223ff
How bright appears the Morning Star 496, 497
Father eternal, Ruler of creation 573
Let all mortal flesh keep silence 324
Of the Father's love begotten 82
Word of God, come down on earth 633

Lift Every Voice and Sing II

Wonder, Love, and Praise

Arise, shine, for your light has come 883
From the dawning of creation 748

Weekday Commemorations

Tuesday, December 31
Frances Joseph Gaudet, Educator and Social Reformer, 1934

Gaudet (b. 1861) descended from African- and Native-American bloodlines. While living in the South in 1894, Gaudet dedicated her life to prison reform. She started with prayer meetings for imprisoned blacks, then extended her prison ministry to whites. She wrote prisoners' letters, delivered their messages, and clothed them. Doing so won her the respect of prison officials, city authorities, and the governor of Louisiana. She supported young offenders in Louisiana and rehabilitated young blacks arrested for misdemeanors. She helped found the Juvenile Court. She also founded an industrial school and the Gaudet Episcopal Home for African-American children.

Saturday, January 4
Elizabeth Ann Seton, Vowed Religious and Educator, 1821

Mother Seton founded the Sisters of Charity, the first community of sisters in the United States. Raised an Episcopalian, she converted to Roman Catholicism in 1805; a year later, she patterned a congregation of seven women religious after the French Daughters of Charity of Saint Vincent de Paul. The sisters' charism plaited social ministry, education, and religious formation. In Maryland in 1810, they opened St. Joseph's Free School for needy girls. Until her death, Elizabeth Seton remained the superior of the Sisters of Charity on which the earliest Anglican religious orders for women rested their rules.

Christmas

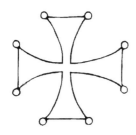

The Holy Name of Our Lord Jesus Christ

January 1, 2020

God's identity is revealed as "merciful and gracious" (Exodus 34:6). Jesus' name has significance: it is the Greek form of the Hebrew name Joshua, meaning "God saves."

Christmas

Color   White

Preface   Of the Incarnation

Collect

Eternal Father, you gave to your incarnate Son the holy name of Jesus to be the sign of our salvation: Plant in every heart, we pray, the love of him who is the Savior of the world, our Lord Jesus Christ; who lives and reigns with you and the Holy Spirit, one God, in glory everlasting. *Amen.*

Readings and Psalm

Numbers 6:22–27

In our opening lesson, **Moses, by God's command, instructs those set aside for priestly ministry to bless Israel, putting God's own name upon them.** These words have come to be known as the "Aaronic blessing," as they were first entrusted to Aaron and his sons. Because there is a threefold form to the blessing, Christians have often here perceived intimations of faith in the triune God.

Psalm 8

The psalmist glorifies the name of the Lord, sovereign of the earth and the magnificent heavens, who has made human life to have mastery over all other earthly creatures.

Galatians 4:4–7

In the fullness of time, **God sent God's own Son, born under the law, to redeem those under the law and to give them a new status as adopted children.** Christians are not to see themselves as God's slaves, but as children and heirs to whom the Spirit has come, enabling them to speak to God in intimate terms, crying "Abba! Father!"

or

Philippians 2:5–11

From one of the earliest Christian hymns we hear **how Christ Jesus accepted the condition of a servant, was obedient even to the point of death, and was then given the name above every name.** It is possible that this poem was adapted by Paul or another disciple from the hopes for a savior of a people who did not yet know Jesus. Jesus has fulfilled humanity's dream of one who will share fully in the mortal condition before his exaltation. To him every knee shall bow and every tongue confess the great name of the Lord now known in person, Jesus.

Luke 2:15–21

Our gospel tells how **the shepherds, after the angelic vision which announced the Savior's birth, come to Bethlehem to see for themselves the child who is to be named Jesus.** They share with Mary and Joseph the words of the angels. In this little infant, laid in a manger, the shepherds perceive the fulfillment of the song of the heavenly hosts. After eight days, in accordance with the law, the baby is then circumcised and given the promised name.

Prayers of the People

Plant within our hearts, O Lord, the love of our Savior, as we lift our voices in prayer, responding to each petition by saying, "Holy is your Name."

O Key of David, unlock our greed and love of material goods, that we may be generous to the hungry, poor, unemployed, and homeless; for this we pray.

Holy is your Name.

O Emmanuel, God with us, visit us in the dark season of the year, revealing your everlasting light, and making us beacons of your grace and integrity in the world about us; for this we pray.

Holy is your Name.

O Prince of Peace, send your Spirit upon the face of the earth, changing weapons of war into resources for peace, revealing the gift of new life when hope has dimmed, and uniting peoples of every language, race, nation, and tribe; for this we pray.

Holy is your Name.

O Savior of the world, reach down from your heavenly throne and grasp our imaginations, that we may bring freshness and vitality to age-old problems, revealing to others the reality of your kingdom; for this we pray.

Holy is your Name.

O Root of Jesse, help us to honor the traditions of our Church and nation, learning from the past to welcome the future with openness and expectancy; for this we pray.

Holy is your Name.

O Giver of life, reveal your eternal promises to those who have died as followers of Jesus, and look with compassion upon those whose faith is unknown or uncertain; for this we pray.

Holy is your Name.

O Cup of Salvation, we thank you for this Eucharistic Meal which we share this day; may the bread we break reveal our participation in the Body of Christ; for this we pray.

Holy is your Name.

Finding our strength in the Holy Name of Jesus, we join with all the apostles and saints in continuing our prayers and thanksgivings.

(Special intentions of the congregation, the diocese, and the Anglican Communion may be added here or before the formal intercessions.)

The Celebrant adds a concluding Collect.

Ideas for the Day

- The rabbis taught that engaging scripture was something like participating in a wrestling match (noting Jacob's bout in Genesis 32). As the NRSV describes it, Mary is "treasuring and pondering" the words that the shepherds had proclaimed. But the force of the Greek has Mary probing, struggling, prodding meaning from what has been said. And the force of the verbs has her continuing to do this over time, so that one wonders if she returned to these words and the ones that would describe her son in the future, again and again, to make sense of his work in the world.

- Purchase loose-leaf paper. Number twenty pieces paper. Using the internet, find twenty different song/hymn lyrics connected to the name of Jesus Christ. Once you find the lyrics, physically write the words on the pieces of paper. Feel free to come up with different designs for how you place the words on the page. Leave space for a picture somewhere on the page. Find twenty corresponding pictures and paste them to each page. On a separate sheet of paper write a two-verse hymn inspired by the lyrics you have researched. Take your papers and research different ways to bind the papers together. Your book will be specific to you, a reflection of your own personal view on the name of Jesus.

Christmas

Christmas

♦ The naming of a person being baptized is an important element in the baptismal rite, as in scripture: "You shall be called by a new name that the mouth of the Lord will give" (Isaiah 62:2). In some traditions a child was literally named at baptism and given the name of a Christian saint. Whether or not the name is given at baptism, one's given name takes on new significance as one is adopted into the family of Christ.

Making Connections

A newborn baby is possibility incarnate. But, if that child goes hungry, is never read to, or allowed to play in the park. If no one teaches them the difference between right and wrong, how to love God and neighbor. If no one shows them that they are a beautiful, beloved child of God. If no one ensures that they go to school and do their homework, then all those possibilities disappear. We have the power—individually and collectively as a community—to help the children in our communities live into the wonderful possibilities God has in store.

Engaging All Ages

In scripture, Jesus is given many names. We may see these symbols at our churches and even on bumper stickers, but do we know what they mean or where they come from? Explore the meanings and origins of names associated with Jesus from birth to resurrection: *Chi Rho* (the first two letters of the Greek spelling of Christ); Alpha and Omega (Rev. 1:8 and 22:13); *INRI* (the Latin inscription on the cross of Calgary—John 19:19—meaning "Jesus of Nazareth, King of the Jews"); *IHS* (monogram derived from first three letters in Greek spelling of "Jesus"—Matt. 1:21); *Ichthus* (Greek letters spell fish and make a rebus "Jesus Christ, God's Son, Savior"); and Agnus Dei (Lamb of God—Rev. 5:12–14).

Hymns for the Day

The Hymnal 1982
Jesus, the very thought of thee 642
How sweet the Name of Jesus sounds 644
Now greet the swiftly changing year 250
O for a thousand tongues to sing 493
To the Name of our salvation 248, 249
Sing praise to our Creator 295
A stable lamp is lighted 104
All hail the power of Jesus' Name! 450, 451
All praise to thee, for thou, O King divine 477
At the name of Jesus 435
From east to west, from shore to shore 77
Jesus! Name of wondrous love! 252

Lift Every Voice and Sing II
Blessed be the name 78
Glorious is the name of Jesus 63
O how I love Jesus 95
There's something about that name 107
God be with you 234
A choral benediction 231

Wonder, Love, and Praise
God be with you till we meet again 801
You're called by name, forever loved 766

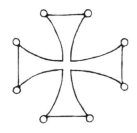

The Second Sunday after Christmas

January 5, 2020

The restoration of human nature through the divine life of Jesus.

Color   White

Preface   Of the Incarnation

Collect

O God, who wonderfully created, and yet more wonderfully restored, the dignity of human nature: Grant that we may share the divine life of him who humbled himself to share our humanity, your Son Jesus Christ; who lives and reigns with you, in the unity of the Holy Spirit, one God, for ever and ever. *Amen.*

Readings and Psalm

Jeremiah 31:7–14

The Hebrew Bible reading was originally composed as **a vision of hope, full of joy, for the restoration of the northern tribes of Israel.** The Lord will bring them all back from exile, including the weak and the infirm. As a father and a shepherd, God will comfort them and give them cause for great gladness.

Psalm 84 or 84:1–8

A song of the pilgrims' happiness as they come to worship in the house of the Lord.

Ephesians 1:3–6, 15–19a

This New Testament lesson opens with **praise to God for God's blessings, together with thanksgiving and prayers that these spiritual graces may continue.** In the beloved Son Christians have, since the beginning of the world, been given a destiny of holiness as God's children. Paul prays for a spirit of wisdom and revelation so that the disciples' hearts may be enlightened to perceive the glorious hope of the saints.

Matthew 2:13–15, 19–23

Our gospel is **the story of Joseph and Mary escaping to Egypt with the infant Jesus. They flee the jealous wrath of King Herod and are able to return to live in Nazareth only after his death.** These movements early in Jesus' life are seen as the fulfillment of prophecy. As God's Son, Jesus is brought out of Egypt just as were the people of Israel. The prophecy concerning Nazareth could have several sources, but the evangelist understands all things to be taking place according to God's plan.

or

Luke 2:41–52

Our gospel tells **the story of Jesus' pilgrimage to Jerusalem as a young man of twelve, and the depths of his understanding in conversation with the teachers in the temple.** To his amazed and concerned parents, who had returned to Jerusalem after missing him on the journey homeward, Jesus responds that he must be in his Father's house. The narrative emphasizes Jesus' wisdom and comprehension of his Jewish heritage and points to his future role as a teacher whose authority will be greater than that of all the scribes and lawyers. When he returns to the temple late in his ministry, it will be to cleanse it before his rejection and death.

or

Matthew 2:1–12

Our gospel is **the story of the wise men from the east, who, guided by a star, come to worship the child born to be king.** Despite the wicked plotting of Herod, the Magi are able to bring their gifts to Jesus without betraying his exact location. Early Christians found in the rich symbolism and motifs of the story the fulfillment of both Old Testament prophecy and the dreams of many peoples. The meaning of this birth, amid terrifyingly human circumstances, enlightens and transcends human history.

Christmas

Prayers of the People

Raising our voices in proclamation and praise, let us rejoice as we offer our prayers to God, responding, "Lord, hear our prayer."

In thanksgiving for the peacemakers who toil in troubled lands, and in families of discontent, that the Prince of Peace may give them words of wisdom as they seek to encourage new means of communication and the mending of relationships; let us pray.

Lord, hear our prayer.

In thanksgiving for those who bring treasures to the poor and needy of the world, offering precious gifts of hope to God's fragile people; let us pray.

Lord, hear our prayer.

For those who exercise leadership throughout our Church, that they may bear in their actions the love of Christ, enlightening the hearts of those who have a hidden faith, and strengthening those of a weak spirit; let us pray.

Lord, hear our prayer.

For N., our President, members of our legislative bodies, and those who serve on the Supreme Court, that they may honor our historic inheritance and take us along new pathways in the service of bettering our nation; let us pray.

Lord, hear our prayer.

For those who have died in the noonday of their lives, and for parents who grieve the loss of children, that they may be comforted by the Father of us all, whose only Son was not spared an early death; let us pray.

Lord, hear our prayer.

In thanksgiving for all the blessings of this life, remembering those who have been our mentors and teachers, and through whose companionship we have experienced the riches of divine grace; let us pray.

Lord, hear our prayer.

As God's adopted children, through the will of Jesus Christ, let us add to these prayers and thanksgivings. *(Special intentions of the congregation, the diocese, and the Anglican Communion may be added here or before the formal intercessions.)*

The Celebrant adds a concluding Collect.

Images in the Readings

Once again this Sunday, **light** is a primary image for the power of God to transform the earth and us in it. Even the smallest light shines through a field of darkness.

Again, becoming **children of God** recurs in the readings. Although many contemporary people think of God as being naturally father of humankind, this was not a cultural idea in the first century, and the Bible understands this extraordinary claim only as a consequence of the incarnation. God is not, as many people imagine, the alien and uncaring other. Rather, thanks to Christ, God loves us as children.

The church is a **watered garden**. A garden is more personal, more beautiful, than a field of crops. We think ahead to Good Friday and the Easter Vigil, when according to John's gospel Jesus is buried and raised to life in a garden.

Ideas for the Day

♦ Jeremiah is often remembered as the gloomiest of prophets, but not today. Within the period of deepest alienation and brokenness in Israel's long history—the Babylonian Exile—Jeremiah rings gladsome changes. The God who had lately seemed so distant and judgmental and uncaring is palpably back, nurturing, feeding, redeeming, loving a people once forlorn back to life. Gospellers a few centuries later will see in this good news a portrait of the One whose birth we continue to celebrate. Jesus will grow up to become the epitome of the shepherd described here, as well as the host of the kind of ingathering, inclusive celebration that Jeremiah envisioned.

- Adoption is often used as a metaphor of our relationship with God. This language is also associated with baptism, which comes from Ephesians heard this week. The prayer (BCP 311) also uses this: "All praise and thanks to you, most merciful Father, for adopting us as your own children, for incorporating us into your holy Church."

- In this season of birth/rebirth, let us be open to new ways of creative expression. We commonly may not think of ourselves as creative people, but in reality, Christianity is a creative process. Just think of all of the different ways we have to be prepared to analyze and synthesize scripture for the purpose of expressing our faith to ourselves and to others. Don't shy away from presenting your faith in new and different ways. Our spiritual growth is contingent upon our ability to adapt to the different surroundings we are confronted with on a daily basis.

Making Connections

Herod causes a great deal of pain and suffering in the slaughter of the Holy Innocents (Mt. 2:16–18), but the story does not end there. It ends with the safe return of Jesus' family, a story of pain and tragedy, where hope triumphs and love has the last word. This is the human story. It is the story of the Kindertransport in World War II. Humanity may do unspeakable horrors, but there will always also be the tremendous beauty of the human spirit shown in those who have the courage to do what is necessary to save the lives of others.

Engaging All Ages

It is hard not to miss the connection with the story in Matthew of the Holy Family fleeing to Egypt with today's plight of refugees around the world. While World Refugee Day is observed on June 20, it would be appropriate to learn how many people continue to flee to other countries or are internally displaced within their own country due to famines, plagues, war, persecution, discrimination, natural disasters like floods and earthquakes, and to escape dire poverty. How can your congregation connect to this justice issue? See **https://episcopalmigrationministries.org/**.

Hymns for the Day

The Hymnal 1982
How bright appears the Morning Star 496, 497
How lovely is thy dwelling-place 517
Once in royal David's city 102
O God of Bethel, by whose hand 709
In your mercy, Lord, you called me 706
Sing praise to our Creator 295
Duérmete, Niño lindo/Oh, sleep now, holy baby 113
In Bethlehem a newborn boy 246
Lully, lullay, thou little tiny child 247
Our Father, by whose Name 587
When Jesus left his Father's throne 480
As with gladness men of old 119
Brightest and best of the stars of the morning 117, 118
Earth has many a noble city 127
Father eternal, Ruler of creation 573
On this day earth shall ring 92
Unto us a boy is born! 98
The first Nowell the angel did say 109
We three kings of Orient are 128
What star is this, with beams so bright 124
Where is this stupendous stranger? 491

Lift Every Voice and Sing II

Wonder, Love, and Praise
Where is this stupendous stranger? 726

Christmas

Weekday Commemorations

Wednesday, January 8
Harriet Bedell, Deaconess and Missionary, 1969

Born in 1875, Bedell attended the New York Training School for deaconesses. She started her mission work among the Cheyenne in Oklahoma, went to Alaska (1916) near the Arctic Circle, and started a boarding school. In 1932, she traveled to Florida to serve the Mikasuk nation to exploit their crafts (basket-weaving and doll-making) to improve their economy. She exerted her ministry of care even after retirement and the devastation of Hurricane Donna. Bedell, named Bird Woman by the Cheyenne, traveled an average of 20,000 miles a year in her missions and was a popular writer of mission tales.

Thursday, January 9
*Julia Chester Emery, Lay Leader
and Missionary, 1922*

Born in 1852 in Dorchester, Massachusetts, Emery served the Episcopal Church's Board of Missions with loyalty, efficiency, and dedication for 40 years. At 22, she became editor of *The Young Christian Soldier*, a missionary publication of the Woman's Auxiliary of the Board. At first, the Auxiliary assembled and distributed "missionary boxes" to supplement salaries of missionaries; Emery's last report in 1916 recorded branches in two-thirds of the Church's missions and parishes with receipts of $500,000. Emery traveled extensively for the Church, including, in 1908, attending the Lambeth Conference in London. In retirement, Emery wrote *A Century of Endeavor*, her history of the Domestic and Foreign Missionary Society.

Friday, January 10
William Laud, Archbishop of Canterbury, 1645

Laud, born in 1573, was beheaded in 1645 after impeachment for treason. He was seen through his life—and ever since—as either a martyr or a bigot, either compassionate toward commoners against landowners or dispassionate, even murderous, toward "puritans." Made Archbishop of Canterbury in 1635, he emphasized the marriage of church and state, headed by royalty as a divine right; raised up the priesthood and sacraments, especially the Eucharist; and demanded reverencing of the altar, which he returned to the eastern wall and fenced in. Laud, who headed the courts of High Commission and the Star Chamber, was fiercely loyal to the Church of England.

Epiphany

Preparing for Epiphany

Theological Themes that Might Shape Liturgy, Catechesis, and Education

In previous "Preparing for . . ." sections, we highlighted the importance of planning a through line that connects the seasons of Advent, Christmas, and the Epiphany. The theme of revelation, light, and illumination that characterizes the season after the Epiphany is built upon the incarnation of Jesus Christ and the inception of his movement in Christmas, which itself hinges on the yearning and anticipation of the Advent season. We hope, we receive, we share. If underscored in this manner, we develop the capacity to build out a more fulsome expression of the Christian witness than might otherwise be possible if we simply acquiesce to the secular commemorations of the season.

Throughout this season, we hear how Jesus' ministry is manifested throughout his context, beginning with the Feast of the Epiphany where the power of Jesus is confirmed by the presence of non-Jewish visitors from afar. The message from the start seems to be clear—Jesus is for all people, and all means all.

Liturgical Possibilities

Rites

As its name might suggest, the season after the Epiphany begins on the Feast of the Epiphany—January 6. Epiphany is not a transferable feast for the majority of congregations. Contrary to what we might like to think, clergy are not Time Lords (obscure Dr. Who reference). Abiding by the framework of the church calendar presents congregations with an opportunity to add additional worship opportunities for their congregations and, because it will likely not be a principal liturgy, gives a little more room for experimentation and innovation. What might

a midweek liturgy look like that is inclusive of families and other non-regular worshipers from the community? A Saint Lydia's style dinner church? A liturgy with experiential prayers of the people?

It is important not simply to transfer the feast of the Epiphany because the first few Sundays mark important, building moments in the life of Jesus. The first Sunday after the Epiphany is the Baptism of our Lord, which marks a pivotal moments in the life of Jesus as he immediately goes into the wilderness before beginning his public ministry. The beginning of that ministry is marked in Year A and B with the calling of his disciples, which makes an important statement about the nature of the Jesus Movement. These stories might be as dramatic as some of the creative ways we find to tell the story of the visit of the magi (though an argument can be made about doves and disembodied voices being incredibly dramatic), they represent concepts that are foundationally important to the Jesus Movement, concepts that will be further developed through the season.

The Season after the Epiphany, unlike the Season after Pentecost (which will be explored later), has a particular character. Prayers of the People, Eucharistic Prayers, and other adjustable portions of the liturgy should be adapted to reflect this character. The celebration of the Epiphany (January 6) should be further differentiated from the season that follows, as it is a major feast.

Another feast the pops up during this season is the Presentation of our Lord Jesus Christ, which, like the Epiphany, is non-transferable. This feast, which some confuse for the Feast of the Circumcision (which occurs on January 1), marks the occasion where Mary and Joseph present the infant Jesus to Simeon the priest and Anna the prophet in fulfillment of the ancient Jewish custom. Candlemas, as the feast is also known, directly appeals to the themes of light and illumination, and presents another opportunity to develop an innovative, attractive liturgy.

Epiphany

Space

What better season to experiment with different kinds of light than the season that follows the Epiphany? Where might additional candles add depth of meaning? How might artificial light be adjusted to create a different experience?

Other Rituals and Resources

As with most seasons, there are other, smaller but meaningful ways to observe the season. A community might observe the burning of the greens, burning of the palms (on the last Sunday after the Epiphany), baptisms, or the blessing of homes. Some resources can be found in the *Book of Occasional Services* or by simply doing a web search.

Through the Eyes of a Child

What Jesus did and said helps us to know who God is and what God is doing for us: on the night of Jesus' birth, the giant comet star let the world know that God is with us; magi from far away saw the star and journeyed to visit Jesus. Jesus called his friends to be with him and to help him in his work. Jesus said and did amazing and wonderful things that no one else could do. He healed many people to show how much God loved them. Jesus, the gift of love, came for all the people of the world. Jesus is like a light, helping us to see better. We are a part of Jesus, and in Jesus we are baptized into God's family, the Church. The wonder and mystery of the magi invite us to wonder about the mystery. Jesus, who are you really?

When it comes to young people—indeed all people—it is important to keep formation as a key principal. Epiphany is filled with opportunities for community to live into traditions that they find important, but has that meaning been conveyed to a younger audience? If you are burning the Advent and Christmas greens, have you explained why that is so and why they aren't merely discarded? If you are blessing homes, have you explained what it is about this season that makes this a particularly appropriate time to do so?

Epiphany is also an opportunity to make worship more sensory by deploying light (sight) and incense (smell) in ways that contribute to deeper worship experience. Even if incense isn't used in worship, how might we teach our children what frankincense and myrrh are in ways that expand their spiritual and liturgical experience?

Through the Eyes of Youth

The Church is called to reveal Jesus to the world, to reaffirm baptismal vows strengthening the ways to seek Christ in all persons, and to continue in the apostles' teachings, breaking of bread, and the prayers. Epiphany is a time to celebrate the mystery of the visit of the magi to the infant Jesus. Epiphany is the sudden realization or comprehension of the essence or meaning of something sacred. Invite the youth to read God's Word every morning; use the lectionary and follow the stories for the season of Epiphany. This is a wonderful season to take each sentence of the Baptismal Covenant and invite the teens to determine how to put it into action, not only for themselves, but for the community.

Through the Eyes of Daily Life

Epiphany is a time to bless the homes of Christians with holy water, incense, and prayers, that those who abide in the home may live lives that are an epiphany of God's coming among us in Jesus, into whose body we have been incorporated at our baptism. (See *The Book of Occasional Services*).

Through the Eyes of Those Outside of the Church

If the Epiphany is about the light of Christ being manifested to the world, it would follow that this is a great opportunity for the local faith community to make some kind of effort to reach out to the community in new ways. If the Epiphany and Candlemas are observed as non-Sunday liturgies, it might worthwhile to engage them as seeker-friendly liturgies, playing into the spiritual themes that resonate across religious experience—light and illumination.

Through the Eyes of the Global Community

Many of the collects during this season speak of covenants and commandments. The Baptismal Covenant calls Christians to strive for justice and peace among all people, and to respect the dignity of every human being (BCP 305). Six of the Ten Commandments, which summarize the 613 commandments of the Torah, remind us that to honor God is to love others as we love ourselves. Many of the commandments of the Torah deal with proper treatment of the poor, the stranger, and the disadvantaged in society, as well as ethical business practices. Jesus' "new Law" outlined in the Sermon on the Mount calls the Christian to an even higher standard: reconciliation in all relationships; truthfulness in business, personal, and political matters; justice and respect for human rights; and love for all people, even those perceived to be enemies. In 1997, the General Convention of the Episcopal Church designated the Last Sunday of Epiphany as World Mission Sunday to increase awareness of and participation in the wider global mission of the Church.

Epiphany

Seasonal Rites for Epiphany

Epiphany Blessing[1]

The following blessing may be used by a bishop or priest whenever a blessing is appropriate. It is a three-fold form with an Amen at the end of each sentence, leading into a Trinitarian blessing. This may be used from the feast of the Epiphany through the following Sunday.

May Almighty God, who led the Wise Men by the shining of a star to find the Christ, the Light from Light, lead you also, in your pilgrimage, to find the Lord. *Amen.*

May God, who sent the Holy Spirit to rest upon the Only-begotten at his baptism in the Jordan River, pour out that Spirit on you who have come to the waters of new birth. *Amen.*

May God, by the power that turned water into wine at the wedding feat at Cana, transform your lives and make glad your hearts. *Amen.* And the blessing of God Almighty, the Father, the Son, and the Holy Spirit, be upon you and remain with you for ever. *Amen.*

The Blessing of the Home

From the time of the Middle Ages it has been a tradition that on the feast of the Epiphany we pray for God's blessing on our dwelling places, marking the entrance to our homes with chalk. Chalk is used as a tangible reminder of the dust of the earth from which we are all made.

We mark the main door of our home with the initials of the magi and the numerals of the new year. The initials remind us of the names of the magi—Caspar, Melchior, and Balthasar—and also stand for the Latin motto: *Christus mansionem benedicat,* "May Christ bless this house." We connect the initials and the numerals with crosses as a sign that we have invited God's presence and blessing into our homes.

Gather everyone to bless the chalk. Then invite everyone to take the chalk home to bless their homes after your gathering with a "The Blessing of a Home"[2] liturgy.

The Blessing of the Chalk

Participants gather around a basket containing pieces of ordinary white or colored chalk.

The Blessing

Leader: God dwells in you.

Participants: And also with you.

Leader: Let us pray. Bless, O Lord, this chalk that it may be a sign of your blessing upon the homes of your people. We pray that, like wise men and women of old, we may serve him as our only King, worship him as the one true God, and honor him with lives of sacrifice and praise, who lives and reigns with you and the Holy Spirit, one God, for ever and ever. Amen.

The Blessing of the Home

The blessing of the house begins with all members of the household at the entrance of the home. A member of the family leads the blessing.

Leader: Peace be to this house.
Participants: And to all who enter here.

The Leader speaks the following while marking the doorway with the chalk as indicated:

1 *The Book of Occasional Services 2003* (New York: Church Publishing, 2004), 24.

2 This is available as a download at **www.churchpublishing.org/faithfulcelebrations3** and is adapted from *Faithful Celebrations: Making Time for God from Advent through Epiphany* edited by Sharon Ely Pearson (Church Publishing, 2018), 129–130.

Epiphany

Leader: Wise ones came to honor the Savior and offer him gifts.

 C Caspar,

 M Melchior,

 B and Balthasar followed the star of God's Son who became human two thousand and twenty years ago.

 ++ May Christ bless our home and all who join us here,

 ++ and remain with us throughout the new year. *Amen.*

 20 + C + M + B + 20

All: May this Epiphany blessing be a reminder of Christ's presence among us and a symbol of God's love and care as we share the blessings and burdens of our daily lives. *Amen.*

Candlemas[3]

Saturday, February 2

Candlemas (Candle Mass) takes its name from the candles carried at the celebration of the Presentation of Christ in the Temple. It celebrates a ritual of Jewish law related to first-born sons that Joseph and Mary carried out (Luke 2:21–40). Luke's gospel tells how Simeon and Anna, devout Jews, honored the infant Jesus as the promised Messiah.

When circumstances permit, the congregation gathers at a place apart from the church so that all may go into the church in procession; however, it can begin just inside the door of the church. All are provided with unlighted candles. These are lit during the opening canticle, which is sung or said.

The Entrance

Celebrant: Light and peace, in Jesus Christ our Lord.

> **Thanks be to God.**

A Light to enlighten the nations,
and the glory of your people Israel.

> **A Light to enlighten the nations,
> and the glory of your people Israel.**

Lord, you now have set your servant free
to go in peace as you have promised.

> **A Light to enlighten the nations,
> and the glory of your people Israel.**

For these eyes of mine have seen the Savior,
whom you have prepared for all the world to see.

> **A Light to enlighten the nations,
> and the glory of your people Israel.**

God our Father, source of all light, today you revealed to the aged Simeon your light which enlightens the nations. Fill our hearts with the light of faith, that we who bear these candles may walk in the path of goodness, and come to the Light that shines for ever, your Son Jesus Christ our Lord. *Amen.*

The Procession

Deacon: Let us go forth in peace.

> **In the name of Christ. Amen.**

All carry lighted candles while an appropriate hymn or canticle is sung, stopping for the following Collect to be read.

O God, you have made this day holy by the presentation of your Son in the Temple, and by the purification of the Blessed Virgin Mary: Mercifully grant that we, who delight in her humble readiness to be the birth-giver of the Only-begotten, may rejoice for ever in our adoption as his sisters and brothers; through Jesus Christ our Lord. *Amen.*

The procession approaches the altar as the following antiphon and Psalm 48:1–2, 10–13 is read.

We have waited in silence on your loving-kindness, O Lord, in the midst of your temple. Your praise, like your Name, O God, reaches to the world's end; your right hand is full of justice.

Great is the Lord, and highly to be praised;
    in the city of our God is his holy hill.
Beautiful and lofty, the joy of all the earth, is the hill
    of Zion the very center of the world and the city
    of the great King.
Let Mount Zion be glad and the cities of Judah
    rejoice, because of your judgments.
Make the circuit of Zion; walk round about her;
    count the number of her towers.
Consider well her bulwarks; examine her stronghold;
    that you may tell those who come after.
This God is our God for ever and ever;
    he shall be our guide for evermore.

---

3 Ibid, 53–55.

Other Notable Days during the Epiphany Season

Martin Luther King, Jr. Day

January 20

A federal holiday, this day will fall on Monday, January 20, 2020. Some schools celebrate the day be teaching their pupils or students about the work and ministry of Martin Luther King and the struggle against racial segregation and racism. It has also become a day where Americans give some of their time on this day as volunteers in action in their communities. For congregations, Sunday, January 19 can be a day of focused prayer, preaching, and education on the legacy Dr. King entrusted to us. Resources can be found at http://www.thekingcenter.org/king-holiday *and* https://www.serve.gov/site-page/mlkday

Lord our God, see how oppression and violence are our sad inheritance, one generation to the next. We look for you where the lowly are raised up, where the mighty are brought down. We find you there in your servants and we give you thanks this day for your preacher and witness, Martin Luther King Jr.
Fill us with your spirit: where our human community is divided by racism, torn by repression, saddened by fear and ignorance, may we give ourselves to your work of healing. Grant this through Christ our Lord. *Amen.*[4]

Week of Prayer for Christian Unity

January 18–25

The Week of Prayer for Christian Unity is an international Christian ecumenical observance for eight days, held between the feasts of Peter and Paul. Resources for study, prayer, music, and worship are offered in advance at https://www.oikoumene.org/en/resources/week-of-prayer *(accessed February 8, 2019).*

Prayers of the People[5]

Leader: Let us raise to the Lord our common prayer for the Church and for the needs of all humanity.

Reader: From the islands and the oceans,
  we worship you, O God, the Creator of life.
Throughout the mountains and the valleys,
  we praise you, O God, the Savior of the world.
With the tongues of all nations,
  we thank you, O God, the Comforter of bodies
  and souls.
We come before you bearing our burdens and hopes.
Today we ask you:

  O God, hear our prayer and grant us your love.

Reader: We pray for those who live in the midst
  of injustice.
Encourage us to lift up their voices and
  strengthen their hope.
We pray for those who continue to perpetuate
  injustice.
May your kindness fill our hearts and make us
  agents of freedom and peace.
We prayer for every institution and person who
  stands for justice.
Let us act justly according to your words.
Today we ask you:

  O God, hear our prayer and grant us your justice.

Reader: We pray for the visible unity of the Church.
Lead us to fulfill Jesus' prayer that we may be one
  and work together to manifest your Kingdom.
Today we ask you:

  *O God, hear our prayer and grant us
  passion for unity.*

Reader: We thank you for the many colors, cultures,
  and customs that we share in this world.
In our differences, unite us by your love.
Enable us to act together to uphold life
and to make this world a just and peaceful household
  for all humanity.
Today we ask you:

  O God, hear our prayer and grant us your peace.

Epiphany

---

4 Christopher L. Webber, editor. *An American Prayer Book* (Harrisburg, PA: Morehouse Publishing, 2008), 124.

5 https://www.oikoumene.org/en/resources/documents/commissions/faith-and-order/xi-week-of-prayer-for-christian-unity/2019, 19-20 (accessed February 8, 2019).

Theological Education Sunday

February 2

> *Theological Education Sunday (TES) is officially recognized on the first Sunday in February. It is a day parishioners set aside to pray and give for all laity and clergy whose ministry is Christian education, wherever that ministry happens—in the home, preschool programs, parishes, colleges, universities, and seminaries. Established in 1999 by the Episcopal Church, this Sunday on the church calendar is an occasion for all parishioners to focus on education as a key aspect of mission. Guest preachers and seminarians sponsored by the congregation are often invited to preach.*

O God of truth, ever beckoning us to loftier understanding and deeper wisdom, we seek your will and implore your grace for all who share the life of divinity schools and seminaries in our day, knowing that, unless you build among us, we who teach and learn will labor but in vain.

Silence

For the men and women who teach, that they may together bring fire and vision to a common task, knowing one field yet eager to related it to all others; just in their academic demands, yet seeing each student as a child of God; fitted to teach not only by great learning but by great faith in humankind and in you, their God:

> **In them and in us, O God,
> kindle your saving truth.**

Silence

For deans and presidents, trustees and development officers, and all others who point the way for theological education in our day, that their chief concern be not budgets and buildings and prestige, but men and women freed to know your whole will and roused to serve you in your Church:

> **In them and in us, O God,
> kindle your saving truth.**

Silence

For janitors and maids, for cooks and keepers of the grounds, for those who prepare our food and wash our dishes, and for the host of other workers and suppliers whose faithfulness ministers to our common life:

> **In them and in us, O God,
> kindle your saving truth.**

Silence

For parents and givers of scholarships, who support theological students, that they may not desire for them more income, or social acceptance, or glory of family or of donor, but look rather for new breadth of intelligence, the spirit made whole, and devoted Christian service in life:

> **In them and in us, O God,
> kindle your saving truth.**

Silence

For the students themselves, that their confusion may be brief, their perspective constantly enlarged, and their minds and spirits alert to all that chapel and classroom, library, and fieldwork assignment can mean in their lives:

> **In them and in us, O God,
> kindle your saving truth.**

Silence

For every member of this community of learning and service, that with them we may be aware of your Holy Spirit leading us all into truth, and may grasp here your special intention for all our learning and striving:

> **In them and in us, O God,
> kindle your saving truth.**

Silence

We know, O heavenly Father, that a seminary education is but the willing and planning of many men and women, each sought by your great love. Grant that we who would earnestly serve you may witness in the world to the reality of your gospel, as it is shown forth in Christ Jesus our Lord. *Amen.*[6]

---

6 John Oliver Nelson, "For Theological Seminaries," in *The Wideness of God's Mercy: Litanies to Enlarge Our Prayer* edited by Jeffrey W. Rowthorn (New York: Church Publishing, 2007), 165–166.

Super Bowl Sunday: Souper Bowl of Caring

February 2

The Souper Bowl of Caring is a national movement of young people working to fight hunger and poverty in their own communities around the time of the Super Bowl football game. In the weeks leading up to or on Super Bowl Sunday, young people take up a collection (many use a soup pot), asking for one dollar or one item of food for people in need. They give 100 percent of their donation directly to the local hunger-relief charity of their choice. Learn more at **https://souperbowl.org/welcome**

We have seen your hand of mercy in the service of those who spread food, shelter, hope, and faith to suffering humankind. Plant more seeds in the bellies of the full, to burst forth in joy, to explode like the ripened grain with life-giving bread. Give us, we beseech you, in the bosoms of our souls, a passion for the powerless and a commitment to place all poverty in the past. *Amen.*[7]

Presidents' Day

Monday, February 17

Almighty God, Who has given us this good land for our heritage; We humbly beseech Thee that we may always prove ourselves a people mindful of Thy favor and glad to do Thy will. Bless our land with honorable ministry, sound learning, and pure manners. Save us from violence, discord, and confusion, from pride and arrogance, and from every evil way. Defend our liberties, and fashion into one united people, the multitude brought hither out of many kindreds and tongues. Endow with Thy spirit of wisdom those whom in Thy name we entrust the authority of government, that there may be justice and peace at home, and that through obedience to Thy law, we may show forth Thy praise among the nations of the earth. In time of prosperity fill our hearts with thankfulness, and in the day of trouble, suffer not our trust in Thee to fail; all of which we ask through Jesus Christ our Lord. *Amen.* (BCP, 820)

Preparing for Lent

The last Sunday of the season of the Epiphany features the story of the Transfiguration in the Gospel reading. This is also the last Sunday the word, "Alleluia" will be used in liturgy and preparations begin for the coming week's Ash Wednesday liturgy as well as the solemn season that follows.

Here are two traditions for making the transition from Epiphany to Lent.

Burying the Alleluia

As we keep the ancient practice of fasting from singing or speaking "alleluia" through the forty days of Lent, you may consider the practice of "burying" the alleluia at the end of the liturgy on the last Sunday before Ash Wednesday. This might mean simply singing an appropriate song at the end of the service or including the actual lowering of a visual alleluia banner (perhaps created by children) while singing. You could bury it in your churchyard or hide it away in a dark place (but remember where you put it!). Bring the alleluia back as part of the first alleluias at the Great Vigil of Easter or your Easter Festive Eucharist.

Farewell to Alleluia

Leader: O God, make speed to save us, hallelujah, hallelujah.

O Lord, make haste to help us, alleluia, alleluia.

All: (Sing an Alleluia hymn such as #178, #460 in The Hymnal 1982 or #41 from Lift Every Voice and Sing II)

Reading I
Leader: After this I heard what seemed to be the loud voice of a great multitude in heaven, saying, "Hallelujah! Salvation and glory and power belong to our God."

And the twenty-four elders and the four living creatures fell down and worshiped God who is seated on the throne, saying, "Amen. Hallelujah!" And from the throne there came a voice saying, "Praise our God, all you his servants, and all who fear him, small and great."

Then I heard what seemed to be the voice of a great multitude, like the sound of many waters and like the sound of mighty thunderpeals, crying out, "Hallelujah! For the Lord our God the Almighty reigns" (Revelation 19:1, 4–6).

Procession *(Carry the Alleluia Poster to its resting place for Lent.)*

7 Marcia King, "For An End to Poverty" in *Lifting Women's Voices: Prayers to Change the World* Margaret Rose, Jenny Te Paa, Jeanne Person, and Abagail Nelson, editors (Harrisburg, PA: Morehouse Publishing, 2009), 6

Epiphany

Epiphany

Reading II

Leader: Let us pray, reading aloud Psalm 137:1–6.

All: By the rivers of Babylon—
    there we sat down and there we wept,
    when we remembered Zion.
On the willows there
    we hung up our harps.
For there our captors
    asked us for songs,
and our tormentors called for mirth, saying,
    "Sing us one of the songs of Zion!"
How could we sing the Lord's song
    in a foreign land?
If I forget you, O Jerusalem,
    let my right hand wither!
Let my tongue cling to the roof of my mouth,
    if I do not remember you,
if I do not set Jerusalem
    above my highest joy.

Farewell to Alleluia *(Silently put away or veil the Alleluia Poster.)*

Prayer

Leader: Let us pray.

All: *(Pray the Lord's Prayer in unison.)*

Leader: God, you teach us to sing in praise. You teach us to pray in silence. Help us who prepare for the season to Lent to come with joy to the celebration of Easter, through Jesus Christ our Lord. *Amen.*

Dismissal *(Depart in silence at the conclusion of this service.)*

Shrove Tuesday

The day before Ash Wednesday was the day households were to use up all milk, eggs, and fat to prepare for the strict fasting of Lent. These ingredients were made into pancakes, a meal which came to symbolize preparation for the discipline of Lent, from the English tradition. "Shrove" comes from the verb "to shrive" (to confess and receive absolution) prior to the start of the Lenten season. Other names for this day include Carnival (farewell to meat) and Mardi Gras (Fat Tuesday of the French tradition). Thus, many congregations have Shrove Tuesday Pancake Suppers.

O Lord, we as we prepare our hearts for our Lenten journey, bless these pancakes we are about to share. As they remind us of the rich ingredients from our kitchens that fill our bellies with satisfaction, may we also remember your time in the wilderness when you did not even have bread or water. Be present with us as we get ready to begin the holy season of Lent, strengthening us to be ready to serve you in the days and weeks to come. *Amen.*

Making Pretzels

The pretzel has been used during Lent for over 1,500 years. It is thought that originally pretzels were made by monks to resemble arms crossed in prayer. These breads were called "little arms." This can have deep spiritual meaning for us during Lent. Since basically only flour and water are used, pretzels can remind us of fasting.

Heavenly Father, we ask you to bless these little breads. Each time we eat them may we be reminded of the special season we are in and that through prayer we will become better people to each other. Let us not forget those who are in need of our prayers daily. Keep your loving arms around us, O Father, to protect us always. *Amen.*

The Epiphany

January 6, 2020

The significance of Jesus' birth is revealed to the world beyond Judea.

Color   White

Preface   Of the Epiphany

Collect

O God, by the leading of a star you manifested your only Son to the peoples of the earth: Lead us, who know you now by faith, to your presence, where we may see your glory face to face; through Jesus Christ our Lord, who lives and reigns with you and the Holy Spirit, one God, now and for ever. Amen.

Readings and Psalm

Isaiah 60:1–6

In our Hebrew scripture lesson **the prophet envisions the end of exile and the glorious restoration of Jerusalem.** Although darkness covers the earth, the Lord will be a light making God's people shine. To this radiance shall come the nations. Rich treasures will be brought from afar to honor God.

Psalm 72:1–7, 10–14

The psalm asks that God endow the king with compassionate justice and righteousness, and that his reign may extend over all nations and throughout all generations.

Ephesians 3:1–12

Here is set forth the great theme of Paul's apostolic commission: the revealed mystery that Christ's salvation extends beyond Judaism to include all peoples. The apostle is near the end of his ministry and in prison at the time of the writing of this letter. Now it is recognized as God's eternal purpose that the Gentiles are to be members of the same body. The wisdom of God is made known through the church even in transcendental realms.

Matthew 2:1–12

Our gospel is **the story of the wise men from the east, who, guided by a star, come to worship the child born to be king.** Despite the wicked plotting of Herod, the Magi are able to bring their gifts to Jesus without betraying his exact location. Early Christians found in the rich symbolism and motifs of the story the fulfillment of both Hebrew scripture prophecy and the dreams of many peoples. The meaning of this birth, amid terrifyingly human circumstances, enlightens and transcends human history.

Prayers of the People

It is in following the Light that we discover the truth. With the love of God to guide our footsteps, let us journey to the new Bethlehem and offer our prayers to the Holy Child, responding, "Hear us, God of Glory."

For the light of hope which illumines the depths of reality and releases our hearts to offer the treasures of our souls; let us pray.

Hear us, God of Glory.

For the fragile stirrings of peace sown in troubled places throughout the world, that freedom may flourish, and its fruits bring hope to those most in need; let us pray.

Hear us, God of Glory.

For the forgiveness of our sins: our greed and narrow-mindedness, our selfishness and misuse of power, our misjudgment of one another, that we may acknowledge our faults and turn to the all-merciful love of God; let us pray.

Hear us, God of Glory.

Epiphany

That we may be humbled in the presence of the poor, bending the knee of our hearts to those who have no defender, and to those whose economic and personal distress pains us to encounter; let us pray.

Hear us, God of Glory.

For those who are suffering with illness and for those who bear a private grief, that the Holy Comforter may bring them relief from their burdens; let us pray.

Hear us, God of Glory.

For all that is to be revealed to us during this new year: the joys, the disappointments, the struggles, the new directions and insights; that through all our journeys we may know the Messiah as our constant companion; let us pray.

Hear us, God of Glory.

For a generosity of spirit, that through the delight of giving treasures rich and rare, we may share a common bounty and support a shared mission; let us pray.

Hear us, God of Glory.

In thanksgiving for the Body and Blood of Christ, a foretaste of that heavenly banquet upon which the faithful departed continually feast; let us pray.

Hear us, God of Glory.

In companionship with the angels of light, we continue our prayers.

(Special intentions of the congregation, the diocese, and the Anglican Communion may be added here or before the formal intercessions.)

The Celebrant adds a concluding Collect.

Images in the Readings

The main image is **light**. The star symbolizes a new light in the cosmos. The dawn pierces the thick darkness that has obscured our vision. During January, the northern hemisphere is experiencing a gradual lightening of the darkest time of the year, an appropriate time for the church to praise Christ as the light. This light shines again in the night of the Easter Vigil.

Made popular in hymns, pageants and crèche sets are the gifts of the magi: **gold, frankincense, and myrrh**. Gold denotes Jesus as a king. Frankincense and myrrh are sweet-smelling resins that were used in offerings to a god and at status burials. These are symbolic gifts for the divine king who has come to die. The birth narratives contain in them the death of Christ.

The ancient political idea was that monarchs were supposed to ensure safety for their subjects. Christ, not Herod, is the true **king** who gives life, rather than death, to the people.

Ideas for the Day

♦ What must it be like to follow a star not knowing precisely where it's headed, how the journey or its outcome will affect you, whether it is sheer folly or mere hardship or the stuff of which dreams are made? The journey/quest theme is pervasive: older than Homer's *Odyssey*, as fresh as *Harry Potter*, *Star Wars*, *Lord of the Rings*, and more. Epiphany is the celebration and commemoration of the successful following of an improbable star. The point was never the star (or ridding the world of Voldemort or Darth Vader), but the things we learn about ourselves as we slog along. We shall not, as T. S. Eliot says, "cease from exploration" until all the stars of all our tomorrows are sighted and followed and realized.

◆ In this season of things revealed, let us find new things to learn. We have untapped skills that we may never realize that we had. It is also possible that we have skills we never get to use because of our current work and family situations. Find ways to put yourself in new and different circumstances so that new facets of who you are can be revealed. Church ministries are wonderful ways to do this. Help out in a soup kitchen, you may discover you have a talent for cooking. Join the church choir, you may find out that your voice is not as bad you thought. Help out with the Altar Guild of your church, you may see that you have a gift for visual design.

◆ Christians are to continue "revealing the mystery" to the world. As God appeared in Jesus, so God appears through the Holy Spirit in the people of God who are the church.

Making Connections

If Herod is the fear in the story, then the Magi are the trust. It is precisely the immensity of God's gift that terrifies Herod and at times, might terrify us too. In those moments we should think of the Magi. Think of their calm spirits and peace of mind. Think of their conviction and their faith. Think of their willingness to trust. Think of their joy at meeting Christ. It is worth remembering that the Magi were the first to recognize that the transformation that Jesus' birth represented was for all people.

Engaging All Ages

From the time of the Middle Ages it has been a tradition that on the feast of the Epiphany we pray for God's blessing on our dwelling places, marking the entrance to our homes with chalk. Chalk is used as a tangible reminder of the dust of the earth from which we are all made. Distribute chalk to the congregation, inviting them to mark the doors of their home (and the church buildings) with the initials of the magi, which stand for the Latin motto: *Christus mansionem benedicat.* 20 + C + M + B + 20 (the current year). Download and distribute "The Blessing of a Home" at **www.churchpublishing.org/faithfulcelebrations3**.

Hymns for the Day

The Hymnal 1982

Hail to the Lord's Anointed 616
How bright appears the Morning Star 496, 497
Now the silence 333
Arise, shine, for your light has come S223ff
O very God of very God 672
O Zion, tune thy voice 543
Now, my tongue, the mystery telling 329, 331
Our God, to whom we turn 681
As with gladness men of old 119
Brightest and best of the stars of the morning 117, 118
Duérmete, Niño lindo / Oh, sleep now, holy baby 113
Earth has many a noble city 127
Father eternal, Ruler of creation 573
On this day earth shall ring 92
Songs of thankfulness and praise 135
Unto us a boy is born! 98
The first Nowell the angel did say 109
We three kings of Orient are 128
What star is this, with beams so bright 124
When Christ's appearing was made known (vs. 1, 2, 5) 131, 132
Where is this stupendous stranger? 491

Lift Every Voice and Sing II

Wonder, Love, and Praise
Where is this stupendous stranger? 726
Arise, shine, for your light has come 883

Epiphany

The First Sunday after the Epiphany: The Baptism of Our Lord Jesus Christ

January 12, 2020

The baptism of Jesus.

Color　　White

Preface　　Of the Epiphany

Collect

Father in heaven, who at the baptism of Jesus in the River Jordan proclaimed him your beloved Son and anointed him with the Holy Spirit: Grant that all who are baptized into his Name may keep the covenant they have made, and boldly confess him as Lord and Savior; who with you and the Holy Spirit lives and reigns, one God, in glory everlasting. Amen.

Readings and Psalm

Isaiah 42:1–9

In our lection from the Hebrew Bible we hear of **the mission of the Lord's servant, the one whom God has chosen to bring forth justice and salvation.** This is the first of the "servant songs" that form a portion of the Book of Isaiah, written at the time when the exile in Babylon was ending and the city of Jerusalem had begun to be restored. The servant is sometimes thought to be a historical individual or is understood as an idealization of Israel. Christians see in the servant a prefiguration of the ministry of Jesus, who will become a light to the nations of the world.

Psalm 29

The majesty of God is described in the likeness of a **mighty thunderstorm.**

Acts 10:34–43

In this reading we learn how **Peter recognizes that the good news, which Jesus began to proclaim after his baptism, now extends to all people.** At first Peter was slow to believe that God wanted him to bring the word to a non-Jew. But God has revealed this to Peter, and Peter gladly responds to Cornelius, a Roman centurion, together with his family and friends. Peter and the disciples are witnesses to Christ's ministry, death, and resurrection and have been commanded to preach forgiveness of sins through Jesus' name.

Matthew 3:13–17

Our gospel is **the story of Jesus' baptism.** John wonders why Jesus should come to him to receive a baptism for the remission of sins, but Jesus tells him that it is right and fitting. After he is baptized, the Holy Spirit is manifest. A voice from heaven proclaims who Jesus is, with words that echo ancient oracles concerning the king and the calling of the Lord's chosen servant.

Prayers of the People

Through Christ we are anointed with the Holy Spirit in baptism. May the same Spirit inspire us as we offer our prayers, responding, "Hear us, God of Glory."

For an overflowing gift of generosity, that we may reflect God's abundant care for all of creation, lifting others out of systemic poverty, increasing the mission work of our churches, and reaping the joy of a philanthropic life; let us pray.

Hear us, God of Glory.

For the courage to walk through the tranquil and turbulent waters of life, knowing that in our baptism we died with Christ in darkness and joined him in the risen light; let us pray.

Hear us, God of Glory.

For N., our President, and all who exercise authority in the nations of the world, that they will faithfully establish justice on earth, and carry the torch of freedom and peace into all their deliberations; let us pray.

Hear us, God of Glory.

For the Church, that it may bear witness to Jesus' forgiveness and love, offering to those outside its walls the light that illumines all darkness and releases humanity from the grip of sin; let us pray.

Hear us, God of Glory.

That we may know our identity through the voice of God, who claims us as his beloved sons and daughters, and invites us to share in his earthly mission; let us pray.

Hear us, God of Glory.

In thanksgiving for the Body and Blood of Christ, a foretaste of that heavenly banquet upon which the faithful departed continually feast; let us pray.

Hear us, God of Glory.

In companionship with the Blessed Virgin Mary, and all the saints whose constant intercession strengthens our faith, let us continue our prayers.
(Special intentions of the congregation, the diocese, and the Anglican Communion may be added here or before the formal intercessions.)

The Celebrant adds a concluding Collect.

Images in the Readings

There can be no life as we know without **water**. Christians see in the waters of baptism the matrix of our new life in Christ. The font is like the Jordan, a river of water that leads us to the new land of promise.

The **dove** functions in several biblical stories as a symbol of the presence of God's Holy Spirit. The white color matches the baptismal garment. Secular culture connects the dove especially with peace, which Acts cites as the message of Jesus' preaching.

The gospel reading uses the image of **Son** to describe Jesus' identity: the first reading uses the image of **servant**, and the second reading speaks of Jesus as **the anointed one**. Each of these images conveys something of the meaning of Jesus for believers. It is instructive to think about Son and Christ as metaphors before these words became literalized as part of Jesus' name.

Once again **light** is an image for the power of God. Early Christians referred to baptism as enlightenment.

Ideas for the Day

- Although the lectionary editors have divided the stories, the narrative of Jesus' baptism is immediately followed by the testing in the wilderness. Jesus sets off, still wet from the water of his baptism to face his first ordeal, the test that asked "What kind of Son of God will you be?" And he went with those words "My Son, the Beloved" ringing in his ears. With that claim and that love pronounced on him, and the commissioning it implies calling him forward, Jesus steps into his ministry, but he does not go alone. He goes armed with the love and the promise of the One who had sent him.

- The words of calling and anointing for ministry heard in connection with Jesus' baptism are the words that frame the church's ministry of all the baptized today: "You are my . . . Beloved; with you I am well pleased." The radical nature of our calling is to bring justice and to serve the cause of right, to be part of God's own mission of liberating the suffering, the oppressed, and the hungry.

- Today, let us go for a hike. Leave the car at the parking lot and begin walking down your selected path. Smell the air that trees are making clean. Breathe in deeply and walk slowly. Engage in the environment away from cars, buildings, and computers. Listen to how the breeze rustles the trees' leaves and branches. Hear the melody that God is creating. Follow the path to the water. Take in the sight of the waterfall flowing in constant renewal. Touch the water. Feel its cold, brisk temperature. Water is life. Life is spirit. It is through baptism that these two are joined. Let the touch of water renew in you that which you already know.

Making Connections

This day is an opportunity for us to reflect on what it means to be a follower of Jesus and how we might deepen and strengthen the Covenant we make at Baptism. Being a Christian is about believing in God, in Christ, in the Holy Spirit, about believing God's promises, and it is about living in such a way that we share the abiding love of God with the world. Our Baptismal Covenant reminds us to share our stories and to do our part to help make this a world a place where the dignity of every human being is respected.

Epiphany

Engaging All Ages

If you are celebrating baptisms on this day (this Sunday is one of the five most appropriate times for baptism in the church (BCP, 312), invite children to surround the font with perhaps a sibling of someone being baptized invited to pour the water in the font. Invite a teen to light a baptism candle from the Pascal candle, giving it to a godparent. This is a sacramental moment that easily involves all ages in the "action" and welcome of new members into the Body of Christ.

Hymns for the Day

The Hymnal 1982
Songs of thankfulness and praise 135
Blessed be the God of Israel 444
Thy strong word did cleave the darkness 381
In Christ there is no East or West 529
Christ, when for us you were baptized 121
From God Christ's deity came forth 443
"I come," the great Redeemer cries 116
O love, how deep, how broad, how high (vs. 1–3, 6)
    448, 449
The sinless one to Jordan came 120
When Christ's appearing was made known (vs. 1, 3, 5)
    131, 132
When Jesus went to Jordan's stream 139

Lift Every Voice and Sing II
Take me to the water 134
In Christ there is no East or West 62

Wonder, Love, and Praise
Blessed be the God of Israel 889

Weekday Commemorations

Monday, January 13
Hilary, Bishop of Poitiers, 367
Hilary was born about 315 in Poitiers in Gaul into a wealthy and pagan family. He wrote of his spiritual journey from unbelief to baptism (at about age 30) to bishop in 350, a job he never sought but that he executed with skill and courage. His bravery was tested about 355, when Emperor Constantius ordered all bishops to condemn Athanasius; Hilary refused and was exiled to Phrygia. Uncomplaining, Hilary used those three years to write On the Trinity, his principal work. In 360, after great churchly agitation, Hilary returned to his see, where he continued to fight against heresy and to care for his diocese.

Tuesday, January 14
*Richard Meux Benson, Priest, and
Charles Gore, Bishop, 1915 and 1932*
Benson and Gore played roles in the revival of Anglican monasticism in the 19th century. Born in London in 1824, Benson studied under Edward Pusey and became well-known for conducting silent retreats. In 1865, Fr. Benson helped establish the Mission Priests of St. John the Evangelist, the first community of men in the Church of England since the Reformation. Gore, ordained in 1876, founded the Community of the Resurrection, which combined traditional religious life with modern demands of ministry. Gore, a principal progenitor of liberal Anglo-Catholicism, believed in making Biblical scholarship available to the church and pricking the conscience of the church to engage in social justice.

Wednesday, January 15
Martin Luther King, Jr. (alt)—see April 4

Friday, January 17
Antony of Egypt, Monastic, 356
Athanasius queried this regarding Antony: "Who met him grieving and did not go away rejoicing?" Antony, born in Egypt to Christians, exemplified the movement of the third century toward monasticism. He followed Christ's invitation to sell all his possessions, and he became an anchorite, or solitary ascetic. Antony dwelt alone for two decades: he prayed, he read, and he worked with his hands. In 305, he walked out of his mountain cave across the Nile and founded a monastery, its cells filled with monks living together in love and peace. He spent his remaining days in the mountains of Egypt, fighting against dissenters through preaching, converting, and performing miracles.

Saturday, January 18
The Confession of Saint Peter the Apostle
Simon Bar-Jona, a boisterous fisher, confessed to Jesus: "You are the Christ." Jesus renamed him Peter, the "rock," on which Jesus built his church. Peter and his brother Andrew were the first disciples; thus, Peter figures keenly in the gospels despite his ill manners. Peter tried to walk on water; Peter wished to build three tabernacles. Peter thrice denied knowing Christ. On the other hand, Peter courageously risked his life to be a disciple, openly declaring his belief in Jesus as the Christ, and he courageously headed the young church's missions. Peter transformed from ordinary Simon, overbearing and impetuous, to an extraordinary church leader, filled with the Holy Spirit.

The Second Sunday after the Epiphany

January 19, 2020

Responding to God's call to be a "light to all nations."

Color   Green

Preface   Of the Epiphany or of the Lord's Day

Collect

Almighty God, whose Son our Savior Jesus Christ is the light of the world: Grant that your people, illumined by your Word and Sacraments, may shine with the radiance of Christ's glory, that he may be known, worshiped, and obeyed to the ends of the earth; through Jesus Christ our Lord, who with you and the Holy Spirit lives and reigns, one God, now and for ever. Amen.

Readings and Psalm

Isaiah 49:1–7

In our Hebrew scripture lesson the servant of the Lord reflects movingly on his mission—its sorrows and frustrations—and God's high calling and promise to be with him. The servant is sometimes thought to be an historical individual or is understood as an idealization of Israel. This song was probably composed as the exiles from Jerusalem were preparing to return to their devastated city. Despite appearances, the Lord will make this servant a light to the nations.

Psalm 40:1–11

A prayer for deliverance and a song of thanksgiving to God who has saved the Lord's servant from great troubles and made it possible to sing God's praise.

1 Corinthians 1:1–9

In this lesson Paul greets the members of the new Christian community in Corinth and offers thanksgiving for their growth in Christ. He is writing from Ephesus some months after his first stay with the Corinthians, and he will shortly be concerned with many of their problems and questions. Now he reminds these disciples of their high calling and expresses his gratitude for their spiritual enrichment.

John 1:29–42

In our gospel passage, **John the Baptist declares who Jesus is. The next day two of John's followers become disciples of Jesus.** One of these disciples is Andrew, who then brings his brother Simon Peter. John has led them to understand that Jesus is God's chosen one, the servant on whom God's Spirit rests. He is the Lamb of God who will be a sacrifice for the sins of the world.

Prayers of the People

O Lamb of God that takes away the sins of the world, cast your eyes of mercy on your people who entrust their prayers to you, responding, "Hear us, God of Glory."

For the light of Christ that never fades away, that it may shine through our words and actions, revealing the saving grace of the Anointed One; let us pray.

Hear us, God of Glory.

That the leaders and peoples of every nation may be willing to pay the price of peace through compromise, compassion, humility, and forbearance; let us pray.

Hear us, God of Glory.

For an increase in vocations to the Religious Communities of our Church, that we may continue to be guided by their life of prayer and sacrificial works; let us pray.

Hear us, God of Glory.

Epiphany

For relief for those who live with debilitating anxiety, and to those who bear the scars of poverty and emotional desolation, that they may experience the fruits of your eternal and holy presence; let us pray.

Hear us, God of Glory.

In thanksgiving for our sacred fellowship with Christ, may we move from strength to strength in our spiritual life so that its fruits may flow into our workplaces, schools, and neighborhoods; let us pray.

Hear us, God of Glory.

For the baptized who have entered into their eternal rest, and for those whose faith is known to God alone, that our Eternal Judge will look kindly on their souls; let us pray.

Hear us, God of Glory.

That the true light that enlightens even the far reaches of the universe and the deep recesses of the sea, will open our eyes to the beauty of creation and encourage us to be good stewards of its bountiful gifts; let us pray.

Hear us, God of Glory.

Let us continue our prayers to the one who calls us to faithfulness and strengthens us for the journey.

(Special intentions of the congregation, the diocese, and the Anglican Communion may be added here or before the formal intercessions.)

The Celebrant adds a concluding Collect.

Images in the Readings

Once again we are given images of **water, light,** and **dove** (see Baptism of Our Lord).

The fourth gospel refers to Jesus as the **Lamb** of God. Several New Testament writers used this image to give salvific meaning to Jesus' execution. The lamb as apocalyptic conqueror, the lamb as suffering servant, and the paschal lamb are all possibilities of what the earliest Christians meant by the image. The medieval church stressed Christ as sacrificial lamb, whose blood takes away sin.

God calls. The Scriptures include many **call** narratives, in testifying that this God is the kind of deity who knows us by name and who calls us into a new identity. All three readings refer to such a call. In the poem from Second Isaiah, the call comes to the prophet even before birth. The church has described baptism as our call to servanthood, and many churches use the imagery of the call in descriptions of their clergy.

Ideas for the Day

♦ At the center of this story of the first disciples is a verb of some significance to the fourth Gospel; variously translated "remain," "stay," or "abide," it is a key to the process of discipling. We don't know what transpired between those two and Jesus that first afternoon and evening, but we do know that their "abiding" with him and he with them changed their lives. During his ministry, Jesus periodically carves out time to "abide" with his followers. In his last speech to them on the night before he dies, Jesus explains the import of the intimacy of abiding in his extended metaphor of the vine and the branches immediately followed by the command to "love one another" (John 15).

♦ This Sunday begins a serialized reading of 1 Corinthians 1–4; therefore, the epistle reading will not usually be in thematic harmony with the other lections. However, it provides an opportunity to dig into Paul's first letter to the Christians in Corinth as a sermon series or Bible study.

♦ Let us live our lives in ways that will be a legacy for those who come after us. The Bible is filled with ordinary people who lived extraordinary lives through their acceptance of a holy path. It is important that we not get caught up in the day to day. There will always be people who will doubt us, people who might make us think silly for having such a steadfast faith. It is important that we persevere. Use the examples shown to us in the Bible to reassure our intentions. We must think and plan ahead. We have to good stewards today, in order to better stewards tomorrow.

Making Connections

Archbishop Rowan Williams has an interesting take on holiness. He does not see it as an exalted status for those select few who seem to lead ideal and exemplary lives. Holiness is about living lives with holes in them. Being holy is not about getting it all right. It is about leaving holes in your life that the light of Christ can shine through. What better way to do this then by being open and vulnerable? Just as Isaiah was called, we too have been called to share God's light with the world.

Engaging All Ages

The star guided the magi to Jesus, and stars were used for navigation and by travelers for thousands of years. The constellations guided runaway slaves in the United States from slavery to freedom. Read *Follow the Drinking Gourd* (Scholastic, 1992) by Jeanette Winter based on an American folksong first published in 1928. The "drinking gourd" refers to the hollowed-out gourd used by slaves (and other rural Americans) as a water dipper. But here it is used as a code name for the Big Dipper star formation, which points to Polaris, the Pole Star, and North. What (or who) do we follow when we have hopes for a better life? How does the light of Christ lead the way for us?

Hymns for the Day

The Hymnal 1982
Christ is the world's true Light 542
Christ, whose glory fills the skies 6, 7
God of mercy, God of grace 538
How wondrous and great thy works,
    God of praise! 532, 533
O Zion, tune thy voice 543
Strengthen for service, Lord, the hands 312
We the Lord's people, heart and voice uniting 51
By all your saints still striving (St. Andrew) 231, 232
In your mercy, Lord, you called me 706
Jesus calls us; o'er the tumult 549, 550
Lord, enthroned in heavenly splendor 307
What wondrous love is this 439
Ye servants of God, your Master proclaim 535

Lift Every Voice and Sing II
I have decided to follow Jesus 136

Wonder, Love, and Praise
Will you come and follow me 757

Weekday Commemorations

Monday, January 20
Fabian, Bishop and Martyr, 250
Although he was not among the candidates for pope in 236, Fabian, a stranger to Rome and layman, was elected without opposition after a dove alighted on his head. He served for 14 years, reforming the office by developing structure among the churches. He set a custom of venerating martyrs at their shrines, and he appointed a committee to record their lives for posterity. He himself became a holy, exemplary martyr when Emperor Decius demanded persecution of the Church across the empire about 240. The Church Fabian had served diligently and with humility stood fast through this time of trouble.

Tuesday, January 21
Agnes [and Cecilia] of Rome, Martyrs, 304 and c. 230
Agnes and Cecilia, two highly venerated early Christians, were martyred during persecutions in Rome. Men propositioned Agnes ("lamb" in Latin) as a girl; when she rejected them, they denounced her as a Christian. She refused to sacrifice to Roman gods, so she was tortured and executed. A Roman basilica, oft visited by pilgrims, bears her name. Cecilia, patron saint of musicians, supported the conversions of her fiancé Valerian and her brother Tiburtius; after they, too, were martyred, Cecilia was arrested as she buried her beloveds. Cecilia was known to passionately sing praises to God; thus, many music schools, societies, and concert series honor her name.

Wednesday, January 22
Vincent of Saragossa, Deacon and Martyr, 304
Vincent, the so-called protomartyr of Spain, exemplifies the saint raised up because of vehement support of Jesus in a time of persecution, torture, and death. Vincent is known for little else than his name, his order (deacon), and the time and place of his martyrdom (early in the fourth century, Saragossa). Vincent and his bishop, Valerius, were persecuted under the rule of the Roman emperors, Diocletian and Maximian, but Vincent preached loudly and fervently in Jesus' name, so he was punished grotesquely then killed at last by Dacia, governor of Spain. Vincent has been venerated as an outspoken follower of Christ.

Thursday, January 23
Phillips Brooks, Bishop, 1893

Writer of songs ("O little town of Bethlehem") and sermons ("Remember the nearness of God to each one of us"), builder of churches in body and building (Trinity-Boston), innovator, youth leader, and bishop, Brooks was a tender friend and pastor. He spent ten years serving in Philadelphia before returning to Boston, where he had been born in 1835. He was appointed rector of Trinity, but three years later, the church building burned; Brooks oversaw its rebuilt altar placed daringly in the center of the chancel, "a symbol of unity." He was elected bishop in 1891, and through the force of his personality and preaching, he provided the spiritual leadership the diocese needed for that time.

Friday, January 24
Florence Li Tim-Oi, Priest, 1992

Named by her father "much beloved daughter," Li Tim-Oi was born in Hong Kong in 1907. When she was baptized as a student, she chose the name of Florence in honor of Florence Nightingale. Ordained deaconess in May 1941, Florence worked in Macao even after Hong Kong fell to Japanese invaders and priests could not travel to Macao to celebrate the Eucharist. Her work came to the attention of Bishop Ronald Hall who decided that "God's work would reap better results if she had the proper title" of priest. She was ordained on January 25, 1944, the Feast of the Conversion of St. Paul, the first woman to be ordained priest in the Anglican Communion.

Saturday, January 25
The Conversion of Saint Paul the Apostle

Saul, an orthodox Jew, studied under the famous rabbi Gamaliel, but soon after Jesus died, Saul connected to the Christian movement. He determined to crush it as heresy. On his way to Damascus to persecute Christians, Saul converted dramatically, becoming Paul and dedicating himself to Jesus. He planted Christian congregations bordering the eastern Mediterranean. His letters manifest his alignment with the mind of Christ, thereby founding Christian theology. Although rather frail physically, he was strong spiritually: "I will all the more gladly boast of my weaknesses that the power of Christ may rest upon me." His martyrdom is believed to have occurred in 64 under Nero.

The Third Sunday after the Epiphany

January 26, 2020

The calling of the disciples, yesterday and today.

Color   Green

Preface   Of the Epiphany, or of the Lord's Day

Collect

Give us grace, O Lord, to answer readily the call of our Savior Jesus Christ and proclaim to all people the Good News of his salvation, that we and the whole world may perceive the glory of his marvelous works; who lives and reigns with you and the Holy Spirit, one God, for ever and ever. Amen.

Readings and Psalm

Isaiah 9:1–4

Our Hebrew Bible lesson is **a hymn of thanksgiving and hope offered at the birth of a new king in Jerusalem.** The prophet hails the one born to be the ruler of his people. His reign will end oppression and bring justice, righteousness, and a lasting peace. Christians see these words coming to fulfillment in Jesus.

Psalm 27:1, 4–9

The psalmist expresses great trust and confidence in the Lord and asks always to be in God's presence.

1 Corinthians 1:10–18

In this lesson we hear that Paul is disturbed by news of factions in the young Corinthian church. Apparently the new converts were dividing into groups based on who it was who baptized them and whose teaching they were following. They must instead be unified in Jesus, in whose name alone they are baptized. Paul is grateful on this account that he himself has baptized very few of them, and that he does not preach with such eloquent wisdom that people would rely on him rather than the cross of Christ.

Matthew 4:12–23

The gospel is **a summary of the early ministry of Jesus: his preaching, the calling of disciples, and his acts of healing.** After the arrest of John the Baptist, Jesus withdrew to Galilee, an area in which many Gentiles lived. The evangelist perceives in this a fulfillment of prophecy and a foreshadowing of the church's mission to bring the light of the gospel to darkened lives. Two sets of brothers are called to leave their nets and become fishers of people.

Prayers of the People

The light of Christ breaks through our hesitancies, and releases our tongues to proclaim the good news of the kingdom, and so we offer our prayers responding, "Hear us, God of Glory."

That the Church may respond with compassion and generosity to those who live with the anguish of unemployment, disrespect, hunger, and fear, releasing them from their anxiety through the supportive ministry and compassion of the household of faith; let us pray.

Hear us, God of Glory.

In thanksgiving for those who have been lights in their generation, especially Peter, Andrew, James and John; may we, following their example, leave comfort and certainty behind as we respond to Jesus' call to follow wherever he leads; let us pray.

Hear us, God of Glory.

In thanksgiving for writers and actors, dancers and singers, doctors and teachers, and all who use their talents in the cause of peace throughout the world; let us pray.

Hear us, God of Glory.

Epiphany

For the leaders of the nations, that concern for justice may guide the daily decisions they must make on our behalf, and that a dedication for the common good may overcome the powerful seduction of a few; let us pray.

Hear us, God of Glory.

In thanksgiving for this Eucharistic Meal through which we receive the Body and Blood of Christ, heavenly food to strengthen us on our earthly pilgrimage; let us pray.

Hear us, God of Glory.

For those whom we no longer see, but who live in the fellowship of the saints, in whose company we hope to reside; let us pray.

Hear us, God of Glory.

Guided by the light of Christ shining in our hearts, we continue our prayers.
(Special intentions of the congregation, the diocese, and the Anglican Communion may be added here or before the formal intercessions.)

The Celebrant adds a concluding Collect.

Images in the Readings

The gospel describes the first disciples as **fish**ermen. This may be a memory of the profession of some in the Jesus movement. As well, it grounds the early Christian imagery of baptism as water, believers as water-dwellers, the net as the gospel, and the boat as the church. The Greek of the early Christian creed, "Jesus [i] Christ [ch], God's [th] Son [u], Savior, [s]" produces the acronym *ichthus*, fish, and fish show up in much Christian iconography.

The gospel introduces the image of "the **kingdom of heaven.**" Arguably the most important image in the New Testament, the kingdom invoked Israelite memory of a time of political independence. Yet this kingdom is, according to Matthew, "of heaven," that is, of a realm beyond this earth and was probably, in accord with Jewish sensibilities, a circumlocution for God. The designation of Jesus as Christ, that is, the one anointed by God for power to reign, relies on the kingdom imagery. It is not an image easily accessible for twenty-first century believers. In the New Testament, *basileia* is not solely a reference to either the church or an afterlife.

The poem in Isaiah mentions **Midian**. Israel remembered its oppression by the Midianites and then under the leadership of Gideon its victory over them. Invoking this memory, first Isaiah likens God's coming salvation to the military victory that set them free. Even the archetypal practice of warriors **plundering** the vanquished is offered as a positive image.

Ideas for the Day

- Immediately after the testing in the wilderness (4:1–11) Jesus begins his ministry in Galilee where he calls his first disciples to "Come, follow me." He will close his ministry twenty-four chapters later, again in Galilee, with the "Go, baptize" command. Between that coming and going, the disciples will have on-the-job training, not only to say the sorts of things Jesus said in his time with them, but to do the sorts of things he did with all sorts of people and to teach others to do the same. In some sense the Church is born in that time between the "Come" and the "Go."

- We begin to focus on mission, ministry, and discipleship in our readings today. Just as Jesus called his disciples (followers) who became his apostles (ambassadors) after the resurrection, he calls us to be his followers. In our baptism we too are called by the Lord to point beyond ourselves to God's eternal presence in creation.

- What things in our daily lives do we need to cast down and set aside so that we can more intently follow our given Christian path? Understanding the dynamics within society regarding financial self-sufficiency, is there something that we can let go of in order to become a more faithful follower? Is there something that we fear that we can finally let go of? So many steps we refuse to take because we fear a particular outcome, yet faith provides the safety net we need to overcome anything we might face. Brothers Andrew and Simon Peter did not know what lay ahead them when Jesus called them to discipleship, yet they accepted the challenge, leaving their lives to the will of God.

Making Connections

The call to follow Jesus deserves a love and desire that jumps in with our whole selves, and it deserves the careful consideration of what it means. The secular world that tells us our lives would be easier without Jesus. Being a Christian is a lot of work and completely worth it because it means holding to beliefs about how every human being is worthy of our care and respect and about how there is always hope, even in the midst of great darkness. These beliefs matter, and they have the power to help us make a difference in the world.

Engaging All Ages

Today might be a good day to hold a ministry and mission "fair" for the congregation. Invite the ministries within your church (altar guild, youth group, teaching, etc.) and those who connect your church outside into the community (social justice, soup kitchen, pastoral care, mission trips, etc.) to set up a display in your parish hall during coffee hour for all ages to visit and learn how they might be called to a new ministry in the name of Christ. Make sure there are opportunities for all ages, not just adults, to be involved.

Hymns for the Day

The Hymnal 1982
How wondrous and great thy works,
   God of praise! 532, 533
My God, thy table now is spread 321
Spread, O spread, thou mighty word 530
Singing songs of expectation 527
The people who in darkness walked 125, 126
Thy strong word did cleave the darkness 381
God is Love, and where true love is 576, 577
I come with joy to meet my Lord 304
Where charity and love prevail 581
Where true charity and love dwell 606
Jesus calls us, o'er the tumult 549, 550
They cast their nets in Galilee 661

Lift Every Voice and Sing II

Wonder, Love, and Praise
Ubi caritas et amor 831
As we gather at your Table 763
Will you come and follow me 757
Put down your nets and follow me 807
Tú has venido a la orilla / You have come down
   to the lakeshore 758

Weekday Commemorations

Monday, January 27
John Chrysostom, Bishop and Theologian, 407
John was dubbed "Chrysostom" due to his "golden mouth," an apt description of this legendary preacher, one of the great saints of the Eastern Church. Born about 354 in Antioch, Syria, John followed a call to desert monasticism, but the desert compromised his health. Upon return to Antioch, he was ordained a presbyter; in 397, he became Patriarch of Constantinople, but his ascetic episcopate led to two banishments. He died September 14, 407, during his second exile. John, the patron saint of preachers, believed, "Preaching improves me." His sermons shed light on liturgy and emphasized the voice of the *laos* (the people). A Prayer of St. Chrysostom speaks significantly in the Book of Common Prayer at the end of Morning and Evening Prayer.

Tuesday, January 28
Thomas Aquinas, Friar and Theologian, 1274
Thomas is the greatest theologian of his time (the high Middle Ages)—and, perhaps, of all time. Born (probably in 1225) to a noble Italian family, he joined the new Dominican Order of Preachers. Teaching in a time of intellectual ferment, he ordered his thinking in the light of the recent rediscovery of Aristotle's works and their effect on Roman Catholic doctrine. Thomas asserted that reason and revelation harmonize: "Grace is not the denial of nature," he wrote. He understood that God's Name in Exodus, "I Am Who I Am," means that God is Being from which everything else derives. Thomas died in 1274; his remains were removed to Toulouse on Jan. 28, 1369.

Friday, January 31
Marcella of Rome, Monastic and Scholar, 410
Born in 325, as a child Marcella studied with Athanasius of Alexandria. As a young widow, she traded richness for asceticism. Marcella made her dwelling a house of prayer, setting an example for a community of women devoted to fasting and serving the poor. With Paula (Sept. 28), Marcella stands as a mother of Roman monasticism. In 382, with Paula, Marcella hosted Jerome at her estate; the three formed a friendship that encouraged Jerome's Latin translation of the scriptures into the Vulgate. Scholars sought Marcella's insight on the Greek and Hebrew scriptures. She died at the hands of Visigoths.

Epiphany

Saturday, February 1
Brigid of Kildare, Monastic, c.523

As Irish as Patrick, and as beloved, Brigid was born
to a Druid household in the mid-fifth century. She
chose early to dedicate her life to Christ as a nun; in
470, she founded a nunnery in Kildare. To secure the
sacraments, Brigid persuaded an anchorite to receive
episcopal ordination and escort his community to
Kildare, thus establishing the only known double Irish
monastery. She effected policy at church conventions
and may have received episcopal orders herself. Stories
of her care for the poor include the healing of a leper
woman and the taming of a wolf. Her feast day shares
sacredness with Imbolg, the Celtic festival of spring.

The Fourth Sunday after the Epiphany

February 2, 2020

The Sermon on the Mount: God's word is revealed. God's way is proclaimed.

Color   Green

Preface   Of the Epiphany, or of the Lord's Day

Collect

Almighty and everlasting God, you govern all things both in heaven and on earth: Mercifully hear the supplications of your people, and in our time grant us your peace; through Jesus Christ our Lord, who lives and reigns with you and the Holy Spirit, one God, for ever and ever. Amen.

Readings and Psalm

Micah 6:1–8

In our lesson from the Hebrew Bible **God contends with the people of God, reminding them of the saving acts done for them and instructing them in the good that God expects.** The very mountains and hills are called as witnesses. God led the people out of Egypt and through the wilderness in safety. Yet they sin. It is not animal or human sacrifices the Lord wishes, but that the people act in justice, with loving-kindness and humility.

Psalm 15

The psalm describes the virtues of one who is worthy to worship the Lord.

1 Corinthians 1:18–31

In this reading **Paul directs the Corinthians' attention to God's way of using what is weak and lowly—even what the world regards as foolish—to accomplish the divine purposes.** Paul emphasizes this understanding because a number of these new Christians had come to think of themselves as especially gifted, powerful, and wise. As the cross has shown, however, God's ideas about what is wise and noble are often quite different from ours. Our only boast can be in the Lord.

Matthew 5:1–12

The gospel lesson is **the opening sayings of the Sermon on the Mount, words of both comfort and challenge.** The values of the kingdom are quite different from worldly standards. Those who are to find blessing will know want and thirst, if not because of their own circumstances, then for the sake of others. Those who hunger for righteousness will find fulfillment, but first they must experience persecution.

Prayers of the People

Knit together with Mary, the Mother of God; Simeon; Anna; and all the righteous, let us offer our prayers, responding to each petition, "Kyrie eleison."

That our young people may be brought up in the mystery of faith, rooted in God's Word, participants in the Holy Meal, honored by the community of the baptized, and participants in the life of the Church; for this we pray.

Kyrie eleison.

In thanksgiving for those who give sacrificially to God's mission in this place, supporting creative programs and good works, ministering to those in need, and revealing the divine kingdom in our time; for this we pray.

Kyrie eleison.

That we may acknowledge our individual suffering, seeing the presence of Christ in the midst of our despair, and helping others who are experiencing their time of testing; for this we pray.

Kyrie eleison.

Epiphany

That those who live in slavery may be freed from their bondage, especially the victims of human trafficking, children throughout the world, and all who are innocent victims of the evil ways of others; for this we pray.

Kyrie eleison.

In thanksgiving for foster parents, who bring hope to young people who long for stable and loving family life; may they be worthy of the trust invested in them; for this we pray.

Kyrie eleison.

That all who are dying may depart this life in peace, trusting in Christ's promise of eternal life; for this we pray.

Kyrie eleison.

Gathered together with all who serve with joy in the house of the Lord, let us continue our prayers.

(Special intentions of the congregation, the diocese, and the Anglican Communion may be added here or before the formal intercessions.)

The Celebrant adds a concluding Collect.

Images in the Readings

In the ancient Near East, some religious practice required parents to sacrifice their firstborn child to the deities, who would then reward the parents with many healthy children. Numbers 18:16 stipulates that instead parents should provide for the sacrifice of animals, the slaughter of which **redeems** the infant. This practice, so alien to us, is fundamental to the New Testament's explanation of the purpose behind the crucifixion of Christ. Kept alive as an infant—recall also Matthew's story of Jesus escaping Herod's slaughter of the innocents—Jesus as an adult will die as a sacrificed lamb in order to redeem us all. Thus the festival of the Presentation is really a meditation on Good Friday.

Simeon's poem about Christ being **light** to the Gentiles—that is, to most of us—led to the medieval practice of people bringing to the church on this day their year's supply of candles to be blessed: thus the popular naming of this day as Candlemas. Perhaps you can use up the remainder of your Christmas candles by having all worshipers hold their lighted candles during the reading of this day's gospel. These tiny lights remind us of the refiner's fire that Malachi anticipates. The white robe of baptism, like the vestment we call an alb, is a sign of our joy in the presence of God. We are to shine with the light of God.

Martin Luther says of Anna's being **eighty-four years** old that since 84 is 12 times 7, Anna's age combines all the meanings of twelve and of seven in the Bible. Thus her age can be seen as signifying the completion of the Old Testament in Christ.

The book of Hebrews expands the metaphor of Jesus being the sacrifice by naming him as the **high priest** who does the sacrificing of the lamb. This reminds us that no image of Christ is profound enough, and so we sometimes turn the image around and use it upside down.

Here is part of today's gospel: that according to the oracle from Malachi, we become like **gold and silver**, precious, shining with the beauty of God.

Ideas for the Day

♦ A slip of the tongue turns Beatitudes into Attitudes. In a way, attitudes are what the beatitudes are lauding. The familiar "Blessed are" or "Happy are" are the English versions of a Greek (and earlier) Hebrew expression which means something more like: "Congratulations, you've arrived!" It should come as no surprise to Matthew's hearers that the subjects of the plaudits are those whose attitudes are not the norm. The God of Israel had been famous for overturning preconceptions for millennia; the Son's inaugural teaching is an extension of the same and meant to be as provocative.

♦ ". . . what does the Lord require of you but to do justice, and to love kindness and to walk with your God?" It is the compassion God shows us that should empower us to show compassion to others. Working toward justice in our community allows us to strengthen our resolve as we walk on our chosen Christian path. Expressing kindness in a variety of ways in different aspects of our life is yet another form of engaging in our faith. In the midst of injustice and people who are unkind, we must remain steadfast. We must be ambassadors of kindness in the world. We never know the impact a single act of kindness can have on the person who receives it.

Making Connections

At the heart of Micah's words is a question that is important for all of us to hear. What does our faith look like? Is the love of God that has been so generously given to us made manifest through our actions? As we look ahead to Lent, might we consider fasting in such a way as to make a difference in the lives of others. Might we seek to smile more, do more small acts of kindness and generosity, so that our lives show God's reconciling Way of Love to the world.

Engaging All Ages

Have the congregation look at the worship bulletin (or Book of Common Prayer) to visually see (and experience) how our liturgy envisions the reign of God. In worship we (1) gather in God's name, (2) hear God's radical Word, (3) respond in prayer and thanksgiving, (4) offer ourselves to God through our offerings, (5) share a foretaste of the heavenly banquet through communion and (6) go forth to love and serve.

Hymns for the Day

The Hymnal 1982
How lovely is thy dwelling-place 517
Angels, from the realms of glory 93
Love divine, all loves excelling 657
How bright appears the Morning Star 496, 497
Sing of Mary, pure and lowly 277
The great Creator of the worlds (vs. 1–4) 489
Blest are the pure in heart 656
Christ, whose glory fills the skies 6,7
Hail to the Lord who comes 259
Let all mortal flesh keep silence 324
Lord God, you now have set your servant free 499
Sing we of the blessed Mother 278
Virgin-born, we bow before thee 258

Lift Every Voice and Sing II

Wonder, Love, and Praise
Lord, you have fulfilled your word 891

Epiphany

Weekday Commemorations

Monday, February 3
Anskar, Bishop and Missionary, 865
As Archbishop of Hamburg, Anskar was papal legate for missionary work among the Scandinavians. The immediate result of his devoted and perilous labors was slight: two churches established on the border of Denmark and one priest settled in Sweden. He also participated in the consecration of Gotbert, first bishop in Sweden. While still a young man, Anskar was consecrated Archbishop of Hamburg in 831, and continued his work among the Scandinavians until 848, when he retired to the See of Bremen and died in 865. The seeds of his efforts were not to bear fruit until over one hundred years later, when Viking devastation, weakness in the Frankish Church, and the lowest ebb of missionary enthusiasm came to an end. The rich harvest of conversion was three generations away. Nevertheless, Anskar is looked upon by Scandinavians as their apostle.

Tuesday, February 4
Manche Masemola, Martyr, 1928
Born in Marishane, South Africa (1913?), into a non-Christian farm family, Masemola worshipped with the Anglican Community of the Resurrection as a girl, but her parents forbade her baptism, beating her as dissuasion. She prophesied that she would die at her parents' hand and be baptized in her own blood. On Feb. 4, 1928, Masemola's parents indeed killed her. Although she had not been baptized, the church recognized her baptism by her desire for same. In 1935, a small band of pilgrims came to her grave; now hundreds visit every August. Her statue stands at Westminster Abbey, a 20th-century martyrs.

Tuesday, February 4
Cornelius the Centurion
The sum total of knowledge about Cornelius comes in chapters 10 and 11 in the Acts of the Apostles. Born a Gentile, he was the first convert to Christianity in his household. The writer of Acts credited Cornelius' conversion with affecting Christianity as it influenced the apostolic council of Jerusalem, held a few years later, to admit Gentiles to full partnership with Jewish converts. As a centurion, Cornelius commanded a company of 100 soldiers in the Roman army; he took responsibility for their discipline, on the battlefield as well as in camp. Some centurions, like Cornelius, were men of deep religious piety. Tradition holds that Cornelius was the second Bishop of Caesarea.

Wednesday, February 5
The Martyrs of Japan, 1597

In the 16th century, Christianity was introduced into Japan, first by the Jesuits under Francis Xavier and then by the Franciscans. The missions raised stories of self-sacrifice as well as success: by the end of that century, Japan was home to an estimated 300,000 baptized believers. Soon, however, these pluses were compromised by rivalries between religious orders; in addition, colonial politics—within Japan and between Japan and Spain and Portugal—caused suspicion about Western intents. Christian missions suffered persecution and suppression in a half century of powerful *shoguns*. The first victims were six Franciscan friars and 20 of their converts in Nagasaki on February 5, 1597.

Wednesday, February 5
Agatha of Sicily, Martyr, 251

Agatha, born (231?) to wealth, dedicated her life to God as a virgin, but men continued to hassle her. Quitianus, the local Roman prefect, tried to overpower her by threatening to expose her as a Christian. She spurned him. He not only denounced her during the Decian persecution but also served as her accuser and judge. Agatha continued to refuse him, so he imprisoned her in a brothel where she maintained her resolve to remain a virgin. Quitianus, impatient, sentenced her to death. She is venerated as the patron saint for those who suffer from sexual harassment and/or assault.

Saturday, February 8
Bakhita (Josephine Margaret Bakhita), Monastic, 1947

Born in Sudan, Bakhita's enslavement at seven traumatized her so badly that she forgot her name. The slavers named her "Bakhita," "fortunate one." She remained a slave for 12 years. Finally in 1883, she was sold to the Italian consul in Khartoum, who gave her to his friend, with whom she traveled to Italy. As a nanny, Bakhita attended a Christian institute with her charge. There, she was baptized as Josephine. She became a Canossian Daughter of Charity in 1896. She said she found God in her heart without ever being evangelized. Bakhita stands as inspiration for all the victimized.

The Fifth Sunday after the Epiphany

February 9, 2020

The Sermon on the Mount: God's people are to give witness to God's grace and power by leading righteous lives.

Color   Green

Preface   Of the Epiphany, or of the Lord's Day

Collect

Set us free, O God, from the bondage of our sins, and give us the liberty of that abundant life which you have made known to us in your Son our Savior Jesus Christ; who lives and reigns with you, in the unity of the Holy Spirit, one God, now and for ever. Amen.

Readings and Psalm

Isaiah 58:1–9a (9b–12)

This passage is **a denunciation of the injustices of those who only act at their religion. There is a promise of the Lord's favor for those who genuinely repent and care for the needy.** Fasts and many prayers are of no purpose and may be misused if they do not involve the liberation of the oppressed and help for the weak and afflicted. When there is justice and sharing, then the light of the Lord will rise out of darkness and all the ruins will be rebuilt.

The same introduction may be used for either the shorter or longer reading.

Psalm 112:1–9 (10)

Blessed are those who are right with the Lord, who are just and generous with those in need.

1 Corinthians 2:1–12 (13–16)

In this lection **Paul teaches the Corinthians that the wisdom of God is very different from the wisdom in which humans pride themselves.** Some of the Corinthians were apparently boasting of their Christianity as though it were powerful in terms of worldly wisdom. They even made fun of Paul for his lack of eloquence. The true power of God is, however, hidden from the ruling forces of the world, for it is discovered in a crucified Lord. This is revealed through God's own Spirit.

If using the longer version, the introduction may continue:

Genuine spirituality manifests itself in wise discernment and a Christ-like cast of mind.

Matthew 5:13–20

In the gospel lesson we learn that **disciples are like salt and as light to the world. They are to live even more righteously than the pious scribes and Pharisees.** Like a city set on a hill or a lamp on a stand, Jesus' followers must show forth their good works to the glory of God. Jesus has not come to abolish the law and the prophets but to fulfill their purpose. Only those who go beyond the keeping of the law and are wholly committed to God's will can enter the kingdom of heaven.

Prayers of the People

In the offering of our prayers, let us draw upon God's holy and life-giving waters to refresh our hearts, responding, "Hear us, God of Glory."

For the courage to live with integrity, that what is visible in our outward actions reveals the Holy Spirit of God residing within our souls; let us pray.

Hear us, God of Glory.

That we may discover the light that is within us, placing it upon the lamp stands of the world, offering a way of hope for those who live under the burden of poverty, abuse, oppression, and degradation of every kind; let us pray.

Hear us, God of Glory.

That the commandments of God may be the pathways upon which we walk, acknowledging their wisdom and fashioning our lives after their challenges, that through them the whole community of God's people may prosper and live in mutual trust and goodness; let us pray.

Hear us, God of Glory.

That the leaders of the Church may be strengthened by the crosses they are called to bear, the burdens of petty concerns and the weight of serious discord, all in the Name of Christ, whose cross leads the faithful to a risen life; let us pray.

Hear us, God of Glory.

For those in positions of public trust, that they may have a vision of the global good over political gain, and the welfare of the whole over the special interests of the few; let us pray.

Hear us, God of Glory.

In thanksgiving for those whose lives enriched our own, and who now live in the communion of saints, in whose company we may one day reside; let us pray.

Hear us, God of Glory.

From the depths of weakness and trembling that live in every human heart, let us continue our prayers and thanksgivings.
(Special intentions of the congregation, the diocese, and the Anglican Communion may be added here or before the formal intercessions.)

The Celebrant adds a concluding Collect.

Images in the Readings

Light is an image on many Sundays. The Sermon on the Mount speaks also of the **lampstand**. Paul would remind us that, contrary to the wisdom of the world, our lampstand is the cross.

Salt is necessary for human life. In recollection of this passage, some early Christian communities placed salt on the tongue of the newly baptized. In the early twentieth century, the British placed an embargo on salt, requiring the Indian people to purchase salt from them, and Gandhi's Salt March became a symbol of the right of Indians to manage their own survival.

The passage from Isaiah speaks about a **fast**. In many religious traditions, people limit or refrain from some necessary human activity as a symbol that their truest life comes only from the divine. In both the Jewish and Christian traditions, fasting must be accompanied with justice for the poor for God to acknowledge its value.

Ideas for the Day

♦ The lectionary editors have it precisely right in their pairing of this gospel portion with Isaiah's good news. Being "salt of the earth" or "light of the world" *is* "the fast" that Isaiah delineates. These actions—freeing captives and undoing oppression and feeding the hungry and clothing the naked—are not behaviors at a remove, but immediate, risky, hands-on interventions done for the sake of another, whoever that other may be. In fact, these are just the sorts of things that Jesus did and that he commends to his hearers in his final encouragement concerning the sheep and the goats at Matthew 25.31ff.

♦ Ministry is bringing Christ's light into the world in the daily life of each Christian and in the corporate witness of the church.

♦ What can God reveal to us through the Spirit? We like to think we have things so well figured out. In fact, our desire to pinpoint and control every waking moment of our life may be blocking what the spirit has to say to us. Spirit moves through people. Being active in our church provides opportunities for us hear what the Spirit is saying in our lives. Active participation in a Sunday service gives you the chance to listen to the Spirit. Sing the hymns with gusto, read the prayers with intention, and greet your fellow congregants with energy and a smile.

Making Connections

The Gospel reading today is meant for any of us who have ever felt "less than." Jesus preaches a message that each of us matters, that each one of us is a beloved child of God. We are the light of the world, and the world needs our light. We are not meant to put it under a bushel basket. We are not meant to hide it away or give into those messages that we are less than. We are to cultivate shame resilience. Episcopalian Brené Brown believes that we do this by "understanding our vulnerabilities and cultivating empathy, courage, and compassion."[1]

Engaging All Ages

Jesus gives us a New Covenant, setting a higher standard than the basis of the Old Testament law. Christians respond to moral problems with the light of Christ rather than relying on guidelines for merely avoiding sinful behavior. For the Christian it is not so much what I must do to keep out of trouble but what I will do to spread the light of Christ in the world. What guides our behaviors and interactions with others?

Hymns for the Day

The Hymnal 1982
Thy strong word did cleave the darkness 381
Lord, whose love through humble service 610
Now quit your care (vs. 3–5) 145
O day of God, draw nigh 600, 601
Lord, make us servants of your peace 593
Praise to the living God! 372

Lift Every Voice and Sing II
Out in the highways and byways of life
    (Make me a blessing) 158
This little light of mine 160, 221

Wonder, Love, and Praise
The church of Christ in every age 779
Gracious Spirit, give your servants 782
We are marching in the light of God 787

Weekday Commemorations

Monday, February 10
Scholastica, Monastic, 543
The patron saint of nuns is twin to Benedict, who founded the Benedictine order. Gregory the Great's *Dialogues* tell Scholastica's story. With a few other women religious, she lived in a small hermitage in Plumbariola, near her brother's monastery at Monte Cassino. The siblings often discussed scriptures and spiritual matters. Near death, she begged her brother to stay with her. He said no. She prayed to God and credited her Lord with the storm that kept her brother by her side that night. She died three days later. Brother and sister are buried together.

Tuesday, February 11
Theodora, Empress, c. 867
This 9th-century Byzantine empress gained credit as a saint in Orthodox churches for her role in restoring icons to objects of veneration. She was married in 830 to Theophilos. Though Christian, he believed that venerating icons was idolatry. They had seven children, but at only 29, he died. Theodora ruled their son, the emperor, as his regent from 842 to 855. In that role, she formed a synod to study iconoclasm; the gathering ended with members bearing icons back into Hagia Sophia. Theodora is also remembered for the gentle way she treated her theological opponents.

Thursday, February 13
Absalom Jones, Priest, 1818
Born a slave in 1746 in Delaware, Jones taught himself to read from the Old Testament. He bought his freedom in 1784 after buying his wife's. He served as a lay minister at St. George's Methodist Episcopal Church, evangelizing alongside his friend Richard Allen. The resulting numbers of blacks at St. George's caused the fearful vestry to segregate them into an upper gallery; the blacks indignantly left the building as one body. Jones and Allen were elected overseers of the Free African Society of black Christians in 1787. They worked ceaselessly for blacks to be included within the Episcopal Church, into which Jones was ordained a priest on September 21, 1802.

---

1 http://brenebrown.com/research/

Epiphany

Friday, February 14
Cyril and Methodius, Missionaries, 869 and 885

These brothers by blood and mission served as apostles to the southern Slavs against mighty barriers from Germany but with equally mighty support from Rome. In 862, the Moravian king asked for missionaries to teach his people in their native tongue; both learned brothers knew Slavonic and accepted the mission, Cyril to the point that he invented an alphabet for transcription. He died in Rome in 869, but Methodius continued despite enmity among Germans and Moravians. While continuing his mission, Methodius translated the Bible into the Slavonic tongue; his funeral, attended by masses, was conducted in Greek, Latin, and Slavonic.

Saturday, February 15
Thomas Bray, Priest and Missionary, 1730

As overseer for the Church in Maryland, Bray, an English country parson, visited the colony in 1702 for the first and only time, but from that visit, Bray gained his *foci*: he felt deep concern over the state of the American churches; over the need for education among clergy and laity, adults and children; for Native Americans and blacks. He founded 39 lending libraries, raised funds for missions, and encouraged young English priests to emigrate to America. He founded societies for Promoting Christian Knowledge and for the Propagation of the Gospel. For his own country and for the colony of Georgia, he championed prison reforms.

The Sixth Sunday after the Epiphany

February 16, 2020

The Sermon on the Mount: Jesus' commandments call for a profound commitment, leading the Christian to witness to a distinctive way of life.

Color   Green

Preface   Of the Epiphany, or of the Lord's Day

Collect

O God, the strength of all who put their trust in you: Mercifully accept our prayers; and because in our weakness we can do nothing good without you, give us the help of your grace, that in keeping your commandments we may please you both in will and deed; through Jesus Christ our Lord, who lives and reigns with you and the Holy Spirit, one God, for ever and ever. Amen.

Readings and Psalm

Deuteronomy 30:15–20

In the Hebrew scripture lesson **Moses presents the people with their choice: love and obey the Lord and find life, or turn away to other gods and know death.** Israel is about to cross over into the promised land, and this is Moses' final charge to them. In historical terms the speech was probably composed many hundreds of years later, near the time of the exile, after Israel had experienced much backsliding from the Lord. But this is still their choice: blessing or curse—life and good, or death and evil.

or

Sirach 15:15–20

Our first reading is **an instruction in the responsibility of human beings for their own actions.** The reading comes from Ecclesiasticus, otherwise known as the Wisdom of Jesus, Son of Sirach, a book composed about two centuries before the birth of Christ. The author reproves any tendency to say, "The Lord made me sin." God gives individuals a choice between good and evil.

Psalm 119:1–8

The psalmist takes great delight in the Lord's statutes and seeks to keep all God's commandments.

1 Corinthians 3:1–9

In this lesson **Paul admonishes the Corinthians for their bickering and divisions.** Missionaries like Paul and Apollos are not to be regarded as leaders of separate sects. They are coworkers in the Lord's field, while it is God who supplies the growth. To think otherwise is immature and is based on worldly rather than spiritual understandings.

Matthew 5:21–37

In our gospel we hear of **Jesus' concern with the heart of human behavior.** Discipleship means far more than observance of the outward forms of the law. Genuinely to fulfill the commandments not to kill, not to commit adultery, and not to swear falsely requires a transformation of one's life. One must be willing to cast away any part of the self which opposes this change of mind and heart.

Prayers of the People

Be with us, O Christ, in the offering of our prayers, as we respond, "Hear us, God of Glory."

That by your blessing and unfaltering presence we may choose life over death, and follow the path whose destination is spiritual prosperity and whose way is uncompromising love; let us pray.

Hear us, God of Glory.

That our ministry with and for each other may take on the yoke of servanthood, the garment of humility that transcends quarreling, false witness, and self-righteousness, so that we may walk the road that leads to Christ, and bear witness to his truth; let us pray.

Hear us, God of Glory.

That the Church, in her desire to foster growth and change, may respond to the needs of those outside her fellowship, proclaiming the liberating power of forgiveness and the glorious freedom that flows from God's glorious mercy; let us pray.

Hear us, God of Glory.

For peace throughout the world, beginning with our families and friends, flowing into the hearts of our political leaders, finding its fulfillment through the nations and peoples of the world; let us pray.

Hear us, God of Glory.

In thanksgiving for those who tend to the needs of the poor, giving aid when needed, training when helpful, teaching when called upon, and who commit to those whom others neglect; let us pray.

Hear us, God of Glory.

In thanksgiving for the promise of eternal life, and for the intercessions of those who have died and who now live upon another shore and in a greater light; let us pray.

Hear us, God of Glory.

In thanksgiving for our children, who unknowingly capture the essence of mystery, drawing us beyond earthly wisdom and revealing the simplicity of faith; let us pray.

Hear us, God of Glory.

In the confidence of God's unending love, let us continue our prayers.
(Special intentions of the congregation, the diocese, and the Anglican Communion may be added here or before the formal intercessions.)

The Celebrant adds a concluding Collect.

Images in the Readings

According to Matthew, Jesus threatened immoral people with **hell**. The idea that God will punish sinners with eternal fire came into intertestamental Jewish tradition from their Zoroastrian neighbors and is included in some New Testament books. Matthew's literalism is seen in the phrases that one's "whole body . . . be thrown into hell." Fear of hell was apparently a central religious motivation during some pieties and periods of the church, and lurid descriptions of torment extended far beyond what many theologians propose: that hell is self-willed distance from God, through life and beyond death. From the second century to the present, some Christians have maintained that eternal punishment contradicts the primary description of a merciful God. The Apostles' and Nicene creeds speak only of judgment and an everlasting life of the world to come, although according to the later Athanasian Creed, "those who have done evil will enter eternal fire."

The word of God is **milk** to us, who are infants. As nursing mothers know, both the infant and the mother need the times of feeding. It is as if God needs to give us the milk we need.

The passage from Deuteronomy evokes the classic *The Pilgrim's Progress*, by John Bunyan, in which the Christian life is described as one **choice** after another. It is God's Spirit who inspires us to choose what God has already chosen for us: in Paul's words, life in God's field, God's building.

Ideas for the Day

- ◆ Jesus had insisted that he didn't come to change any part of the law (5:17), but like the Pharisees, he knew that ancient practices, no matter how sacred, must always be nimble enough to be adapted for new generations whose needs and ethos reflected a different time. So his long initial speech in Matthew—the Sermon on the Mount—is a conscious return to Mosaic teaching on another mountain in the distant past but a refreshing of that early covenant for a new generation that will usher in a new covenant and a new way of being people of God.

- ◆ "I planted, Apollos watered, but God gave growth. So neither he who plants, nor he who waters is anything, but only God who gives growth." It is important to stay out of God's way when it comes to growth. We must find ways to facilitate spiritual growth in ourselves. We do this by engaging in our faith actions, seeking ways to participate in our larger community. We must balance self-care with care for others so that God can find expression through us. It important to recognize and respect others for their current level of spiritual growth. It is not for us to judge but to facilitate spiritual growth by providing space, allowing them to freely walk on their own Christian path.

Making Connections

Choose life. We are called to follow in the way of Jesus, the Way of Love. Sometimes the loving, life-giving, liberating choice is not easy. It means saying no to other things. Yes to exercise and time with our families means resisting the temptation to stay in bed longer or work more. Yes to caring for ourselves and those we love means no to relationships that are toxic or destructive. Choosing life means engaging deeply with those around us, and that means taking the risk that we will have our hearts broken or we will lose someone for whom we care deeply.

Engaging All Ages

Two actions occur during our liturgy that give us examples as to how to follow Jesus' commandments. The passing of the peace expresses the command of Jesus to leave one's gift at the altar and be reconciled with one's sibling and then offer the gift. Since it follows the confession and absolution, the peace is an acting out of the need to forgive as we have been forgiven. The offertory at the Eucharist continues the ancient temple practice of offering gifts at the altar as an act of commitment to and reconciliation with God. How do we raise awareness of these actions instead of seeing them as a chance to say "hello" to a neighbor or "pass the plate" in our worship?

Hymns for the Day

The Hymnal 1982
If thou but trust in God to guide thee 635
Come, gracious Spirit, heavenly Dove 512
God of grace and God of glory 594, 595
Lord, be thy word my rule 626
Now that the daylight fills the sky 3, 4
Praise to the living God! 372
I come with joy to meet my Lord 304
Lord, make us servants of your peace 593
Where charity and love prevail 581
Blessed Jesus, at thy word 440
"Forgive our sins as we forgive" 674
Go forth for God; go to the world in peace 347
Strengthen for service, Lord 312

Lift Every Voice and Sing II
I will trust in the Lord 193

Wonder, Love, and Praise
Come now, O Prince of peace 795
Ubi caritas et amor 831

Epiphany

Weekday Commemorations

Monday, February 17
Janani Luwum, Archbishop and Martyr, 1977

In 1969 Janani Luwum became Bishop of Northern Uganda, where he was a faithful visitor to his parishes as well as a growing influence at international gatherings of the Anglican Communion. In 1974, as Archbishop of the Church of Uganda, Rwanda, Burundi, and Bog-Zaire, he had contact and confrontation with the Ugandan military dictator, Idi Amin. By early February 1977 the Archbishop's residence was searched for arms by government security forces; on the 15th, he was summoned to the palace. He said to the bishops and others accompanying him "They are going to kill me. I am not afraid." he was never seen alive again.

Tuesday, February 18
Martin Luther, Pastor and Church Reformer, 1546

Martin Luther was born November 10, 1483, at Eisleben, in Germany. His intellectual abilities were evident early, and his father planned a career for him in law. Luther's real interest lay elsewhere, however, and in 1505, he entered the local Augustinian monastery. He was ordained a priest on April 3, 1507. In October 1512, Luther received his doctorate in theology, and shortly afterward he was installed as a professor of biblical studies at the University of Wittenberg. His lectures on the Bible were popular, and within a few years he made the university a center for biblical humanism. As a result of his theological and biblical studies, he called into question the practice of selling indulgences. On the eve of All Saints' Day, October 31, 1517, he posted on the door of the castle church in Wittenberg the notice of an academic debate on indulgences, listing 95 theses for discussion. As the effects of the theses became evident, the pope called upon the Augustinian order to discipline their member. After a series of meetings, political maneuvers, and attempts at reconciliation, Luther, at a meeting with the papal legate in 1518, refused to recant. Luther was excommunicated on January 3, 1521.

Luther translated the New Testament into German and began the translation of the Old Testament. He then turned his attention to the organization of worship and education. He introduced congregational singing of hymns, composing many himself, and issued model orders of services. He published his large and small catechisms for instruction in the faith. During the years from 1522 to his death, Luther wrote a prodigious quantity of books, letters, sermons, and tracts. Luther died at Eisleben on February 18, 1546.

Wednesday, February 19
Agnes Tsao Kou Ying, Agatha Lin Zhao, and Lucy Yi Zhenmei, Catechists and Martyrs, 1856, 1858, and 1862

These lay catechists refused to renounce their faith in the mid-1800s, a time of conflict in China between Christianity and imperial colonialism. Agnes was martyred with a missionary priest as they catechized women and children. At 18, Agatha asked to be released from a marriage contract so that she could dedicate her life to the church. She ran a school for girls. She was arrested in 1857 for evangelizing among her pupils and executed a year later. Lucy was born a Roman Catholic on Dec. 9, 1815. Like Agatha, she taught and catechized girls and women in her parish without pay. She was beheaded without trial.

Thursday, February 20
Frederick Douglass, Social Reformer, 1895

Born a slave in 1818, Douglass broke the law by teaching himself to read. At 14, he converted to Christianity in the African Methodist Episcopal Church, whose music bolstered his struggle for freedom. Douglass spoke on tours in the North sponsored by the American Anti-slavery Society, but his renown as an orator magnified his fear of capture. When Douglass fled to England, his American friends bought his freedom so he could return to America, where he edited the North Star, a pro-abolition journal. Douglass championed the rights of African Americans and of all women and children.

Saturday, February 22
Margaret of Cortona, Monastic, 1297

After her mother died and her father remarried, Margaret ran away from her farm home and became servant, then mistress to a wealthy man, who promised to marry her. When he died, she and their son sought succor with the Franciscans, who homed her with a group of devout women. She became a Tertiary of the Franciscans, dedicating her life to the Passion of Christ. She established a home and hospital for the needy and gathered the women she lived with as nurses. She was publicly active in her ministry, including challenging the Bishop of Arezzo for his martial and luxurious lifestyle

The Last Sunday after the Epiphany

February 23, 2020

The Transfiguration of our Lord.

Color   White

Preface   Of the Epiphany

Collect

O God, who before the passion of your only-begotten Son revealed his glory upon the holy mountain: Grant to us that we, beholding by faith the light of his countenance, may be strengthened to bear our cross, and be changed into his likeness from glory to glory; through Jesus Christ our Lord, who lives and reigns with you and the Holy Spirit, one God, for ever and ever. Amen.

Readings and Psalm

Exodus 24:12–18

In the Hebrew scripture lesson **Moses is called up to Mount Sinai, and the glory of the Lord appears.** There he is to receive the commandments written on stone tablets. The Lord's presence is essentially indescribable, but it is known in the cloud and fire. The cloud both hides and reveals the Lord's glory, and the scene suggests the awesome majesty of a volcanic mountain.

Psalm 2

God is sovereign in all the earth and shall prevail. The one who rules from Zion will be God's own Son.

or

Psalm 99

The holy and mighty Lord reigns on high. God spoke to Israel's leaders from a pillar of cloud and has forgiven them their misdeeds.

2 Peter 1:16–21

This lesson presents **the apostle Peter as he recalls his vision of Jesus in majesty on the holy mountain and the heavenly voice that announced this was God's beloved Son.** Peter was among those who were eyewitnesses to this revelation. It makes more sure the prophetic message that is like a lamp for us. But no one should make this prophecy a matter solely of their own interpretation, for it has come through the Holy Spirit.

Matthew 17:1–9

Our gospel is **the story of Jesus' transfiguration.** The narrative is richly woven with themes and symbols drawn from Israel's past and its hopes for the future. Moses and Elijah represent the law and the prophets, whose promises Jesus fulfills. The chosen disciples see divine glory reflected in Jesus' human person. They hear a voice from the cloud declaring that he is the beloved Son.

Prayers of the People

Let us go to the mountain of God's generosity, offering our prayers as we respond, "Hear us, God of Glory."

That we may offer ourselves to the refashioning hands of the Divine Potter, who centers, molds, and changes us into vessels of grace; let us pray.

Hear us, God of Glory.

That we may admit our faults, our desire to keep things as they are and to return to things that never were, so that when Christ invites us into a transformed life, we may readily answer his call; let us pray.

Hear us, God of Glory.

Epiphany

For a vigorous spirit of mutual cooperation and unity, that we may treasure the common ground which we share with the whole Anglican Communion, and work together to share in the fruits of God's kingdom across our nations, cultures, tribes, and peoples; let us pray.

Hear us, God of Glory.

For the cessation of war, that armaments of destruction may be made into tools for development, and that resources spent on the fields of battle may instead support the basic necessities of life; let us pray.

Hear us, God of Glory.

For a commitment to a life of simplicity, that we may preserve for generations to come the beauty of land and seas and sky, and the complexity of every living creature; let us pray.

Hear us, God of Glory.

That those who have died may experience the blessed rest of everlasting peace; let us pray.

Hear us, God of Glory.

Continue to mold us into your perfect wholeness as we add to these prayers.

(Special intentions of the congregation, the diocese, and the Anglican Communion may be added here or before the formal intercessions.)

The Celebrant adds a concluding Collect.

Images in the Readings

Once again the readings include the central biblical images of **light** and **mountain**.

Yet God is not only brilliant light: important for the readings is the image of the **cloud**. Although contemporary people tend to think of clouds as relating to weather conditions, in the Bible the cloud is a sign of the presence of God. It is as if God covers the earth, brings life, effecting much yet suddenly vanishing. Christians can add that from God as cloud rains down the waters of baptism.

We are so accustomed to the language of being children of a God who is like a Father that we miss the astonishment of the early church, when this imagery was a religious surprise. Christ is to God as a **son** is to a father, and we are not pitiful creatures struggling to life in a hostile environment but rather children cared for by a beneficent God. "Son of man," on the other hand, is the biblical name for the apocalyptic judge, thus only paradoxically the beloved Son of God.

Ideas for the Day

As we began the season after the Epiphany, so we draw it to a close. Back then, at his Baptism, at the beginning of his ministry, a voice from heaven had declared, "This is my Son, the Beloved, with whom I am well pleased" (3:17). Now, as that season ends and just before we bend our way into Lent, we hear the same declaration from that same voice with the added proviso: "Listen to him." In the gospel, Jesus is now turning his steps and his attention toward Jerusalem where suffering and death and final victory await. Perhaps this is the disciples'—and our—final encouragement before their own trial begins.

The Sundays after the Epiphany are framed both by the Feast of the Epiphany, with its star in the heavens and Jesus' face shining like the sun at the Transfiguration. The light of God's revelation in Jesus becomes clearer in the ensuing weeks as disciples are called and his word is proclaimed.

What are the ways God reveals God's self to us? Create a list of seven things that bring you personal joy such as hiking, biking, reading novels, writing music, aerobics, painting, sculpting, singing, writing poetry, and teaching, among many other possibilities. Thinking of your church community, create a list of seven ways that you can bring joy to others. Pick a week in the future. Assign a personal "joy" and a community "joy" to each day of the week and find a way to achieve those moments. God is joy, God is love, God is peace.

Making Connections

"Get up and do not be afraid." Our communities are not going to change themselves. Transformation happens because we are engaged participants. It happens when we are in relationship, seeking to join with God's restoring and reconciling work in the world. Transformation happens when the hungry are fed, the naked are clothed, when the stranger is welcomed and we love our neighbors. Transformation happens when we strive for peace and justice, when we respect the dignity of every human being, when we strive to follow the Way of Love even more faithfully in all the facets of our lives.

Engaging All Ages

Like Moses, Elijah, and Jesus, it is in those mountaintop, seeing-the-light experiences that we begin to understand what the Lord is calling us to do in our covenant relationship. Martin Luther King, Jr.'s "I Have a Dream" speech could be called a contemporary mountaintop experience. What does it take to have a mountaintop experience? Are there times in our lives when we have been changed by an experience or have seen life in a new way? How can we be open to seeing the face of God?

Hymns for the Day

The Hymnal 1982
Songs of thankfulness and praise 135
Alleluia, song of gladness 122, 123
We sing of God, the mighty source of
     all things 386, 387
Christ is the world's true Light 542
Christ, whose glory fills the skies 6, 7
From God Christ's deity came forth 443
Christ upon the mountain peak 129, 130
O light of Light, Love given birth 133, 134
O wondrous type! O vision fair 136, 137

Lift Every Voice and Sing II
I love to tell the story 64

Wonder, Love, and Praise

Weekday Commemorations

Monday, February 24
Saint Matthias the Apostle
Little is known of Matthias beyond his selection as a disciple. In the nine days between Jesus' ascension and the day of Pentecost, the disciples gathered in prayer. Peter reminded them that the defection and death of Judas had left the fellowship with a vacancy. The Acts of the Apostles records Peter's suggestion that one of the followers from the time of Jesus' baptism until his crucifixion "must become with us a witness to his resurrection." After prayer, the disciples cast lots between nominees Barsabbas Justus and Matthias; the lot fell to Matthias. Tradition holds him as exemplary, a suitable witness to the resurrection, but his service is unheralded by history and unsung by psalms.

Tuesday, February 25
Emily Malbone Morgan, Lay Leader and Contemplative, 1937
Morgan was born in 1862 in a prominent Anglican family in Hartford, Connecticut, where Adelyn Howard inspired her. Homebound, Howard sought spiritual companionship and offered intercessory prayer. Morgan responded by gathering together the women who formed the Society of the Companions of the Holy Cross in1884. The community of Episcopal laywomen was devoted to prayer, discipleship, and social justice. Morgan, concerned about working women who had no hope of a break, developed vacation houses in the Northeast for these tired women and their daughters. In 1901, the Society established Adelynrood, a permanent home in Byfield, Massachusetts.

Wednesday, February 26
Photini, the Samaritan Woman, c. 67
One of the most significant conversations in Jesus' life occurred at Jacob's well in Sychar. Against social mores, Jesus asked a Samaritan woman for a drink. He revealed to her the first important "I am" declarations in John's Gospel, including his Messianic title. She was the first to preach the gospel that Jesus is the Christ. Unnamed in the Book of John, Orthodox Christian tradition called her Photini, "the enlightened one." It is said that she was martyred at the hands of the emperor Nero. A Greek Orthodox church, consecrated to Photini in 1893, sits at the site of the well.

Epiphany

Epiphany

Thursday, February 27
George Herbert, Priest and Poet, 1633
This is what he preached: "Nothing is little in God's service." Herbert penned prose and poetry, describing the latter as "a picture of the many spiritual conflicts that have passed betwixt God and my soul . . ." Born in 1593, Herbert studied divinity as a young man; in 1626, he took Holy Orders. He served as rector of parishes in Fugglestone and Bemerton. According to Izaak Walton, his biographer, Herbert was a model of the saintly parish priest. He wrote *A Priest in the Temple: or The Country Parson* and *The Temple*; two of his poems, "Teach me, my God and King" and "Let all the world in every corner sing," became well-known hymns.

Friday, February 28
Anna Julia Haywood Cooper, Educator, 1964
In 1870, Cooper, daughter of a black slave and a free white, attended St. Augustine's, founded by the Episcopal Church to educate African American teachers and clergy. She became an Episcopalian and married one of the first African American Episcopal priests in North Carolina. Widowed, she moved to Washington, D.C., where she taught mathematics, advocated for African American women, and organized the Colored Women's League and the first Colored Settlement House. She challenged the church to support its African American members struggling under segregation. She received her doctorate in 1925 at 67 and lived to 105.

Lent

Preparing for Lent

Theological Themes that Might Shape Liturgy, Catechesis, and Education

Just as Advent, Christmas, and the season after the Epiphany should be thought of and planned with a through line in mind, Lent, Holy Week, and Easter should be as well. These three portions of the Church year represent the Paschal cycle (as opposed to the Incarnation cycle) and are moveable (as opposed to fixed).

Lent, as Advent is to Christmas, is our time of intentional preparation to receive with freshness and renewed vitality, the mystery of the resurrection of Christ. It is during this forty-day period (forty-six including the Sundays) that we contemplate the suffering of Jesus Christ and that suffering makes the resurrection not only possible, but powerful.

The way we prepare to receive the mystery is by observing a period of penitence. Penitence is an opportunity to reflect on how far we have wandered from grace, how much stand in need of God's forgiveness, and then how we might live a life more closely aligned with God's desires for us. The danger of our Lenten penitence is that, if not carefully observed, this season can quickly devolve into a competition of works-righteousness. Grace must remain at the heart of our Lenten practice and devotion. It is the grace of God that leads us to return God once we have wandered away.

Because Lenten practice can be so countercultural, this is a great opportunity to engage in some intentional formation around Lent. Exploring the concepts of prayer and reflection, fasting and abstinence, almsgiving and charity can really support and strengthen the spirituality of our faith communities. There are also opportunities to engage in some formation around the specific rites that occur during this season only, particularly during Holy Week. Simply holding a liturgy and expecting people to gather its meaning without any type of context or framework can no longer be taken for granted. These liturgies are layered with meaning. We owe it to those who will come to worship to help them explore the depths of this season.

Liturgical Possibilities

Rites

Lent begins with the Proper Liturgy for Ash Wednesday, which, after reading the portion of Matthew's Gospel that prohibits the outward showiness of religion, invites the congregation to be marked with an ashen cross as a sign of their mortality and penitence. I have found it right for these two portions of the liturgy to stand in a creative tension, asking the penitent listener to critically examine the spiritual efficacy of their Lenten practice.

As far as the Sundays in Lent are concerned, there are many options to make the liturgy reflect the penitential nature of the season. Observing the Great Litany is an appropriate to open the season on Lent I (Book of Common Prayer and *Enriching our Worship*). A community might also choose to open their liturgy with the Penitential Order. If the Penitential Order is included, it might also be helpful to include the Decalogue—God's commandments—as a way to further explore the ways we have failed to live up to the love of God and our need for God's forgiving grace.

Lenten liturgy should be simpler, solemn, but not overly sad. Lent is a season of nuance where we hold in tandem both our sinfulness and God's grace-filledness. Our Orthodox siblings refer to this tension as "luminous sadness." Altering the adjustable portions of the liturgy to reflect this might help to draw more of our focus into this tension.

Lent

It is also important to allow Lent to speak to the truths of our faith in ways that allow us to enter them differently. This might be a wonderful opportunity for a congregation to explore liturgical resources from another, minority community, not only as a way to repent for the sin of cultural superiority but also to open the eyes of our hearts to see God at work in worlds we don't know about.

Adult Baptism is most appropriately observed during Easter, so utilizing the season of Lent as a time to prepare adult catechumens is especially appropriate. The *Book of Occasional Services* is filled with wonderful resources that can help to make this moment really meaning both for the congregation and the individual catechumens.

Space

As with Advent, adjusting the space where possible can help to dial up the distinctiveness of this season. Veiling crosses and other religious imagery (statuary, iconography, etc.) might also help to draw our focus to the way that sin prevents us from seeing God with greater clarity. The point is to draw a contrast between Lent and the season of Easter that is to follow.

Other Rituals and Resources

A community might opt to observe Stations of the Cross during Lent. There are resources for this in the *Book of Occasional Services* as well as *Saint Augustine's Prayer Book*. Given that this service has so much flexibility, a nod towards creativity and innovation might help to make this service take on fresh meaning for a new community. It is also appropriate to more intentionally offer the Sacrament of Reconciliation to the community.

Through the Eyes of a Child

It can be tempting to shield younger people from the message of Lent; however, this would be unwise. Children are capable of engaging in topics; and often the refusal to allow them to engage and wonder about tough topics speaks more to an insecurity on behalf of their guardians. Teaching skills like reflection, asking for and receiving forgiveness and then extending that forgiveness to others are great life skill generally, and Christianity centers these practices as incredibly important.

Lent is also a time to empower parents to the primary agents of faith formation by giving them the tools to help their children develop a Lenten discipline. Maybe it is journaling, reading the Bible, writing notes and cards, or prayer daily. Whatever the practice, helping parents instill these values in their children will go a lot further in developing their spirituality than almost any other program the church can offer.

Lent is a time for forgiveness: looking at the things we have done that are wrong, asking God's and other people's forgiveness, and making a promise not to do them again. It is a time for giving up the things that keep us from being loving people; a time for doing extra things that will help us grow closer to God; a time to be more aware of what it means to love as God loves us; a time to ask God to help us to be more loving, remembering that God is always ready to strengthen us; and a time to think about our baptism and what it means to be a child of God. Encourage parents to help their child read the Bible every day. Invite them to reflect on the stories, particularly inviting reflection on the life of Jesus as he approaches the cross.

Through the Eyes of Youth

Communicating passion during the passion, the church is called to recognize Christ in the poor, the stranger at the gate; follow the Creed as rule of life; faithfully follow daily practices that imitate Christ for the sake of others; and explore the Penitential Order and how we can be reconciled within our families, our schools, our communities, our church. Demonstrating an outward and visible sign of Lenten participation, invite youth to lead a Lenten ingathering that serves the poor either in the church community or local areas. Invite the youth to serve at soup kitchens, at shelters, at the Salvation Army, or any other program or institution that serves the poor and hungry and homeless. Invite the youth to define evil, reflect upon the ways they see evil in the world, and how the mission and ministry of the church responds. Offer overnight or day "retreats" for youth that include contemplation, reflection, and action.

Through the Eyes of Daily Life

As with young people, so with those who are more mature. Lent is a great time to encourage and stress the importance of the development of a spiritual life that goes beyond the outwardness of religion (hear Jesus' injunction from Ash Wednesday with new ears). Tools and resources should be created and distributed that help our faith communities understand how to develop a more vibrant spiritual life. The *Way of Love* materials from the Episcopal Church Evangelism Office and Church Publishing Incorporated are a great place to start.

The season of Lent is marked by self-examination and repentance, culminating in the Rite of Reconciliation; by prayer and meditating on Holy Scripture; by fasting (not eating between sunrise and sunset on Fridays to remind us what food we need most for life); and by acts of self-denial, best understood as acts or positive practices that enhance an ever-growing and loving relationship with God. However, the main emphasis during Lent is for each person to prepare for the renewal of baptismal vows and covenant at the Easter vigil.

Through the Eyes of Those Outside of the Church

If the Church can invite people to be among us when we celebrate the joyous mysteries of Christ, how much more meaning might it hold if we invite people to be a part of us when we walk through the hard parts of our story, particularly because of how they resonate with the lived reality of a great many. Many people experience suffering—emotional, physical, economic, social/political—and how the church explores these complex experiences might help the message of the Church land on new ears.

Through the Eyes of the Global Community

Ethical issues are raised in the Litany of Penitence (BCP 267–269) during the Ash Wednesday liturgy:

- Exploitation of other people;
- Dishonesty in daily life and work;
- Indifference to injustice, human need, suffering, and cruelty;
- Prejudice and contempt toward those who differ from us;
- Waste and pollution of God's creation.

As we explore more fully the Baptismal Covenant and the covenant of the Torah during Lent, we become increasingly aware of how far we have strayed from God's ways.

Lent

Seasonal Rites for Lent

Lenten Blessings[1]

In Lent, in place of a seasonal blessing, a solemn Prayer over the People is used, as follows:

The Deacon or, in the absence of a deacon, the Celebrant says:

Bow down before the Lord.

The people kneel and the Celebrant says one of the following prayers:

Ash Wednesday

Grant, most merciful Lord, to your faithful people pardon and peace, that they may be cleansed from all their sins, and serve you with a quiet mind; through Christ our Lord. *Amen.*

Lent 1

Grant, Almighty God, that your people may recognize their weakness and put their whole trust in your strength, so that they may rejoice for ever in the protection of your loving providence; through Jesus Christ our Lord. *Amen.*

Lent 2

Keep this your family, Lord, with your never-failing mercy, that relying solely on the help of your heavenly grace, they may be upheld by your divine protection; through Christ our Lord. *Amen.*

Lent 3

Look mercifully on this your family, Almighty God, that by your great goodness they may be governed and preserved evermore; through Christ our Lord. *Amen.*

Lent 4

Look down in mercy, Lord, on your people who kneel before you; and grant that those whom you have nourished by your Word and Sacraments may bring forth fruit worthy of repentance; through Christ our Lord. *Amen.*

Lent 5

Look with compassion, O Lord, upon this your people; that, rightly observing this holy season, they may learn to know you more fully, and to serve you with a more perfect will; through Christ our Lord. *Amen.*

Ash Wednesday Prayer

This collect is appropriate for a service with children, at home, at Morning Prayer, with grace, or at bedtime.

God of all mercy, you love all that you have made. You forgive the sins of all who are truly sorry. Create and make in us clean hearts, that we, humbly confessing our sins and knowing our brokenness, may receive forgiveness and blessing; through Jesus Christ our Lord, who lives with you and the Holy Spirit, one God, for ever and ever. *Amen.*[2]

1 *The Book of Occasional Services 2003* (New York: Church Publishing, 2004), 23–24.

2 Anne E. Kitch. *The Anglican Family Prayer Book* (Harrisburg, PA: Morehouse Publishing, 2004), 133.

Lent

Lent

Let's Go! An Ash Wednesday Service for Children[3]

This interactive children's service for Ash Wednesday is suitable for children aged four through ten. The service consists of four interactive stations and a fifth station for the Imposition of Ashes and Eucharist. The fourth station includes the shrouding of an Alleluia Banner that can be created on the last Sunday of the Season after the Epiphany or at a Shrove Tuesday Pancake Supper. Ideally it should be cloth and large enough to hang from a banner or chart stand. Choose a location for each station; place the appropriate props at each station. Create a simple tune to go with the words of the chant to use as you process to the stations. Review and memorize a simple version of the two Bible stories. Prepare a take-home Lenten Box for each child: small wooden boxes, each one with a small container of water, of oil, of ashes and a votive candle. Tie a purple ribbon around each box.

Scenery/Props:

Station One—Water: small table, container of water

Station Two—Oil: small table, container of oil

Station Three—Light: small table, candle, matches or lighter. (A slight darker location if possible; lighting the candle should make a noticeable difference.)

Station Four—Alleluia Banner: Alleluia Banner, banner or chart stand, purple net

Station Five—Ashes/Eucharist: container of ashes, small altar/table (a small child height table placed in front of the main altar works well), purple cloth, cross, Bible, chalice and paten, Lenten Boxes, bread, wine; Lenten Boxes: small wooden boxes, small containers of water, small containers of oil, votive candles, small containers of ashes, purple ribbon.

Gather/Introduction:

Welcome the children and sit together in the area where you will conclude with the Eucharist. Say a short prayer. Using language personalized for your parish and children explain that we are now in the season of Lent. Share what Lent is, how it is different from other seasons, why we have Lent, and some of your parish customs. Teach the words of the song and practice the first verse a few times.

Process to Station One—Water . . . singing . . . Come into God's presence singing: "Alleluia, Alleluia, Alleluia."

Tell the story of Jesus' baptism. (Matthew 3:13–17, Mark 1:4–11, Luke 3:15–17, 21–22.) Invite the children to wonder about all the ways we use water.

Leader: Jesus wanted John to baptize him. Jesus went right under the water so he saw and felt and heard water everywhere! Jesus must have felt clean and refreshed! When we are baptized, it is just the same for us. We are clean and refreshed. Jesus shows us how to get ready to follow him.

Invite the children to dip their fingers into the water. They might want to touch their foreheads with their wet fingers. Share a simple prayer of thanks.

Process to Station Two—Oil . . . singing . . . Come into God's presence singing: "Water that cleans, water that cleans, water that cleans."

Tell the story of the anointing at Bethany (John 12:1–8.)

Leader: Jesus received a very special gift—Mary's gift of extravagant love. Jesus loved Mary. Mary may have felt tears because of so much love. Jesus shows us how to show love to the people around us.

Invite the children to dip a finger into the oil and, if they are comfortable, anoint one another on the backs of their hands. Share a simple prayer of thanks.

Process to Station Three—Light . . . singing . . . Come into God's presence singing: "Blessed by the oil, blessed by the oil, blessed by the oil."

Leader: Long, long ago, the people felt afraid and uncertain. They were very lonely. Jesus said to them, "I am the Light. I am always with you." When we light a candle, we know Jesus is close, and we feel his love in our hearts. Jesus shows us how to shine in the world.

Invite the children to watch as you light the candle. (If you are feeling brave, have a votive for each child to light.) Share a simple prayer of thanks.

---

3 This service was developed by Elizabeth Hammond and is part of the *Skiturgies* collection from Church Publishing. **www.skiturgies.com**

Process to Station Four—Alleluia Banner . . . singing . . . Come into God's presence singing: "Jesus the Light, Jesus the Light, Jesus the Light."

Leader: Alleluia is one of our special church words. It is a word of celebration. We don't say the word Alleluia during Lent, and we won't say it again until Easter.

Invite the children to help you hang/place/ attach the banner to a stand or a wall. Shroud it with the purple net. Explain to the children that the net allows us to still see the word but not say it. (If appropriate for your congregation allow the banner to stay in full view throughout Lent.)

Process to Station Five — Ashes/Eucharist . . . singing . . . Come into God's presence singing: "We are in Lent, we are in Lent, we are in Lent."

Show the container of ashes and talk about their significance and why we use ashes on this day. Invite the children to be anointed with ashes. The children may want to help say the words each time someone is anointed: "Remember that you are dust . . ."

Set the table together with a purple cloth, cross, Bible, chalice and paten. Continue with a Eucharist, a very simple retelling of the Last Supper. Invite the children to serve/share the bread to/with each other. Have an adult administer the chalice. End with a simple prayer of thanks.

Show the Lenten boxes. Remind the children of the stories we shared today. Invite them to find a special place at home for their box. Share a simple final prayer. Offer a blessing.

The Catechumenate

Enrollment of Candidates for Baptism[4]

The enrollment of candidates for Baptism at the Great Vigil of Easter normally takes place on the First Sunday in Lent. After the Creed, the catechumens to be enrolled are invited to come forward with their sponsors. A book for them (and their sponsors) should be available to sign at the conclusion of this enrollment.

Catechist: I present to you these catechumens who have been strengthened by God's grace and supported by the example and prayers of this congregation, and I ask that *they* be enrolled as *candidates* for Holy Baptism.

Catechist: I present to you these catechumens who have been strengthened by God's grace and supported by the example and prayers of this congregation, and I ask that *they* be enrolled as *candidates* for Holy Baptism.

Celebrant: Have they been regular in attending the worship of God and in receiving instruction?

Sponsors: They have. (*He* has.)

Celebrant: Are they seeking by prayer, study, and example to pattern their lives in accordance with the Gospel?

Sponsors: They are. (*He* is.)

Celebrant: As God is your witness, do you approve the enrolling of *these catechumens* as *candidates* for Holy Baptism?

Sponsors and the Congregation: They have. (*He* has.)

Celebrant: Do you desire to be baptized?

Catechumens: I do.

Celebrant: In the Name of God, and with the consent of this congregation, I accept you as candidates for Holy Baptism, and direct that your names be written in this book. God grant that they may also be written in the Book of Life.

---

4 *The Book of Occasional Services 2003,* 122–123.

Welcoming Those Who Are Preparing for the Reaffirmation of the Baptismal Covenant[5]

This rite is used at the principle Sunday Eucharist for those baptized persons who have returned to the life of the Church after a time away, from those baptized in other traditions, or those seeking to reaffirm their baptism at the Rite of Confirmation. This takes place at the time of the Prayers of the People

Member of the Community: N., We present to you these persons *(or N., N.,)* who are baptized members of the Body of Christ and we welcome them to our community as they undertake a process of growth in the meaning of their baptism.

Celebrant: (to each baptized person) What do you seek?

Renewal of my life to Christ.

Celebrant: In baptism, you died with Christ Jesus to the forces of evil and rose to new life as members of his Body. Will you study the promises made at your baptism, and strive to keep them in the fellowship of this community and the rest of the Church?

I will, with God's help.

Celebrant: Will you attend the worship of God regularly with us, to hear God's word and to celebrate the mystery of Christ's dying and rising?

I will, with God's help.

Celebrant: Will you participate in a life of service to those who are poor, outcast, or powerless?

I will, with God's help.

Celebrant: Will you strive to recognize the gifts that God has given you and discern how they are to be used in the building up of God's reign of peace and justice?

I will, with God's help.

Celebrant: (to the sponsors/companions/friends) You have been chosen by this community to serve as companions to these persons. Will you support them by prayer and example and help them to grow in the knowledge and love of God?

We will, with God's help.

Celebrant: (to the congregation) Will you who witness this new beginning keep *(N., N.)* in your prayers and help them, share with them your ministry, bear their burdens, and forgive and encourage them?

We will, with God's help.

In full view of all, the baptized write their names in the church's register of baptized persons.

Celebrant: (extending both hands toward the baptized, with sponsors placing a hand on the candidates' shoulders) Blessed are you, our God, our Maker, for you form us in your image and restore us in Jesus Christ. In baptism, N., N., were buried with Christ and rose to new life in him. Renew them in your Holy Spirit, that they may grow as members of Christ. Strengthen their union with the rest of his Body as they join us in our life of praise and service; through our Savior, Jesus Christ, who lives and reigns with you and the Holy Spirit, now and for ever.

Amen.

Celebrant: Please welcome the new members of the community.

We recognize you as members of the household of God. Confess the faith of Christ crucified, proclaim his resurrection, and share with us in his eternal priesthood.

Lenten Litany[6]

This litany can be used during a weekly Lenten study or at the end of a meal.

Create in us a clean heart, O God.
And renew a right spirit within us.

*Create in me a clean heart, O God.
and renew a right spirit within me.*

Have mercy on me, O God,
according to your loving-kindness
In your great compassion blot out my offenses.

Renew a right spirit within me.

Wash me through and through from my wickedness
And cleanse me from my sin.

Renew a right spirit within me.

---

5 Ibid, 139–141.

6 Adapted from Psalm 51 by Anne E. Kitch. *The Anglican Family Prayer Book* (Harrisburg, PA: Morehouse Publishing, 2004), 134–136.

For I know my transgressions
and my sin is ever before me.

Renew a right spirit within me.

Purge me from my sin, and I shall be pure;
Wash me, and I shall be cleaned indeed.

Renew a right spirit within me.

Give me the joy of your saving help again
And sustain me with your bountiful Spirit.

Renew a right spirit within me.

Glory to the Father, and to the Son,
and to the Holy Spirit.

*Create in me a clean heart, O God.
and renew a right spirit within me.*

World Day of Prayer

Friday, March 6

Sponsored by Church Women United, a Christian group of women that strives to work for justice and peace, the origin of World Day of Prayer dates back to 1887, when Mary Ellen Fairchild James, a Methodist from Brooklyn, New York, called for a day of prayer for home missions. Each year, Church Women United selects a women's group from different parts of the world, to write a prayer service for the day. Then, everyone, men and women alike, are encouraged to attend a prayer service using what the group wrote. The theme for 2019 is "Rise! Take Your Mat and Walk" and will be written by the women of Zimbabwe based on John 5:2–9a. The prayer service will be available here: http://worlddayofprayer.net/index.html

International Women's Day

Sunday, March 8

Grant, O God, that all may recognize women as equal partners in creation and prophesy. By the grace of the Holy Spirit, empower women at home, at work, in government, and in the hierarchies of churches, temples, mosques, synagogues, and all other places of worship. Provide safety and protection, O Gracious Divinity, and inspire just laws against all forms of violence against women. We ask this through Christ our Savior, *Amen.*[7]

World Water Day

Sunday, March 22

Held annually as a means of focusing attention on the importance of freshwater and advocating for the sustainable management of freshwater resources, the theme for 2020 is "Climate Change)."[8] *Learn more:* www.unwater.org/campaigns/world-waterday/en

"We thank you, Almighty God, for the gift of water. Over it your Holy Spirit moved in the beginning of creation. Through it you led the children of Israel out of their bondage . . . In it your Son Jesus received the Baptism of John and was anointed by the Holy Spirit as the Messiah, the Christ, to lead us, through his death and resurrection, from the bondage of sin into everlasting life" (BCP, 306).

Lent

7 "Equal Partners" by Chris Knight. *Lifting Women's Voices: Prayers to Change the World* Margaret Rose, Jenny Te Paa, Jeanne Person, Abagail Nelson, editors. (New York: Morehouse Publishing, 2009), 101–102.

8 Learn more at www.unwater.org/what-we-do/inspire-action/ (accessed March 28, 2018).

Ash Wednesday

February 26, 2020

God hates nothing he has made and forgives us when we are truly repentant. We ask God to give us new and contrite hearts, asking for God's perfect forgiveness through Jesus Christ our Lord.

Color   Violet / Lenten Array

Preface   Of Lent

Collect

Almighty and everlasting God, you hate nothing you have made and forgive the sins of all who are penitent: Create and make in us new and contrite hearts, that we, worthily lamenting our sins and acknowledging our wretchedness, may obtain of you, the God of all mercy, perfect remission and forgiveness; through Jesus Christ our Lord, who lives and reigns with you and the Holy Spirit, one God, for ever and ever. Amen.

Readings and Psalm

Joel 2:1–2, 12–17

In our Hebrew Bible reading **the prophet pictures the day of the Lord as a time of judgment and darkness, but he holds out the hope of mercy if the people will repent.** Some looked to the day of the Lord's coming as an event of great triumph and joy in Israel. But because of sin the sky will become black with swarms of locusts. The trumpet must be blown, calling for a solemn fast, a time for weeping, rending of hearts, and turning back to a compassionate Lord.

or

Isaiah 58:1–12

The lesson from the Hebrew Bible is **a denunciation of the injustices of those who only act at their religion. There is a promise of the Lord's favor for those who genuinely repent and care for the needy.** Fasts and many prayers are of no purpose and may be misused if they do not involve the liberation of the oppressed and help for the weak and afflicted. When there is justice and sharing, then the light of the Lord will rise out of the darkness and all the ruins will be rebuilt.

Psalm 51:1–17

A confession of sin and guilt and a prayer for a clean heart.

2 Corinthians 5:20b—6:10

In this lesson **Paul urges the new disciples to be reconciled to God in this time of deliverance, and he reminds them of all the hardships he has patiently endured for their sake and for the gospel.** The disciples' task is to respond to God's reconciling work in Christ who has taken upon himself their sinfulness so that they might have a right relationship with God. In order that he might offer his service without presenting any personal obstacles, Paul has accepted many of the paradoxes that were part of Jesus' own ministry. Although himself poor, he brings true riches to many.

Matthew 6:1–6, 16–21

In our gospel **Jesus describes genuine charity, prayer, and fasting.** For religious people the temptation is always strong to want to be recognized as full of piety more than to want honestly to be seeking God and the good of others. Praise and rewards for an outward show of religion all pass away. The real treasure is found in our relationship with God.

Lent

Images in the Readings

Although cited only in the reading from Isaiah 58, **ashes** are the primary image for the day. Since the eleventh century, the ashes, made by burning last year's palms, cycle around from the triumphant celebration of Jesus' entry into Jerusalem to the humiliation of sinners covering their heads with the burnt greens. Ashes also bring to mind the fire of the Easter Vigil. Honesty is always good, if sometimes painful: this day we are honest about sin and death. The ash cross marks one's forehead as if it is the brand of one's owner. We journey forward wearing the sign of the cross.

The gospel reading is the source for the three **disciplines of Lent** that have proved useful for many of Christ's disciples. To increase one's giving to the poor, to intensify one's rituals of prayer, and to decrease one's focus on the self: the idea is that such disciplines open up the self to God and to the neighbor.

The **acceptable time**, the day of salvation, are ways Paul describes the here and now of the life of the baptized. Ash Wednesday calls us each day into life in Christ.

Several beloved hymns call Christ our **treasure**. The treasure described in both Matthew and Paul— "poor, yet making many rich"—is the countercultural value of the baptized life.

Ideas of the Day

♦ In *Goodnight iPad* by Ann Droyd, a parody of the classic picture book *Goodnight Moon*, the grandmother says goodnight to all of her family's electronic devices so that her family can sleep for an evening. The action of turning off (or turning from) that which distracts us is so simple and so hard. At times we need others to support such actions. Ash Wednesday invites us to reflect on our humanity ("You are dust and to dust you shall return") and wonder where in our lives we need to turn off or turn from distraction in order to turn back to God.

♦ The Isaiah reading calls the people to fast by outward acts of justice and mercy rather than in ritualistic fashion. It reminds us of the kind of life the covenant calls us to. We act out our commitment to God in a life leading toward justice and liberation for every person. Just as in the gospel, we practice piety as a means of sharing God's love, not as an outward sign of virtue.

♦ We are humbled in the act of kneeling and accepting the imposition of ashes. We can no longer take life for granted or assume that the world was created just for us. Only from this humble stance can we move to the next step in the Ash Wednesday liturgy and review the ways we have "strayed from thy ways like lost sheep."

Making Connections

"I invite you, therefore, in the name of the Church, to the observance of a holy Lent, by self-examination and repentance; by prayer, fasting, and self-denial; and by reading and meditating on God's holy Word. And, to make a right beginning of repentance, and as a mark of our mortal nature, let us now kneel before the Lord, our maker and redeemer" (BCP, 265). This powerful summons calls us to mark this season with intention. Discipline. Repentance. It is startling. At what other time in the year are we invited, in the name of the church, to do anything that publicly or forcefully? Should we do that more often?

Engaging All Ages

An Ash Wednesday experiment: Find some large marshmallows, a stick, and a safe (but open) flame—outdoor fire pits are good for this. Char that marshmallow until it is black. Once the marshmallow has cooled enough, peel off the charred outer skin, noticing how easy it slips away. What do you notice about the innards of the once solid puffy snack? That's right—it is now gooey. What choices can you make that will help you to peel away things in your life that make it hard to connect with Jesus or others in a loving manner this Lenten season?

Hymns for the Day

Note: There is no Entrance Hymn on this day (see BCP, p. 264).

The Hymnal 1982
Eternal Lord of love, behold your Church 149
O bless the Lord, my soul! 411
The glory of these forty days 143
Before thy throne, O God, we kneel 574, 575
Kind Maker of the world, O hear 152
Lord Jesus, Sun of Righteousness 144
Creator of the earth and skies 148
Lord, whose love through humble service 610
Now quit your care 145
O day of God, draw nigh 600, 601
Lead us, heavenly Father, lead us 559
God himself is with us 475
Jesus, all my gladness 701

Lift Every Voice and Sing II
Bless the Lord, O my soul 65
Come, ye disconsolate 147
Close to thee 122
Give me a clean heart 124
In God we trust 55
I've decided to make Jesus my choice 68

Wonder, Love, and Praise
Almighty Lord Most High draw near 888
Bless the Lord, my soul 825
Gracious Spirit, give your servants 782

Lent

The First Sunday in Lent

March 1, 2020

Saying "no" to evil so that the Christian can say "yes" to Christ.

Color Violet / Lenten Array

Preface Of Lent

Collect

Almighty God, whose blessed Son was led by the Spirit to be tempted by Satan: Come quickly to help us who are assaulted by many temptations; and, as you know the weaknesses of each of us, let each one find you mighty to save; through Jesus Christ your Son our Lord, who lives and reigns with you and the Holy Spirit, one God, now and for ever. Amen.

Readings and Psalm

Genesis 2:15–17; 3:1–7

From the Hebrew Bible we hear **the story of the creation of the first man and woman in the Garden of Eden and their disobedience and consequent loss of innocence.** Tempted by the serpent, first the woman and then the man eat from the forbidden tree of the knowledge of good and evil. The story expresses the understanding that human beings are the crown of God's creation, and yet there is something tragically wrong with them. From later Christian perspective, however, this transgression is seen as part of God's greater plan for the maturity and salvation of humanity. The free choice of disobedience and the learning of good and evil will, through redemption, make possible a more profound relationship with God.

Psalm 32

A psalm of thanksgiving for the forgiveness of sin.

Romans 5:12–19

In this lesson **Paul tells how the history of human sinfulness and death has been transformed by the free gift of Jesus Christ.** The act of disobedience of the one person, Adam, began the reign of sin and death. This was later compounded by the role of law which, by instructing people not to sin, actually caused trespassing to abound. But now the righteousness and obedience of the one man Jesus Christ means acquittal and new life for all.

Matthew 4:1–11

Our gospel is **the story of the temptations of Jesus by the devil.** After his baptism Jesus is led into the wilderness and confronted with temptations which are inescapable in his ministry. He might seek to show that he is the Son of God by satisfying material needs or wielding miraculous power. Or he could seek to control allegiance through the pomp and might of a worldly kingship. But Jesus' obedience is God's way for him.

Prayers of the People

Let us offer our prayers to God, who justified us through the death of his Son and rescued us from the disobedience of our forebears, as we respond, "Kyrie eleison."

That as you led your people through the waters of the Red Sea and in the desert of their awakening, so lead us through this season of Lent into the unfolding gift of your divine imagination; let us pray.

Kyrie eleison.

For those who are preparing to receive rites of initiation at the Great Vigil of Easter and throughout the season of resurrection, that they may come to a deeper knowledge of the faith, and profess with their lips and with their lives the liberating joy of living a Christian life; let us pray.

Kyrie eleison.

For the courage to face our demons of confusion, desolation, and darkness, that through the agonizing quest for truth we may summon the faith and strength to put them to flight; let us pray.

Kyrie eleison.

For our country, the world, and all its leaders, that we may strive for the common good over personal gain, sharing territory and lands across tribal, religious, and ethnic divides, offering security to all, and honoring the image of God in those who differ from us; let us pray.

Kyrie eleison.

For our absent sisters and brothers, that they may feel called to return to our community of faith, where we wait to welcome them with thanksgiving and joy; let us pray.

Kyrie eleison.

For all who have died and for all who are experiencing the many faces of loss, that they may know that nothing separates us from the love of God revealed through Christ Jesus; let us pray.

Kyrie eleison.

That we may be faithful in prayer, fasting, and the generous giving of alms, so that we may prepare our souls for the celebration of the Paschal Feast; let us pray.

Kyrie eleison.

With gratitude for God's unfailing love and forgiveness, we add to these prayers.
(Special intentions of the congregation, the diocese, and the Anglican Communion may be added here or before the formal intercessions.)

The Celebrant adds a concluding Collect.

Images in the Readings

Matthew writes that Jesus fasted for **forty days and forty nights.** In the Bible, forty is always the time between, the necessary span before the gracious conclusion. It is forty, days or years, that numbers the rain of Noah's flood, Moses on Mount Sinai, Israel in the wilderness, the spies scouting out Canaan, Israel in the hands of the Philistines, the taunting by Goliath, the reign of Saul, David, and Solomon, Ezekiel lying on his right side, Nineveh's repentance, and Jesus' appearance after Easter. For us, it is forty days until the celebration of the resurrection.

The **Tree of Knowledge of Good and Evil**—a stark contrast with the wondrous Tree of Life that appears again in Revelation 22—is a fascinating, ambiguous symbol, perhaps signifying the human tendency to replace God's way with one's own way, God's word with human knowledge. It is a mystery tree that according to the story represents all that is wrong in human life.

Who initiated sin? In Genesis it is **the woman**, in Paul it is **Adam**—characters whom we recognize as being essentially ourselves. The storyteller of Genesis 3 joined with many others in antiquity by blaming the woman for all the troubles of humanity. In accord with a Christian theological interpretation of this story, all people are Adam, creatures of earth, and all people are Eve, bearers of life.

The gospel describes the **devil** as the tempter, the power that seeks to lure us away from God. It is this devil that much Christian tradition has used to explain the talking serpent of Genesis 3. The tradition of art has not given us profound enough depictions of this primordial evil, but in the usual image of a creature part human, part monster, we can see another picture of ourselves.

Lent

Lent

Ideas of the Day

- For many, the story of Adam and Eve is loaded with the baggage of "original sin," shame, and blame, which do more harm than good. What would it look like to instead ground today's sacred stories of temptation and sin in the knowledge that we are all beloved children of God? Sin, most simply defined, is that which separates us from the love of God. What would it feel like to turn away from shame and reflect on what separates you from the love of God?

- The gospel points out the contrast between Adam (representing humankind) and Jesus. Jesus is tempted in the wilderness, but he does not fall into sin. We need to realize that this account of the temptation of Jesus is symbolic and poetic. Jesus was undoubtedly tempted all his life. The painful reality of that temptation is expressed profoundly in the wilderness scene. But Jesus did not give in to temptation; he reversed the story and destiny of Adam and Eve in the garden.

- During Lent in Year A, the readings provide a primer in Christianity as outlined in Paul's letters to the Romans and Ephesians. These epistle readings pick up the theme from Hebrew Scripture readings and the gospel.

Making Connections

We are tempted every day to say "If only . . ." Eve in the garden and A. L. Kennedy's Mary in *The Little Snake* (Canongate Books Ltd, 2016) are intrigued by the serpents and their suggestions about the possibility of more. Of different. We wish there were just one change, one shift, one thing done or left undone that could be righted, and then . . . *then* we could be at peace. The gospel today reminds us that these are false solutions. They are about right now, but not about eternal peace with God. Even in the worst of times, in a desert after a fast, Jesus reminds us to trust. Step away from the "if only" solutions and let God's angels tend to you, even in your suffering.

Engaging All Ages

Rough camping can be a good Lenten practice. If you can't get far away, camping for one night in the backyard or maybe camping out in your living room will work. Strip away some of the comforts and conveniences (often taken for granted) in order to connect and meditate on the story of the Israelites in the desert, Jesus in the wilderness, and those who find themselves displaced from home and shelter. Sleep on the ground. Eat bread and water, or rice and water. Use no electricity to heat or cool. Use no devices. What do you notice?

Hymns for the Day

The Hymnal 1982
Creator of the earth and skies 148
Wilt thou forgive that sin, where I begun 140, 141
Praise to the Holiest in the height 445, 446
Forty days and forty nights 150
From God Christ's deity came forth 443
Lord, who throughout these forty days 142
Now let us all with one accord 146, 147
O love, how deep, how broad, how high 448, 449
The glory of these forty days 143

Lift Every Voice and Sing II
It is well with my soul 188
Sweet hour of prayer 178

Wonder, Love, and Praise

Weekday Commemorations

Monday, March 2
Chad of Lichfield, Bishop, 672

Ordained to the bishopric irregularly, that is, not following Roman Catholic custom, Chad appeared before Theodore, the new Archbishop of Canterbury. Chad tendered his resignation, saying, "Indeed, I never believed myself worthy of it." Such humility prompted Theodore to re-ordain Chad and to appoint him Bishop of Mercia and Northumbria. Chad traveled his diocese by foot until Theodore commanded that he ride when needed. Chad was a devout administrator, who built a monastery at Barrow, near his see in Lichfield. Not three years after his ordination, Chad fell victim to the plague that killed many in his diocese. Of his death, the Venerable Bede wrote: "He joyfully beheld . . . the day of the Lord . . . ."

Tuesday, March 3
John and Charles Wesley, Priests, 1791, 1788

Born four years apart (John, 1703; Charles, 1707), the Brothers Wesley entwined their lives until their deaths, three years apart (Charles, 1788; John, 1791). They were the 15th and 18th children of Samuel, a rector of Epworth, Lincolnshire. They preached sermons and wrote theology, but they are best known through their hymns (Charles wrote more than 6,000). They were educated at Christ Church, Oxford, where they convened friends to adhere strictly to the discipline and worship of the Prayer Book (thus, they were called "Methodists"). They adhered confidently to the doctrine of the Church of England, which they loved. The schism of Methodists from the Church occurred after the deaths of the Wesleys.

Saturday, March 7
Perpetua and Felicity, Martyrs, 202

Vibia Perpetua and her companions—Felicitas, Revocatus, Secundulus, and Saturninus—were martyred for their faith as Christians. Early in the third century, Emperor Septimius Severus decreed that everyone must sacrifice to his divinity. Perpetua could not and would not: she and her companions were arrested. In prison, Perpetua had visions. At her public hearing before the Proconsul, she declared, "I am a Christian," even refusing entreaties of her father. On March 7, the troop was sent to the arena for mangling by a boar, bear, leopard, and a vicious cow. Perpetua exhorted the companions "to stand fast in the faith." Eventually, she guided the hand of the executioner sent to drive a sword through her throat.

Lent

The Second Sunday in Lent

March 8, 2020

Lent

Saying "yes" to Jesus.

Color Violet / Lenten Array

Preface Of Lent

Collect

O God, whose glory it is always to have mercy: Be gracious to all who have gone astray from your ways, and bring them again with penitent hearts and steadfast faith to embrace and hold fast the unchangeable truth of your Word, Jesus Christ your Son; who with you and the Holy Spirit lives and reigns, one God, for ever and ever. Amen.

Readings and Psalm

Genesis 12:1–4a

The opening lesson is **the story of God's call of Abraham (who was then known as Abram) to leave his own country and become the father of a great nation.** Trusting in the Lord, Abram and his family forsake all that is familiar to them to set out for an unknown land. This story is a primary illustration of the way God acts in history by calling individuals to venture forth in faith.

Psalm 121

A song of trust in the Lord, the unsleeping guardian of Israel.

Romans 4:1–5, 13–17

In this passage **Paul describes Abraham as an individual who through faith found a right relationship with God. He is the father of all who trust in the Lord.** Paul uses the example of Abraham as a centerpiece for his argument that righteousness with God comes through faith and not by works of the law. The promise given to Abraham and his descendants was not made because of good works or legal obedience. It rests on grace alone.

John 3:1–17

In our gospel story **Nicodemus, one of the Pharisees, comes during the night to talk with Jesus.** Nicodemus is a figure used by the evangelist to represent a type of person who wants to believe but has difficulty understanding spiritual realities. Jesus tells him that individuals cannot enter the kingdom of God unless they are born anew through water and the Spirit. The inner meaning of the passage partly turns on the fact that "born anew" can also be understood as "born from on high" and the same Greek word means both wind and spirit. Jesus then tells Nicodemus of the Son of Man come down from heaven who will be lifted up, both on the cross to die for the world and to return to heaven in glory.

or

Matthew 17:1–9

Our gospel is **the story of Jesus' transfiguration.** The narrative is richly woven with themes and symbols drawn from Israel's past and its hopes for the future. Moses and Elijah represent the law and the prophets, whose promises Jesus fulfills. The chosen disciples see divine glory reflected in Jesus' human person. They hear a voice from the cloud declaring that he is the beloved Son.

Prayers of the People

Let us pray to the one who renews our life and restores our fortunes, as we respond, "Kyrie eleison."

That we may be willing to make extraordinary journeys in response to the gospel, leaving behind old patterns of living, and embracing the new path that God is setting before us, knowing that he will watch over us and preserve us from the Evil One; let us pray.

Kyrie eleison.

For the grace to recognize the power of envy and jealousy that reside in our hearts, and to dispel the demons that masquerade as their glory, trusting that God's transforming hand will conform us to the Body of Christ; let us pray.

Kyrie eleison.

That we may honor the worker, paying a fair wage for honest labor; let us pray.

Kyrie eleison.

That we may see our salvation through the lens of faith, focusing on the endless mercy of Jesus Christ, through whom we have been justified and given the gift of everlasting life; let us pray.

Kyrie eleison.

For all who have died, and for all who are afraid to die to the memories which enslave them to the past, that stones may be removed from every tomb which keeps us from sharing in Christ's promise of abundant life; let us pray.

Kyrie eleison.

That this Eucharistic Meal may strengthen us in our lenten resolve to live more deeply into the heart of God's word; let us pray.

Kyrie eleison.

That candidates for baptism and confirmation and their families may marvel at the presence of God throughout history and in the midst of our current age; let us pray.

Kyrie eleison.

As a people born of water and the Spirit, let us join in the continuation of our prayers.

(Special intentions of the congregation, the diocese, and the Anglican Communion may be added here or before the formal intercessions.)

The Celebrant adds a concluding Collect.

Images in the Readings

John's language of being born again suggests the image of the **mother**. Historically, the church described itself as this mother and the font as the womb from which birth in God arises. Recently, also God is described as the mother who births a new creation. But birth is not easy, and Lent allows us forty days to reenvision that birth.

Abram's immigration to the land of promise offers the image of the **journey**. Lent provides forty days for the annual journey back to the mystery of the resurrection and the new life to which we are called.

Paul's language of justification assumes that God is a **judge** who requires of us a life of righteousness. That justification comes via faith does not eliminate the necessity for such a radical reorientation of the self before God. It is instructive to hold the image of judge next to that of the mother: each image is a nuance of the other.

Ideas of the Day

- Birth is messy, painful, loud, disruptive, and miraculous. Every episode of the BBC show *Call the Midwife* centers around a birth and the midwives who accompany the mother as she pushes her baby into the world. Not one of the babies is born of their own choosing, nor are they born alone. Their life is bestowed as a gift. When Jesus speaks of being born of the Spirit, what does that look like and feel like? Messy? Painful? Loud? Disruptive? Miraculous? How do we receive this gift? Who are the midwives accompanying birth of the Spirit?

- Abram had the faith to move to a strange, alien land. He could face the unknown. All ages know about fear in facing the unknown—how do we deal with our fears and anxieties? What does faith mean in our movement into new situations and new life?

- Faith leads us into relationship with God: "For God so loved the world that he gave his only Son, that whoever believes in him should not perish but have eternal life."

Lent

Making Connections

The blessing in the Genesis reading is present throughout the Episcopal Church's liturgical resource "*I Will Bless You, and You Will Be a Blessing*." It explores the threefold character of blessing: (1) acknowledging what is already present—God's goodness; (2) setting things apart for God's purposes; and (3) prayers for divine grace to fulfill those purposes. Just as the blessing of bread and wine at the Eucharist sets those elements apart from ordinary usage and designates them for a particular, sacred purpose that grows forward into the future, so the public affirmation of divine blessing of relationships, ministries, buildings, and work set them apart from others. The blessing of Nicodemus to us continues in the example he set for us to seek out Jesus, even in the darkness of our secrets or fears and find him there.

Engaging All Ages

Look outside your window. What is happening with the weather, the trees or grasses, the sky, the animals? Is it bare or are things beginning to bud and turn green? Is there snow or a heat wave? The earth moves and shifts in seasons. So do our lives. Some seasons follow the expected schedule, but others take too long or pass too quickly. Lent is a season of turning, reorienting, and centering our lives back on Jesus. Sometimes this turning is easy; sometimes it is difficult and requires many tries. What action or attitude of Jesus do you need to turn back to?

Hymns for the Day

The Hymnal 1982
I to the hills will lift mine eyes 668
Now let us all with one accord 146, 147
Praise our great and gracious Lord 393
The God of Abraham praise 401
How firm a foundation, ye saints of the Lord 636, 637
I call on thee, Lord Jesus Christ 634
And now, O Father, mindful of the love 337
Lift high the cross 473
O love, how deep, how broad, how high 448, 449
The great Creator of the worlds 489
When Christ was lifted from the earth 603, 604

Lift Every Voice and Sing II
We've come this far by faith 208

Wonder, Love, and Praise

Weekday Commemorations

Monday, March 9
Gregory of Nyssa, Bishop and Theologian, c. 394
Born about 334 in Caesarea, a brother to Basil the Great, Gregory became besotted by Christ and his Passion. His faith was heartened when he was 20 by the transfer of relics of the 40 Martyrs of Sebaste, but he dismissed ministry to become a rhetorician like his father. Nevertheless, Basil convinced Gregory to become Bishop of Nyssa; ordination made Gregory miserable because he felt unworthy, knowing little of tact or budgets. Basil and Macrina, their sister, died in 379; his siblings' deaths opened the way for Gregory to develop as a philosopher and theologian (his *Great Catechism* is one of his most respected treatises). In 381, Gregory was honored as a "pillar of the church."

Thursday, March 12
Gregory the Great, Bishop and Theologian, 604
Gregory, born a patrician in 540, is one of only two popes, with Leo the First, to be popularly called "great." Both men reigned during barbaric invasions of Italy, and Gregory served during "plague, pestilence, and famine." He became Prefect of Rome in 573 and Ambassador to Constantinople in 579; in 590, Gregory succeeded Pope Pelagius. Gregory's pontificate was marked by vigorous service: he defended Rome against the Lombards and fed the people from the papal granaries in Sicily. He ordered the Church's liturgy and chant; his legacy remains. He also supported evangelism of the Anglo-Saxons, "which led to him being called 'Apostle to the English.'" He is buried in St. Peter's Basilica.

Friday, March 13
James Theodore Holly, Bishop, 1911
Born a free black, Holly was ordained a deacon in Detroit in 1855 and a priest in Connecticut in 1856. That year, he founded an antecedent to the Union of Black Episcopalians. He and Frederick Douglass worked together to promote the "extension of the church among colored people." Holly took his ministry to Haiti, where his wife, mother, and two children died. Holly continued to speak of God's love to Haitians. To build the church in Haiti, Holly was consecrated a missionary bishop in 1874, becoming the first African American bishop in the Episcopal Church.

The Third Sunday in Lent

March 15, 2020

The baptismal waters become for the Christian "a spring of water gushing up to eternal life." (John 4:14)

Color   Violet / Lenten Array

Preface   Of Lent

Collect

Almighty God, you know that we have no power in ourselves to help ourselves: Keep us both outwardly in our bodies and inwardly in our souls, that we may be defended from all adversities which may happen to the body, and from all evil thoughts which may assault and hurt the soul; through Jesus Christ our Lord, who lives and reigns with you and the Holy Spirit, one God, for ever and ever. Amen.

Readings and Psalm

Exodus 17:1–7

In our Hebrew Bible story **the people are at the point of rebellion because they are without water in the wilderness.** Moses decries their readiness to challenge the Lord through their lack of trust, and he asks God what is to be done. The Lord instructs Moses to strike a rock with his staff so that water will pour from it. This place he names Massah (meaning Challenge) and Meribah (meaning Dispute).

Psalm 95

A call to worship the Lord our God, with a warning not to put God to the test.

Romans 5:1–11

In this lection we hear how **Paul bids disciples to rejoice in the reconciliation and hope which are theirs because of the sacrifice of Christ on behalf of sinners.** Through faith we have justification; we are given a right relationship with God. Now even our sufferings can lead to endurance, and this to a perseverance which strengthens our hope. Since God was willing to show such a love while we were still God's enemies because of sin, how much more we are assured that we are to be saved.

John 4:5–42

Our gospel tells **the story of Jesus' meeting with the Samaritan woman by Jacob's well.** The narrative is rich with themes. Jesus is willing to break with custom in order to talk with one who is both a woman and a foreigner. True worship of God is tied to no particular place. He himself offers living water which wells up to eternal life. The woman learns that Jesus is the expected Messiah, and later others from the town come to believe that he is the world's Savior. During an interval in the story, Jesus speaks with his disciples concerning his true food and drink, and tells them that the time of harvesting for eternal life is at hand.

Prayers of the People

Come, let us adore Christ, who refreshes us with springs of living water and calls us to be a people of prayer and thanksgiving, as we respond, "Kyrie eleison."

For the Church throughout the world, that all who lead the people of God during the present age may have courage to endure the disputes and sufferings of our time, and to have the vision to see the places in which God is revealing his presence in our midst; let us pray.

Kyrie eleison.

That we may not fear those whose ways are destructive to society, or who condemn the faith we cherish, or who commit acts which grieve the heart of Christ, that instead we may extend the hand of charity to all people, and witness to the power of transforming love; let us pray.

Kyrie eleison.

For leaders of government, that they may drink from the waters of holy peace and bring to the world's peoples the hope of a new and more prosperous life; let us pray.

Kyrie eleison.

That we may extend the lamp of charity to all whom we have harmed and to all who have brought darkness to our souls, knowing that all have fallen short of God's glory, and that all are invited into a redeemed and grace-filled life; let us pray.

Kyrie eleison.

For Christians throughout the world who are offering their finest gifts of bread and wine on the Sabbath day, that through the power of the Holy Spirit, the Body and Blood of Christ will be received across every distinction of race, class, and nationality; let us pray.

Kyrie eleison.

For an ever-deepening sense of God's presence in all our lives, but most especially in those who will receive rites of initiation this Easter season; let us pray.

Kyrie eleison.

For all who have died in the hope of the resurrection, and those whose faith is known to God alone; let us pray.

Kyrie eleison.

Confident that we are all within reach of the saving embrace of Jesus, let us continue our prayers.

(Special intentions of the congregation, the diocese, and the Anglican Communion may be added here or before the formal intercessions.)

The Celebrant adds a concluding Collect.

Images in the Readings

The primary image for this Sunday is **water**. Water: that life as we know it on earth requires water is perhaps the reason that water figures in countless stories in all cultures, stories of rivers and seas, wells and rain. The Bible is overflowing with water stories, some of which we will hear at the Easter Vigil. In our time, daily showers, public fountains, swimming pools, and water parks provide society with the refreshment of water. Yet we are told that the next world wars will be over water, and current Christian ecologists urge care for the waters of the earth. In medieval Christian art, a picture of Moses striking the rock so that water can flow was set next to a depiction of Christ on the cross being pierced with the sword, as the water of life flowed from his side.

Another image for the day is the **rock**. In the Psalms, God is called Rock twenty-two times. That water can flow from rock provides us with a double image for God.

Ideas of the Day

♦ Knowing someone's reputation is different from knowing that person. The conversation between Jesus and the Samaritan woman, whom society at the time did not believe should interact, is challenging, honest, and breaks through facades. It is Jesus' longest conversation the Bible. Jesus truly sees the Samaritan woman beyond her reputation and offers her living water—both are holy gifts. Afterward the Samaritan woman shares with her people her experience with Jesus. We all need to be truly seen. We all need living water. What assumptions get in our way?

♦ The concept that lies behind the Old Testament readings during Lent is the idea of a quest or journey. God is always calling us into a new land and into new adventures. We resist, yet we long to move on. There is tension and tragedy in our response. Our own individual lives are filled with stories of being in the wilderness and the decisions that have come out of them. What have the signs been? Where are we moving now?

♦ Today's gospel could be centered on water, refreshment, faith, and the meaning of baptism. In baptism we recognize that water is still a sign of God's power and presence with us. Can we recognize ourselves with the Israelites in their demand for signs? How is the Eucharist and other sacraments signs of God's presence?

Making Connections

Last week, under the cover of darkness in fear of risking his reputation, a highly regarded Pharisee named Nicodemus approached Jesus with questions about life. This week, in the light of day, with no regard for his own reputation, Jesus approaches an unnamed outcast woman with a request for water, and more words of new life. Sometimes we are approaching God from a position of privilege, and sometimes we are being sought by God on the fringes of belonging. The Holy Spirit is in all of this, pushing the culturally prescribed boundaries and expectations aside to offer salvation to all who would ask.

Engaging All Ages

Frequently this time of year is when gardeners begin to work in earnest to prepare for their spring and summer gardens. They begin to clean out the greenhouse, repair tools, and brush cobwebs off their mucking boots and wheelbarrows. They order mulch and turn the compost pile. They also begin "starting seeds" in tiny paper pots with no more than three tablespoons of soil, often setting them under heat lamps to begin their germination process. Consider starting some seeds of your own or think about what spiritual tools might need cleaning.

Hymns for the Day

The Hymnal 1982
To God with gladness sing 399
Come, thou fount of every blessing 686
Glorious things of thee are spoken 522, 523
Guide me, O thou great Jehovah 690
O Food to pilgrims given 308, 309
O God, unseen yet ever near 332
Rock of ages, cleft for me 685
Shepherd of souls, refresh and bless 343
Surely it is God who saves me 678, 679
Hail, thou once despised Jesus 495
O Love of God, how strong and true 455, 456
There is a balm in Gilead (vs. 1–2) 676
You, Lord, we praise in songs of celebration 319
As longs the deer for cooling streams 658
Draw nigh and take the Body of the Lord 327, 328
I heard the voice of Jesus say 692
In your mercy, Lord, you called me 706
Jesus, Lover of my soul 699

O Jesus, joy of loving hearts 649, 650
O love that casts out fear 700
The first one ever, oh, ever to know 673

Lift Every Voice and Sing II
Come, thou fount of every blessing 111
There is a balm in Gilead (vs. 1–2) 203
Jesus, Lover of my soul 79
Grant me a blessing 166

Wonder, Love, and Praise
Camina, pueblo de Dios / Walk on, O people of God 739
As panting deer desire the waterbrooks 727

Weekday Commemorations

Tuesday, March 17
Patrick of Ireland, Bishop and Missionary, 461
Patrick was born in a Christian family on the north-west coast of Britain about 390. As a teen, Patrick was kidnapped to Ireland and forced to served as a shepherd; as a young man, he escaped back to Britain, where he was educated as a Christian and took holy orders. A vision returned him to Ireland about 432. Patrick's missions of conversion throughout Ireland continued until his death. He adapted pagan traditions to Christian: he had Christian churches built on sites considered sacred; he had crosses carved on druidic pillars; and he reassigned sacred wells to Christian status. "St. Patrick's Breastplate," while attributed to him, is probably not his except as it expresses his zeal.

Wednesday, March 18
Cyril of Jerusalem, Bishop and Theologian, 386
Holy Week: brought to you by Cyril. Also, Lent and inquirers' classes. Born in Jerusalem about 315, he became a bishop there around 349. He was banished and restored to this post three times due to disputes in church and state. Early in his episcopate, Cyril wrote *Catechetical Lectures*, comprising an introduction and 18 *Catecheses* based on the articles of the creed of the Church of Jerusalem. Likely, Cyril instituted observances of Palm Sunday and Holy Week as a practical way to organize devotions for locals and pilgrims around Jerusalem's sacred sites. Most likely, pilgrims took the practices home with them, exploiting the liturgies' development throughout the Church, as still seen in the 1979 Book of Common Prayer.

Lent

Thursday, March 19
Saint Joseph

The Gospel of Matthew honors Joseph as open to mysticism while also a man of compassion and devotion. Even so, he may have been perturbed when pressed to be Mary's protector and to be a father to Jesus. He accepted and provided nurturance; he protected Jesus and Mary by escorting them to Egypt to escape Herod's commanded slaughter of boy children. Joseph reared his son as a faithful Jew. Joseph himself, a descendant of David, was a pious Jew, a carpenter by trade. As such, he is enrolled as the patron saint of workers for not only working with his hands but also mentoring his son in this trade. Joseph exemplifies a loving husband and father, a man who trusted God.

Friday, March 20
Cuthbert, Bishop, 687

Cuthbert, born about 625, entered a monastery after having a vision of angelic light and learning that Aidan of Lindisfarne had died at the time of this vision. Cuthbert was Prior of Melrose Abbey from 651 to 664 and of Lindisfarne for a dozen years. He made it his habit to visit far–flung villages and to preach to the poor people who needed his discipline as a model to withstand the pull of the pagan. He became Bishop of Hexham in 684 but kept his see at Lindisfarne. Cuthbert was the most popular saint of the pre-Conquest Anglo-Saxon church. Today, his relics and tomb remain at Durham.

Saturday, March 21
Thomas Ken, Bishop, 1711

Born in 1637, Ken became known as a man of integrity during royal upheavals. He publicly rebuked the Prince of Orange's dastardly treatment of his wife and denied hospitality to the mistress of Charles II in 1683. In 1688, under James II, Ken refused to read the king's Declaration of Indulgence; he and his six cohorts were sent to the Tower, acquitted in court, then considered heroes. After the revolution of 1688, Ken refused to swear allegiance to William of Orange and so was deprived of his see. The accession of Queen Anne saw Ken in line again with the Church of England. He wrote the doxology that begins "Praise God from whom all blessings flow."

The Fourth Sunday in Lent

March 22, 2020

The Christian is given the gift of enlightenment through the Holy Spirit.

Color   Violet / Lenten Array

Preface   Of Lent

Collect

Gracious Father, whose blessed Son Jesus Christ came down from heaven to be the true bread which gives life to the world: Evermore give us this bread, that he may live in us, and we in him; who lives and reigns with you and the Holy Spirit, one God, now and for ever. Amen.

Readings and Psalm

1 Samuel 16:1–13

In this Hebrew scripture story **the Lord sends Samuel to anoint David to be the new king over Israel.** God has rejected Saul as king but he remains in power and Samuel must go secretly on his mission. As so often happens in the Bible, one who seems least likely in the eyes of others is chosen by God to carry out the divine will.

Psalm 23

The Lord is shepherd and guide. God is present in the time of danger and is generous and merciful.

Ephesians 5:8–14

In this New Testament lesson **disciples are called to be a people of the light, forsaking all the works of darkness.** Their present life is to be in sharp contrast with their actions before they became Christians. All that is done is to be exposed to the light. The passage closes with what was probably part of an ancient hymn used at baptisms.

John 9:1–41

Our gospel is **the story of Jesus' healing of a man born blind. Jesus brings light into a dark world.** Many people of the time regarded the man's blindness to be a result of sin, but Jesus helps him to see, at first physically, and then spiritually as well. The man withstands the criticism of the religious officials and worships Jesus as the Son of Man and his Lord.

Prayers of the People

As a sign of our obedience, let us bend the knee of our hearts, and make an offering of prayer and thanksgiving to God, as we respond, "Kyrie eleison."

For those preparing for baptism and other rites of initiation, and those who will renew their baptismal vows at the Great Vigil of Easter, that they may find in the Church a place of spiritual integrity, renewal and hope, forgiveness and restoration; let us pray.

Kyrie eleison.

That Christians throughout the world who are being persecuted for being followers of Christ may be protected by the strong armor of faith, and sustained by the fervent prayers of all the baptized; let us pray.

Kyrie eleison.

That the work of God may be made visible through our weaknesses and shortcomings, bearing witness to others of the power of the Holy Spirit to overcome the heartache and despair that visits every human heart; let us pray.

Kyrie eleison.

That we who celebrate this Eucharistic Meal may receive the mercy of the Lamb, who shares our burdens, removes our sin, and restores us to the company of the faithful; let us pray.

Kyrie eleison.

For all who are preparing for Holy Week and the Great Paschal Feast of Easter, especially choirs, altar guilds, church staff, and clergy, that their efforts may inspire our participation; let us pray.

Kyrie eleison.

That those who have died may rest in peace, and we who hear of war and famine remain restless until the day of peace has come; let us pray.

Kyrie eleison.

Knowing that Jesus opens the eyes of the blind, gives voice to the voiceless, and frees those who are imprisoned by fear, let us with confidence continue our prayers.

(Special intentions of the congregation, the diocese, and the Anglican Communion may be added here or before the formal intercessions.)

The Celebrant adds a concluding Collect.

Images in the Readings

The primary image for the day is **light**. According to Genesis 1, light is the first creation of God. In John, Christ not only brings light, he is the very light of God. And so the synoptics describe the crucifixion as effecting an eclipse, and when Judas leaves the company for the betrayal, the author of John writes, "And it was night" (13:30). The Ephesians reading emphasizes that the light that is Christ is now the light within each believer.

Another image for the day is the **anointing**. In ancient times, and still today in the British monarchy, consecrated oil is poured on the head of the one chosen to lead. In some Christian churches, an anointing is a necessary part of the baptismal ritual. What was dry and brittle is now limber with life.

David was a **shepherd**. According to Israelite memory, the people were nomadic herders before becoming urban dwellers. So David embodies the good old tradition, a more innocent time. Other ancient Near Eastern cultures also used the metaphor of the shepherd to describe their king. The sheep are the source of the people's life, and the shepherd ensures that livelihood.

Ideas of the Day

♦ So many questions! What happened? Whose fault is it? How is that possible? The man who was born blind can now see. Those who hold societal position cannot see. (Or can they?) Many of us have been taught, "There are no bad questions." Even if there are no bad questions, we sometimes do not hear the answers to the questions we are asking because they are not the answers we want to hear. We want answers that fit neatly within the way we know the world. Jesus and the formerly blind man answer each question in ways that point to God's action in the world.

♦ Through the anointing of the Holy Spirit at baptism the Christian can see to follow Jesus. The early church saw the healing of the man born blind as a metaphor of enlightenment: the Christian is called to see things differently.

♦ How do our goals for life stack up against the strange words of Jesus in today's gospel that were acted out in his own life and in the lives of the apostles? This is not a time for answering questions or resolving doubts. Rather, it is a time to raise questions. Everyone must find their own understanding of what the gospel proclaims, but we can do so only as our own views of life area challenged and confronted.

Making Connections

In a beautiful reflection on the reading from 1 Samuel to his confirmands, Harvard Wilbur (Episcopal priest, 1924–2008) wrote about grief and moving forward after loss. "How long will you grieve over Saul?" is the question. So many people lose hope and become discouraged when "the persons and things to which you gave your energies and hopes have failed you." Wilbur reminds us that God will break-in to the narratives playing in our heads and hearts, as he did with Samuel when he told him "Fill your horn with oil and go." It is essential, but rarely easy, that we accept disappointment and loss, because it is a part of life. "The same can be said to those of us who find ourselves walking through the rubble of once glorious dreams. Stop your grieving. Gather your resources. Do what needs to be done."[1]

---

1 From a confirmation church bulletin circa 1986 from St. James Episcopal Church in Wichita Kansas.

Engaging All Ages

Lent is season of simplicity—a season when we remind each other to depend on God and not on our "stuff" or accomplishments to bring us love or joy. In our churches we mark this season with a particular color and by changes around our altars and our buildings. What changes have you noticed? Is there anything different about the cross(es), the altar, or the robes that people wear? What could you change in your home to reflect the simplicity of Lent? Are there material items that you are ready to part with?

Hymns for the Day

The Hymnal 1982

My Shepherd will supply my need 664
The King of love my shepherd is 645, 646
The Lord my God my shepherd is 663
God moves in a mysterious way 677
Seek the Lord while he wills to be found S217ff
Awake, O sleeper, rise from death 547
I want to walk as a child of the light 490
Lord Jesus, Sun of Righteousness 144
O splendor of God's glory bright 5
Christ, whose glory fills the skies 6, 7
Deck thyself, my soul, with gladness 339
Eternal light, shine in my heart 465, 466
God of mercy, God of grace 538
How wondrous and great thy works,
    God of praise! 532, 533
I'll praise my Maker while I've breath 429
I heard the voice of Jesus say 692
Lord God, you now have set your servant free 499
O for a thousand tongues to sing 493

Lift Every Voice and Sing II
The Lord is my shepherd 104
The Lord is my light 58

Wonder, Love, and Praise
So the day dawn for me 750
When from bondage we are summoned 753, 754
Lord, you have fulfilled your word 891

Weekday Commemorations

Monday, March 23
Gregory the Illuminator, Bishop and Missionary, c.332

Gregory, Apostle of the Armenians, was born about 257. Following his father's assassination of the Persian king, baby Gregory was removed to Caesarca in Cappadocia and raised as a Christian. He married and fathered two sons. About 280, he returned to Armenia and, after much effort, converted the king to Christianity, thereby ending paganism in his native land. About 300, Gregory was ordained a bishop at Caesarea; his cathedral at Valarshapat remains the center of Armenian Christianity. As the first nation-state to become officially Christian, Armenia set a precedent for adoption of Christianity by Emperor Constantine; as a buffer between empires in Rome and Persia, Armenia suffered through the vicissitudes of power and protection.

Tuesday, March 24
Óscar Romero, Archbishop and Martyr, 1980 and the Martyrs of El Salvador

In and out of seminaries due to poverty, Romero (born in 1917 in San Salvador) was eventually sent to Rome to study theology. After ordination, he returned home to work among the poor. Appointed archbishop in 1977, Romero contended with radicals, who distrusted his conservative sympathies. He protested—even unto Pope John Paul II—the government's torturous injustice to the poor; he pled with America to stop military aid. Assassinated while celebrating Mass in 1980, Romero was canonized by the Roman Catholic Church in 2018. His fellow martyrs include Maryknoll and Ursuline sisters, Jesuit priests, and lay missioners and staff.

Wednesday, March 25
The Annunciation of Our Lord Jesus Christ to the Blessed Virgin Mary

Mary's willingness to assent to God's call paved the path for God to accomplish the salvation of the world. March 25 is the day to commemorate the story of how God made known to a young Jew that she was to be the mother of his son. Her acceptance is the reason generations have called her "blesséd." The Annunciation serves as a significant theme in the arts of the East and the West, a theme running through countless sermons and poems. The General Council of Ephesus in 451 affirmed the term, coined by Cyril of Jerusalem, for the Blessed Virgin: Theotokos ("the God-bearer"). Mary serves as God's human agent within the mystery of the Incarnation.

Thursday, March 26
Harriet Monsell, Monastic, 1883

Monsell, recently widowed, was fired up by the work of the Community of Saint John Baptist, which sheltered and rehabbed women caught by poverty and/or human trafficking. She was installed as superior in 1852 and served until ill health forced retirement in1875. The Community focused on life contemplative and active with devotions plus worship with the Daily Office. The Community also tried to produce a Breviary in English. Mother Harriet prayed fervently for her sisterhood to reveal the mind of Christ to "ardent seekers." Mother Harriet's Community continues its prayerful ministry in the Episcopal Church and the Church of England.

Friday, March 27
Charles Henry Brent, Bishop, 1929

Brent served as a senior chaplain to the American Expeditionary Forces in World War I; at war's end, he accepted election as Bishop of Western New York. He had turned down three prior elections so he could remain in the Philippines. Elected Missionary Bishop, Brent had been posted there in 1901. He crusaded against the opium trade in the islands as well as Asia. For 20 years, Brent stood tall in the Episcopal Church, focusing on Christian unity. In 1927, he led the church in the movement that resulted in the first World Conference on Faith and Order, over which he presided. One of his prayers is included in the Book of Common Prayer.

Saturday, March 28
James Solomon Russell, Priest, 1935

Russell, born a slave in 1857 in Virginia, was the first student in what became Bishop Payne Divinity School, also in Virginia. In 1888, a year after his ordination in the Episcopal Church, he and his wife opened a school for academic and industrial education; religion was a mandatory subject. During his 52 years of ordained ministry, Russell worked tirelessly to encourage black candidates to stand for ordination in order to care for the growing number of black Episcopalians. Russell, elected the first African-American bishop in the Episcopal Church (1927), fought adamantly against the idea of subordinate racial bishops.

The Fifth Sunday in Lent

March 29, 2020

In baptism the Christian is freed from the tomb of sinfulness. Dry bones take on flesh and those who were dead are filled with the breath of God. The raising of Lazarus points ahead to the Resurrection.

Color   Violet / Lenten Array

Preface   Of Lent

Collect

Almighty God, you alone can bring into order the unruly wills and affections of sinners: Grant your people grace to love what you command and desire what you promise; that, among the swift and varied changes of the world, our hearts may surely there be fixed where true joys are to be found; through Jesus Christ our Lord, who lives and reigns with you and the Holy Spirit, one God, now and for ever. Amen.

Readings and Psalm

Ezekiel 37:1–14

In our first reading **the prophet has a vision of the bones of a dead and hopeless people being restored to new life in their homeland.** The Lord calls upon Ezekiel as son of man to prophecy that the people who have experienced exile and many hardships will live again. The Spirit of the Lord restores their spirit and breath, and they rise from death. Although this passage can be understood to anticipate the hope of individual resurrection, Israel did not yet have this belief.

Psalm 130

The psalmist calls to the merciful Lord and waits upon God for forgiveness and redemption.

Romans 8:6–11

In this lesson **Paul draws a contrast between minds dominated by fleshly and worldly things and those in whom Christ lives and are set on the Spirit.** The person at enmity with God is incapable of fulfilling the intention of the law, but one in whom Christ dwells is animated by the Spirit of God, and that Spirit, through which God raised Jesus from the dead, also gives to believers true life in our mortal bodies.

John 11:1–45

The gospel is **the story of Jesus' raising of Lazarus from the dead.** This is the last and greatest of Jesus' signs, and it points beyond itself to the hope of a new life after death for all. Only slowly do Jesus' friends begin to understand what he is saying to them and the deeper meaning of their own words. Soon the one who has raised Lazarus will himself be put to death, and then become the way of resurrection to eternal life.

Prayers of the People

Confident that with our hearts set on the glorious act of redemption revealed by God's beloved One, we receive the gift of new life, we offer our prayers and respond, "Kyrie eleison."

That the arms of Christ will reach into our spiritual tombs, releasing us from the fires of sin and division, of death and despair, and set our eyes upon the eighth day of our inheritance; let us pray.

Kyrie eleison.

That the breath of God may rush into the hearts of the faithful, filling them with respect for the wisdom of their forebears, and the courage to walk where their feet had never trod; let us pray.

Kyrie eleison.

For the unemployed and those who live with financial anxiety, for children born into poverty and those whose wealth does not buy contentment, for those in troubled marriages and the lonely who suffer in silence, that all may be held by the risen Christ, who broke through the walls of darkness; let us pray.

Kyrie eleison.

For the healing of our environment and for the vision to see ourselves as a global community, interdependent, economically woven, spiritually bonded, technologically linked, and physically united as a speck in the universe; let us pray.

Kyrie eleison.

In thanksgiving for our life together, our persistence in listening to the divine word, and our commitment to proclaim the life-giving love of God; let us pray.

Kyrie eleison.

That we who celebrate this Eucharistic Meal may receive the mercy of the Lamb, who shares our burdens, removes our sin, and restores us to the company of the faithful; let us pray.

Kyrie eleison.

For those who have died in the faith of Christ, that they may reside in paradise; let us pray.

Kyrie eleison.

In the certain hope of the resurrection from the dead, let us continue our prayers.

(Special intentions of the congregation, the diocese, and the Anglican Communion may be added here or before the formal intercessions.)

The Celebrant adds a concluding Collect.

Images in the Readings

Many medieval churches housed burials and contain even glass-cased skeletons, but most contemporary churches avoid picturing those bones that are left after the flesh has rotted away. Our culture avoids dealing directly and honestly with death: many people are even replacing the verb "died" with the term "passed," as if with everyone going off to heaven, there really is no death. In contrast, this Sunday presents us with the images of the **grave**, the **stink** of bodily decomposition, and the pile of **bones**. Furthermore, Paul's use of the term **flesh** as a metaphor for the misused human life intensifies this Sunday's honesty about human mortality. These texts represent the Bible's stark attention to the reality of death, both the "death" that is sin and the finality of death when our bodies die. For this Sunday, you might borrow a skeleton from a science classroom to hang prominently in the sanctuary. When we fully acknowledge the natural fact of death, we are ready to praise God's life as gift.

Ideas of the Day

+ Jesus weeps with his followers before miraculously resuscitating Lazarus. In his tears, we see that Jesus knows what it feels like to mourn the death of a loved one. Jesus knows that Lazarus's regained life does not fully erase four days of mourning beforehand. Even though we believe in resurrection, when a loved one dies, first we grieve. We feel the raw human emotion of sadness. In our grief we know, and draw comfort from knowing, that God is with us. Even though we believe God can transform the direst of situations, when our hope is lying in tatters, we need to know that God is with us.

+ In baptism the Christian is freed from the tomb of sinfulness. Dry bones take on flesh and those who are dead are filled with the breath of God. The raising of Lazarus points ahead to the resurrection.

+ Even physical death does not end our growing relationship with the Creator. This covenant is a far deeper one than was understood by Abram as he struggled in the land of Canaan. The relationship is eternal.

Making Connections

In today's story Jesus, for very specific reasons, delayed going to see to his friends in need. When he finally arrived, even though things seemed to be going as he had planned, he was troubled. Across our translations the Greek reads "greatly disturbed in spirit," "greatly agitated," or "deeply angered." And following the unwrapping of the body, Jesus had to go into hiding. Sacrificing oneself for others costs us not just in death, but in life. Doing what is required is not always easy. Even Jesus struggled with the pressures of caring for friends, the community, dealing with authorities, and ultimately dying. In this dark season of Lent, knowing the resurrection of Easter is on the horizon, we can trust that our struggles are shared, and we are not alone.

Engaging All Ages

Have you ever tried something new—like playing an instrument or ice skating? Were you perfect at it from the beginning? No! Part of learning something new is the willingness to be awkward and imperfect while you practice. Silence and stillness are two spiritual disciplines that anyone can practice—if they are willing to practice badly at first. It is hard to be still and silent—especially at the same time, but it can be done. This week see if you can practice stillness and silence in five-minute increments twice a day, each day. What did you notice? Did it get easier? How did you feel afterwards?

Hymns for the Day

The Hymnal 1982
From deepest woe I cry to thee 151
Out of the depths I call 666
Breathe on me, breath of God 508
Go forth for God; go to the world in peace 347
Put forth, O God, thy Spirit's might 521
Come down, O Love divine 516
Come, gracious Spirit, heavenly Dove 512
Come, Holy Spirit, heavenly Dove 510
Holy Spirit, ever living 511
O splendor of God's glory bright 5
Spirit divine, attend our prayers 509
Awake, O sleeper, rise from death 547
Eternal light, shine in my heart 465, 466
I am the bread of life (vs. 4, 5) 335
Lord, whose love through humble service 610

O bless the Lord, my soul 411
O for a thousand tongues to sing 493
O Love of God, how strong and true 455, 456
Thine arm, O Lord, in days of old 567
Thou art the Way, to thee alone 457
When Jesus wept 715

Lift Every Voice and Sing II
Let it breathe on me 116
Spirit of the living God 115
Come, Holy Ghost 112
Spirit of God, descend upon my heart 119
Take my hand, precious Lord 106

Wonder, Love, and Praise
Filled with the Spirit's power 741

Weekday Commemorations

Tuesday, March 31
John Donne, Priest and Poet, 1631
John Donne is one of the greatest of the English poets. Most famous for "Any man's death diminishes me, because I am involved in mankind. And therefore never send to know for whom the bell tolls: It tolls for thee." Born into a wealthy and pious Roman Catholic family in 1573, he was educated at Oxford and Cambridge and studied law at Lincoln's Inn. His sermons reflect the wide learning of the scholar, the passionate intensity of the poet, and the profound devotion of one struggling in his own life to relate the freedom and demands of the Gospel to the concerns of a common humanity, on every level, and in all its complexities.

Wednesday, April 1
Frederick Denison Maurice, Priest, 1872
Maurice's journey of faith did not describe a straight line: he dissented (refusing to agree to the Thirty-nine Articles of Religion) as often as he assented (working toward unity in the Church). Born in 1805, he studied civil law at Cambridge. He became an Anglican and was ordained in 1834. In 1838, he wrote *The Kingdom of Christ*, which delved into divisions within the Anglican Church and which served as a source for ecumenism within the wider church. He taught English literature and history at King's College, London, in the 1840s but was dismissed because he led the Christian Socialist Movement. In his lifetime, Maurice encouraged Anglicans' concerns with society's problems.

Lent

Thursday, April 2
James Lloyd Breck, Priest, 1876

Called "The Apostle of the Wilderness," Breck was born in Philadelphia (1818). He was influenced by William Augustus Muhlenberg, who inspired him as a teenager to become a missionary. In 1844, with three classmates from General Theological Seminary, Breck founded a religious community at Nashotah, Wisconsin. From that frontier, Episcopal missionaries were the first responders to settlers. The seminary flourished, but the concept of a religious "house" did not, so Breck removed to St. Paul, Minnesota, to work for the church. His St. Columba's Mission laid a foundation for the Chippewa nation to raise up its own Episcopal priests. Breck founded Seabury Divinity School before establishing other theological schools and five parishes in California.

Friday, April 3
Richard of Chichester, Bishop, 1253

Before being elected Bishop of Chichester in 1244, Richard studied at Oxford under teachers including Robert Grosseteste. Richard also studied law in Paris and Bologna. After earning a doctorate, Richard returned to Oxford as University Chancellor. Afterwards, Richard was appointed chancellor to and by his friend, the Archbishop of Canterbury, Edmund Rich, whose biography Richard penned. In 1243, Richard was ordained a priest, and, a year later, removed to England from Orleans, where he had been living in political exile, and became Bishop of Chichester. His bishopric was disturbed often by politics: King Henry III opposed his election, but finally—threatened by the pope—Henry acknowledged Richard as bishop in 1246. For eight years, he served his diocese before contacting a fever while campaigning for a new crusade.

Friday, April 3
Mary of Egypt, Hermit and Penitent, c.421

Most of what is known about Mary, a fifth-century hermit, comes from a seventh-century text by Sophronius of Jerusalem. He described Mary as an Alexandrian prostitute who went to Jerusalem to seduce pilgrims. She repented of her sins and became a solitary contemplative and ascetic in the desert beyond the Jordan River for 47 years. Many stories are told about Mary, including that her grave was dug by a lion, a symbol for Christ. Her life of repentance is commemorated by Orthodox churches during Lent. Goethe cast Mary as one of three saints who pray for the forgiveness of Faust.

Saturday, April 4
Martin Luther King, Jr., Pastor and Martyr, 1968

In December 1955, King led the Montgomery bus boycott after Rosa Parks was arrested for refusing to relinquish her seat to a white man. Born January 15, 1929, the son and grandson of Baptist preachers, King earned bachelor's, master's, and doctor's degrees. He articulated his righteous indignation over treatment of blacks and proved a prophet, heard by blacks and whites alike. He founded the Southern Christian Leadership Conference. His campaign for civil rights included empowering the poor and opposing the Vietnam War. After preaching at Washington Cathedral on March 31, 1968, he headed to Memphis to support sanitation workers' stand. On April 3, he declared to them that, one day, they would be "free at last." He was assassinated the next day.

Holy Week

Preparing for Holy Week

Theological Themes that Might Shape Liturgy, Catechesis, and Education

Holy Week as its name might suggest, is the holiest week in the Christian calendar. It begins on Palm Sunday (or the Sunday of the Passion) and concludes on the Eve of Easter. It is a week of high drama that invites the faithful to walk with Jesus through the final moments of his pre-Resurrected life in ways that create new containers of meaning for our own lives.

While there are liturgies that might be observed through Holy Week, there are three proper liturgies which should be observed by every faith community (even if it means partnering with another faith community to do so). These liturgies, when observed according to the rubrics of the Book of Common Prayer highlight important, often uncomfortable truths of the Christian faith. The proper liturgies comprise the Triduum—Maundy Thursday, Good Friday, and the Easter Vigil.

It can be incredibly tempting to either distill the events of this week into carefully crafted equations that somehow sort out our salvation or to ignore the disturbing bits altogether. Either extreme would be an incredible miscalculation and a missed opportunity. The events of Holy Week and how God uses these events to bring out the salvation of humanity and the restoration of Creation are concepts with which the biblical witness is deeply interested in engaging without having to settle on anything neat and polished. Holy Week doesn't explain salvation so much as it allows us to experience it by walking it.

The Incarnation, the mystery we celebrated in Christmas, is brought into starker focus during Holy Week. Jesus' ministry of healing, gathering, reconciliation, and social disruption is seemingly brought to a close by the executionary power of an insecure empire. The response of the temporally powerful to the divine power of Christ was to attempt to kill it by putting Jesus Christ to death. We walk through these moments, bringing into focus the ways we as individuals and as a society continue to reject the divine power of Christ which seeks to reshape us and our world.

While these liturgies can be hard to engage, it is appropriate for all generations to experience them in their fullness. The truths we experience as we walk with Jesus through The Triumphal Entry, the scene in the Temple, the Upper Room, the Garden of Gethsemane, and then his final steps to Calvary are important to the development of a robust faith.

Liturgical Possibilities

Rites

As we explore the rites of this week, it should be noted that it would be appropriate to hold some sort of liturgy or even to celebrate the Eucharist on the Monday, Tuesday, and Wednesday of Holy Week while observing the other highlights of the week Palm Sunday, Maundy Thursday, Good Friday, and the Easter Vigil.

The week begins on Palm Sunday which is itself a long, dramatic liturgy. Whereas some faith communities have chosen to iron out the wrinkles of this service (choosing to read the Passion Gospel at the end of the service), this service is meant to be jarring. The jubilant "Hosannas" of the Liturgy of the Palms is almost immediately followed by the roughness of the "Crucify Him" in the Gospel. Let it be.

Maundy Thursday should be observed using the proper liturgy in the prayer book, which is surprisingly light on "must dos." This presents the planner with options as to how to celebrate this night. There is something to be said about the standard, liturgical celebration of the evening, which aligns with the typical Sunday celebration of the Eucharist, but with options to observe foot washing and the ritual

Holy Week

stripping of the altar as well as the observance an an Agape Feast beforehand, why not avail oneself to all of these options to make this service a distinct way of marking this moment in the week? Some congregations may choose to observe the Maundy Thursday Vigil, which puts us in the shoes of the disciples who are asked by Jesus to "stay awake" while he goes away to pray.

The Good Friday liturgy makes a moment of great importance for the Christian witness—the death of Christ. Everything about this service is a paradox from the observance of the Veneration of the Cross (and instrument of death that becomes a tool and symbol of life) to the Solemn Collects, which lovingly pray for the world even as the world responded to Love (and continues to respond to love) with death.

The Holy Saturday liturgy is extremely brief and will likely not draw a huge crowd, but its emphasis on uncertainty, waiting, and expectation continue to pick up on themes that were explored during Advent and continue to resonate with the human experience—the eager longing for the revelation of the fullness of the Christ.

The Easter Vigil marks the culmination of the Triduum and Holy Week. It is a resounding response to the human cruelty exposed on Good Friday— neither death nor the tomb have any power over Christ, and the love of God cannot be extinguished even by the most cruel machinations of humanity. As it retells the story of salvation, each community has a wealth of options regarding how this important liturgy is observed.

Space

Holy Week intentionally takes us on a journey, so it would be appropriate to use space to indicate this. For example, beginning the Palm Sunday liturgy in one spot for the Liturgy of the Palms and then processing to another for the Liturgy of the Word would be something to consider. Additionally, given that the liturgies through the week are likely not going to be attended by the normal Sunday (or certainly not the Easter Sunday) crowds, what might it mean to engage space in a more dynamic way? Innovation aside, there are a lot of space-related questions to consider for Holy Week, and proper planning and rehearsal are key to ensure sufficient ritual effect without becoming a distraction.

Other Rituals and Resources

In addition to the Proper Liturgies and the celebration of the Holy Eucharist, a faith community might decide to observe a communal commemoration of the Stations of the Cross or Tenebrae service during the course of the week. There are resources in the *Book of Occasional Services* for these and other services.

Through the Eyes of a Child

Talking about death and grief with children is critical to their faith; however, even though it is Holy Week and not yet Easter, it is necessary to give the proclamation, "Christ has died, and Christ has risen from the dead." Children will be thinking bunny rabbits, Easter eggs and baskets, and time home from school; this is the time to instill in them through prayer and practice the importance of Holy Week in their faith. For example, you might want to do a "foot washing" at home after sharing the story of Jesus and the last supper. You might encourage the children to participate in a "Good Friday" service. Talk about how sad the disciples and Mary the Mother of Jesus must have been to see Jesus die. Attend an Easter Vigil service and remind them of the story of our salvation, from Old Testament times to the present. The children will want to act out the Good Friday/Easter story in much the same way they enjoy the Christmas story.

Through the Eyes of Youth

The Church is called to proclaim that before his death Christ invited us to remember how much God loves us, so much so that bread and wine mysteriously become what we share at Eucharist when we eat and drink of his flesh and blood, and that through his death new life would be offered for all humanity.

♦ We fear that we will lose our awareness of a connection with God, or even that we have "lost" God or that our connection with him is invalid. We must be willing to let go of former experiences, no matter how powerful, and continually redefine what it means to be a follower of God at every stage, to be in new life.

♦ It is not easy to speak about God with friends; many of them see the Church as a reality that judges youth, that opposes their desire for happiness and love. It is a constant Good Friday struggle.

Holy Week is the time to stay current and connected to the youth. Consider with the youth ways in which twenty-first century discipleship calls us to go to the cross. What are the crosses youth will need to bear in the twenty-first century? Practice noticing all kinds of people and responding to them as Christ is in them.

Through the Eyes of Daily Life

During Holy Week some communities gather each day to meditate on Jesus' final days before his death on the cross. Begin the journey with Jesus, following his path to Jerusalem through prayer with others or in solitude. At the heart of the Maundy Thursday liturgy is Jesus' commandment to love one another. As Jesus washed the feet of his disciples, we are called to follow his example as we humbly care for one another, especially the poor and unloved. At the Lord's table, we remember Jesus' sacrifice of his life, even as we are called to offer ourselves in love for the life of the world. Plant the cross on your heart, so that in its power and love you can continue to be Christ's representative in the world at work, school, and play.

Through the Eyes of Those Outside of the Church

If there were any season for the Church to play up its distinctiveness, Holy Week is one of them. Our faith is not one that is incapable of handling the hard parts of life. Not only can our faith hold them with care, but Christianity teaches us to interpret our own experiences through the saving lens of Jesus Christ. Holy Week is simply a weird week and as such presents opportunities for the Church to celebrate the love of Christ in ways that invite others to inquire more deeply about the message of the Gospel.

Through the Eyes of the Global Community

Two collects heard during Holy Week set the focus for social justice:

+ Palm Sunday: Mercifully grant that we may walk in the way of his suffering (BCP 272).
+ Monday in Holy Week: Almighty God, whose most dear Son went not up to joy but first he suffered pain, and entered not into glory before he was crucified: Mercifully grant that we, walking in the way of the cross, may find it none other than the way of life and peace (BCP 220).

These collects remind us that we are called:

+ To identify with the suffering peoples of the nation and the world and not to remain aloof;
+ To have compassion for "all sorts and conditions" of people (BCP 814).

Holy Week

Holy Week Blessing[1]

The following blessing may be used by a bishop or priest whenever a blessing is appropriate from Palm Sunday through Maundy Thursday.

Almighty God, we pray you graciously to behold this your family, for whom our Lord Jesus Christ was willing to be betrayed, and given into the hands of sinners, and to suffer death upon the cross, who lives and reigns for ever and ever. *Amen.*

Tenebrae[2]

The name Tenebrae (the Latin word for "darkness" or "shadows") has for centuries been applied to the ancient monastic night and early morning services (Matins and Lauds) of the last three days of Holy Week, which in medieval times came to be celebrated on the preceding evening.

Apart from the chant of the Lamentations (in which each verse is introduced by a letter of the Hebrew alphabet), the most conspicuous feature of the service is the gradual extinguishing of candles and other lights in the church until only a single candle, considered a symbol of our Lord, remains. Toward the end of the service this candle is hidden, typifying the apparent victory of the forces of evil. At the very end, a loud noise is made, symbolizing the earthquake at the time of the resurrection (Matthew 28:2), the hidden candle is restored to its place, and by its light all depart in silence.

This service is most appropriate for Wednesday of Holy Week.

Maundy Thursday

Thursday, April 9

Anointing One Another

In the Old Testament, anointing commonly signified a transmission of power and blessing. In the New Testament, it came to be a sign of love, of identity as a Christian, and of the reception of the gifts of the Holy Spirit. These flowed from the Church's understanding of Jesus as the "Messiah" or "Christ," which means "the anointed one." This ritual may take place on Maundy Thursday or any time during Holy Week.

Directions: following the reading, pass a small bowl with perfumed oil around, with each person drawing the sign of the cross on the palm of the person next to them. Conclude with the litany, divided between those gathered (Group A and Group B).

While he was at Bethany in the house of Simon the leper, as he sat at the table, a woman came with an alabaster jar of very costly ointment of nard, and she broke open the jar and poured the ointment on his head. But some were there who said to one another in anger, "Why was the ointment wasted in this way? For this ointment could have been sold for more than three hundred denarii, and the money given to the poor." And they scolded her. But Jesus said, "Let her alone; why do you trouble her? She has performed a good service for me. For you always have the poor with you, and you can show kindness to them whenever you wish; but you will not always have me. She has done what she could; she has anointed my body beforehand for its burial. Truly I tell you, wherever the good news is proclaimed in the whole world, what she has done will be told in remembrance of her." (Mark 14:3–9)

Leader: We will remember the soothing,

And not forget the jarring.

---

1 *The Book of Occasional Services 2003* (New York: Church Publishing, 2004), 26.

2 The actual service of Tenebrae can be found in *The Book of Occasional Services 2003*, 75–92.

Leader: We will remember the sweetness,

> **And not forget the sour.**

Leader: We will remember the jagged desperateness of Judas,

> **And own it; it is our story too.**

Leader: We will remember

> Group A: **The passion of love,**
>
> Group B: **The smell of perfume,**
>
> Group A: **The pain of rejection,**
>
> Group B: **The stench of blood money.**

Leader: And help us on the journey, to help us hold the tensions, to help us face both the delight and the difficulty,

> **We will say "Yes" to God's generosity in creation, we will say "Yes" to God's judgment poured out on humankind, we will say "Yes" to God's justice in Jesus.**

Good Friday

Friday, April 10

The Stations of the Cross for Children[3]

This is a script for a meditation for children, either gathered on the floor, or walking from station to station. Any of the following props may be used and passed around so that children can feel, smell, and taste the story.

Needed are: charoset (chopped apples, honey, and cinnamon) parsley, and salt water (Seder foods); a chalice and wine, flat bread, a bowl with oiled water; rough jute rope, rich purple fabric; a crown of thorns; a large bowl with water for Pilate; nails; Veronika's veil (gauzy fabric with a face vaguely chalked on it); a sponge with vinegar; cotton balls with fragrant oil; linen.

If you wanted to celebrate the beginning of our nation, where would you go to do it? *(Elicit answers: Boston, perhaps, or Philadelphia, or Washington DC.)*

And how would you celebrate? *(Probably with parades, fireworks, food for sure!)*

In Jesus' time, where do you think the Jewish people went to celebrate their liberation? *(To the city of Jerusalem).*

And do you know the name of the holiday that still marks their freedom? *(It is called Passover.)*

When Jesus lived, all the people would go up to Jerusalem for Passover. There they sang and danced and prayed and ate! At the Seder meal, they would tell their children the story of how God had saved them from slavery in Egypt.

"Why is this night different from all other nights?" the children would ask.
"On this night, God opened the Red Sea waters and the Jewish people passed through the sea on dry ground, but the Egyptians who chased them drowned in the sea!"

"Why do we eat charoset?" the children would ask.
"Because of the mortar for the bricks our mothers and fathers had to make in their hard labor in Egypt!"

"Why do we eat bitter herbs dipped in salt?" the children would ask.
"Because of the bitterness and tears of our slavery!"

"Why do we eat unleavened bread?" the children would ask.
"Because there was no time to wait for the bread to rise the night we escaped from Egypt!"

Every spring, from the time Jesus was a boy, the Jewish people have gathered at Passover meals to tell that same story with the children. They say, "Next year, may we celebrate this meal in Israel, our home!"

They sing: **"Da da ye nu, da da ye nu, da da ye nu, dayenu, dayenu!"**[4]

> (It would have been enough for us!)
> If God had split the sea for us, Dayenu!
> If God had sustained us in the wilderness for forty years, Dayenu!
> If God had brought us before Mount Sinai, Dayenu!
> If God had given us the Torah, Dayenu!
> If God had led us to the land of Israel, Dayenu!

In Jesus' time, the people waited for a king to come and free them from the Romans who ruled over them in their own homeland. This king would come at Passover, entering the holy city riding on a colt. He would be like a god, able to heal blindness, and other miracles. So, when Jesus came onto Jerusalem on a colt, many thought he was the Messiah, and they made a huge parade, and shouted "Hosanna! Hosanna!" They made a path with their palms and their clothes.

3　Susan K. Bock. *Liturgy for the Whole Church: Multigenerational Resources for Worship* (New York: Church Publishing, 2008), 93–94.

4　Music for this hymn can be found at **www.chabad.org/multimedia/media_cdo/aid/255530/ jewish/Dayenu.htm**

The children sang the loudest, and when people tried to quiet them, Jesus said, "If you silence them, the stones will start to sing!"

The people thought that Jesus would lead them into a great war, a war they could win, and that, after all these years they would be free at last! But there was no war, and the people became sad, scared, and angry. The same people who had welcomed him with such joy and love began to want to kill Jesus.

Jesus knew what was happening. He knew the people wanted him dead. He was sad, scared, and angry, too, because he had thought things would surely turn out differently than this. But he trusted God and listened to God every minute so that he would know what to do next.

Jesus gathered his friends in a small room and they shared their last meal together. As always, he blessed the bread and the wine, but this time he said something different. He said, "From now on, when you eat or drink like this, know I am with you. Remember how I loved you, and how I died on this night."

After supper, Jesus got up from the table and washed his friends' feet, to show them how they ought to serve each other.

Here, the children may share bread and wine, and pass the bowl of oiled water around to smell and feel. You may want to do a real foot washing while a simple song is sung.

One of Jesus' closest friends, Judas, was so angry that he left and told the police where to find Jesus so they could arrest him. The police paid Judas 30 pieces of silver for this information. Later, when Judas looked at his money and counted it, he realized that no amount of money is worth your love and loyalty.

In the garden of Gethsemane, Jesus was praying, and Roman soldiers came to arrest him. They tied his hands together, like a criminal, though Jesus had never used his hands to hit or hurt anyone but only to heal and soothe. The soldiers dressed him in a fancy purple robe and a crown that they made of thorns.

These items may be passed around.

They blindfolded him, and spat at him, and beat him, and shouted, "Some king you are! If you're a prophet, then tell us who just hit you!"

They took him to Pilate, who really wanted to know the truth about things. He said to Jesus, "Who are you?" Jesus was silent. Jesus knew that what was happening to him was not fair, and that, if he spoke, he might be able to save himself. But sometimes we need to be silent, and he knew this was one of those times.

Pilate washed his hands in a bowl of water in front of all the people as a sign that he would not be guilty for whatever might happen to Jesus.

Jesus was led to a hill. He was made to carry his own cross. He was so tired and hungry and sad that he had trouble carrying it. Many people gathered to watch the spectacle. Some made fun of him, some wept, and some helped him, like Veronika.

The legend of Veronika is that the image of Jesus' face remained on her veil when, breaking with tradition and safety, she ran to him, removed her veil, and wiped his face.

Simon helped him carry his cross.

They nailed him to a cross, and his life slipped slowly away from him. He wondered why this was happening to him and where was his God now that he needed God more than ever. He became very thirsty, and some soldiers held up a vinegar-soaked sponge for him to suck on.

The sponge with vinegar may be passed around.

Just before he died, Jesus gathered up his last little bit of strength and shouted to God in the saddest, loudest cry anyone ever heard. And he died.

He was taken down from the cross and wrapped in white linen. Then he was put in a small cave for a tomb, and a huge stone was rolled in front of it. The next day, some women came with oil and spices to anoint Jesus' body.

The oil-soaked cotton and piece of linen may be passed around.

Only, when they got there, they found that the body was gone! They were angry and confused and ran to tell Peter and the others what they had discovered. This is a Holy Week story, whose end comes at Easter. I wonder how the story will turn out.

The Sunday of the Passion: Palm Sunday

April 5, 2020

We enter into Jesus' death through baptism so that "just as Christ was raised from the dead by the glory of the Father, so we too might walk in newness of life." (Romans 6:4b)

Color   Red / Oxblood

Preface   Of Holy Week

Collect

Almighty and everliving God, in your tender love for the human race you sent your Son our Savior Jesus Christ to take upon him our nature, and to suffer death upon the cross, giving us the example of his great humility: Mercifully grant that we may walk in the way of his suffering, and also share in his resurrection; through Jesus Christ our Lord, who lives and reigns with you and the Holy Spirit, one God, for ever and ever. Amen.

Readings and Psalm

The Liturgy of the Palms

Psalm 118:1–2, 19–29
A festival hymn sung in procession in praise of the Lord's salvation.

Matthew 21:1–11
In this gospel lesson **Jesus comes to the holy city of Jerusalem and is hailed as the promised Son of David.** He has a young donkey brought to him, and, as did the kings of old in royal celebrations, Jesus rides on it, while the crowds spread their garments and branches in the way and shout in his honor. The evangelist perceives this as a fulfillment of the prophet Zechariah's words concerning the coming king. Here is both great drama and irony as Jesus enters the city he would save, while the people who will soon call for his blood spread the rumor that the prophet from Galilee has arrived.

The Liturgy of the Passion

Isaiah 50:4–9a
Our reading tells of **the servant who speaks for the Lord and suffers persecution, but still trusts in God's help and vindication.** This is the third of the "servant songs" that come from a period late in Israel's exile. The servant might be thought to be the faithful of Israel, the prophet himself, or another historical or idealized figure. The people are weary and tired of the Lord's calling, but the servant steadfastly continues. Christians have long perceived in these words a foretelling of Jesus' mission.

Psalm 31:9–16
A psalm of trust by one who looks to the Lord for mercy and protection.

Philippians 2:5–11
From one of the earliest Christian hymns we hear **how Christ Jesus accepted the condition of a servant, was obedient even to the point of death, and was then given the name above every name.** It is possible that this poem was adapted by Paul or another disciple from the hopes for a savior of a people who did not yet know Jesus. He has fulfilled humanity's dream of one who will share fully in the mortal condition before his exaltation. To him every knee shall bow and every tongue confess the great name of the Lord now known in person, Jesus.

Matthew 26:14–27:66

Our gospel reading is **the story of Jesus' last supper with his disciples, his betrayal in the Garden of Gethsemane, and then his arrest and trials before the Jewish council and Pilate, followed by his final sufferings and death.**

or

Matthew 27:11–54

Our gospel is **the story of Jesus' trial before Pilate, his final sufferings and death.**

Prayers of the People

Jesus stretched out his arms of love and embraced human suffering, drawing the peoples of the world into his wounded heart, that they might share in his resurrection. With great devotion and gratitude we lift our voices in prayer, responding, "Christ, have mercy."

For Christians throughout the world who are being imprisoned and persecuted for their belief in Christ, that faith may be their shield, courage a mantle upon their shoulders, and love a lantern to their footsteps; Lord, have mercy.

Christ, have mercy.

That we may pass over from weapons of war to the armaments of peace: food, education, meaningful work, security, water, and health care; Lord, have mercy.

Christ, have mercy.

For N., Archbishop of Canterbury; N., our Presiding Bishop; N., Bishop of our diocese; and N., our priest, [N., our deacon] that through their words and presence we may be guided faithfully through our Holy Week pilgrimage; Lord, have mercy.

Christ, have mercy.

That we may confess the sovereignty of Christ, sharing his unique expression of love, and inviting the un-churched to join in the Paschal Feast; Lord, have mercy.

Christ, have mercy.

That we may prepare ourselves to welcome into the community of faith those who will be baptized this Easter season, and to support and affirm those who will be confirmed, received, or who will reaffirm their faith; Lord, have mercy.

Christ, have mercy.

For those who have departed this life in the fellowship of Jesus and his apostles, that they may reside in his eternal presence; Lord, have mercy.

Christ, have mercy.

Lord, have mercy upon us who humbly put our trust in you, as we continue our prayers and supplications. *(Special intentions of the congregation, the diocese, and the Anglican Communion may be added here or before the formal intercessions.)*

The Celebrant adds a concluding Collect.

Images in the Readings

Two opposite images of Christ come in the readings. First, Christ is **king.** In Matthew's passion narrative, he is acclaimed as the Son of David; he is the apocalyptic Son of Man, who will judge the world at the end of time; he is accused of falsely presenting himself as Messiah, yet affirmed by believers as the Christ; he is mocked as the "king of the Jews"; and ironically, even when dead, his body is attended by Roman guards. Much in American culture resists "king" as a positive image. Yet the hope that someone has ultimate power, absolute justice, and endless mercy persists in human imagination.

In an image that derives from the first and second readings. Christ is **servant.** God will vindicate the servant, even though he is now suffering. We are to adopt the mind of Christ Jesus, who became a servant, indeed a slave, for us. Once again, much in American culture resists "servant" as a positive image. Martin Luther's essay "The Freedom of the Christian" can help us here: through our baptism, we are both free, slaves to none, and simultaneously servants to all.

Ideas of the Day

- St. Peter and St. Paul's Church in Godalming, Surrey owned a donkey, Rusty. Rusty was kept a few miles from the church. Rusty was expected to appear at the church three times a year: for the Christmas Pageant, the Beating of the Bounds, and the Palm Sunday procession. Rusty was so stubborn and ornery that his keeper was only able to coax him to the church for some of his scheduled appearances. When he did arrive, he was stolid and slow. Imagine Jesus our savior upon such an animal. Was there laughter among the hosannas? Curiosity with the waving of the palms?

- Holy Week is a seven-act drama that begins on Palm Sunday and ends with Easter Eve. During this week we dramatize the last week of Jesus' life, and in that story-sharing we begin to experience Christ leading us through our own darkness, death, and guilt to a new understanding of forgiveness and life of resurrection. Today the drama begins with a triumphant entry of pageantry and concludes with the words, "Crucify him!" We are carried along with the crowd in celebration as well as condemnation.

Making Connections

Most often, when someone we know—or know of—dies, we start telling their story differently. A life that might have been described by events, travels, relationships, or cultural engagements has a death epilogue attached, which becomes the lead. It can come across as "hindsight" or "back-filling"—to go in and add details that seemed to be of little significance at the time. A conversation with a waiter the week before. A sweater ordered online that arrives the week after. A letter unmailed, on the counter. We look for clues, for reasons. Words and moments to capture as a way to redeem, or at least to better understand, the death. Notice the discrepancies, including the absence of some details, of the Passion narratives across our Gospels. Consider how your final meals, words, even court appearances and death itself, might impact your legacy and the proclamation of your faith in the conversations that follow.

Engaging All Ages

Today is a day of rejoicing—it is the day before things take a dark turn and Jesus is betrayed and killed—it is a day filled with hope and celebration! Take your palm and lay it flat on a piece of paper, then trace around your hand with a pencil or pen. Next, write in each finger a short prayer or word of praise to Jesus. Do this as many times as you like. Cut them out and string them together like party decorations, then hang them somewhere they can be seen each and every morning—a reminder that though hard things happen, resurrection *will* come.

Hymns for the Day

The Hymnal 1982
Palm Sunday Anthems 153
All glory, laud, and honor 154, 155
Ride on! ride on in majesty 156
Alone, thou goest forth, O Lord 164
Hail, thou once despised Jesus! (vs. 1–2) 495
To mock your reign, O dearest Lord 170
Cross of Jesus, cross of sorrow 160
Morning glory, starlit sky (vs. 4–6) 585
The flaming banners of our King 161
The royal banners forward go 162
What wondrous love is this 439
Ah, holy Jesus, how hast thou offended 158
And now, O Father, mindful of the love (vs. 1–2) 337
Let thy Blood in mercy poured 313
My song is love unknown 458
Nature with open volume stands 434
O sacred head, sore wounded 168, 169
When I survey the wondrous cross 474

Lift Every Voice and Sing II
Ride on, King Jesus 97
Simon of Cyrene 49
O sacred head, sore wounded 36

Wonder, Love, and Praise
Mantos y palmas esparciendo /
    Filled with excitement 728
O sacred head, sore wounded 735

Monday in Holy Week

April 6, 2020

We pray that we may find the way of the Cross to be the way of life and peace.

Color   Red / Oxblood

Preface   Of Holy Week

Collect

Almighty God, whose most dear Son went not up to joy but first he suffered pain, and entered not into glory before he was crucified: Mercifully grant that we, walking in the way of the cross, may find it none other that the way of life and peace; through Jesus Christ your Son our Lord, who lives and reigns with you and the Holy Spirit, one God, for ever and ever. Amen.

Readings and Psalm

Isaiah 42:1–9

In our reading from the Hebrew scriptures we hear of **the mission of the Lord's servant, the one whom God has chosen to bring forth justice and salvation.** This is the first of the "servant songs" that form a portion of the Book of Isaiah written at the time when the exile in Babylon was ending and the city of Jerusalem had begun to be restored. The servant is sometimes thought to be an historical individual, or is understood as an idealization of Israel. Christians see in the servant a prefigurement of the ministry of Jesus, who will become a light to the nations of the world.

Psalm 36:5–11

The psalmist celebrates the expansive love of God expressed in faithfulness and justice. God is a river of delight in whose light we see light.

Hebrews 9:11–15

Christ has inaugurated a new covenant, accomplishing all that was anticipated by the rites and rituals of the first covenant, that is, redemption from sin and transgression and the purification of conscience for the right worship of the living God.

John 12:1–11

Six days before the Passover, Jesus gathers with his friends in Bethany at the home of Lazarus, whom he had raised from the dead. **Mary, the sister of Martha and Lazarus, anoints Jesus' feet with costly perfume,** wiping his feet with her hair. This extravagant devotion is criticized by Judas Iscariot, but Jesus defends the action in ways that seem to prefigure his fast approaching death.

Ideas of the Day

- The smell of Grandma's cookies, of your beloved's perfume, or lilacs on the first spring day—all of us have scents that bring back a flood of memories and emotions. Mary fills her home with the scent of the perfume with which she anointed Jesus' feet. The smell of oil used to anoint a corpse, not a king, indicates that Mary, as a close follower of Jesus, understands what is next to come. How did that sweet scent linger after the death of Jesus? What scents remind of our sacred stories?

- In the Old Testament, anointing commonly signified a transmittal of power and blessing. In the New Testament, it came to be a sign of love, of identity as a Christian, and of the reception of the Holy Spirit. These flowed from the Church's understanding of Jesus as the "Messiah" or "Christ," which means "the anointed one."

Making Connections

In a story whose original version is likely beyond recovery, a woman interrupts a gathering, anoints either Jesus' head or feet, and is declared a sinner and/or redeemed for all time through the telling of this story. For those who know the ending (spoiler alert), it also hints that if we don't anoint Jesus now, we won't get to, because he will rise from the tomb before we have a chance. In one version the most basic hospitality is withheld from Jesus: water for his feet, a kiss of greeting, and anointing. We don't know why. We might, if we are being honest, recall many occasions when we arrived to church for a meeting, study, or worship—longing to have the filth of our day washed away, a loving greeting, and an anointed benediction before being thrown back to the proverbial wolves, but went away without. And also we might not have offered those to others. Why is that?

Engaging All Ages

"All people may take refuge in the shadow of your wings" (Psalm 36:7). Not every hen wants to raise baby chickens. A hen has to decide that she wants to turn "broody" and sit on her eggs for twenty-one days until they hatch. Once the baby chick hatches, the momma hen becomes incredibly protective, often tucking the babies under her wings so that they cannot be seen by predators or curious humans. But momma hens do not just sit on their own eggs; they will sit and raise whoever's eggs are in the nest when they go broody. Who has God sent to go "broody" over you in your life? Who has been a refuge for you?

Hymns for the Day

The Hymnal 1982
We sing the praise of him who died 471
Ancient of Days, who sittest throned in glory 363
Jesus shall reign where'er the sun 544
Thy strong word did cleave the darkness 381
Weary of all trumpeting 572
Come, thou fount of every blessing 686
Cross of Jesus, cross of sorrow 160
Draw nigh and take the Body of the Lord 327, 328
Glory be to Jesus 479
Holy Father, great Creator 368
Let thy Blood in mercy poured 313
God himself is with us 475
Jesus, all my gladness 701
Jesus, the very thought of thee 642
Just as I am, without one plea 693
There's a wideness in God's mercy 469, 470

Lift Every Voice and Sing II
Come, thou fount of every blessing 111
Just as I am 137

Wonder, Love, and Praise

Holy Week

Tuesday in Holy Week

April 7, 2020

Through God, Jesus' shameful death on the Cross has become the means of life for us.

Color Red / Oxblood

Preface Of Holy Week

Collect

O God, by the passion of your blessed Son you made an instrument of shameful death to be for us the means of life: Grant us so to glory in the cross of Christ, that we may gladly suffer shame and loss for the sake of your Son our Savior Jesus Christ; who lives and reigns with you and the Holy Spirit, one God, for ever and ever. Amen.

Readings and Psalm

Isaiah 49:1–7

The servant of the Lord reflects movingly on his mission—its sorrows and frustrations—and God's high calling and promise to be with him. The servant is sometimes thought to be an historical individual, or is understood as an idealization of Israel. This song was probably composed as the exiles from Jerusalem were preparing to return to their devastated city. Despite appearances, the Lord will make this servant a light to the nations.

Psalm 71:1–14

The psalmist prays that God will continue to be his refuge and stronghold.

1 Corinthians 1:18–31

In this lesson **Paul directs the attention of the Corinthians to God's way of using what is weak and lowly—even what the world regards as foolish—to accomplish the divine purposes.** Paul emphasizes this understanding because a number of these new Christians had come to think of themselves as especially gifted, powerful, and wise. As the cross has shown, however, God's ideas about what is wise and noble are often quite different from ours. Our only boast can be in the Lord.

John 12:20–36

In this gospel passage **Jesus presents teaching concerning the meaning of his death. After his prayer to God a voice from heaven is heard.** Greeks wish to see Jesus, but he will not draw all others to himself until after he has died and risen. Then, like a seed which falls into the earth, he will bear much fruit. Now is the hour for the Son of Man to be glorified—glorified both by his willingness to be lifted up on the cross to die for others, and afterward to be lifted up to heaven. Disciples must learn to follow Jesus in his way—not walking in darkness but in the light.

Ideas of the Day

- We have many tools to help us see clearly: glasses, booster seats, windshield wipers, binoculars. "We want to see Jesus." This request in the gospel is our own urgent and lifelong request as followers of Jesus. What are we holding onto that is preventing us from seeing Jesus: what expectations, prejudice, traditions, assumptions, firmly held beliefs? If we let them go, we are not always going to like what we see. We are going to be uncomfortable. We are going to be able to see Jesus at work in the world in ways we never expected. How can we lay our impediments at the cross this Lent in order that we can see Jesus' resurrection in our life this Easter?

- Jesus talks about the importance of believing in his words. Many people refuse to believe in Jesus despite the many signs they have witnessed. What signs do we have presented before us today that God calls us to respond to but we might ignore or refuse to acknowledge our responsibility for?

Making Connections

The rhizotron is a larger lab version of the experiments done in primary schools where you watch a seed transform into roots and a plant behind glass. In the rhizotron scientists are able to see enormous cuts of agriculture in an outdoor setting, including the interaction with other plants and animals. The analogy of the Christian life as a seed finds its way across our texts and stories. In the season of Lent we talk about denying ourselves of pleasures or habits, a sacrifice that is supposed to make room for a Lenten discipline or practice. But the gospel calls for death, not discomfort. The seed swells and bursts, its contents completely consumed by new life, and it is gone. Roots sink, life springs up. Are we really called to repeat this death daily, and what is the "great harvest" that follows? "After Jesus had said this, he departed and hid from them." No wonder.

Engaging All Ages

Are you preparing for Easter Sunday? What are you doing to get ready? Do you have new clothes? Are you decorating your house or preparing for a big meal? During the first Holy Week Jesus and his friends were also preparing for a big meal—the Passover supper. During this feast, stories are shared of how God has been faithful to the Jewish people even in desperate situations. As you prepare for Easter, make a list of all the times God has been faithful to you or your family—add to it all week. Read the list aloud during your Easter meal.

Hymns for the Day

The Hymnal 1982

My song is love unknown (vs. 1–2, 7) 458
Christ, whose glory fills the skies 6, 7
God of mercy, God of grace 538
How wondrous and great thy works,
    God of praise! 532, 533
Beneath the cross of Jesus 498
Cross of Jesus, cross of sorrow 160
In the cross of Christ I glory 441, 442
Nature with open volume stands 434
We sing the praise of him who died 471
When I survey the wondrous cross 474
I heard the voice of Jesus say 692
I want to walk as a child of the Light 490
O Jesus, I have promised 655
The great Creator of the worlds 489
When Christ was lifted from the earth 603, 604

Lift Every Voice and Sing II

Near the cross 29
The old rugged cross 38

Wonder, Love, and Praise

Holy Week

Wednesday in Holy Week

April 8, 2020

We ask God for the grace to accept our present sufferings joyfully, secure in the glory that will be revealed.

Color   Red / Oxblood

Preface   Of Holy Week

Collect

Lord God, whose blessed Son our Savior gave his body to be whipped and his face to be spit upon: Give us grace to accept joyfully the sufferings of the present time, confident of the glory that shall be revealed; through Jesus Christ your Son our Lord, who lives and reigns with you and the Holy Spirit, one God, for ever and ever. Amen.

Readings and Psalm

Isaiah 50:4–9a

Our first reading tells of **the servant who speaks for the Lord and suffers persecution, but still trusts in God's help and vindication.** This is the third of the "servant songs" that come from a period late in Israel's exile. The servant might be thought to be the faithful of Israel, the prophet himself, or another historical or idealized figure. The people are weary and tired of the Lord's calling, but the servant steadfastly continues. Christians have long perceived in these words a foretelling of Jesus' mission.

Psalm 70

A prayer for help and vindication.

Hebrews 12:1–3

The author of the Book of Hebrews exhorts hearers to persevere in the face of adversity, looking to the example of Jesus and encouraged by all those through the generations who have sought to be faithful to God in difficult circumstances.

John 13:21–32

At his final supper with his disciples Jesus is troubled by the knowledge of Judas's impending betrayal but tells his disciples that God is at work in the glorification of the Son of Man. Judas Iscariot departs into the night to do what he has determined to do.

Ideas of the Day

♦ Betrayal in books creates an exciting who-done-it page-turning energy. The reader hopes that the betrayer will get what they deserve by the end of the book. In our own lives, betrayal can break our hearts, causing us to sever relationships or put up armor so that no one else can hurt us. Although troubled in spirit, Jesus responds to betrayal in another way. He knew who would betray him when he washed *all* of his disciples' feet. Although it troubled his spirit, Jesus shared bread with the one he knew would betray him. Jesus chose to love his betrayer.

♦ Jesus foretells his betrayal by Judas and Peter's denial of him before the last cock crow. How have we denied Jesus by our words and actions in our daily life?

Making Connections

In the Episcopal Church's baptismal liturgy the question is asked: "Do you renounce Satan and all the spiritual forces of wickedness that rebel against God?" The answer is: "I renounce them." If you have declared this renunciation, what did you mean by that? Do you have a personal understanding of Satan and the spiritual forces of wickedness? If so, is that the energy that you suspect entered Judas in order that the scriptures might be fulfilled, and Jesus might meet his destiny? What if Judas was the most connected to the authorities, the strongest in stature and character, and the only friend at that table whom Jesus could trust to do this very difficult task? Because the betrayal had to be done—didn't it?

Engaging All Ages

Several times in the scripture we hear about the "great cloud of witnesses." This is a reference to those who have died but who in their lifetimes were great examples of what it means to love and follow God. Sometimes we know these people personally, but not always. Take some time to think about who is in your great cloud of witnesses. Does it include a grandparent, a particular saint, writer, or artist? What about a friend or minister? Make a collage, drawing, or list of these people while giving thanks for their witnesses.

Hymns for the Day

The Hymnal 1982
Alone thou goest forth, O Lord 164
Bread of heaven, on thee we feed 323
Let thy Blood in mercy poured 313
To mock your reign, O dearest Lord 170
Hail, thou once despised Jesus 495
Lo! what a cloud of witnesses 545
The head that once was crowned with thorns 483
Ah, holy Jesus, how hast thou offended 158
Bread of the world, in mercy broken 301
O love, how deep, how broad, how high 448, 449

Lift Every Voice and Sing II

Wonder, Love, and Praise

Holy Week

Maundy Thursday

April 9, 2020

We pray that Jesus will give us grace to receive the Sacrament of his Body and Blood thankfully, remembering that in these holy mysteries we have been given a promise of eternal life.

Holy Week

Color   Red / Oxblood, or White

Preface   Of Holy Week

Collect

Almighty Father, whose dear Son, on the night before he suffered, instituted the Sacrament of his Body and Blood: Mercifully grant that we may receive it thankfully in remembrance of Jesus Christ our Lord, who in these holy mysteries gives us a pledge of eternal life; and who now lives and reigns with you and the Holy Spirit, one God, for ever and ever. Amen.

Readings and Psalm

Exodus 12:1–4 (5–10), 11–14

In our first reading **instructions are given, and the meaning of the Passover meal is told: it is a remembrance and reenactment of Israel's beginnings as a people when they were saved out of slavery in Egypt.** The details indicate that several different traditions stand behind the Passover memorial. Perhaps it was the Israelites' attempts to keep ancient spring rites, derived from their shepherding and agricultural backgrounds, which caused the Egyptians to persecute them. With these traditions the story of God's judgment on Egypt and victory for God's people has become richly entwined.

Psalm 116:1–2, 12–19

An offering of thanksgiving and praise by one who has been rescued from death.

1 Corinthians 11:23–26

In this lection **Paul recalls the tradition he received concerning the supper of the Lord on the night he was betrayed.** The apostle reminds the Corinthians, who have shown an alarming tendency to divide up into factions, of the message he first delivered to them. This meal is a remembrance and reenactment of the Lord's offering of himself and forming of the new covenant. It proclaims the Lord's saving death and looks forward to his coming.

John 13:1–17, 31b–35

Our gospel tells how **Jesus washes his disciples' feet during his last meal with them.** This action symbolizes the love and humility of Christ in stooping down to wash those whom he loves from their sins. He has set for them an example, for he must soon depart. His disciples are to be characterized by servant love for one another.

Prayers of the People

In the company of Jesus and in unity with his faithful followers in years past and in our present day, let us offer our prayers responding, "Kyrie eleison."

For the gift of humility, that we may mirror the servanthood of Jesus, bending the knee of our hearts to all whose feet have journeyed a long distance, and whose hands have washed away the burdens of others; let us pray.

Kyrie eleison.

For peace throughout the world, especially in
_____ and all places where the lust for power
fosters tyranny and war; let us pray.

Kyrie eleison.

For the courage to face our own unfaithfulness: the
kisses of deception, the subtle betrayals, our spiritual
sleepiness; that in turning to Christ we may receive the
grace that changes lives; let us pray.

Kyrie eleison.

For those who keep watch this night, that in watching
they may be found, in seeking they may be filled with
the Spirit, and in waiting they may find peace; let us
pray.

Kyrie eleison.

For those who keep watch every night: the hungry,
the homeless, the fearful, that Christ may find them in
their own gardens of Gethsemane and not leave them
in despair; let us pray.

Kyrie eleison.

In thanksgiving for this Eucharistic Meal, which
gathers us into the fellowship of all the beloved,
uniting us with Jesus, whose Divine Presence we now
share; let us pray.

Kyrie eleison.

In companionship with Peter, John, and all the
apostles, let us continue our prayers.
*(Special intentions of the congregation, the diocese,
and the Anglican Communion may be added here or
before the formal intercessions.)*

The Celebrant adds a concluding Collect.

Images in the Readings

A primary image for Maundy Thursday is the **servant**.
We recall from Passion Sunday's Servant Song that the
image of servant is not a readily accessible symbol in
today's society. Even the wait staff in many restaurants
now presents itself not as servants but as personal
friends. John's gospel offers us a lowly, even dirty, task
as appropriate for a true servant.

The readings are filled with **body**: the body of
the dead lamb, cooked and eaten; the body of Christ,
shared in the bread; the body of the neighbor's actual
feet. For people who like to keep their individual
space, it is countercultural to share in one another's
body in this public way.

The first reading says that it is the lamb's **blood**
that reminds God not to punish the Israelites, and Paul
says that the wine is a new covenant in Jesus' blood.
In the ancient world, life was seen as residing in the
blood. Thus pouring out of blood is giving up of life.
Isn't it interesting that small children lick a bleeding
wound, in hopes of keeping their blood inside their
body?

In all three readings, the people of God experience
themselves as a **meal** community. Humans must eat to
live, and humans eat together to become and maintain
community. The Israelites are to keep the Passover
meal "as a perpetual ordinance"; Paul assumes and
corrects the meal practice of the Corinthians; John
describes the last loving meal Jesus had with his
disciples before his arrest. So it is over the centuries
most Christian assemblies have shared a meal at their
weekly meeting. The liturgy of the Three Days begins
with this meal.

Holy Week

Holy Week

Ideas of the Day

♦ When we are babies and children, we are fully dependent on the help of others. As adults, many of us have lost the ability to receive something so intimate as having our feet washed. To receive can be very uncomfortable. To receive means we are dependent and not in control. Jesus teaches that we must learn to receive and are dependent upon God's love. k.d. lang's "Wash Me Clean" embraces the humility and grace of receiving. How do we pray these words or others in order that we may also embrace the spiritual discipline of receiving?

♦ Commemorate this day with an agapé meal, or love feast, as a community event. The setting should be plain and food simple, in keeping with the solemnity of the Lenten fast that continues through this week. A meal of soup, cheese, olives, dried fruit, bread, and wine are appropriate. Eat the meal in silence while someone reads passages from scripture or poetry that allows for introspection while eating, or have soft music playing in the background.

Making Connections

The foot washing of the disciples and the command to "love one another. Just as I have loved you" appear only in John's gospel. Both call us into spaces of supreme discomfort. We have so many excuses to not participate in the foot washing: it's embarrassing, it's too intimate, your socks have holes, you don't like the person doing it, your toes are weird, you don't want someone touching you, you don't have time, that's just for the religious people in the congregation, and so on. The same goes for why it is so hard to love one another without condition: it is embarrassing, too intimate, we don't even *like* one another, they are weird or disagree with me, and we don't have time. That's for the religious people in our congregation. Thomas Merton said, "Pride makes us artificial. Humility makes us real."[1] Lent gives us a chance to become real.

Engaging All Ages

The word "Maundy" comes from the Latin *mandatum*, which means "commandment." We often wash one another's feet during the Maundy Thursday liturgy to honor the commandment that Jesus gave his disciples when he washed their feet and said, "So if I, your Lord and Teacher, have washed your feet, you also ought to wash one another's feet. For I have set you an example, that you also should do as I have done to you" (John 13:14–15). Feel awkward about foot washing? Practice with a loved one at home and encourage one another, then bravely wash another's feet at church.

---

1 Thomas Merton, *No Man is an Island* (New York: Shambhala Publications, 2005), 119.

Good Friday

April 10, 2020

We ask God to look with kindness at us his family, for whom our Lord Jesus Christ died on the Cross and lives and reigns forever with God and the Holy Spirit.

Color

Preface

Collect

Almighty God, we pray you graciously to behold this your family, for whom our Lord Jesus Christ was willing to be betrayed, and given into the hands of sinners, and to suffer death upon the cross; who now lives and reigns with you and the Holy Spirit, one God, for ever and ever. Amen.

Readings and Psalm

Isaiah 52:13–53:12

Our opening lesson is **the poem of the Lord's servant who suffers and bears the sins of many.** The passage is the fourth and last of the "servant songs" that form a portion of the Book of Isaiah written when the exile was coming to an end. The servant is sometimes thought to be an historical individual, or is understood as an idealization of the faithful of Israel. This "man of sorrows," who was "despised and rejected," "wounded for our transgressions," and one whom the Lord at last vindicates, is perceived by Christians to be a prefigurement of Jesus.

Psalm 22

A psalm of lamentation and a plea for deliverance by one who feels deserted and pressed in on every side, expressing final confidence in God and God's goodness.

Hebrews 10:16–25

In this reading we hear that **God has established the promised new covenant through which our sins are forgiven and God's laws are written on our hearts.** Given such confidence, we are to be unswerving in our hope and strong in our encouragement of one another.

or

Hebrews 4:14–16; 5:7–9

In our New Testament reading **we are encouraged to have full confidence in drawing near to God because Jesus, our great high priest, knows our every weakness and temptation and makes intercession for us.** Having learned obedience through suffering, he has become the source of salvation for all who obey him.

John 18:1–19:42

Our gospel is **the story of Jesus' trials before the Jewish council and Pilate, followed by his final sufferings and death.**

Prayers of the People

For the principal liturgy on this day, use the Solemn Collects as directed in the Book of Common Prayer. The following form might be appropriate for a simpler and shorter service in places where more than one service is offered.

Jesus' love is for the loveless, his death for those who betray him still, his sacrifice for all who would turn to him. Let us turn again to Christ, our Lord, offering our prayers as signs of repentance and rebirth, responding, "Kyrie eleison."

That we may die to self, to all that keeps us from finding unity with our sisters and brothers, to all that alienates us from living in the light of truth; let us pray.

Kyrie eleison.

That we may die for others, living a life of simplicity, so that others may receive a fair share of the world's resources; reassessing our values so that there may be time and energy for that which is dear; living into the gifts which God has given us, and empowering others to do the same; let us pray.

Kyrie eleison.

That we may not run from our personal corners of darkness, but see them as avenues through which the Spirit of hope draws us into the God of love; let us pray.

Kyrie eleison.

That we, the people of God, the Body of Christ, may bring release to those held in captivity, compassion to the abused and neglected, and hope to all for whom Christ died; let us pray.

Kyrie eleison.

That those who have departed this life may be with us through the Sacrament of Christ's Body and Blood, the eternal banquet of God's unending love; let us pray.

Kyrie eleison.

That those who grieve may, with Mary, experience the hope to which all the faithful are called, knowing that in Christ death has been conquered and life is the victor; let us pray.

Kyrie eleison.

Let us continue our prayers, stirring up one another to love and good works, holding fast the confession of our hope, unwavering in our faith.
(Special intentions of the congregation, the diocese, and the Anglican Communion may be added here or before the formal intercessions.)

The Celebrant adds a concluding Collect.

Images in the Readings

The **cross** was the electric chair of the Roman Empire, the means of execution for low-class criminals. Some cultures have used the shape of the cross as a sign of the four corners of the earth. Christians mark the newly baptized with this sign, God coming through suffering and death, aligned with all who are rejected, and surprisingly in this way bringing life to the whole earth. In the suggested sixth-century hymn "Sing, My Tongue," the cross is paradoxically likened to the archetypal Tree of Life.

In John's passion narrative, Jesus of Nazareth is called King of the Jews, the Son of God, and most significantly, I AM, the very **name** of God. Christians see in the man dying on the cross the mystery of God's self-giving love. Along with the witnesses in John's passion, we can sing with the hymn writer Caroline Noel, "At the name of Jesus every knee shall bow, every tongue confess him king of glory now."

In the Israelite sacrificial system, the **lamb** represented the life of the nomadic herders, and killing the lamb symbolized a plea that God would receive the animal's death as a gift that would prompt divine mercy. The New Testament often uses the image of the lamb as one way to understand the meaning of Jesus' death. The book of Revelation recalls Good Friday and Easter in its paradoxical vision of a lamb seated on a throne and standing as if slaughtered.

But any single image—such as the lamb—is not sufficient. Thus we are given the opposite image, Christ as the **high priest** who does the slaughtering. According to Israelite religion, the people needed an intermediary to approach God. Christ then is the mediator who prays to God for us. Yet for John, Christ is the God whom our prayers address.

Good Friday lays each image next to another one, for no single metaphor can fully explain the mystery of Christ.

Ideas of the Day

♦ Good Friday is our companion when darkness has set in and transformation has yet to break in. God has lived it. Good Friday is our story when we hear a life-limiting diagnosis, when we stand with our loved ones looking at the ashes of their home, when we feel so empty we cannot get out of bed, when we do not know what to feel or do or think when tragedy occurs, and when the last embers of our dreams have died. Good Friday entreats us to bring our brokenness to the cross that Jesus carried, not for a quick fix, but to know that we are never alone. We are in Holy company.

♦ The vigil at the foot of the cross can be shared in various ways, but the congregation should experience it, whether it be in a three-hour vigil or in a briefer liturgy of reading, prayer, meditation, and discussing the feelings of the participants.

Making Connections

The gospel for Good Friday reveals the failures of Jesus' closest friends and followers: their failure to prevent his arrest, to claim him as their leader, to choose his release, to shield him from shame, and to stay by his side in death. In the end it was Joseph of Arimathea, a secret disciple of Jesus and Nicodemus, who also sought Jesus' teaching in the dark, who tended to Jesus following his death. All of the others seemed to be in hiding, managing their own fears, grief, and worry. On this dark day, through this tragic story, we are reminded that we also fail to choose Jesus. But we do not know who else is out there, listening, following, and claiming his death. Even in our unfaithfulness we are bold to ask at the end of the Good Friday liturgy that Jesus would, now and in the hour of our death, give mercy and grace to the living, pardon and rest to the dead, and peace and concord to the church.

Engaging All Ages

At the end of the Maundy Thursday liturgy the sanctuary lamp is blown out above the aumbry or tabernacle. We do this to remember how dark and lonely the world would feel without Jesus' life or love as well as the absence of Jesus in our presence through the sacrament. At home, consider fasting from media of any kind or the use of electricity where possible (no microwaves, electric lights, e-readers, televisions, electric stoves, or ovens) using only candlelight for illumination. If you can't commit to a full day or evening, what about for an hour? How much darker do things feel?

Hymns for the Day

Note: There is no Entrance Hymn on this day (see BCP, p. 276).

The Hymnal 1982
Ah, holy Jesus, how hast thou offended 158
O sacred head, sore wounded 168, 169
To mock your reign, O dearest Lord 170
Alone thou goest forth, O Lord 164
Cross of Jesus, cross of sorrow 160
From God Christ's deity came forth 443
There is a green hill far away 167
At the cross her vigil keeping 159
Go to dark Gethsemane 171
In the cross of Christ I glory 441, 442
Lord Christ, when first thou cam'st to earth 598
Morning glory, starlit sky 585
Sing, my tongue, the glorious battle 165, 166
Sunset to sunrise changes now 163
Were you there when they crucified my Lord?
    (vs. 1–3) 172
When I survey the wondrous cross 474

Lift Every Voice and Sing II
O sacred head, sore wounded 36
Calvary 32
Near the cross 29
Lead me to Calvary 31
O how he loves you and me 35
The old rugged cross 38
There is a fountain 39
He never said a mumbalin' word 33
Were you there? (vs. 1–3) 37
He will remember me 34

Wonder, Love, and Praise
O sacred head, sore wounded 735
Faithful cross, above all other 737
When Jesus came to Golgotha 736

Holy Saturday

April 11, 2020

We ask God that we may wait with Christ for the coming of the third day and rise with him to newness of life.

Color　　　Red / Oxblood

Preface　　Of Holy Week

Collect

O God, Creator of heaven and earth: Grant that, as the crucified body of your dear Son was laid in the tomb and rested on this holy Sabbath, so we may await with him the coming of the third day, and rise with him to newness of life; who now lives and reigns with you and the Holy Spirit, one God, for ever and ever. Amen.

Readings and Psalm

Job 14:1–14

Job reflects on the brevity of human life. Nature may renew itself but not mortals who have but an impossible hope that they might meet God after the grave.

or

Lamentations 3:1–9, 19–24

Our first reading is **a poem of lamentation and complaint** from one who feels besieged by God and circumstance, yet chooses to affirm the steadfast love of the Lord and a belief that confidence in God is ultimately well placed.

Psalm 31:1–4, 15–16

A song of trust by one who looks to the Lord for mercy and protection.

1 Peter 4:1–8

Believers are encouraged to live lives devoted to the will of God, steering clear of all forms of dissipation. Because Christ has suffered in the flesh, his followers must be willing to do likewise, disciplining themselves for the goal of life in the spirit. Of primary importance is the practice of love for one another.

Matthew 27:57–66

A man of privilege and a disciple, Joseph of Arimathea, wraps the body of Jesus in clean linen and places the corpse in his own newly hewn tomb. Other disciples of Jesus witness the burial. Jesus' religious opponents appeal to Pilate to place a guard at the tomb lest Jesus' disciples steal his body, and Pilate gives them permission to seal the tomb.

or

John 19:38–42

Nicodemus and Joseph of Arimathea prepare Jesus' body for burial according to custom, interring Jesus' corpse in a new tomb in a garden where nobody had previously been laid.

Prayers of the People

Washed in the waters of Christ's death and resurrection, that we might enter the community of faith, let us praise our Lord by offering our prayers and thanksgivings as we respond, "Hear us, O risen Christ."

Risen Lord, mold us into your new creation, that we may seek the radiance of your light as found in the lives of the saints, and as revealed through the generosity of our sisters and brothers; let us pray.

Hear us, O risen Christ.

Eternal Christ, help us journey through this life with compassion and vision, entering into the sufferings of the world, that we might know the depth of your truth and the dwelling place of your love; let us pray.

Hear us, O risen Christ.

Saving Lord, stretch out the strong arms of your grace and lift up those who are hungry and downtrodden, lonely and forgotten, so that all of humanity may be reconciled to you and to one another; let us pray.

Hear us, O risen Christ.

Christ our Passover, may the nations of the world seek after peace and thirst anew for the freedom of men and women everywhere; may we pass from domination to mutual trust, from economic intimidation to a responsible use of the world's resources, from thoughts of destruction to a respect for all life; let us pray.

Hear us, O risen Christ.

Jesus, Bread of Heaven, nourish us in this Holy Sacrament of your unending Presence, that we may become for one another your bread of hope and your cup of joy; let us pray.

Hear us, O risen Christ.

Jesus, Savior, Risen Lord, we thank you for all the blessings of this life: for family and friends who reveal your love, for those who have died in the faith, for those who have entered our communities through baptism, for all things which enliven our spirits, and especially for the Paschal Flame that outshines every darkness; let us pray.

Hear us, O risen Christ.

Rejoicing in the garments of new life, let us continue our prayers.
(Special intentions of the congregation, the diocese, and the Anglican Communion may be added here or before the formal intercessions.)

The Celebrant adds a concluding Collect.

Images in the Readings

At the beginning of the Vigil, Christ is symbolized by the candle, which gives **light** to our darkness and remains bright even when we all share in its flame. The early church called baptism enlightenment. Sharing this light outdoors in darkness makes the image emotionally effective.

Each reading offers an image with which to picture salvation: the earth is God's perfect creation; we are saved in the ark during the flood; we are granted a reprieve from sacrifice; we escape the enemy army; we are enlivened by spring rains; we are instructed by Woman Wisdom; we are given a new heart; our bones are brought back to life; we enjoy a homeland; swallowed by the fish, we do not drown but are coughed up on dry ground; we wear party clothes; when thrown into a furnace, we emerge untouched by the fire; we are risen with Christ; and although we do mistake Christ for the gardener, he appears to us and enlivens our faith.

Ideas of the Day

- Jesus is dead. His followers are lamenting. Joseph of Arimathea, a disciple, follows the proper burial rituals for Jesus' body. He lays Jesus in a tomb, a sign of respect. This ritual is intimate and personal, like when we bury our own loved ones. The ritual is a known next step after a tragedy that has fully thwarted Jesus' followers' understanding of Jesus and the world. On Holy Saturday, we are invited to lament our beloved Jesus' death. We are invited into the rituals of grief and mourning. We are invited to imagine a world in which Jesus is dead.

- The church remains darkened. The bare altar and sanctuary is stark. A quiet liturgy of Morning Prayer can be offered.

Holy Week

Making Connections

The Hebrew Scriptures say you have been laid low. Afflicted. Down, dead in darkness. The psalmist suggests refuge and rescue, the Epistle says be ready, and the Gospels say be still. Sit in this tomb. In the dead, damp, darkness. Be food for the worms. Let yourself feel the impending decay. Feel the waiting. In the stillness of this day, let the longing wash over you. Today—this Holy Saturday. But do not forget the promise. Yes, this is the day after. But it is also the day before.

Engaging All Ages

Today is a great day to dye eggs. Whether you make natural dyes from vegetables and fruits or use food coloring and vinegar, make sure to include a wax crayon (or a piece of clear-white wax). Before you dye your eggs, create designs on the eggs with your piece of wax. Once you drop the eggs into the dye, the design will slowly appear, as the colors soak into the shell all around the wax. Think or talk about a time when God was slow to appear in your life. What was that experience like? How did you handle the waiting?

Hymns for the Day

The Hymnal 1982

From deepest woe I cry to thee 151
Immortal, invisible, God only wise 423
Out of the depths I call 666
O love, how deep, how broad, how high
    (vs. 1–4, 6) 448, 449
O Love of God, how strong and true (vs. 1–3) 455, 456
My song is love unknown (vs. 1–2, 6–7) 458
O sorrow deep! 173
Were you there when they crucified
    my Lord? (vs. 1–3) 172

Lift Every Voice and Sing II

Lead me to the calvary 31
Were you there? (vs. 1–3) 37

Wonder, Love, and Praise

The steadfast love of the Lord never ceases 755

Holy Week

Easter

Preparing for Easter

Theological Themes that Might Shape Liturgy, Catechesis, and Education

Eastertide is God's ultimate rejection of violence and clear declaration of the core values of the Kingdom of God—abundant life, reconciliation, joy, peace. These themes are explored throughout the Easter season. Like Christmas, the religious celebration of Easter is often shrouded by a broader, albeit less clear, celebration of Easter in the wider culture. This is seen in the marked uptick in attendance on Easter. How we choose to celebrate this holy season can either draw a distinction between broader celebrations of springtime and a more meaningful celebration of the Resurrection of Jesus Christ.

The season of Easter lasts fifty days through Ascension Day and up to and including Pentecost. The length of the season underscores the importance of the event we are celebrating. It also presents many opportunities for celebration in our faith communities, including long after the neighborhood Easter egg hunts are over and the discount store has begun putting up red, white, and blue decor for the impending celebration of Independence Day.

Liturgical Possibilities

Rites

The season begins on Easter Sunday, the first of seven Sundays of Easter. In stark contrast to the liturgies that occurred during Lent, and especially Holy Week, Easter should be filled with celebratory music and plenty of opportunities for the congregation to respond to liturgical actions with joy. Eucharistic Prayer D, though the longest of those in the prayer book, might be a suitable choice here (chanted if possible, Mozarabic if you're daring). The next week,

the Octave of Easter, is suitable for daily Eucharistic celebration, another nod toward the sheer importance of this event.

There are some liturgical variations that might occur during this season too, including the omission of the Confession and Absolution. Whatever the decision is here, a note in the bulletin (if printed bulletins are present) or some other form of communication might be a helpful form of catechesis, emphasizing grace, love, and reconciliation as themes of the season.

In addition to Easter Sunday, there are at least two other major feasts during Eastertide—Ascension Day and Pentecost. Ascension Day, which occurs midweek, 40 days into the Easter season is another opportunity to observe Eucharist as a community. Pentecost, which falls on the eighth Sunday of Easter, or fifty days after the Resurrection, celebrates the coming of the Holy Spirit on the community of disciples and the continued presence of the Holy Spirit as the animating force of the Church. It is a perfect day for baptisms and for worshipers to renew their own baptismal vows.

Space

The Paschal candle is one of the central foci of the Easter season. Having it lit and prominently placed is important to convey a central theme of Easter—the unconquered Light of Christ.

Other Rituals and Resources

Easter is a suitable season to welcome new people who have circled into the faith community in the past year. As Easter celebrates the new life that is possible in Christ, newcomers to our faith communities represent the new life that comes when we encounter and are transformed by the presence of another.

Through the Eyes of a Child

Jesus is risen from the dead! Easter has brought us everlasting life because of Jesus' resurrection. The alleluias are said and sung. God's love is stronger than anything, even death. Because of God's love, we do not have to be afraid of death. Easter is about new life, coming from what we thought was death and bringing unexpected possibilities and surprises. Easter eggs, Easter chicks, Easter flowers all remind us of the new life in Christ. We received new life at our baptism, and during Easter we think about what that baptism means in our lives. Reflect with the children on the ways we keep our baptismal promises:

+ How do we keep the promises we make?
+ How do we show our love for God?
+ How do we show love for each other?

Make an alleluia banner for the table, and talk about why Jesus' resurrection would make us so happy. Take a walk and look at all the new life you begin to spot during the walk. Read stories of transformation and new life, such as *The Very Hungry Caterpillar*[1] by Eric Carle. Name the baptismal promises and reflect on them with pictures of how you live each of them out with your family and friends, at home and at school.

As with Christmas, though to a lesser extent, Easter still occupies a privileged place in our social memory. Children will hear messages of Easter that may conflict with or complicate the message the Church teaches. A robust celebration of Easter that includes children where possible or that empowers the parents and guardians of children to become evangelists for the Resurrection is of utmost importance. Liturgical ritual is filled with opportunities to draw children into the mystery. Therefore, planning the liturgy with a mind toward the inclusion of younger people might be key. How can we use the liturgy to teach children about the cultivation of joy? The power of hope? The unstoppable love of God?

Through the Eyes of Youth

This is the time to encourage youth to Easter reflection and action. Reflect upon the individual baptismal promises found in the Easter Vigil and invite the youth to respond to new ways that they can serve within the congregation:

+ Take Easter flowers to shut-ins.
+ Become part of a lay eucharistic visiting team.
+ Color Easter eggs for the young children and engage them in an Easter egg hunt.
+ Invite someone to church who does not have a "home" church.
+ Through the Sundays of Easter put closure on their Lenten project.

Above all, give youth an opportunity to witness to the fact that they believe Jesus has risen from the dead.

+ Go: "Where does God need us to go—in school, in our neighborhood, town, and beyond?"
+ Visit: "Who are the friendless, lonely, outcast people in our lives and how do we connect with them?"
+ Listen: "Who are the people that no one pays attention to?"
+ Care: "Why, God, are your people suffering?"
+ Ask: "What can we do for needy people near and far?"
+ Pray: "God, open our eyes and ears and hearts. Who will help us to live for others?"
+ Invite: "Who will go with us? Which adults and teens can we invite to follow, to encounter, and to become Christ today?"

---

1 Philomel Books; 1 edition (March 23, 1994).

Through the Eyes of Daily Life

On this day the Lord has acted! On the first day of the week God began creation, transforming darkness into light. On this, the "eighth day" of the week, Jesus Christ was raised from the dead. We celebrate this new creation in the waters of baptism and in the feast of victory. Reflect on your baptism and how you live out the promises in every facet of your life. Throughout this season, we hear stories of the men and women who recognized who Jesus really is after failing to do so during his earthly life. We are enlightened by their visions and their visits with the Risen Christ as they proclaim that our Lord is alive and is life for the world. As we begin the Great Fifty Days of Easter filled with hope and joy, be prepared to go forth to share the news that Christ is risen!

While a fifty-day party might sound like a lot of fun, sustaining the energy for that long of a timespan might prove more daunting than originally thought. However, the rich themes of Easter can have direct bearing on the lives of the faithful. Structuring liturgy, formation, and fellowship in ways that allow people to get the themes of Easter into their bones might be extremely helpful here. While Lenten calendars might help us structure our fast and devotion, what might an Easter calendar that helps us structure our celebration and gratitude look like?

Through the Eyes of Those Outside of the Church

As with Christmas, how the Church chooses to mark Easter can either distinguish the Church as an alternative community centered around a different set of values or just another repository of prevailing culture. Not only should our liturgical celebration be joyous and meaningful, but we might think seriously about what it means to turn our worshipers into evangelists of the Resurrection, empowering them with tools to be a blessing to those they meet outside of church. Expecting people to come to church to experience the fullness of the Resurrection is a wasted opportunity. Instead, it might be helpful to turn what might a rote celebration of a religious ritual into an opportunity to serve the world in the name of him who died and rose again.

Through the Eyes of the Global Community

The collects for Easter petition the living power of Jesus to open up new life to all. Our prayers and action can reflect God's desire of reconciliation for all. During the Easter season, direct attention is placed in prayer to alleviate the extreme poverty of the world. The Christ-centeredness of the Sustainable Development Goals (SDGs) is an example of how making a commitment to others is a commitment to Jesus (John 10:10). For the sake of the poor and suffering of the world, our conversion (turning our lives around) at the individual, congregational, diocesan, churchwide, and global level a difference can be made (Luke 18:18–23). Focus on one SDG for the whole liturgical cycle so that during the Easter season, a particular geographic area can be chosen to learn about the people, worship, and need in that area of the world or domestically. The Easter season can be a time to build direct relationships with another location in the Anglican Communion. Enter into mission with another, to help alleviate extreme poverty.

Easter

Easter Season Blessings[1]

The following blessing may be used by a bishop or priest whenever a blessing is appropriate. It is a three-fold form, with an Amen at the end of each sentence, leading into a Trinitarian blessing.

May Almighty God, who has redeemed us and made us his children through the resurrection of his Son our Lord, bestow upon you the riches of his blessing. *Amen.*

May God, who through the water of baptism has raised us from sin into newness of life, make you holy and worthy to be united with Christ forever. *Amen.*

May God, who has brought us out of bondage to sin into true lasting freedom in the Redeemer, bring you to your eternal inheritance. *Amen.*

And the blessing of God Almighty, the Father, the Son, and the Holy Spirit, be upon you and remain with you forever. *Amen.*

Blessings Over Food at Easter[2]

These blessings are appropriate for a parish meal following the Easter Vigil or over foods brought to the church for blessing.

Over Wine

Blessed are you, O Lord our God, creator of the fruit of the vine: Grant that we who share this wine, which gladdens our hearts, may share forever the new life of the true Vine; you Son Jesus Christ our Lord. *Amen.*

Over Bread

Blessed are you, O Lord our God: you bring forth bread from the earth and make the risen Lord to be for us the Bread of life: Grant that we who daily seek the bread which sustains our bodies may also hunger for the food of everlasting life, Jesus Christ our Lord. *Amen.*

Over Lamb

Stir up our memory, O Lord, as we eat this Easter lamb that, remembering Israel of old, who in obedience to your command ate the Pascal lamb and was delivered from the bondage of slavery, we, your new Israel, may rejoice in the resurrection of Jesus Christ, the true Lamb who has delivered us from the bondage of sin and death, and who lives and reigns forever and ever. *Amen.*

Over Eggs

O Lord our God, in celebration of the Pascal feast we have prepared these eggs from your creation: Grant that they may be to us a sign of the new life; and immortality promised to those who follow your Son, Jesus Christ our Lord. *Amen.*

Over Other Foods

Blessed are you, O Lord our God; you have given us the risen Savior to be the Shepherd of your people: Lead us, by him, to springs of living waters, and feed us with the food that endures to eternal life; where with you, O Father, and with the Holy Spirit, he lives and reigns, One God, forever and ever. *Amen.*

1 *The Book of Occasional Services 2003* (New York: Church Publishing, 2004), 26.

2 Ibid, 97–98.

Earth Day Litany[3]

Wednesday, April 22

We have forgotten who we are.
We have become separate from the movements
    of the earth.
We have turned our backs on the cycles of life.
We have forgotten who we are.

We have sought only our own security.
We have exploited simply for our own ends.
We have distorted our knowledge.
We have abused our power.
We have forgotten who we are.

Now the land is barren
And the waters are poisoned
And the air is polluted.
We have forgotten who we are.

Now the forests are dying
And the creatures are disappearing
And the humans are despairing.
We have forgotten who we are.

We ask forgiveness.
We ask for the gift of remembering.
We ask for the strength to change,
all for the love of our Creator. *Amen.*

Rogation Days[4]

The Rogation Days are traditionally observed on the Monday, Tuesday, and Wednesday before Ascension Day. They may, however, be observed on other days, depending on local conditions and the convenience of the congregation.

In ancient times, the observance consisted of an outdoor procession, which culminated in a special celebration of the Eucharist. In more recent centuries, the procession has frequently taken place on a Sunday afternoon, apart from the Eucharist.

Hymns, psalms, canticles, and anthems are sung during the procession. The following are appropriate:

Canticle 1 or 12 (Benedicite)
Psalm 102 (Refrain: "Bless the Lord, O my soul")
Psalm 104 (Refrain: "Hallelujah")

At suitable places the procession may halt for appropriate Bible readings and prayers.

In addition to the readings listed on page 930 of the Book of Common Prayer, any of the following passages are appropriate:

Genesis 8:13–23
Leviticus 26:1–13 (14–20)
Deuteronomy 8:1–19 (11–20)
Hosea 2:18–23
Ezekiel 34:25–31
James 4:7–11
Matthew 6:25–34
John 12:23–26

In addition to the prayers in the Book of Common Prayer, the following can be used:

Almighty and everlasting God, Creator of all things and giver of all life, let your blessing be upon this (see, livestock, plough, forest, _____) and grant that *it* may serve to your glory and the welfare of your people; through Jesus Christ our Lord. *Amen.*

---

3 United Nations Environment Programme. "Only One Earth," a United Nations Environment Programme publication for Environmental Sabbath/ Earth Rest Day, June 1990. UN Environment Programme, DC2–803, United Nations, New York, NY 10017. Used by permission.

---

4 *The Book of Occasional Services*, 103–104.

A Prayer for Renewing our Stewardship of Creation[5]

Creator of all, we come to a time in our lives where we are filled with the understanding that we are part of all you have made. We thank you for the variety of your creation. Its complexity fills us with wonder and stretches our imaginations. Make yourself known to us as we strive to be good stewards of our environment, for as you placed Adam and Eve in a garden in Eden, you have set us in this world to help it flourish and live in harmony and peace with all living things. We acknowledge our past sins against creation with sorrow. Rekindle your light shining through us, so that we may know the work you have given us on this earth and declare your glory; through Jesus Christ, who with you and the Holy Spirit, upholds your creation through all ages. *Amen.*

A Mother's Day Prayer[6]

Sunday, May 10

On this Mother's Day, we give thanks to God for the divine gift of motherhood in all its diverse forms. Let us pray for all the mothers among us today; for our own mothers, those living and those who have passed away; for the mothers who loved us and for those who fell short of loving us fully; for all who hope to be mothers someday and for those whose hope to have children has been frustrated; for all the mothers who have lost children; for all women and men who have mothered others in any way—those who have been our substitute mothers and we who had done so for those in need; and for the earth that bore us and provides us with our sustenance. We pray this all in the name of God, our great and loving Mother. *Amen.*

An Ascensiontide Litany[7]

Thursday, May 21

Christ was baptized as one of us, but he destroyed sins as God.
He was tempted as a human, but he conquered as God.
He wants us to rejoice, for he has overcome the world.

He hungered, but he fed thousands. He is the living bread that comes down from heaven.
He thirsted, but he cried, "If anyone thirsts, let them come to me and drink." He promised that fountains would flow from those who believe.

He was wearied, but he is the rest of those who are weary and heavy-laden.
The demons acknowledge him, but he drives them out. He plunges into the sea the legions of foul spirits and sees the prince of demons falling like lightning.

He prays, but he hears prayers.
He weeps, but he makes tears to cease.

He asks where Lazarus was laid because he was human; but he raises Lazarus because he was God.
He is sold, and very cheap—for only thirty pieces of silver; but he redeems the world at a great price—the cost of his own blood.

As sheep he is led to the slaughter, but he is the Shepherd of Israel—and now of the whole world.
He is bruised and wounded, but he heals every disease and infirmity.

He is lifted up and nailed to the tree, but he restores us by the tree of life.
He lays down his life, but he has the power to take it up again.

He dies, but he gives life; and by his death he destroys death.
He is buried, but he rises again.

He descends into hell, but he raises souls from death.
He ascends to heaven, and he will come again to judge the living and the dead. Amen.

Easter

---

5 *Changes: Prayers and Services Honoring Rites of Passage* (New York: Church Publishing, 2007), 45.

6 Leslie Nipps, "For Mother's Day" in *Women's Uncommon Prayers* (Harrisburg, PA: Morehouse Publishing, 2000), 364.

---

7 "The Mystery of Christ—An Ascensiontide Litany" from *The Wideness of God's Mercy: Litanies to Enlarge Our Prayer,* edited by Jeffrey W. Rowthorn (New York: Church Publishing, 2007), 89–90.

Easter

A Prayer for Memorial Day[8]

Monday, May 25

Lord God, in whom there is life and light: Accept our thanks for those who died for us, our prayers for those who mourn, our praise for the hope you have given us. Refresh our hearts with dedication to heroic ideas, with appreciation for the honesty of the just, with obedience to upright laws. Forgive us when our patriotism is hollow, when our nationalism is arrogant, when our allegiance is halfhearted. Stir within us thanksgiving for all we have inherited, vigilance for the freedoms of all people, willingness to sacrifice for fellow citizens. Comfort us with the joy that Christ died for all those who died for us, bringing life and immortality to light for all who believe in Him. *Amen.*

---

8 "The Last Monday in May" from *An American Prayer Book,* edited by Christopher L. Webber (Harrisburg, PA: Morehouse Publishing, 2008), 141–142.

The Great Vigil of Easter

April 11, 2020

Celebrating Christ's glorious resurrection, we pray that we may be renewed in body and mind, being raised from the dead of sin by God's life-giving Spirit.

Color   White

Preface   Of Easter

Collect

Almighty God, who for our redemption gave your only begotten Son to the death of the cross, and by his glorious resurrection delivered us from the power of the enemy: Grant us so to die daily to sin, that we may evermore live with him in the joy of his resurrection; through Jesus Christ your Son our Lord, who lives and reigns with you and the Holy Spirit, one God, now and forever. Amen.

or

O God, who made this most holy night to shine with the glory of the Lord's resurrection: Stir up in your Church that Spirit of adoption which is given to us in Baptism, that we, being renewed both in body and mind, may worship you in sincerity and truth; through Jesus Christ our Lord, who lives and reigns with you, in the unity of the Holy Spirit, one God, now and forever. Amen.

Readings and Psalm

Genesis 1:1—2:4a

Our lesson is **the story of creation.** As this ancient narrative opens, the Spirit of the Lord hovers like a great mother bird over the shapeless world. God then forms the heaven and the earth and all its creatures in six days. The seventh day is set aside as a day of rest. God's ultimate creative act is human life, made in God's own image, to whom rulership and responsibility over all other life are given.

Psalm 136:1–9, 23–26

A psalm in praise of a good Creator, a God of enduring mercy.

Genesis 7:1–5, 11–18; 8:6–18; 9:8–13

Noah and his household are commanded by the Lord to enter the ark, together with pairs of all animals. Forty days and nights of rain and flood cover the earth in water. Finally the waters subside, and the Lord makes a covenant with Noah, promising never again to destroy the earth by flood. As a sign of this covenant, God hangs God's own warrior's bow in the clouds, the rainbow which stretches in the sky's vast expanse.

Psalm 46

The earth may be moved and kingdoms shaken, but God is our refuge.

Genesis 22:1–18

This reading is **the story of Abraham's willingness in obedience to the Lord's command to sacrifice his only son, Isaac, and the Lord's blessing of him.** The narrative illustrates Abraham's readiness to abandon all to serve the Lord. Originally it probably also was used as a model story encouraging the substitution of animal for human sacrifices. Ancient Israel was given a better understanding of God's will, and because of his obedience, Abraham received God's promise to him and his descendants.

Psalm 16

Contentment, refuge, and joy are found in the presence of the Lord, who does not abandon God's faithful servant at death.

Exodus 14:10–31; 15:20–21

This reading is **the story of the deliverance of Israel from bondage in Egypt.** The people are terrified when they see the pursuing army and complain that it would have been better to live in slavery than to die in the wilderness. Moses urges them to have courage, for they will see the salvation of the Lord, who has called them to freedom to serve the one true God. The Lord then brings them safely through the sea and destroys the army of the Egyptians.

Exodus 15:1b–13, 17–18 (The Song of Moses)

A song of praise to God for deliverance from captivity in Egypt and from the peril of pursuing armies.

Isaiah 55:1–11

In this lesson we hear how **the return from exile will be a time of prosperity and abundance when God's covenant will be renewed.** The prophet pictures the great day: for a people who have been near death there will be food and drink without cost. God's covenant with David is to be extended to all Israel, and other nations will come to see her glory. The life-giving word of the Lord will not fail to produce its fruit and, together with Israel, the natural world will rejoice and reflect God's power.

Isaiah 12:2–6 (The First Song of Isaiah)

A song of praise and thanksgiving to God, the Holy One of Israel.

Baruch 3:9–15, 3:32–4:4

The lesson is a poem of praise to Wisdom, God's companion in the process of creation and God's precious gift to humankind. All who find her will be blessed, and she is embodied most especially in the Torah, the book of God's commandments.

or

Proverbs 8:1–8, 19–21; 9:4b–6

In this lesson **Wisdom calls to all who will hear, offering understanding, direction, and insight into the way of righteousness and justice.** She is God's gift to the wise and simple alike, and those who learn her ways will prosper.

Psalm 19

A hymn which glorifies the Creator God, with special praise for God's law and a prayer for avoidance of sin.

Ezekiel 36:24–28

A time is coming when God will place a new heart and spirit within the people, who will cleave to God and walk in righteousness. Ezekiel prophesies the restoration of the dispersed and humiliated people of Israel.

Psalm 42

The psalmist laments his inability to come to the house of God and thirsts for the presence of the Lord.

and

Psalm 43

A plea to God by one who is persecuted and in distress, to be able to come and worship in the Lord's temple.

Ezekiel 37:1–14

The prophet has a vision of the bones of a dead and hopeless people being restored to new life in their homeland. The Lord calls upon Ezekiel as son of man to prophesy that the people who have experienced exile and many hardships will live again. The Spirit of the Lord restores their spirit and breath, and they rise from death. Although this passage can be understood to anticipate the hope of individual resurrection, Israel did not yet have this belief.

Psalm 143

The psalmist prays earnestly for the help of God's presence.

Zephaniah 3:14–20

In this lesson **the prophet foretells a time when the judgment of Israel will be ended and the mighty Lord will bring victory and renewal to the people.** The city of Jerusalem and its holy Mount Zion may rejoice and sing. All enemies will be defeated and the crippled healed. The fortunes of Israel will be restored, and the nation will be praised by all peoples.

Psalm 98

A song of thanksgiving and praise to the victorious Lord, who has made righteousness known and shown faithfulness to God's people.

Romans 6:3–11

In this reading we hear that, **as Christian disciples have been joined with Christ in his death through baptism, so they are to know a resurrection life like his.** In union with Christ we have died to our sinful selves and have begun to experience a new way of life. In one sense our freedom from death still awaits us in the future, but, in another sense, we already know what it means to be alive to God in Christ Jesus and to realize the true meaning of life.

Psalm 114

A song of praise to the Lord, who has brought the people safely out of Egypt and through the wilderness to the promised land.

Matthew 28:1–10

Our gospel tells of Jesus' resurrection. It is about daybreak as the women come to the grave. No human eye sees Jesus rise, but there is an earthquake and an angel of the Lord rolls away the stone covering the tomb. He tells the two Marys that Jesus is going before his disciples to Galilee. With both fear and joy in their hearts, they run to tell the disciples and, on the way, are met by their risen Lord.

Ideas of the Day

♦ We are all, at times, like the two Marys at Jesus' tomb. We are not sure how something went so horribly wrong; we are in mourning, despair, sadness, and darkness; no longer sure where faith in Jesus will lead; merely putting one foot in front of the other. In the darkness of their friend's death, the unimaginable happened: Jesus defied all that they knew was possible. He rose from the grave and created beauty and joy out of despair and death. He invited the Marys into the holy mystery of Resurrection, asking them to spread the good news that God can and will turn life upside down with God's audacious love.

♦ A movement from one space to another might heighten the sense of this dramatic shift from darkness into light, from remembering God's past deeds done on behalf of God's people and turning toward future promises of God. Read the first four readings around the baptismal font. Move to the altar for the five promises since it represents the promise of the kingdom of God that is coming (Luke 22:18). Use the parish hall, an area outdoors, the columbarium, or other places that make sense in light of the texts.

Making Connections

Water carries us across this grand retelling of our salvation history. The wind of God swept over it, which engulfed us, then washed up on the sand that counted God's people. We escaped through its parting, are called to it—out of our thirst. With it we are sprinkled clean, and when broken are gathered back together in the promised Land to be protected from its storms. We are baptized by water to death and raised from it into life. Jesus appears like lightning after death; a new brightness of God's light. Water and fire; body and spirit. May we so burn with heavenly desires, without fear, and go in peace to meet Jesus in Galilee.

Engaging All Ages

Have you ever heard the term "living wet"? This phrase refers to what it means to live as a baptized person in the world. Our baptism should matter to us every day, helping us to live the Christian life in every situation. During the Easter Vigil we all have the chance to renew our baptismal promises, where we can all recommit to "living wet." What part of the baptism service is your favorite? What parts of the covenant are the most challenging to you? Which ones are the most exciting?

Easter

It is preferable to sing the appointed Psalm or Canticle after each lesson, but the following suitable hymns and songs may be sung instead.

Hymns for the Day

The Hymnal 1982
I sing the almighty power of God 398
Let us, with a gladsome mind [P] 389
Many and great, O God, are thy works 385
Most High, omnipotent, good Lord 406, 407
Most Holy God, the Lord of heaven 31, 32
O blest Creator, source of light (vs. 1–4) 27, 28
A mighty fortress is our God [P] 687, 688
Eternal Father, strong to save 608
Lord Jesus, think on me 641
O sorrow deep! 173
The God of Abraham praise 401
Sing now with joy unto the Lord [Canticle] 425
God moves in a mysterious way 677
Surely it is God who saves me [Canticle] 678, 679

The stars declare his glory 431
God, you have given us power to sound 584
The stars declare his glory [P] 431
As longs the deer for cooling streams 658
Before thy throne, O God, we kneel 574, 575
Breathe on me, Breath of God 508
Go forth for God; go to the world in peace 347
Put forth, O God, thy Spirit's might 521
New songs of celebration render 413
Surely it is God who saves me 678, 679

Lift Every Voice and Sing II
Go down, Moses 228
Let it breathe on me 116
Spirit of the living God 115

Wonder, Love, and Praise
Wisdom freed a holy people 905
Even when young, I prayed for wisdom's grace 906
As panting deer desire the waterbrooks 727

The Sunday of the Resurrection: Easter Day

April 12, 2020

Celebrating Christ's glorious resurrection, we pray that we may be renewed in body and mind, being raised from the death of sin by God's life-giving Spirit.

Color   White

Preface   Easter

Collect

O God, who for our redemption gave your only begotten Son to the death of the cross, and by his glorious resurrection delivered us from the power of our enemy: Grant us so to die daily to sin, that we may evermore live with him in the joy of his resurrection; through Jesus Christ your Son our Lord, who lives and reigns with you and the Holy Spirit, one God, now and forever. Amen.

Readings and Psalm

Acts 10:34–43

In this lesson **Peter realizes that the good news of the gospel is meant for all people, and he proclaims the crucified and risen Jesus.** At first Peter was slow to believe that God wanted him to bring the word to a non-Jew. But God has shown this to be the divine will, and Peter gladly responds to Cornelius, a Roman centurion, together with his family and friends. The risen Jesus has appeared to chosen witnesses, and all who trust in him receive forgiveness of sins in his name.

or

Jeremiah 31:1–6

In our Old Testament lesson, **Jeremiah foretells a time when all the families of Israel will belong to the Lord.** Rejoicing, peace, and prosperity will prevail, and pilgrimages to Zion for worship will be renewed. The tenor of the prophetic language is expansive and inclusive; the joy of the Lord will be for all.

Psalm 118:1–2, 14–24

A festival hymn sung in procession in praise of the Lord's salvation and deliverance from death.

Colossians 3:1–4

Those who have shared in the experience of Christ's resurrection are to set their minds on the things that are above. Although disciples still live on earth in anticipation of the glory to come, in another sense they have already died to their former ways of sin. The true meaning and destiny of their lives is hidden with Christ in God.

or

Acts 10:34–43

In this lesson **Peter realizes that the good news of the gospel is meant for all people, and he proclaims the crucified and risen Jesus.** At first Peter was slow to believe that God wanted him to bring the word to a non-Jew. But God has shown this to be the divine will, and Peter gladly responds to Cornelius, a Roman centurion, together with his family and friends. The risen Jesus has appeared to chosen witnesses, and all who trust in him receive forgiveness of sins in his name.

Easter

John 20:1–18

Our gospel tells of **the discovery of the empty tomb and Jesus' appearance to Mary Magdalene.** While it is still dark, Mary comes and finds that the stone used to cover the tomb has been moved away. She runs and brings Peter and another disciple whom Jesus loved. Although no human eye catches sight of Jesus' rising from death, these first witnesses see the discarded grave wrappings and the other disciple perceives and believes. Mary remains weeping at the graveside and talks with a man she assumes to be the gardener. He speaks her name, and she knows her Lord.

or

Matthew 28:1–10

Our gospel tells of **Jesus' resurrection.** It is about daybreak as the women come to the grave. No human eye sees Jesus rise, but there is an earthquake and an angel of the Lord rolls away the stone covering the tomb. He tells the two Marys that Jesus goes before his disciples to Galilee. With both fear and joy in their hearts, they run to tell the disciples and, on the way, are met by their risen Lord.

Prayers of the People

Christ has burst through the tomb of death, victorious over its power, revealing the triumph of light over every darkness. In thanksgiving, we offer our prayers, responding, "Hear us, O risen Christ."

In thanksgiving for the resurrection of Jesus, who empties our spiritual tombs and reveals the way to abundant life; let us pray.

Hear us, O risen Christ.

For the leaders of the nations, especially N., our President, that they may guide the world to a greater fulfillment of its quest for freedom, justice, and peace; let us pray.

Hear us, O risen Christ.

For the innocent in troubled places and wherever strife stifles harmony, that the actions of the global community may free all who are suffering or imprisoned unjustly; let us pray.

Hear us, O risen Christ.

For the Church, for the bishops throughout our Anglican Communion, and especially N., our Presiding Bishop, and N., Bishop of our diocese; and for each of us, that we may embrace the mystery of the Pascha, and give witness to the living Christ in our midst; let us pray.

Hear us, O risen Christ.

In thanksgiving for the faithful departed, those who have left us an inheritance of God's blessings, and who now join in the chorus of angels and the saints in paradise; let us pray.

Hear us, O risen Christ.

In thanksgiving for all who have gathered here today to share in this Holy Eucharist, that we may each be changed by the message of new life, and the Food of eternal hope, growing richly and fully into the forgiving compassion of Jesus; let us pray.

Hear us, O risen Christ.

Christ, Morning Star, shine in us and through us as we continue our prayer.
(Special intentions of the congregation, the diocese, and the Anglican Communion may be added here or before the formal intercessions.)

The Celebrant adds a concluding Collect.

Images in the Readings

Matthew's accounts of the crucifixion (27:51) and the resurrection (28:2) include **earthquakes**. The eastern Mediterranean area is prone to earthquakes. Although we explain earthquakes in geological terms, often at theophanies or in apocalyptic material in the Hebrew Scriptures earthquakes are interpreted as manifestations of the power of God. Matthew means to say that the entire world was shaken by the actions of God at the tomb.

In biblical symbolism, **angel**s are messengers of God, extensions of the power of God. The description of angels attending God suggests that heaven resembles an ancient royal court, in which the monarch has servants who carry out the sovereign's will. Like the Elohist source of the Old Testament, Matthew has people seeing an angel, rather than seeing the being of God. Luther's morning and evening prayers ask for God's presence in the form of "your holy angel."

The language of being **raised** from death relies on the commonplace human idea, evident in speech and story, that up is good and down is bad. The ancient three-tier universe placed divine powers on the top level, humans in the middle—between life and death—and the dead below the earth. In today's readings, God raised Jesus (Acts), we go up to Zion (Jeremiah), Christ is above at the right hand of God (Colossians), and the angel descends like lightning. Current scientific understandings of the universe teach us that there is no "up." Thus this language must function for us symbolically: up is life, down is death.

Ideas of the Day

- Everything has changed. God's love knows no bounds. Jesus was dead, and now he is alive. Alleluia! In the song "Holy Now," Peter Mayer sings of how his childhood of empty religious actions and stories was fully transformed into sacraments. He proclaims that those same religious actions and stories, water, a child's face, the morning, a red-winged bird, are all holy now. Jesus' resurrection is the lens through which we can see not just heaven but the world here and now. Jesus' resurrection directs our gaze at God at work in the world as we see that everything is holy.

- The power of the resurrection is that we find ourselves always asking questions about it in our quest for Christ. The mystery of the resurrection constantly calls us into deeper and deeper questions. Through our questions we move from ghosts into glimpses of eternity. Thus the Easter story needs to be heard, to be experienced, and most of all, to be shared actively by the Christian family gathered in proclamation.

- Celebrating Christ's glorious resurrection, we pray that we may be renewed in body and mind, being raised from the death of sin by God's life-giving Spirit.

Making Connections

It is not "Stir-up Sunday" made popular in England, primarily about puddings. But one of the collects from which to choose on this great day beseeches God to "Stir up in your Church that Spirit of adoption which is given to us in Baptism, that we, being renewed both in body and mind, may worship you in sincerity and truth" (BCP, 222). That spirit of adoption, of being claimed as God's own completely regardless of any separation we inflict or impose on one another about who is—or is not—welcome at the table. What does it mean to be stirred up as a church? How might that break down walls and barriers we erect between people, which prevents our bodies from being renewed and our worship from being sincere?

Engaging All Ages

Hunting for eggs has become an Easter tradition for many. Plastic eggs filled with candy have become the norm, but occasionally an egg gets missed and is empty on the inside. These are the true Easter eggs. On the very first Easter morning a different sort of hunt was on—the hunt for hope. With the Jesus' death just a couple of days past, all of his friends were sad and scared. Sunday morning Mary Magdalene went to the tomb expecting it to be filled, but to her surprise it was empty! Jesus had risen, and hope was alive! When have you been surprised by hope?

Easter

Hymns for the Day

The Hymnal 1982

At the Lamb's high feast we sing 174
Christ is arisen 713
Christ Jesus lay in death's strong bands 185, 186
Come, ye faithful, raise the strain 199, 2000
Good Christians all, rejoice and sing 205
Jesus Christ is risen today 207
Look there! the Christ, our brother, comes 196, 197
The Lamb's high banquet called to share 202
The strife is o'er, the battle done 208
Hail thee, festival day 175
In Christ there is no East or West 529
Sing, ye faithful, sing with gladness 492
"Welcome, happy morning!" age to age shall say 179
Awake and sing the song 181
Come away to the skies 213
O Zion, tune thy voice 543
Thou hallowed chosen morn of praise 198
Alleluia, alleluia! Hearts and voices
      heavenward raise 191
Love's redeeming work is done 188, 189
The day of resurrection 210
We know that Christ is raised and dies no more 296
Christ the Lord is risen again 184
Christians, to the Paschal victim 183
Lift your voice rejoicing, Mary 190
O sons and daughters, let us sing (vs. 1–3, 5) 203
On earth has dawned this day of days 201

Lift Every Voice and Sing II

Amen 233
Christ has arisen 41
This is the day 219
In Christ there is no East or West 62
Great is thy faithfulness 189
In the garden 69
He 'rose 40

Wonder, Love, and Praise

Christ is risen from the dead 816, 817
Day of delight and beauty unbounded 738
God's Paschal Lamb is sacrificed for us 880

The Second Sunday of Easter

April 19, 2020

We pray that all the people who have been reborn into Christ's Body the Church may live their faith.

Color White

Preface Easter

Collect

Almighty and everlasting God, who in the Paschal mystery established the new covenant of reconciliation: Grant that all who have been reborn into the fellowship of Christ's Body may show forth in their lives what they profess by their faith; through Jesus Christ our Lord, who lives and reigns with you and the Holy Spirit, one God, forever and ever. Amen.

Readings and Psalm

Acts 2:14a, 22–32

In this lesson **Peter preaches the fundamental message of the resurrection.** The time is just after the Pentecost experience and the coming of the Holy Spirit. The author of Acts presents a picture of Peter in Jerusalem telling the news about Jesus of Nazareth. Speaking to a Jewish audience, Peter seeks to show that a passage from the Psalms that promises protection from the powers of death could not have applied to King David, but instead was a prophecy about Jesus' resurrection.

Psalm 16

Contentment, refuge, and joy are found in the presence of the Lord, and God's faithful servant will not be abandoned at death.

1 Peter 1:3–9

This reading tells of **the new birth Christians have received through baptism which brings them a living hope through Jesus' resurrection and an imperishable inheritance.** The letter is addressed to former pagans living in the country we now know as Turkey. They have been experiencing some form of persecution. They are encouraged to regard their trials as a testing, and to think of their faith as more precious than gold, which passes purified and unharmed through fire.

John 20:19–31

Our gospel presents **two appearances of the risen Lord to his disciples.** The first takes place on the very evening of the day of his resurrection. The disciples are gathered in fear, but Jesus brings them peace, gives them their mission, and bestows on them the Holy Spirit. A week later, Thomas, who had been absent when Jesus first appeared and who doubted his resurrection, now knows Jesus by his wounds and worships him as his Lord and God. Future disciples will not have Jesus' physical presence, but they will be blessed in their belief.

Prayers of the People

Let us rejoice in the living hope that has been given to us through the resurrection of Jesus Christ, as we respond to each petition by saying, "Hear us, O risen Christ."

In thanksgiving for the fellowship we share with Christians throughout the world, who hold high the light of Christ that overpowers death and reveals the promises of the God's eternal reign; let us pray.

Hear us, O risen Christ.

Grant us your abiding and merciful presence, so that in the time of trial we will not be shaken, but may walk the path of your glory to the fullness of your joy; let us pray.

Hear us, O risen Christ.

Show us your wounds, that we may see your face in the faces of the poor and hungry, the abused and rejected, the lonely and despised, and respond with the sacrificial generosity by which you redeemed humanity from sin and evil; let us pray.

Hear us, O risen Christ.

Help us to be a people of forgiveness, moving beyond our feelings of betrayal and rejection, to forgive those who have pierced our hearts, and to receive forgiveness from those whom we have wounded, so that together we may receive the victory of love for which Christ gave his life; let us pray.

Hear us, O risen Christ.

Direct the Church on the road to mutual respect, fidelity, and peace honoring different cultures, languages, races and peoples, so that we may discover the beauty of the global community for which Christ stretched forth his arms of love; let us pray.

Hear us, O risen Christ.

Bread of life and cup of our eternal joy, fill us with these riches of your grace, that we may know your constant presence with those who dwell on earth, and with those whose dwelling place is in paradise; let us pray.

Hear us, O risen Christ.

In companionship with all the baptized, let us continue our prayers.
(Special intentions of the congregation, the diocese, and the Anglican Communion may be added here or before the formal intercessions.)

The Celebrant adds a concluding Collect.

Images in the Readings

Usually depictions of the crucified Christ include the marks on his **hands and side**. Our archeological knowledge that for crucifixions nails were driven through the wrist ought not negate the symbolism of the palm, which is central to a person's hand. Neither need we get fascinated by the accounts of the stigmata, for we all carry the mark of the crucified and risen Christ on our palm each time we receive the body of Christ at communion. In John 19:34, blood and water flow from the wound on Jesus' side, and church tradition has seen in this detail not an erroneous description of human anatomy, but rather the proclamation that baptism and eucharist flow from the death of Christ.

Each year on the second Sunday of Easter we meet **doubting Thomas**. He is all of us, and we doubters are glad to share with all other doubters the peace of the risen Christ.

That Christ is **king** is an image behind the reading from Acts: King David testifies to this power; Jesus is now on David's throne; Christ is the anointed one, the Messiah.

God is the Father of our Lord Jesus Christ, and in baptism we have been given a new **birth**, to live as children of this heavenly father. The imagery continues: only children receive the full inheritance.

Ideas of the Day

♦ Thomas the Twin is hungry for connection to the Holy and not afraid to say things that might be embarrassing or awkward, qualities that give him the nickname "Doubting Thomas." Those qualities also open Thomas for an encounter with the resurrected Jesus, where we witness a deep connection between them. Jesus invites Thomas to see and touch his wounds. Although he could have, Jesus did not erase the scars of his suffering or hide the pain he experienced. Jesus is not calling us to airbrush our life. Jesus is calling us as we are into authentic relationships.

Easter

- The Great Fifty Days of Easter, beginning with Easter Week, are the time when those who have reaffirmed their baptismal vows or have been baptized at the Easter Vigil reflect on the meaning of their baptism. Through the lectionary texts they explore the mysteries of their faith. The early church called this period of the process *mystagogia*. Today the whole church enters into this period of uncovering anew the mysteries of faith expressed in sacrament, word, and life lived for others. Each time we celebrate the Holy Eucharist using Eucharistic Prayer A, we say these words: "We proclaim the mystery of faith: Christ has died. Christ is risen. Christ will come again" (BCP, 363).

- All epistle readings are taken from 1 Peter during the Easter season. You may wish to use these seven weeks as a time to look at this letter more fully in relation to baptismal renewal. 1 Peter 1:3–5 seems to have been a baptismal hymn with 1:13–21 an outline of a preparatory homily which treats the exodus as a type of baptism. 1:22—2:10 might be a second homily following the baptism. 1 Peter 2:11—3:7 represents a series of admonitions to the newly baptized, applying the Christian ideal to the moral life of various classes. 3:18—4:6 contains elements of a creed which may have been recited at the baptismal ceremony. 5:5b–9 is probably a fragment of another hymn. Other elements in the epistle may also have had a connection with the baptismal liturgy.

Making Connections

Shalom. Peace. Peace be with you. The only gospel to tell the story of Thomas's doubt, John was keen to set the tone as one of anxiety. Both times Jesus visited them in Jerusalem the doors were locked for fear of the authorities. Belief. Doubt. Seeing. Blindness. Fear clutters up all of those. It is essential to John's listeners that they understand that to see did not mean to literally set their eyes upon something as proof, but that they have the ability to perceive what is important, essential, holy behind the reality of what they are looking at. Without fear. Where does our inability to be at peace interfere with our embracing of this resurrected Jesus?

Engaging All Ages

Christians are an Easter people. This doesn't mean that Christians celebrate Easter with candy and fancy clothes every day, but it does mean that we are people who believe in resurrection. We believe that God's love can create new life for everyone in hearts, in attitudes, in actions. Being Easter people means that we believe in second chances and new beginnings. Do you have a story about a new beginning or a second chance? Tell the story; how did God bring new life to your heart, attitude, or actions?

Hymns for the Day

The Hymnal 1982
Christ the Lord is risen again 184
Good Christians all, rejoice and sing 205
Jesus is Lord of all the earth 178
Jesus lives! thy terrors now 194, 195
Sing, ye faithful, sing with gladness 492
This joyful Eastertide 192
Glorious the day when Christ was born 452
Hope of the world, thou Christ of great compassion 472
Awake, arise, lift up your voice 212
By all your saints still striving (2: St. Thomas) 231, 232
How oft, O Lord, thy face hath shone 242
O sons and daughters, let us sing 206
We walk by faith and not by sight 209

Lift Every Voice and Sing II
We walk by faith 206

Wonder, Love, and Praise

Weekday Commemorations

Tuesday, April 21
Anselm, Archbishop of Canterbury and Theologian, 1109

Anselm, born in Italy about 1033, took monastic vows in 1060 in Normandy and became Archbishop of Canterbury in 1093. Although his greatest gifts lay in theology and spiritual direction, he served in a time of conflict between Church and State. Anselm exploited the so-called "ontological argument" for God's existence: God is "that than which nothing greater can be thought." Anselm is also the most famous exponent of the "satisfaction theory" of the atonement, explaining Christ's work in terms of the contemporary feudal society. Supporting his thinking and arguing was profound piety, captured in the words, "unless I first believe, I shall not understand."

Wednesday, April 22
Hadewijch of Brabant, Poet and Mystic, 13th century

Hadewijch produced an influential body of spiritual writings. She was probably a Beguine. Her learned writings in her native Dutch as well as theological work in both Latin and French suggest she benefited from wealth. Credited as a creator of Dutch lyrical poetry to extol love between the poet and God, she also wrote couplets on religious themes. In *Book of Visions*, she dialogues with Christ. Hadewijch was widely known in the 14th and 15th centuries. Today, she, who defined Love as female, is recognized for influencing male mystics such as Meister Eckhart and John of Ruusbroec.

Thursday, April 23
Toyohiko Kagawa, Social Reformer, 1960

Kagawa, who was born in Kobe in 1888, converted from Buddhist to Christian at 15. "O God, make me like Christ," he prayed. Studying at seminaries in Japan and in Princeton, he was drawn to social reform. He lived in a windowless, 6-foot-square box in Kobe's slums from 1910 to 1924. He was imprisoned twice for flouting the law to found trade and credit unions among dock and factory workers and subsistence farmers. He was also arrested for publicly apologizing to the people of China for Japan's invasion. Kagawa saw himself as an evangelist, not merely an organizer.

Saturday, April 25
Saint Mark the Evangelist

All New Testament references to a man named Mark may not be to the same man, but if they are, he was the son of a woman householder in Jerusalem— perhaps the house in which Jesus ate his Last Supper. Mark may have been the naked young man who fled when Jesus was arrested in the Garden of Gethsemane. Paul referred to Mark in a letter to the Colossians as the cousin of Barnabas, with whom he was imprisoned; Paul was not satisfied by the reasons Mark gave for not accompanying Paul and Barnabas, so Paul refused Mark's company on a second journey. Early tradition names Mark as the author the Gospel of Mark.

The Third Sunday of Easter

April 26, 2020

We pray that God will open the eyes of our faith so that we may recognize Christ in all his redemptive work.

Color   White

Preface   Easter

Collect

O God, whose blessed Son made himself known to his disciples in the breaking of bread: Open the eyes of our faith, that we may behold him in all his redeeming work; who lives and reigns with you, in the unity of the Holy Spirit, one God, now and forever. Amen.

Readings and Psalm

Acts 2:14a, 36–41

This reading is **a summary of the preaching and other activities of the early Christian community in Jerusalem.** The crucified one, Jesus, has been made Lord and Christ. Now is the time for repentance, forgiveness, and the gift of the Spirit. There are many signs and healings as the church grows. The new disciples share fully with one another and meet for teaching, eucharistic meals, and prayers.

Psalm 116:1–4, 12–19

An offering of thanksgiving and praise by one who has been rescued from death.

1 Peter 1:17–23

In this lesson we hear that **the price of Christian freedom from the old ways of futility has been paid with the sacrificial blood of Christ. Although now we await the judgment of God the Father in awe, we have the faith and hope of people who have been born anew.** The letter from which this passage comes was addressed to former pagans, and may first have been read at an Easter baptismal service. Having been purified by Christ's imperishable offering, disciples are now to love one another from the heart.

Luke 24:13–35

Our gospel is **the story of how two disciples were met by a stranger on the road to Emmaus. That evening, as he breaks bread with them, they know the stranger to be Jesus.** While they are walking together, Jesus interprets the scriptures to them, showing that it was necessary that Christ should suffer. Later he disappears from their sight. While their Lord is no longer physically present, the church now knows that Jesus will disclose himself in scripture and the breaking of bread, and sometimes through a stranger.

Prayers of the People

Silver and gold did not buy us our freedom, but the self-sacrificing love of the Lamb. In thanksgiving for this blessed gift, we offer our prayers, responding to each petition by saying, "Hear us, O risen Christ."

Open our ears and eyes to hear your word in the midst of the daily routine, to see in others your holy presence, discovering through the voices of the poor and downtrodden your cry for justice; let us pray.

Hear us, O risen Christ.

Enlarge our ministry to welcome the uninitiated to receive the sacrament of baptism, opening the door for them to share in the death and resurrection of Christ, and the freedom to begin life anew; let us pray.

Hear us, O risen Christ.

Imbue our souls with your Body and Blood, the gladness and joy that fill our souls, and from which our love for one another overflows in mercy; let us pray.

Hear us, O risen Christ.

Easter

Release the gift of peace wherever it is entombed in fear, that resources spent to create armaments for war may instead be given for medical centers, schools, agricultural development, and employment opportunities; let us pray.

Hear us, O risen Christ.

Encourage the Church to develop new ways of communicating its message, receiving guidance from the past as new expressions are developed to speak to the present age and the generations to come; let us pray.

Hear us, O risen Christ.

Give the dying an assurance of eternal life, bring comfort to the grieving, and grant the freedom of redemption to those who have entered into their eternal rest; let us pray.

Hear us, O risen Christ.

Dear people of God, let us remember that gold and silver are false treasures compared to the risen Christ, in whom we continue our prayers.
(Special intentions of the congregation, the diocese, and the Anglican Communion may be added here or before the formal intercessions.)

The Celebrant adds a concluding Collect.

Images in the Readings

The **meal** of Emmaus is one of the many Lukan accounts of eating with Jesus, and Luke's accounts follow the biblical theme that God feeds the people. To be true to the biblical image of the life shared with Christ, the bread that we break, the wine that we share, and our methods of distribution ought to make clear that holy communion is a meal. A loaf of bread or a large circular flat bread, home baked or purchased from a local store and broken for all to see, presents a quite different image of salvation than do medieval quarter-sized tasteless hosts bought from an ecclesiastical supply company. Think about the image presented by your eating and drinking.

The **preaching** of Peter and the teaching of Christ along the road are images of our receiving the "living and enduring" saving word.

The passage from 1 Peter presents an array of images, one rushing along after another. A significant image for the book of 1 Peter is **exile**: the baptized are living in an alien land. When Christians become too comfortable in what Acts calls "this corrupt generation," we are called to be ransomed out of it and purified by obedience to the truth.

Ideas of the Day

♦ In *Sam and Dave Dig a Hole* (Candlewick Press, 2014) by Mac Barnett and Jon Klassen, Sam and Dave do just that, dig a hole in search of something "spectacular." They are so engrossed in their digging that over and over again they miss seeing their dog pointing them to what they are seeking. Eventually they tire and nap. Mid-nap they are awoken by something spectacular. How often do we miss the spectacular in our lives because of preconceived notions of procedure? How often are we given the gift of something spectacular despite ourselves?

♦ From the reading in Acts we hear that as a result of Peter's preaching, many persons were converted to Christ's way and baptized. The account then describes the kind of close communal life the Christians shared. What are the marks of Christian community that you see from this passage? How does your Christian community life up to the ideal described in Acts? What are you doing that blocks or enhances the Christian life-style?

♦ The account of the risen Christ appearing to two of the disciples on the road to Emmaus makes a good launching device for discovering how we meet Christ today. Note that before the disciples recognize the risen Christ they have to be exposed to an understanding of how God encountered people in the past. "And beginning with Moses and all the prophets, he interpreted . . . the scripture . . ." (Luke 24:27). Their mood changes as they enter into searching dialogue with the man on the road. In a sense, they have to open themselves personally to experience the Good News. Finally they experience the presence of Christ in the breaking of the bread with the stranger.

Making Connections

In a series of post-resurrection appearances found only in Luke's gospel, the travelers say to one another, "Were not our hearts burning within us while he was talking to us on the road, while he was opening the scriptures to us?" Have you ever sat at in a pew, a parlor, or a circle and heard someone open up a sacred story in such a way as to set your heart on fire? Have you wondered how it could be that you have heard a particular passage or prayer over a lifetime but never actually listened with your heart? What distinguished that teacher or storyteller? What was in the space, or not in the space, that made way for you to hear the story with new ears? How might this inform how *you* tell the stories to others?

Engaging All Ages

Look around your church. What has changed since Lent? What are the new colors? What do the cross and the altar look like? You will most likely see gold or white linens, maybe brass candlesticks and cross. Things are still "dressed up" for Easter. Have you noticed part of the Liturgy of the Word is different? We do not say the Confession during the Easter season because we are practicing living in a world that looks like God's dream for us: there is no sin, sadness, harm, or hatred. What do you think God's dream for humanity is? Draw a picture or write a poem.

Hymns for the Day

The Hymnal 1982
All who believe and are baptized 298
Baptized in water 294
Over the chaos of the empty waters 176, 177
The head that once was crowned with thorns 483
We know that Christ is raised and dies no more 296
Hail, thou once despised Jesus! 495
Lord, enthroned in heavenly splendor 307
Now the green blade riseth 204
This is the feast of victory for our God 417, 418
Come, risen Lord, and deign to be our guest 305, 306
He is risen, he is risen! 180
Shepherd of souls, refresh and bless 343

Lift Every Voice and Sing II
Baptized in water 121

Wonder, Love, and Praise
Baptized in water 767
As we gather at your Table 763

Weekday Commemorations

Monday, April 27
Zita of Tuscany, Worker of Charity, 1271
Zita, a Christian, never forgot that she was born in poverty (in Tuscany, 1271). As an adult, she gave away most of her income. At 12, she went to work for the Fatinelli family in Lucca, but she continued to practice her faith, embodying Paul's advice to work "for the Lord, not for your masters." Although her diligence met with scorn, she was not dissuaded and eventually earned the household's respect. As keeper of the keys of the household staff, she came to be venerated throughout Lucca. In popular piety, Zita is entreated to find lost keys.

Wednesday, April 29
Catherine of Siena, Mystic, 1380
Catherine Benincasa was the youngest of twenty-five children of a wealthy dyer of Siena. At six years of age, she had a remarkable vision that probably decided her life's vacation. Walking home from a visit, she stopped on the road and gazed upward, oblivious to everything around her. "I beheld our Lord seated in glory with St. Peter, St. Paul, and St. John." She went on to say, later, that the Savior smiled on her and blessed her. From then on, Catherine spent most of her time in prayer and meditation, despite her mother's attempts to force her to be like other girls. Eventually, she was accepted as a Dominican postulant.

Friday, May 1
The Apostles Saint Philip and Saint James
Philip and James are known but a little—and that through the gospels. James has been called "the Less" to distinguish him from James the son of Zebedee and from Jesus' brother James—or maybe he was young, or short. He was listed among the Twelve as James the son of Alpheus, and he may also be the person labeled in Mark's gospel as "James the younger," who witnessed the crucifixion. In John's gospel, Philip has a greater presence: Jesus called Philip as a disciple right after naming Andrew and Peter; in turn, Philip convinced his friend Nathaniel to see the Messiah. Philip, at the Last Supper, declared, "Lord, show us the Father, and we shall be satisfied."

Saturday, May 2
Athanasius of Alexandria,
Bishop and Theologian, 373

Athanasius significantly determined the direction of the Church in the fourth century. Born about 295 in Alexandria, he was ordained a deacon in 319. He attended the first council at Nicaea in 325 as secretary and adviser to Alexander, the Bishop of Alexandria. Athanasius won approval for the phrase in the Nicene Creed that expresses the godhead of Christ, "one Being with the Father." Athanasius succeeded Alexander in 328. He defended the Nicene Christology against powers political and clerical, and he was exiled five times. He wrote volumes, from treatises to theology, sermons, and letters. His *On the Incarnation of the Word of God* is a classic.

Easter

The Fourth Sunday of Easter

May 3, 2020

Ministry as a way of revealing the risen Christ through word, action, and prayer.

Color White

Preface Easter

Collect

O God, whose Son Jesus is the good shepherd of your people: Grant that when we hear his voice we may know him who calls us each by name, and follow where he leads who, with you and the Holy Spirit, lives and reigns, one God, forever and ever. Amen.

Readings and Psalm

Acts 2:42–47

The new community of believers in the resurrected Jesus devote themselves to teaching and fellowship, to sharing in eucharistic meals, and to the prayers. There are many signs and healings as the church grows. Followers of Christ express their commitment to one another even to the point of pooling their possessions. Their fellowship is characterized by joy and generosity, and many are drawn to them because of the richness of their common life.

Psalm 23

The Lord is shepherd and guide. God is present in the time of danger and is generous and merciful.

1 Peter 2:19–25

In this reading we learn that **disciples are called to bear undeserved suffering with patience, even as Christ has set an example for us, so that we might die to sin and live for righteousness.** This word is addressed primarily to those who are servants, but can well be applied to all Christians who endure pain despite having done no wrong. Their Lord has transformed the meaning of suffering and through his wounds brought healing. This letter was evidently written at a time when the Christians in Asia Minor were experiencing various forms of persecution.

John 10:1–10

Our gospel presents **two related images in which Jesus is first the shepherd in charge of the sheep and then the gate through which the sheep enter.** These teachings are set in the context of controversy. Jesus' words are directed against religious officials who do not know or truly care for their people. But Jesus knows his own sheep by name. They hear his voice and find the fullness of life.

Prayers of the People

We offer our prayers to Jesus, who is the Good Shepherd and guardian of our souls, responding to each petition by saying, "Hear us, O risen Christ."

For the parishes and missions of our diocese, that we will devote ourselves to the teaching and fellowship of Christ, to the breaking of bread, and the offering of prayers; let us pray.

Hear us, O risen Christ.

That an outpouring of generosity will flow from the gratitude and thanksgiving that dwell in our hearts, moving the Church, the household of faith, to provide relief to those in any want or need; let us pray.

Hear us, O risen Christ.

For the courage to share the faith we hold, and the willingness to listen humbly to those whose interpretation of the faith differs from our own; let us pray.

Hear us, O risen Christ.

For all who exercise leadership, that their actions may reflect the ways of the Servant, whose obedience to God released the power to overcome every darkness, and whose sacrifice opened the gates to eternity; let us pray.

Hear us, O risen Christ.

In thanksgiving for our merciful Jesus, who loves us beyond our shame and guilt, frees us from the tombs of our past, and invites us to receive his gift of overwhelming forgiveness; let us pray.

Hear us, O risen Christ.

That we may not fear the day of judgment, but entrust ourselves to the one who judges justly; let us pray.

Hear us, O risen Christ.

For all the faithful departed, who now behold the Lord Jesus in his risen glory; let us pray.

Hear us, O risen Christ.

Let us continue our prayers in the Name of the One in whom we sing the triumphant strain, "Alleluia, alleluia, alleluia."
(Special intentions of the congregation, the diocese, and the Anglican Communion may be added here or before the formal intercessions.)

The Celebrant adds a concluding Collect.

Images in the Readings

To deepen our contemplation of the metaphor of Christ as **shepherd**, it is good to review the positive use that the Bible makes of the image of **sheep**. The Jewish Scriptures remembered their people as having been sheep and goat herders. Sheep, signified the communal life of the people, constituted a source of food and clothing and functioned as the primary sacrificial gifts to God. The single wandering lamb from the parable of the lost sheep is not the image in John 10. Nor is a barefooted white-robed man a realistic depiction of the shepherd, who by the first century was thought of as lower-class and religiously unclean. In Genesis 29, Rachel is a shepherd.

Still today some herders in Iran, after gathering the sheep into an enclosure at night, lay themselves down to sleep at the opening of the pen. The wolf cannot enter through the opening, because the body of the herder has become the **gate**. In some medieval churches, the main doorway was elaborately decorated with biblical scenes, sometimes also surrounded with the signs of the zodiac, as if the door was a symbol of Christ, proclaimed in the Bible and encompassing the universe. The body of our Lord, taken in holy communion, is a gate to eternal life.

The image in Acts 2 of the Christian **commune** connects with the church's actual history and present situation, in that the baptized, living with generous hearts, contribute to all who have need. It is appropriate that at every meeting of Christians for worship there be a collection of money, goods, or services for the needy.

Ideas of the Day

♦ Social dancers develop a special way of hearing music. First, they learn the basic beat of a style of music, which guides their basic steps to build their dance around. Then, they learn to identify a voice or instrument that guides their movement in, out, and around the beat to create something more than the basic dance step. When their movement responds perfectly to that leading voice, the results are a beautiful dance. Jesus, the gatekeeper and the shepherd, calls us with a voice we learn to recognize. Jesus calls us to dance in this world.

◆ We need to approach the statements from the Gospel of John with an understanding and appreciation of poetry. The resurrection of Jesus has shaped our understanding of life and of all creation. To know Jesus, the man from Nazareth, was to know personally the presence of the God of Abraham, Isaac, and Jacob. To know the risen Christ is to experience the same personal relations with the God of creation, history, and eternity. To know this risen Christ in daily life is like being given a cool drink of spring water on a hot day. It is like knowing that we are not alone but a part of a "living vine" of God's people. And so John describes our relationship to the resurrection in words of poetry and analogy.

Making Connections

Jesus as gate is an interesting follow up to Jesus as shepherd. As shepherd, there is the lovely suggestion that Jesus leads the sheep—from up front. Not the usual corralling and herding, just walking ahead. And the sheep follow because he knows them, and they know him. There are so many times when Jesus walks, and we do not follow. He leads us directly into controversy to be peacemakers, into brokenness to be reconcilers. As the gate, we know that he is not just leading us but is our way back. But sometimes we do not want to go. We prefer to listen to the voices that would rob us of those opportunities. These thieves say, "Be afraid. Stay. Do nothing. Waste time and resources on these other things, and with these other leaders. You need to take care of number one. It's too hard, and too dangerous."

Engaging All Ages

Taking care of sheep is a daily and often messy job. During lambing season sheep give birth at all hours of the day or night. Their hooves and wool coats need regular caring for, and of course they need healthy food, water, and space to wander and exercise. Sheep are very docile and kind animals, which is why they are incredibly vulnerable to predators. What does it say about Jesus as the Good Shepherd in that he is like someone whose main goal is to care for and protect the most vulnerable creatures?

Hymns for the Day

The Hymnal 1982
Good Christians all, rejoice and sing! (vs. 1, 3–5) 205
My Shepherd will supply my need 664
The King of love my shepherd is 645, 646
The Lord my God my shepherd is 663
I come with joy to meet my Lord 304
Christ the Lord is risen again 184
Shepherd of souls, refresh and bless 343
Sing, ye faithful, sing with gladness 492
The strife is o'er, the battle done 208
Jesus, our mighty Lord 478
Praise the Lord, rise up rejoicing 334
Savior, like a shepherd lead us 708

Lift Every Voice and Sing II
The Lord is my Shepherd 104

Wonder, Love, and Praise
Come now, O Prince of Peace, make us one body 795

Weekday Commemorations

Monday, May 4
Monnica, Mother of Augustine of Hippo, 387
Tucked into *The Confessions of Saint Augustine* is the story of his mother Monnica, who was born in North Africa around 331. Within her deepening life of prayer, she converted her husband Patricius to Christianity, and she longed to bring her son to Christ as well. He was baptized in Milan in 387. Monnica became sick as she and her two sons awaited a ship in the port of Rome to return them home to Africa. As she lay dying, she asked that her sons remember her "at the altar of the Lord." Her mortal remains were buried in 1430 at the Church of St. Augustine in Rome.

Easter

Tuesday, May 5
Martyrs of the Reformation Era

On this date, the Church of England commemorates all of the English saints and martyrs of the Reformation Era—not just Anglican martyrs like Thomas Cranmer, Hugh Latimer, and Nicholas Ridley but also those Roman Catholics who were killed by Anglicans as well as other Christians who were persecuted by fellow Christians, most notably the Anabaptists and the Quakers. Baptized Christians are incorporated into God's one Church and, thus, heirs of both martyrs and their executioners. Such a double heritage encourages efforts to heal divisions for a future in Christ in which all are one.

Friday, May 8
Julian of Norwich, Mystic and Theologian, c.1417

Little is known of Julian's life. Born about 1342, the only writing of hers we have is *Revelations of Divine Love*, the description of her "showings," or visions, which she experienced after an illness when she was 30. Prior to her illness, Julian had desired three gifts from God: "the mind of his passion, bodily sickness in youth, and three wounds—of contrition, of compassion, of willful longing toward God." Although she forgot about the first two until after her illness, the third was always with her. After recovering, she became an anchorite at Norwich, living alone in a hut attached to the Church of St. Julian (hence, her name) and gaining fame as a mystic.

Saturday, May 9
Gregory of Nazianzus, Bishop and Theologian, 389

This Cappadocian Father loved God, *belle lettres*, and humankind. Born about 330, he studied rhetoric in Athens; with his friend Basil of Caesarea, he compiled the works of Origen. He was ordained a presbyter against his will in 361 and attempted a life of austerity; however, the times were against living peacefully. He became Bishop of Sasima ("a detestable little place," he wrote) before moving to Constantinople in 379 with hope renewed. There, he preached five sermons on the doctrine of the Trinity: therein rests his reputation. Among the Fathers of the Church, he is known as "The Theologian."

The Fifth Sunday of Easter

May 10, 2020

One cannot be Christian alone; apart from the Body, we can do nothing.

Color　　White

Preface　　Easter

Collect

Almighty God, whom truly to know is everlasting life: Grant us so perfectly to know your Son Jesus Christ to be the way, the truth, and the life, that we may steadfastly follow his steps in the way that leads to eternal life; through Jesus Christ your Son our Lord, who lives and reigns with you, in the unity of the Holy Spirit, one God, forever and ever. Amen.

Readings and Psalm

Acts 7:55–60

A deacon of the church, Stephen, preaches salvation history before the high priest and the council, culminating in a vision of Jesus standing at God's right hand. Those gathered are so provoked by this testimony that, enraged, they drag him from the city and stone him to death. Those stoning Stephen lay their cloaks at the feet of a young man named Saul, who will later become the apostle Paul. Stephen prays God to forgive those putting him to death, as did Jesus from the cross.

Psalm 31:1–5, 15–16

A psalm of trust by one who looks to the Lord for mercy and protection.

1 Peter 2:2–10

This reading presents **a series of images from the Old Testament, describing Christians as a chosen people called by God to God's service.** It is possible that the passage was once used during an Easter season baptismal liturgy. Newborn disciples are to purify themselves and, as living stones, to join themselves to Jesus, the rejected one, who now is the cornerstone of the spiritual temple. They are the new Israel, called out of darkness into light.

John 14:1–14

In our gospel passage Jesus speaks with his disciples shortly before his passion and tells them that he is the way, the truth, and the life. He is the way because he himself is going the way of the sacrifice of his death, so to prepare a place for his disciples. In this way followers will discover the truth that Jesus so intimately reflects the character of God that those who have seen him have seen the Father. All who come to the Father through Jesus will find true life.

Prayers of the People

Let us call upon God to hear our prayers and to grant us those things that are in accord with the divine will, responding, "Hear us, O risen Christ."

For Christians who are imprisoned and persecuted for their faith that, like Stephen, they may follow the light that casts out all fear; let us pray.

Hear us, O risen Christ.

That we may do the works that Jesus revealed in his ministry, the healing of the sick, the raising up of the lowly, the giving of sight to the blind, and the blessing of the poor and the grieving; let us pray.

Hear us, O risen Christ.

Easter

For those who are spiritually lost, or who question their faith, or whose souls are wrapped in the shadows of doubt, that they may share their misgivings with Jesus, who gently unfolds the truth and reveals a way; let us pray.

Hear us, O risen Christ.

That the Church, the community of the baptized, may vigorously proclaim the alleluias of Easter, revealing the light of Christ, whose victory over death breaks the chains of darkness and despair; let us pray.

Hear us, O risen Christ.

In thanksgiving for the beauty that is set before our eyes, and for the mysteries yet unseen, that we may honor the expansiveness of creation and be guardians of its splendor; let us pray.

Hear us, O risen Christ.

In thanksgiving for missionaries throughout the world, who reveal God's Word in challenging times and places; let us pray.

Hear us, O risen Christ.

That the Lord may comfort those in the waning days of life, and bring to life eternal those who have died in the hope of the resurrection; let us pray to the Lord.

Hear us, O risen Christ.

As a chosen people who share the royal priesthood of Christ, let us add to these petitions.
(Special intentions of the congregation, the diocese, and the Anglican Communion may be added here or before the formal intercessions.)

The Celebrant adds a concluding Collect.

Images in the Readings

For some Christians and pieties, the image of Christ as the **Way** has been used to condemn most other people. John's community did indeed think of itself as enjoying the greatest **truth** and **life** eternal. However, we are called to recognize the Way as the good news that God loves the whole world, as the wideness of God's mercy.

John's metaphor of the Father's **house** and its many dwelling places has been literalized for many Christians, as if heaven were a king's mansion with outbuildings provided for the lesser inhabitants. In a different application of this image, the house is the room in which we weekly gather: here God dwells. Here God serves up our meals. 1 Peter uses the image of house to be a metaphor for the believing community.

1 Peter is filled with images. Several medieval mystics used the image of the eucharist being **milk**. The central image of this passage is Christ as the **cornerstone**, the living stone, of the house that is the church. Many cornerstones are engraved with the date of construction. For Christians, this date is the year of our baptism. Perhaps those congregations that publish members' birthdays could replace these dates with their baptismal anniversary.

Ideas of the Day

♦ Jesus' words of the future offer both comfort and mystery to his followers and call for a response. The song "Woyaya," written by Sol Amarfio, describes the tension of embracing the Holy Mystery of faith in God. "Woyaya" is translated "We are going." The simple lyrics change between what the singers or followers know, "we are going," and what heaven or the holy knows, where they are going and when. As followers in the way of Jesus how do we pray these words in our lives?

♦ The church will reveal the risen Christ to the world and to each other through the community of faithful gathered and scattered as the Body of Christ. We are "made one body with him, that he may dwell in us, and we in him" (BCP, 336).

♦ The Holy Spirit empowers the church. The text for this Sunday might be called a "Prayer of Consecration" for the church. The Body of Christ becomes a living sacrament to the world, an "outward and visible sign" of Christ's redeeming presence in history. In the great "priestly prayer of Christ" from today's Gospel, Jesus asks the Father to "sanctify the truth" in all who follow as Christ's disciples. When we consecrate something, we recognize its holiness. Jesus prays that his disciples (us and the Church) will be consecrated so that we too will be outward and visible signs of God's presence in the world.

Making Connections

We can do even greater things than Jesus himself did. That's what John says. It must be true, that the millions of followers of Jesus have the power to heal, feed, and miraculously turn the hearts of far more people than Jesus alone can do. Our invitation from Presiding Bishop Michael Curry to practice "The Way of Love" challenges us to enter into reflection, discernment, and commitment around the practices of Turn—Learn—Pray—Worship—Bless—Go—Rest. Bishop Curry believes that "we will grow as communities following the loving, liberating, life-giving way of Jesus. His way has the power to change each of our lives and to change this world."

Engaging All Ages

Jesus tells us that people will know we are followers of his by how we love one another and how we love others. On a sheet of paper write down all the ways that Jesus showed loved to people on earth. Next, tear or cut out each of the descriptions. Fold them up and place them in a bowl. Play a game of "Be Like Jesus" charades. Which of the actions were hardest to act to out in the game? What about in real life? Who do you have a hard time showing love to?

Hymns for the Day

The Hymnal 1982
Come away to the skies 213
When Stephen full of power and grace 243
By all your saints still striving (St. Stephen) 231, 232
Christ is made the sure foundation 518
Open your ears, O faithful people 536
God of the prophets 359
The Church's one foundation 525
We the Lord's people, heart and voice uniting 51
Come, my Way, my Truth, my Life 487
Father, we praise thee, now the night is over 1, 2
He is the Way 463, 464
Praise the Lord through every nation 484, 485
Thou art the Way, to thee alone 457

Lift Every Voice and Sing II

Wonder, Love, and Praise
When from bondage we are summoned 753, 754
Here, O Lord, your servants gather 793

Weekday Commemorations

Monday, May 11
Johann Arndt and Jacob Boehme,
Mystics, 1621 and 1624
Arndt (b. 1555) and Boehme (b. 1575), prominent Lutheran mystical writers, influenced contemporaries as well as descendants. A peacemaker, Arndt devoted his life to serving God as a diligent pastor. *True Christianity*, his major work, seeks to de-emphasize the legal aspect of salvation and highlight abiding in Christ through praying and reading Scripture. Boehme had mystical visions in his youth, one of which led him to write *The Rising of the Dawn* in 1600; later, he produced many more works on mystical theology and cosmology. He influenced radical pietists, including the Quakers, and English Romantics, notably William Blake.

Wednesday, May 13
Frances Perkins, Social Reformer, 1965
Perkins, born in 1880 and confirmed an Episcopalian in 1905, served President Franklin Roosevelt, also Episcopalian, as Secretary of Labor—the first woman in a Cabinet and the only member throughout Roosevelt's 12 years in office. With Roosevelt, Perkins shaped New Deal legislation, including banning child labor and establishing the Social Security program. They outlined lofty goals in 1933 for American society and accomplished all but universal healthcare. An eloquent laywoman, she attended church as well as monthly retreats at an Episcopal convent. In creating a just world order, she served as the face of Christ to this nation.

Friday, May 15
Pachomius of Tabenissi, Monastic, 348
The founder of monastic life wherein members live in community rather than as hermits, Pachomius had encountered caring, loving Christians while imprisoned. He was baptized upon release, after which he led an ascetic life of manual labor and prayer while caring for the poor. Followers—especially the young, very old, or ill—were drawn to his definition of a monasticism not so strict and hard. He and his disciples wrote the first rubric for that monastic life, quite controversial then. Within a generation of Pachomius' death, his monastic federation included several thousand monks and nuns, spreading from Europe to Palestine.

Easter

The Sixth Sunday of Easter

May 17, 2020

One cannot be Christian alone; apart from the Body we can do nothing.

Color　　White

Preface　　Easter

Collect

O God, you have prepared for those who love you such good things as surpass our understanding: Pour into our hearts such love towards you, that we, loving you in all things and above all things, may obtain your promises, which exceed all that we can desire; through Jesus Christ our Lord, who lives and reigns with you and the Holy Spirit, one God, forever and ever. Amen.

Readings and Psalm

Acts 17:22–31

This lesson is **Paul's address in a public forum to the curious citizens of Athens.** The apostle has arrived in the intellectual and cultural center of the Greek world. The author of Acts has him deliver a kind of sample sermon for a pagan audience. Troubled by their worship of many gods, Paul uses their altar dedicated to an unknown god as an opportunity to tell them of the one true Lord of heaven and earth, and of the time of judgment and the man he raised from the dead.

Psalm 66:8–20

A hymn of praise and thanksgiving to God, who rules in majesty and delivers the people.

1 Peter 3:13–22

This reading offers **guidance for all Christians, counseling a readiness to suffer patiently for doing what is right.** The First Letter of Peter was written at a time when Christians in Asia Minor were experiencing persecution. The author has given advice to particular groups of people and now urges all disciples to live together in love and humility, always being willing to speak in defense of their Christian hope. They should keep their consciences clear, and, if they do suffer, they are to remember how Christ, the just one, died for the unjust.

John 14:15–21

In our gospel **Jesus promises his followers that those who love him will be guided by the Holy Spirit and will also see him.** The evangelist presents Jesus in final conversation with his followers. Soon he will be taken away from them by death, but God will send another Counselor. The world (that is, Godless society) cannot receive this Spirit of truth nor come to perceive Jesus as still living. Yet those who follow the commandments of love will find new life in intimate association with Jesus and the Father.

Prayers of the People

We offer our prayers and thanksgivings to God, who in the midst of our trials and adversities gives us the faith to endure, responding, "Hear us, O risen Christ."

In thanksgiving for the holy commandments of the Lord's truth, and Jesus' eternal gift of love, that we may follow them as pathways to sanctification; let us pray.

Hear us, O risen Christ.

That we may be a community of joyous believers, bearing one another's burdens, forgiving each other's sins, responding to the needs of all, so that the world may see and know that all things are being made new through the Risen One; let us pray.

Hear us, O risen Christ.

Easter

In thanksgiving for this Eucharistic Meal, where Christ our Passover is sacrificed for us and invites us to share in heaven's feast; let us pray.

Hear us, O risen Christ.

In thanksgiving for the faith of Abraham and Sarah, and of all the faithful departed whose every breath was lived in response to God's promises; let us pray.

Hear us, O risen Christ.

That we may give honor to those considered least in our society, knowing that Jesus reveals the divine will through their lives and in the course of their abiding faithfulness; let us pray.

Hear us, O risen Christ.

That children may receive a full measure of food, education, parental love, and a religious upbringing; let us pray.

Hear us, O risen Christ.

In thanksgiving for those who volunteer their time for the ministry of Christ in this church, in our diocese, and throughout the world; let us pray.

Hear us, O risen Christ.

As adopted children of Jesus, through our passage in the waters of baptism, let us continue our prayers and thanksgiving.
(Special intentions of the congregation, the diocese, and the Anglican Communion may be added here or before the formal intercessions.)

The Celebrant adds a concluding Collect.

Images in the Readings

John calls the Spirit of truth our **Advocate**. This image implies a trial and the probability of judgment. Standing before God, we need someone to speak on our behalf. The reading from 1 Peter also includes the image of a trial in which we must defend our stance.

In John 14, Jesus uses adoption imagery for those who receive the Spirit of truth. Yet Paul's sermon at the Areopagus calls all his pagan hearers God's **offspring.** For centuries, Jewish and Christian theologians have discussed how humans are both like and unlike God, how we enact our relationship to the

Divine. A dominant teaching has been that, just as God cares for creation, so as God's offspring we are to be dedicated to that care.

The church is the **ark**, floating above the chaos of the seas, brought in safety to the harbor. One early Christian bishop directed his clergy to hold the baptismal candidates down under the water three times until they rose up gasping for air. The water of baptism not only gently washes the infant; it also joins the candidate to the death and resurrection of Christ. The eighteenth-century Welsh Methodist poet Ann Griffiths wrote, "We'll yet escape the drowning / Because God is our ark."

Ideas of the Day

- ◆ A common elementary school Valentine's Day custom is for students to give each person in their class a card. They give them to their friends, those they barely know, and those they do not like. Every student shows love to each member of the community. Jesus is calling all followers to embrace love as more than a feeling, to embrace love as an action. To follow holy commandments is an outward sign of the inward grace we have received: God's love. Jesus is calling all of us to practice the spiritual discipline of love.

- ◆ Continuing from last Sunday, the church will reveal the risen Christ to the world and to each other through the community of the faithful: "I am the vine, you are the branches. Those who abide in me and I in them bear much fruit, because apart from me you can do nothing" (John 15:5).

Making Connections

Jesus is leaving, but he promises his followers that he will not leave them alone. He promises that those who do the sometimes hard, always blessed, work of loving God, and being loved back by God, will never be alone—not their generation, nor the one to follow, nor the ones to follow them. The forces of evil do not see the risen Jesus, but the disciples recognize him in their love for one another. We have been promised an indwelling of the Holy Spirit, and advocate who will make her home within us, and assure us peace. That is Good News.

Easter

Engaging All Ages

"Peace I leave with you; my peace I give to you."
What does the peace of Jesus look, feel, or sound
like? We often hear about being peacekeepers
and peacemakers—what is the difference? One is
about forcing good behavior to keep everyone safe
(peacekeeping) and the other is about working to
prevent bad behavior through in understanding and
trust (peacemaking.) If peacemaking is successful,
peacekeeping isn't necessary. The peace of Jesus is the
knowledge that everyone is beloved by God. No one
is left out of God's love. What would the world be like
if everyone believed that they and their neighbor were
deeply loved equally?

Hymns for the Day

The Hymnal 1982

Alleluia, alleluia! Hearts and voices heavenward
raise 191
As those of old their first fruits brought [Rogation] 705
Now the green blade riseth 204
O Jesus, crowned with all renown [Rogation] 292
All things bright and beautiful 405
Creating God, your fingers trace 394, 395
Many and great, O God, are thy works 385
This is my Father's world 651
We plow the fields, and scatter 291
We sing of God, the mighty source 386, 387
O Love of God, how strong and true 455, 456
Sing, ye faithful, sing with gladness 492
Come down, O Love divine 516
Come, gracious Spirit, heavenly Dove 512
Creator Spirit, by whose aid 500
O thou who camest from above 704
To thee, O Comforter divine 514

Lift Every Voice and Sing II
He Lives 42
More love to thee, O Christ 87

Wonder, Love, and Praise
God the sculptor of the mountains 746, 747

Weekday Commemorations

Tuesday, May 19
Dunstan, Archbishop of Canterbury, 988

Although the phrase, "contemplatives in action," sounds
like a contradiction in terms, the work of Bishops
Dunstan, Aethelwold of Winchester, and Oswald of
Worcester (his former pupils), manifested just that. After
King Edgar named Dunstan Archbishop of Canterbury
in 960 (about age 50), Dunstan exploited the vigorous
currents of the Benedictine monastic revival by raising
the monastic prayer life to the attention of the English
Church. The three men sought better education and
discipline among clergy, the end of landed family
influence in the Church, restoration and establishment
of monasteries, revival of the monastic life for women,
and closer ordering of the liturgy. Effects of the
"Monastic Agreement" lasted long.

Wednesday, May 20
Alcuin of York, Deacon, 804

Born in York about 730 into a noble family related to
Willibrord, first missionary to the Netherlands, Alcuin
inherited a strong tradition and zeal for learning from
the early English church. At the cathedral in York,
Alcuin was schooled under Archbishop Egbert, a pupil
of Bede's. As a deacon (770), Alcuin headed the school.
In 796, he became Abbot of Tours, where he remained
until he died. He was a man of learning, charm,
and integrity. As director of Charlemagne's Palace
School at Aachen and under Charlemagne's authority,
Alcuin oversaw reform of the liturgy as well as the
adaptation and editing of service books from Rome,
thus preserving many Collects, including the Collect
for Purity, which opens the Eucharist.

Thursday, May 21
Ascension Day

Friday, May 22
Helena of Constantinople,
Protector of the Holy Places, 330

Helena was mother of Emperor Constantine of Rome
and a devout Christian who cared for the poor. About
325, when she was granted the title of Empress of the
Western Empire, she traveled to the Holy Land to seek
places cited in the Gospels. Her most important finds
were the Cross of the Crucifixion and the site of the
Resurrection. Legend has it that she had the latter area
excavated, and three crosses imprinted with "Jesus,
King of the Jews" were discovered. The church Helena
built there became the Church of the Holy Sepulcher.

Ascension Day

May 21, 2020

The risen Jesus is lifted up into heaven and no longer seen by the disciples.

Color   White

Preface   Ascension

Collect

Almighty God, whose blessed Son our Savior Jesus Christ ascended far above all heavens that he might fill all things: Mercifully give us faith to perceive that, according to his promise, he abides with his Church on earth, even to the end of the ages; through Jesus Christ our Lord, who lives and reigns with you and the Holy Spirit, one God, in glory everlasting. Amen.

or this

Grant, we pray, Almighty God, that as we believe your only begotten Son our Lord Jesus Christ to have ascended into heaven, so we may also in heart and mind there ascend, and with him continually dwell; who lives and reigns with you and the Holy Spirit, one God, forever and ever. Amen.

Readings and Psalm

Acts 1:1–11

In the opening passage of the Acts of the Apostles the author summarizes the last events and instructions of Jesus' earthly ministry before he is lifted up into heaven. The book is formally dedicated to Theophilus, who may have been an early convert to Christianity. Jesus tells his followers to wait for their baptism in the Holy Spirit, after which their missionary work will spread from Jerusalem out to all the world. Jesus will one day come again, but his disciples now have a message to bring to all peoples.

Psalm 47

A hymn of praise to the mighty king who is raised up and enthroned on high.

or

Psalm 93

God reigns, the Lord of all creation, and has established the earth and subdued the great waters.

Ephesians 1:15–23

In this lesson **Paul gives thanks for the faith and love of the Ephesians and prays that they may see with their inward eyes the power of God, who has raised and enthroned Jesus far above all earthly and heavenly dominions.** How vast is the treasure that God offers to those who trust in God! The Lord Christ now reigns as head of the church, which is his body and which experiences the fullness of his love.

Luke 24:44–53

In our gospel **Jesus leaves his followers with the promise of the Holy Spirit and is carried up into heaven.** The disciples are to await their empowerment from on high before beginning their mission to the world. Joyfully they return from Bethany, the town where Jesus had stayed before his passion. They enter the temple and praise God.

Prayers of the People

Come, let us pray with thanksgiving to him who ascended with great triumph to God's heavenly kingdom, responding to each petition by saying, "Hear us, Ascended Lord."

Open our minds to understand the truth of holy scripture, fashioning our lives to proclaim its saving message, and bearing witness to the power of forgiveness and mercy; for this we pray.

Hear us, ascended Lord.

Easter

Send us into places of poverty and despair, that we may feed the hungry, comfort those who are ill, be present to the lonely, offer hope to the downtrodden, and reveal the healing power of the Risen and Ascended Christ; for this we pray.

Hear us, ascended Lord.

Turn our hearts toward your will, that we may choose new life, receive the grace of your forgiveness, and bear witness to your loving and sacrificial hope; for this we pray.

Hear us, ascended Lord.

Move the leaders of Church and government to guide us into a simplicity of living, discovering our worth through virtuous living, and leaving behind the false promises of the world's wealth; for this we pray.

Hear us, ascended Lord.

Give us faith to perceive that Christ dwells with his Church on earth and prepares for us a heavenly mansion, especially remembering today _____ and all who have died; for this we pray.

Hear us, ascended Lord.

In thanksgiving for the faith of the apostles, whose devotion to Jesus inspires our holy and life-giving commitment to proclaim his message today; for this we pray.

Hear us, ascended Lord.

With the freedom of an enlightened heart, we join in the inheritance of the saints as we continue our prayers and thanksgivings.
(Special intentions of the congregation, the diocese, and the Anglican Communion may be added here or before the formal intercessions.)

The Celebrant adds a concluding Collect.

Images in the Readings

Ascension Day plays with the ancient cosmological picture of the three-tier universe, the highest level of which is **heaven**, or "the heavens." Over the centuries, Christians have speculated in quite different ways about what this heaven is. By the nineteenth century, heaven came to be described as a kind of family summer camp, perfection in populist human terms. However, in the Bible, heaven is often a synonym for God, a way to speak about divine majesty and mercy. In Acts, the ascending Jesus is covered with a cloud, which in the Hebrew Scriptures usually refers to the elusive presence yet cosmic power of God. It is important that today's references to heaven not suggest that it is a place that is far away. The risen Christ is here in the assembly of believers.

Luke has two men in **white robes** speaking with the disciples. The Christian church has regularized the wearing of white robes as the sign of baptism. We all can speak of the power of the ascended Christ.

In Ephesians, the **body of Christ** is the church imagined like Atlas, a giant standing on earth holding up the skies, the head being Christ, and the body being the church that fills the world. Today we blend this understanding of "body of Christ" with the bread we eat and the assembly gathered to worship.

Ideas of the Day

- In Godly Play there is a practice referred to as "Changing the Light." After a candle has been used in storytelling or prayer, it is carefully extinguished with a snuffer so that the wafting smoke is visible. The storyteller notes that even though the flame is no longer there, the light is not extinguished; it is changed. The Light goes with them as they leave. In the Ascension of Jesus, Jesus' presence is changed in a way that is hard to understand. He ascends and is no longer with the disciples in the same way that he was. Yet Jesus is with them.

- The revelation we celebrate today is that the direct experience of God revealed to humankind in Jesus of Nazareth continues to be experienced when the Body of Christ, the Church, gathers in witness, love, and mission. Jesus brought power and hope to people. As he talked, healed, and loved them, they felt the direct presence of God. To be in the company of Jesus was to be in the company of God. The appearances of Jesus to the disciples during this Easter season are more than seeing a vision or acknowledging tht death could not destroy the Lord. We are told that the faithful will continue to experience his presence even though we can no longer see him. The Holy Spirit will come, and we will again feel the same healing power that frees us from our enslavement to sin and guilt.

♦ In sharing the feast of the Ascension, we need to keep in mind the poetic nature of the statement of the Creeds and of the Acts account. The power and presence of Christ are eternal experiences, not limited to time and space. The presence of Christ is a much our experience as it was the experience of the disciples. Christ "reigns" eternally with God, the creative power that calls us into being.

Making Connections

In the Catechism we say that what we believe about ascension is this: "that Jesus took our human nature into heaven where he now reigns with the Father and intercedes for us" (BCP, 850). It is through this that we can believe that God truly knows our experience on earth, as humans. Our passion and sorrow. Our feelings of isolation and joy. This is where the incarnation still works for us, if you will, in the revelation not only as God on earth, but as us in heaven. When Luke was written most people believed the world was divided into three parts—heaven, the earth, and the underworld. What do you believe? Why?

Engaging All Ages

Rogation Days are the three days before Ascension Day. In some cultures farmers have their crops blessed by a priest during these days, while in other cultures congregations process around the parameters of their village or their church grounds, asking for God's blessing and protection over them in the coming year. (This is often called "beating the boundaries.") Consider walking the parameters of your church grounds, your neighborhood, your apartment building, or property. Stop at each corner and ask God to bless and protect the land and all those who live, work, rest, and worship within that space.

Hymns for the Day

The Hymnal 1982
And have the bright immensities 459
Hail thee, festival day! 216
A hymn of glory let us sing 217, 218
Alleluia! sing to Jesus! 460, 461
Hail the day that sees him rise 214
See the Conqueror mounts in triumph 215
The Lord ascendeth up on high 219
Crown him with many crowns 494
Hail, thou once despised Jesus 495
It was poor little Jesus, yes, yes 468
Lord, enthroned in heavenly splendor 307
O Lord most high, eternal King 220, 221
Rejoice, the Lord is King 481
Rejoice, the Lord of life ascends 222

Lift Every Voice and Sing II
Go preach my gospel 161
He is king of kings 96

Wonder, Love, and Praise
God the sculptor of the mountains 746, 747

Easter

The Seventh Sunday of Easter: The Sunday after Ascension Day

May 24, 2020

The church consecrated as the Body of Christ.

Easter

Color White

Preface Ascension

Collect

O God, the King of glory, you have exalted your only Son Jesus Christ with great triumph to your kingdom in heaven: Do not leave us comfortless, but send us your Holy Spirit to strengthen us, and exalt us to that place where our Savior Christ has gone before; who lives and reigns with you and the Holy Spirit, one God, in glory everlasting. Amen.

Readings and Psalm

Acts 1:6–14

In this reading **we hear of Jesus' promise of empowerment for mission by the Holy Spirit, after which he is envisioned being lifted up into heaven.** The author of Acts pictures the missionary work of the church spreading outward from Jerusalem. In obedience to Jesus' command, the disciples return to the city and, with others of Jesus' followers and relatives, prayerfully await the coming of the Spirit. Although Jesus will one day appear again, his community now has a ministry to bring the good news to the world.

Psalm 68:1–10, 32–35

A psalm of praise to the mighty God who has brought the people out of Egypt and saved Israel from her enemies. God reigns on high.

1 Peter 4:12–14; 5:6–11

In this lesson we learn that **when Christians find it necessary to suffer for their faith, they are to know that they are sharing in Christ's sufferings.** They can even find cause for rejoicing, recognizing that this may well be a sign that God's Spirit is with them. The advice was given during an outbreak of persecution of Christians in Asia Minor. The disciples are urged to make sure that they only suffer in a right cause and are then unashamed to confess Christ's name.

John 17:1–11

In our gospel **Jesus asks the Father that his glory may be made fully known in his Son, and he prays for his disciples, through whom this glory now shines.** These words are part of what is called Jesus' high-priestly prayer offered before his death. God's glory has been shown forth in Jesus' ministry and will be radiant in his crucifixion and resurrection. Now and afterward Jesus' followers will realize that all which Jesus has given to them has come from the Father.

Prayers of the People

Let us offer our prayers in the Name of Jesus, who dwelt among us, died and rose again for our salvation, and ascended into the heavenly realm, responding, "Hear us, ascended Lord."

That we may place our lives in the sacred heart of Jesus, who claims us as his own, and reveals his glory through our lives; let us pray.

Hear us, ascended Lord.

That our hands may feed the poor and tend the sick, that we may create a church where all are welcomed and where visitors are seen as blessings, and that we may ascend beyond earthly hesitations to grasp the divine inspiration that is implanted within us; let us pray.

Hear us, ascended Lord.

For those who fear the discovery of secret sins and the private guilt that has many names, that they may have confidence in the priestly gift of reconciliation, the courage to admit their shortcomings, and the greater courage to accept God's tender forgiveness; let us pray.

Hear us, ascended Lord.

For an end to violence and abuse, and to all things that harm God's creation and rob humanity of its inherent dignity; let us pray

Hear us, ascended Lord.

That N., our President, members of Congress, and those who sit on the Supreme Court may take seriously the authority invested in them, leaving partisanship behind, and exercising leadership that best responds to the people of our nation and world; let us pray.

Hear us, ascended Lord.

For those who have died, and whom we commend to eternal life, remembering especially _____; let us pray.

Hear us, ascended Lord.

In thanksgiving for our families and friends, and for the communion of saints, we continue our prayers. *(Special intentions of the congregation, the diocese, and the Anglican Communion may be added here or before the formal intercessions.)*

The Celebrant adds a concluding Collect.

Images in the Readings

John writes about the **name** of God. When we say, "Stop in the name of the law," we mean that our very invoking of "the law" brings with it the powerful authority behind the law. So the name of God conveys divine mercy and might. Jews still today, careful not to misuse God's name, invoke *Hashem*, "the Name," as a circumlocution for God. Christians can call upon the name of the LORD by invoking Jesus Christ.

Eternal life, John writes in this chapter, is knowing God now.

As did the gospel of the first Sunday of Lent, 1 Peter speaks in a literal way about the **devil**. One of the primary questions raised by the world's religions

is why there is evil in the world and within the human heart. Borrowed from dualistic religions, the image of the devil personifies the power of evil into a kind of perpetually troublesome anti-God. Christians trust in the mighty hand of God to protect them against this adversary.

Ideas of the Day

- *Man man zou* is a common Mandarin expression used when saying goodbye. Directly translated as "walk slowly," it is a ritual phrase that means "stay a bit" or "take care as you go." It communicates that the person who is taking leave is close to your heart and you enjoy their presence. Before his death and after his resurrection, Jesus is preparing his disciples to say goodbye. In Luke, he prays for them before his resurrection. In Acts he gives them the promise of his Holy Spirit before he ascends.

- On this last Sunday of Easter, lead the congregation in a liturgy of baptismal renewal based on 1 Peter if you have been focused on this epistle throughout this season. See the Second Sunday of Easter for some ideas.

- As this Sunday follows the Feast of the Ascension, review those times during the past year when the congregation has experienced acts of healing, caring, and forgiving. Share stories of these events and talk about how the ascended Christ is feeding and healing us in our own day through those experiences. Our stories continue the gospel narrative. Our stories show how the reign of Christ continues even in our own time.

Making Connections

The words in John's farewell prayer, attributed to Jesus, help us understand the theology of the early Johannine community. The intimacy between Jesus and God. The love of Jesus for all persons, especially those "given to him" and his desire that they be protected in his absence. It is a hope that none are lost as aliens in this world, but found, held together, and dedicated to the service of truth. It is a prayer of oblation, where he offers himself and his followers into the service of God. This is a beautiful idea, and well-timed send off into Pentecost, where we will be launched into stories of service and discipleship armed with, and protected by, this great love.

Easter

Engaging All Ages

As we get ready for Pentecost and Ordinary Time, it is good to think about how Paul and Silas behaved in prison (Acts 16:16–34). When their chains and handcuffs fell off, they didn't take advantage of the situation and try to escape. Instead they remained where they were. Their decision to do the right thing was rooted in their identity as baptized followers of Jesus, and it was such a powerful example of love that the prison guard and his household chose to follow Jesus that day. Who in your life has been a witness in this way—showing God's love through outward and visible actions?

Hymns for the Day

The Hymnal 1982

All hail the power of Jesus' name 450, 451
Crown him with many crowns 494
Praise the Lord through every nation 484, 485
Rejoice, the Lord is King 481
Alleluia! sing to Jesus! 460, 461
Hail, thou once despised Jesus 495
Lord, enthroned in heavenly splendor 307
Christ is alive! Let Christians sing 182
If thou but trust in God to guide thee 635
Rejoice, the Lord of life ascends 222
The head that once was crowned with thorns 483
Thou, who at thy first Eucharist didst pray 315

Lift Every Voice and Sing II

Go preach my gospel 161

Wonder, Love, and Praise

Come now, O Prince of peace 795
No saint on earth lives life to self alone 776
The church of Christ in every age 779
Unidos, unidos / Together, together 796
We are all one in mission 778

Weekday Commemorations

Monday, May 25
Bede, Priest and Historian, 735

Of his life's work, Bede wrote, "I always took delight in learning, teaching, and writing." He was ordained a deacon at 19, a presbyter at 30. Bede, the greatest scholar of his time in the Western Church, also boasted of exemplary character as a model monk, a devout Christian, and a man of manners. The title "Venerable," added a century after his death, was unusual but deserved. Bede commented on the scriptures based on patristic interpretations, and his treatise on chronology was a standard. His most famous work, *The Ecclesiastical History of England*, remains the primary source for Anglo-Saxon culture of the period 597–731.

Tuesday, May 26
Augustine of Canterbury, First Archbishop of Canterbury, 605

Pope Gregory the Great sent a mission to the pagan Anglo-Saxons in 596, led by Augustine, the prior of Gregory's own monastery in Rome. They carried a silver cross and an iconic image of the Christ. About 601, King Ethelbert was converted and became the first Christian king in England; around the same time, Augustine was ordained bishop somewhere in France and named "Archbishop of the English Nation" (the chair of St. Augustine in Canterbury Cathedral dates from the thirteenth century). A remnant of Gregory and Augustine's correspondence from this time deals with "unity in diversity" in the young English Church, foundational to the modern ecumenical movement.

Thursday, May 28
Mechthild of Magdeburg, Mystic, c.1282

Mechthild, a medieval mystic, was the first to write in German. She belonged to the Beguines, who lived in a quasi-monastic community bound to vows so long as they lived there. Mechthild wrote *The Flowing Light of the Godhead*: seven books written over 30 years proved her ease with courtly (erotic) poetry and popular literature. Her writing alternates between passionate descriptions of love for God and burning denunciations of a lax church and its clergy. Blind at the end, Mechthild dictated her last chapters to sisters in her Cistercian convent, known for their scholarship and education.

The Day of Pentecost

May 31, 2020

The gift of the Holy Spirit empowers Christians for ministry in the world.

Color   Red

Preface   Pentecost

Collect

Almighty God, on this day you opened the way of eternal life to every race and nation by the promised gift of your Holy Spirit: Shed abroad this gift throughout the world by the preaching of the Gospel, that it may reach to the ends of the earth; through Jesus Christ our Lord, who lives and reigns with you, in the unity of the Holy Spirit, one God, forever and ever. Amen.

or this

O God, who on this day taught the hearts of your faithful people by sending to them the light of your Holy Spirit: Grant us by the same Spirit to have a right judgment in all things, and evermore to rejoice in his holy comfort; through Jesus Christ your Son our Lord, who lives and reigns with you, in the unity of the Holy Spirit, one God, forever and ever. Amen.

Readings and Psalm

Acts 2:1–21

This lesson tells **the story of the Holy Spirit filling the apostles and empowering them to share the message of the gospel with people of different languages.** Clearly this was a most dramatic moment in the life of the early church, an experience described in terms of wind and fire. From this time forward the mighty works of God done in Jesus will be told to all the peoples of the earth, crossing barriers of language and culture.

or

Numbers 11:24–30

As Moses struggles with the responsibilities of leadership, God pours out the divine Spirit upon seventy elders selected to assist Moses in his duties. The Spirit of God is manifested in a temporary spell of ecstatic prophecy. Two men who have not been selected for a leadership role and who remain in the camp, Eldad and Medad, also demonstrate the signs of the outpouring of God's Spirit, illustrating how God's actions cannot be confined by human appointment.

Psalm 104:24–34, 35b

The psalm describes the wonders of the world created and renewed by the Lord's Spirit.

1 Corinthians 12:3b–13

In this reading we hear that **Christians are all one body and are inspired by the same Spirit which is manifested in a variety of gifts and forms of service.** It is the glory of the Christian community that its members have different gifts to offer for the common good. Disciples also come from diverse backgrounds and conditions. Yet the many members form one body, and the only Holy Spirit was poured out for all to drink.

or

Acts 2:1–21

This lesson tells **the story of the Holy Spirit filling the apostles and empowering them to share the message of the gospel with people of different languages.** Clearly this was a most dramatic moment in the life of the early church, an experience described in terms of wind and fire. From this time forward the mighty works of God done in Jesus will be told to all the peoples of the earth, crossing barriers of language and culture.

John 20:19–23
The gospel describes **an appearance of the risen Lord in which he bestows the Holy Spirit on his disciples.** He brings his disciples peace and tells them of their mission. The ministry which the Father had given Jesus is now carried forward in the world by his followers. The disciples have power over the forgiveness of sins in order to guide others to repentance and faith.

or

John 7:37–39
Jesus offers himself as a spiritual rock from which living waters will flow for all who will believe and drink.

Prayers of the People

Through the waters of baptism we have been joined together in the fellowship of Christ, and in the power of the Spirit we are sent forth to proclaim words and deeds of love, beginning with the offering of our prayers; responding, "Come, Holy Spirit."

Wisdom from on high, be with the leaders of the nations, giving them discernment and patience as they guide the people they serve; for this we pray.

Come, Holy Spirit.

Mighty Wind and Holy Fire, unsettle the hearts and minds of this church and diocesan community, that we may be challenged anew to hear your word and boldly live its message; for this we pray.

Come, Holy Spirit.

Blessed Advocate, may our ministries reflect your love for the poor in spirit, the needy, the sinner, those who are victims of injustice, oppression, violence and abuse, and for all whom the Son of God gave his life; for this we pray.

Come, Holy Spirit.

Spirit of many tongues, may the peoples of the world find a common language of the heart where cultural and racial diversity find holy ground, and nations suffering under bonds of oppression discover the way to peace; for this we pray.

Come, Holy Spirit.

Breath of Life, open our eyes to the crying needs of our environment, that we, and all the nations of the world, may prudently and tenderly nurture our fragile home; for this we pray.

Come, Holy Spirit.

Holy Comforter, pour your grace into the souls of all who have died, that they may know your abiding presence; for this we pray.

Come, Holy Spirit.

Spirit of thankfulness, we offer our gratitude to church school teachers and members of the choir whose devotion and creativity enrich the life of our community; for this we pray.

Come, Holy Spirit.

Filled with the power of the Holy Spirit urging us to be people of passionate witness, let us continue our prayers.
(Special intentions of the congregation, the diocese, and the Anglican Communion may be added here or before the formal intercessions.)

The Celebrant adds a concluding Collect.

Images in the Readings

Anthropologists describe **fire** as one of the markers of the human species. For tens of thousands of years, humans gathered around fire for light, warmth, protection, community, and better food. Many passages in the Bible liken God to fire. The Holy Spirit of God appeared on Sinai in flames of fire, which on Pentecost appeared on the forehead of each believer. Moses experienced God in fire; through fire the Israelites presented offerings to God; God led the people through the wilderness with a pillar of fire. Seraphim are fire spirits, extensions of the divine. Yet fire is also a sign of divine judgment: the angel in Eden hides the tree of life from humanity with a sword of fire, and John the Baptist predicts that fire will consume the chaff. Fire both occasions human life and has the power to destroy. Think fire, think God.

The Hebrew noun *ruah* can be translated into English as **spirit**, breath, or wind. Spirit is the most amorphous of these words. In Christian theology, the Spirit that we experience is the Spirit of the risen Christ, a spirit of service, a spirit of love, a spirit of resurrection beyond death.

In the narrative in Numbers, **seventy** elders receive the Spirit. In the Bible, seventy is a number that connotes totality, seven times ten. In Genesis 10, there are seventy nations in Israel's world, Jacob moves to Egypt with seventy family members, and there are many more seventies. Luke says that seventy were sent out to preach the word.

Ideas for the Day

♦ Perhaps you have seen a post-game interview where the player is rushed with astonishment and excitement, as well as still full of adrenaline from the surprising win. The surroundings are noisy and chaotic, and the player is clearly still breathing heavily. What comes out of that player's mouth is all over the place: a mix of clichés and sometimes nonsensical statements while the confetti flutters down. This might be something like the experience of Pentecost: a plurality of experiences all rushing into heart and mind at the same time. How do we engage the energy and motivation of the Spirit of God that is so evident at Pentecost in our daily practices of lifelong discipleship?

♦ The Rev. Eric Law asks an interesting question in response to the reading from the Acts of the Apostles. He asks, "Is this a miracle of the tongue or a miracle of the ear?" Such an important question in our time of "isms" and in our time when power is so misused. For the disciples, who had no power, they were given the miracle of the tongue—they were called upon to speak. For those outside, in the midst of the party, those with the power—they were called to listen. Funny how we find that in most cases those with power speak and those without power are made to listen. The Holy Spirit has something different in mind.

Making Connections

The Holy Spirit's arrival on the first Pentecost is described as a rushing, mighty wind. The psalmist says it is God's steadfast love and not great strength that saves us. Big winds can be scary in their power to shake loose tree limbs and blow roofs off. Yet wind supports life when it generates electricity and carries seeds to colonize valleys and forests. The song "Blowing in the Wind" written by Bob Dylan in 1962 asks, "How many ears must one man have, before he can hear people cry?" Meditate on images of the wind and how to be the calm center that hears the cries of others.

Engaging All Ages

Pentecost is a red-letter day. There are Roman calendars from 509 BCE that record important dates in red. Do you have calendars with red-letter days? What are those days? Are they important? Why? There are other similar experiences of red: the blinking of the traffic light or the octagonal sign with the word "STOP" swimming in a sea of red. The television and film trope of the big red button. Pentecost is like all of these. Push the button! Stop and reflect on the important dates in the Christian tradition, in your own church, and in your life.

Hymns for the Day

The Hymnal 1982
Come down, O Love divine 516
Come, Holy Ghost, our souls inspire 503, 504
Come, thou Holy Spirit bright 226, 227
Creator Spirit, by whose aid 500
Holy Spirit, font of light 228
O day of radiant gladness 48
O Holy Spirit, by whose breath 501, 502
O Spirit of the living God 531
Praise the Spirit in creation 506, 507
Spirit of mercy, truth, and love 229
This day at thy creating word 52
To thee, O Comforter divine 514
We the Lord's people, heart and voice uniting 51
Praise to the living God! 372
Go forth for God; go to the world in peace 347
Gracious Spirit, Holy Ghost 612
Holy Spirit, Lord of love 349
Lord, you give the great commission 528
O thou who camest from above 704
On this day, the first of days 47
Sing praise to our Creator 295
'Tis the gift to be simple 554
Breathe on me, Breath of God 508
Holy Spirit, ever living 511
I heard the voice of Jesus say 692
All who believe and are baptized 298
Baptized in water 294
Descend, O Spirit, purging flame 297
Over the chaos of the empty waters 176, 177
Spirit of God, unleashed on earth 299

Easter

Lift Every Voice and Sing II

Come, Holy Ghost 112
I'm goin'-a sing when the Spirit says sing 117
Sprit of God, descend upon my heart 119
There's a sweet, sweet Spirit in this place 120
Let it breathe on me 116
Baptized in water 121

Wonder, Love, and Praise

If you believe and I believe 806
Loving Spirit, loving Spirit 742
Veni Sancte Spiritus 832
Lord, you give the great commission 780
O God of gentle strength 770, 771
We all are one in mission 778
Baptized in water 767

Weekday Commemorations

Monday, June 1 (transferred)
The Visitation of the Blessed Virgin Mary

The Feast commemorates the visit of the Virgin Mary to her cousin Elizabeth (Luke 1:39–56). The pregnant Elizabeth greeted Mary, "Blessed are you among women, and blessed is the fruit of your womb." Mary responded with a song of praise, a thanksgiving known as the Magnificat: "My soul proclaims the greatness of the Lord." The dramatic scene places the unborn John the Baptist, who was to prepare the way of the Lord to all Israel, in proximity with the Lord himself. The gospel weaves in the story that when Mary heard her cousin's greeting, John leapt for joy in his mother's womb.

Tuesday, June 2
The Martyrs of Lyons, 177

Sanctus. Attalus. Maturus. Blandina. Pothinus. A deacon, a recent convert, a slave, a bishop—these are the some of the martyrs of Lyons, who refused to deny their faith. "I am a Christian," Blandina declared before the mob. Before persecution began in 177, Christians had lived under the guidance of Pothinus, Bishop of Lyons, in parts of Gaul, which had drawn them from Asia and Greece. After public torments, the Christians were subjected to public spectacle. Blandina, the last one living, was finally beaten, torn, burned with irons; having been wrapped in a net, she was thrown to a wild bull. Her endurance impressed the mob.

Wednesday, June 3
The Martyrs of Uganda, 1886

Mwanga, king of Buganda, grew angry that some of his people put fealty to the Christ ahead of loyalty to him. He ordered 32 young men to burn on this day at Namugongo because they refused to renounce their faith. Martyrdoms, including those of Bishop Hannington and his Companions, had begun in 1885, and many Christians were put to death in days to come as Mwango determined to end Christianity in his land. However, the killings produced the opposite. Martyrs went to their deaths singing hymns and praying for their enemies. Their example encouraged new missions and also served as righteous history when persecutions were renewed in the 1970s by a Muslim dictatorship.

Thursday, June 4
John XXIII (Angelo Giuseppe Roncalli),
Bishop, 1963

John XXIII (born in 1881) grew up in the Roman Catholic Church and was ordained a priest in 1904. His early passion for social justice for workers and the poor stayed with him throughout his ministry. As an archbishop in 1925, he helped reduce tension between Eastern Rite and Latin Rite Catholics in Bulgaria; he represented the papacy when anti-religious sentiments ran high in Greece and Turkey. While in Turkey, he helped Jews flee Nazis. Roncalli was elected Pope in 1958. Within two years, he called the Second Vatican Council, thereby beginning to revitalize the Roman Catholic Church.

Friday, June 5
Boniface, Bishop and Missionary, 754

He was born Winfred in Devonshire, England, about 675 and decided to be a missionary after being professed a monk then ordained to the presbyterate. He traveled to Frisia (Netherlands) but met little success; before traveling next in 719, he first went to Rome for approval from Pope Gregory, who named him Boniface. Thereafter, Boniface dedicated his life to reforming, planting, and organizing churches, monasteries, and dioceses in Hesse, Thuringia, and Bavaria. In 722, Gregory ordained Boniface a bishop and, in 732, an archbishop; he was given a fixed see at Mainz in 743. After resigning his see, Boniface and his fellow missionaries were murdered by pagans.

Pentecost

Preparing for Pentecost

Theological Themes that Might Shape Liturgy, Catechesis, and Education

In both the Incarnation (Advent, Christmastide, and Epiphanytide) and the Paschal (Lent, Holy Week, and Eastertide) the Church walks through and celebrates the defining moments of the life of Christ, mining these events for meaning and spiritual nourishment. In the long season that follows Pentecost (often referred to as Ordinary Time), we apply these teachings to our presence in the world, living the values of the Kingdom of God in light of what we've experienced in the months prior.

Jerome Berryman's *Godly Play* curriculum refers to Ordinary Time as the "great, green, growing season." Inasmuch as this half of the Christian year invites us to continue to plumb the depths of the teachings of Jesus, this is an apt description. This is also a wonderful time of year to emphasize the teachings of Jesus as practical ways that we live out the mysteries we've celebrated in the major events of his life.

Liturgical Possibilities

Rites

While the weekly celebration of the Holy Eucharist in the six months that follow Pentecost can come across as repetitive, there is something to be said about the sanctifying rhythm of this pattern. Unlike Christmas and Easter, those who attend worship during this part of the year represent those who are most disposed toward the further development of their spirituality. Celebrating the Eucharist in ways that speak to that depth might include varying the ways the congregation experiences the Psalms (chanted or not, choir with congregation, etc.) as well as the way they hear the Eucharistic Prayer.

There are also a whole slew of Major Feasts during this season that cannot rubricly be transferred to Sundays (except in the instance of a pastronal/matronal feast day) and therefore present more opportunities to explore mysteries of the church. In the absence of large crowds, the midweek celebration of the Feast of the Transfiguration (Thursday, August 6, 2020) might be a great way to frame an intergenerational formation event—learning, prayer, and sacrament.

There are many ways that different congregations will choose to break up what might be seen as the monotony of Ordinary Time. A word of caution might be to be intentional both in restraining innovation and preserving a pattern. Finding a balance is important during this season.

Space

Depending on the flexibility of space and the occasion of the day, periodically mixing up the space during this season might be a helpful way to assist people in seeing similar liturgies through a different light (literally). If your congregation is one that travels heavily during the summer, that might be a time of greater innovation and liturgical variation.

Other Rituals and Resources

The *Book of Occasional Services* and *Enriching Our Worship* (where permitted) are filled with resources that might be helpful in providing some additional liturgical resources.

Through the Eyes of a Child

Indwelling inspiration: breathing in and out reminds us that our very life is dependent upon the gift of the Holy Spirit. Words and thoughts for young children include: mighty wind, teacher that leads into all truth, New Covenant proclaiming renewal, tongues of fire, witnesses all gathered with new awareness of God and each other. God promises to be with us always,

Pentecost

and we are strengthened from within by the Holy Spirit, whose power, like a strong wind, we can feel even though we cannot see it. Now the church will continue to grow and learn more about Jesus, even after his death and resurrection. Mission, building and rebuilding the church (what some call "congregational development") with and for children is critical during the season of Pentecost. This is the time the children will wonder, what are the adventures of building the early church? How was the early church built? The travels of St. Paul with maps and cities where Paul founded churches, as well as the travels of St. Peter, St. James, and St. John can be inspiring for children as they enjoy the concept of building something new.

With the noticeable absence of large, culturally-observed, religious holidays, some may find it difficult to convey Christian truths to younger members of our communities. There is something to be said about instilling simply, Christian values and practices such as prayer, generosity, and service throughout this season. Christianity is not just about the big events that punctuate the life and ministry of Jesus Christ. Christianity is also that body of teaching that helps us understand how to live compassionately and justly in the world. This is an important lesson to teach younger generations.

Through the Eyes of Youth

Developing an authentic faith in the understanding of "God as Three" (Creator, Redeemer, Sustainer) is a vital part of youth spirituality. Youth are developing their identity, and part of that identity is formed through the gifts God has given them, including gifts of the spirit. Questions to consider with youth:

♦ What will we be, and what will we leave to the next generation?

♦ Are we building our lives on firm foundations, building something that will endure?

♦ Are we living our lives in a way that opens up space for the Spirit in the midst of a world that wants to forget God, or even rejects him in the name of a falsely conceived freedom?

Pentecost is a perfect time to invite the youth to reflect upon the gifts that God has given them, not only the gifts they see in themselves, but the gifts they see in each other. Retreats can be most helpful to give the young people some time to remember the gifts the Spirit gave to the disciples, and the gifts that the Spirit gives to them.

Through the Eyes of Daily Life

On the fiftieth day of Easter, we celebrate the Holy Spirit as the power of God among us that heals, forgives, inspires, and unites. Images of wind and fire describe the Spirit poured out on disciples of all nations. In John's gospel, the risen Christ breathes the Spirit on his followers on Easter evening. In the one Spirit we were baptized into one body, and at the Lord's table, the Spirit unites us for witness in the world. The Spirit calls us to follow in the way and in the pattern and in the shape of the life of Jesus.

The slow, steady growth of faith is a central focus of Ordinary Time. Liturgy, particularly in places where there is not formal Christian formation, should strive not only to create a worshipful encounter with God, but also to teach spiritual practices. The Way of Love materials from the Church Center (and Church Publishing Incorporated) might be helpful to apply here.

Through the Eyes of Those Outside of the Church

Without any major reason to look at the church, many beyond the church simply will not. That doesn't mean that we should de-emphasize evangelism and services in ways that speak to the reality of the Kingdom of God. Again, Ordinary Time is a fine time to live out the values of the Kingdom of God; therefore, empowering the faithful to be agents and bearers of Good News in practical, tangible ways is a helpful practice.

Through the Eyes of the Global Community

The Day of Pentecost opened the way of eternal life to every race and nation. On this day it is appropriate to study racism, sexism, and all other attitudes and actions that deny God's love for all people. It is common to see in the gift of the Spirit at Pentecost a sign that reveals God's purposes to heal and restore creation, including overcoming the disorder and confusion of languages that was told to have happened at Babel. The Spirit of God crosses over the boundaries of language and culture to create a new people of God, a human family renewed and made whole. Consider the global perspective of how the Church has made its journey from the time of Paul to today and how the message of Christ has spread throughout the world in its many forms and traditions.

Seasonal Rites for Pentecost

Seasonal Blessings[1]

The following blessings may be used by a bishop or priest whenever a blessing is appropriate for the following season and noted Sundays.

The Day of Pentecost

May the Spirit of truth lead you into all truth, giving you grace to confess that Jesus Christ is Lord, and to proclaim the wonderful works of God; and the blessing of God Almighty, the Father, the Son, and the Holy Spirit, be among you, and remain with you always. *Amen.*

Trinity Sunday

May God the Holy Trinity make you strong in faith and love, defend you on every side, and guide you in truth and peace; and the blessing of God Almighty, the Father, the Son, and the Holy Spirit, be among you, and remain with you always. *Amen.*

All Saints

May God give you grace to follow his saints in faith and hope and love; and the blessing of God Almighty, the Father, the Son, and the Holy Spirit, be among you, and reemain with you always. *Amen.*

Graduation Prayers

A Graduation Collect[2]

Precious Father, we especially pray for out teenagers and young adults at this time of school graduations; where they are lost, find them; when they are afraid, bring them comfort and love; and where they are confused, show them your will. Protect them, Father, and be with parents as they ride the roller coaster of these years with their children. May they have the courage, the strength, the wisdom through your Holy Spirit to help guide them and in many cases just to hold on, and to be there as their children take on adult responsibilities in a chaotic, sinful world. We now place them under your loving wings. *Amen.*

Graduating from High School[3]

In every beginning is an ending, O Lord, and in every end something new begins. These young people will soon/have graduate/d from high school, and are ready now for new learning and experiences. Grant that childhood's innocence and hope may remain alive in them, bringing joy as they mature. Grant that they may hear your still small voice in their heart saying, "This is the way; walk in it." Help them preserve old friendships while creating new ones. Grant that we who love them may help them to find their own voice, their own words, and their own work in Christ's true way, who knows the persons they were created to be; we pray this in Jesus' name. *Amen.*

---

1 *The Book of Occasional Services 2003* (New York: Church Publishing, 2004), 27–28.

2 "Protect Them and Lead Them" by Stephanie Douglas in *Women's Uncommon Prayers* (Harrisburg, PA: Morehouse Publishing, 2000), 155.

3 Adapted from *Changes: Prayers and Services Honoring Rites of Passage* (New York: Church Publishing, 2007), 22.

Pentecost

Go in Peace: For a Young Adult Leaving Home[4]

Departure from home for college, work, or military service can give rise to complex feelings of anxiety and loss. This rite is designed to equip the young adult/s with the assurances and well wishes of those who have supported them through childhood and/or their youth. A quilt, blanket, or afghan may be presented by the family or congregation during the rite.

Leader: The Lord be with you

And also with you.

Reader #1: A reading from Isaiah 43:1–3a:
Do not fear, for I have redeemed you;
    I have called you by name, you are mine.
When you pass through the waters, I will be with you;
    and through the rivers, they shall not
    overwhelm you;
    when you walk through fire you shall not be
    burned, and the flame shall not consume you.
For I am the Lord your God,
    the Holy One of Israel, your Savior.
The Word of the Lord.

Thanks be to God.

Leader: (addressing the community) A young adult's departure from home is a significant even in their life and in the lives of their families. As _____ prepares to leave home for _____, we gather to mark the significance of their leaving.

(addressing young adult/s) Are you prepared to leave the familiarity of family and friends in order to begin this important new chapter in your journey to adulthood?

Young Adult/s: Yes, with God's help.

Leader: We know that you will face opportunities and challenges and that you will experience joys and disappointments. We know that you will encounter new ways, new images, and new models that you will test and learn from. We ask that, in your learning and growing, you will be mindful of the people and experiences that brought you to this crossroads and of the God whose love will journey with you wherever you go.

Leader: (addressing the community) What symbol will accompany _____ on their journey into new experiences?

Parent/s or Community: This gift represents our assurance that you will be surrounded by our love wherever you go. *(The parent/s or community place the quilt, blanket, or afghan around the young adults' shoulders.)*

Leader: Let us pray. Almighty God, be with _____ at this important crossroads in their journey into a future of wondrous possibility. Bless their efforts, guide their choices, confirm their gifts, and support their growth that they may faithfully discern your will for their life. Be with us that we may appropriately share in their joys, support them in their disappointments, and confidently commend them to your loving care. In the name of Jesus, your Son and our Savior, who journeys with _____ wherever they go.

Amen! May it be so!

An Independence Day Litany[5]

Saturday, July 4

This litany is designed for use on days of national celebration (like Independence Day), or in times of national crisis.

Mighty God: the earth is yours and nations are your people. Take away our pride and bring to mind your goodness, so that, living together in this land, we may enjoy your gifts and be thankful.

Amen.

For clouded mountains, fields, and woodland; for shoreline and running streams; for all that makes our nation good and lovely;

We thank you, God.

For farms and villages where food is gathered to feed our people;

We thank you, God.

For cities where people talk and work together in factories, shops, or schools to shape those things we need for living;

We thank you, God.

---

4 Adapted from Linda Witte Henke, *Marking Time: Christian Rituals for All Our Days* (Harrisburg, PA: Morehouse, 2001), 74–76.

5 "Litany for the Nation" from *An American Prayer Book* edited by Christopher L. Webber (Harrisburg, PA: Morehouse Publishing, 2008), 39–41.

For explorers, planners, diplomats; for prophets who speak out, and for silent faithful people; for all who love our land and guard our freedom;

>> *We thank you, God.*

For vision to see your purpose hidden in our nation's history, and courage to seek it in human love exchanged;

>> *We thank you, God.*

O God, your justice is like a rock, and your mercy like pure following water. Judge and forgive us. If we have turned from you, return us to your way; for without you we are lost people. From brassy patriotism and a blind trust in power;

>> *Deliver us, O God.*

From public deceptions that weaken trust; from self-seeking high political places;

>> *Deliver us, O God.*

From divisions among us of class or race; from wealth that will not share, and poverty that feeds on food of bitterness;

>> *Deliver us, O God.*

From neglecting rights; from overlooking the hurt, the imprisoned, and the needy among us;

>> *Deliver us, O God.*

From a lack of concern for other lands and peoples; from narrowness of national purpose; from failure to welcome the peace you promise on earth;

>> *Deliver us, O God.*

Eternal God: before you nations rise and fall; they grow strong or wither by your design. Help us to repent our country's wrong, and to choose your right in reunion and renewal.

>> *Amen.*

Give us a glimpse of the Holy City you are bringing to earth, where death and pain and crying will be gone away; and nations gather in the light of your presence.

>> *Great God, renew this nation.*

Teach us peace, so that we may plow up battlefields and pound weapons into building tools, and learn to talk across old boundaries as brothers and sisters in your love.

>> *Great God, renew this nation.*

Talk sense to us, so that we may wisely end all prejudice, and may put a stop to cruelty, which divides or wounds the human family.

>> *Great God, renew this nation.*

Draw us together as one people who do your will, so that our land may be a light to the nations, leading the way to your promised kingdom, which is coming among us.

>> *Great God, renew this nation.*

Great God, eternal Lord: long years ago you gave our fathers this land as a home for the free. Show us there is no law or liberty apart from you; and let us serve your modestly, as devoted people; through Jesus Christ our Lord.

>> *Amen.*

Prayers for Summer Travels

Going Away to Camp[6]

In the beauty of your world, O God, you show us how great your love is. Be with _____ as they go away to camp. Open their eyes to the wonder of creation and, in it, let them draw nearer to you. Let their play be joyful. Let them encounter wonder and surprise as they learn. Let their rest be peaceful. Keep them well and safe, in the knowledge that they are deeply loved by you and by us, who hold them dear in our hearts forever. We pray in Jesus' name. *Amen.*

Going on a Pilgrimage[7]

Holy One, you led your people, night and day, by fire and cloud, so lead _____ by the light of your love. Go before them to prepare a safe path. Stay beside them to instill purpose and joy in their mission. Follow after them to leave peace in the wake of wherever they have stayed. Give your angels charge over their journey. At their returning, may all they have seen be engraved on their hearts, and their sense of home enlarged forever, through Jesus Christ, our Savior and Guide. *Amen.*

_____

6 *Changes: Prayers and Services Honoring Rites of Passage* (New York: Church Publishing, 2007), 16.

7 *Changes*, 23.

Pentecost

Labor Day[8]

September 7

Lord God, our Creator: We deserve to labor among thorns and thistles, to eat by the sweat of our brow, to work without reward. For we confess we have spoiled you creation by our sin, we have marred your work by our neglect, we have hurt your work by our rebellion. We pray you, bless our labor by him who was once a carpenter, by him who came to be our servant, by him who saved us to serve. For his sake keep us and all who labor from false dealing and unfair practice, from excessive profit and unjust gain, from slovenly service and irrational demands. Help us to labor with love, to labor with joy, to labor with faithfulness. Teach us that the best labor we give you is loving service to others. In Christ's name we ask it. *Amen.*

Back to School

Marking the Beginning of a School Year[9]

God of all wisdom, we praise you for wisely gifting us with sons and daughter. Give to each one a clear sense of your love, that they may feel your presence supporting them throughout this school year. Guide their choices, direct their quest for knowledge, bless their relationships, and use their successes and failures as opportunities to grow in understanding of who you have them be. Continue, we pray, to shape them as branches of the one true vine, that they may ever walk in the way of Christ, grow strong in your Spirit's love for all people, and know the complete joy of life in you. In the name of Christ, we pray. *Amen.*

The Blessing of Backpacks[10]

Children are invited to gather in the chancel with their backpacks. Following the blessing, small wooden crosses may be given out for the children to place inside the backpacks.

God of Wisdom, we give you thanks for schools and classrooms and for the teachers and students who fill them each day. We thank you for this new beginning, for new books and new ideas. We thank you for sharpened pencils, pointy crayons, and crisp blank pages waiting to be filled. We thank you for the gift of making mistakes and trying again. Help us to remember that asking the right questions is often as important as giving the right answers. Today we give you thanks for these your children, and we ask you to bless them with curiosity, understanding, and respect. May their backpacks be a sign to them that they have everything they need to learn and grow this year in school and in Sunday School. May they be guided by your love. All this we ask this in the name of Jesus, who as a child in the temple showed his longing to learn about you, and as an adult taught by story and example your great love for us. *Amen.*

Remembering September 11, 2001[11]

A prayer to be used in observances of the anniversary of September 11, 2001.

God the compassionate one, whose loving care extends to all the world, we remember this day your children of many nations and many faiths whose lives were cut short the fierce flames of anger and hatred. Console those who continue to suffer and grieve, and give them comfort and hope as they look to the future. Out of what we have endured, give us the grace to examine our relationships with those who perceive us as the enemy, and show our leaders the way to use our power to serve the good of all for the healing of the nations. This we ask through Jesus Christ our Lord who, in reconciling love, was lifted up from the earth that he might draw all things to himself. *Amen.*

The Feast of St. Francis

October 4

A Litany for St. Francis Day[12]

With all our heart and with all our mind, we pray to you, O God:

> *Lord, make us instruments of your peace.*

---

8   "The First Monday in September" from *An American Prayer Book* edited by Christopher L. Webber (Harrisburg, PA: Morehouse Publishing, 2008), 148–149.

9   Linda Witte Henke. "From the Vine" in *Marking Time: Christian Rituals for All Our Days* (Harrisburg, PA: Morehouse Publishing, 2001), 63.

10   Wendy Claire Barrie (New York: Church Publishing, 2011). From *Skiturgies: Pageants, Plays, Rites, and Rituals.* **www.skiturgies.com**.

---

11   Frank W. Griswold. "Remembering September 11, 2001" from *An American Prayer Book* edited by Christopher L. Webber (Harrisburg, PA: Morehouse Publishing, 2008), 113.

12   The Intercessions from "Liturgy for the Feast of St. Francis" by Wendy Claire Barrie from *Skiturgies: Pageants, Plays, Rites, and Rituals* (New York: Church Publishing, 2011). **www.skiturgies.com**

For our President and for all who are in authority, and for the people and leaders of every nation, that we may truly respect each other and learn to live together peacefully, we pray to you, O God:

> *Where there is injury, let us sow pardon.*

For this community gathered, for our families and friends, our neighbors and co-workers, especially for those whom we have hurt, we pray to you, O God:

> *Where there is injury, let us sow pardon.*

For all those who seek you, God, and for those who shut you out, that they may be touched by your presence, power and grace, we pray to you, O God:

> *Where there is doubt, let us sow faith.*

For the poor, for prisoners, for refugees, for those who are oppressed and persecuted, that they may be delivered from danger and fear, we pray to you, O God:

> *Where there is despair, let us sow hope.*

For the people of God throughout the world, that the good news of God's redeeming love may be known in all places, we pray to you, O God:

> *Where there is darkness, let us sow light.*

For those who are sick, unhappy, lonely or bereft, that they may be healed and comforted, we pray to you, O God:

> *Where there is sadness, let us sow joy.*

For those who have died, especially those we now name, we pray to you, O God. *(People may add their own petitions)*

For what is in our hearts today, we ask you to hear us, O God. *(People may add their own petitions)*

For all the gifts of your creation, and for the trust and joy you have given us in these our pets, we thank you and praise you, O God. *(People may add their own thanksgivings.)*

> *Grant that we may not so much seek*
> *to be consoled as to console,*
> *to be understood as to understand,*
> *to be loved as to love,*
> *for it is in giving that we receive,*
> *it is in pardoning that we are pardoned,*
> *and it is dying that we are born to eternal life.*
> *Amen*

A Blessing of Pets[13]

The Lord be with you.

> *And also with you.*

O Lord, how manifold are your works!

> *You stretch out the heavens like a tent.*
> *You set the earth on its foundations.*
> *You make springs gush forth in the valleys*
> *and give drink in every animal.*

You plant trees where birds may build their nests.

> *You cause the grass to grow for the cattle*
> *and plants for people to use.*
> *You open your hand and give all creatures*
> *their food in good season (Psalm 104).*

We have come together to acknowledge with gratitude the goodness of God in all creatures, great and small, and to seek God's blessing on the pets that are our companions in life. Let us pray:

On this day, O God, we offer thanks for these, our pets, who are your daily instruments of joy and comfort in our lives. Even as you demonstrate care for us, so also move us to demonstrate care for these and all your creatures, knowing that, in do doing, we are privileged to share in your love of creation. We pray in the name of Jesus, in whose power we are made a new creation.

> *Amen! May it be so!*

[As the leader approaches each pet, the pet's owner speaks the pet's name aloud so that all those gathered may hear. The leader then raises his/her hand above the pet and speaks a word of blessing.]

May God Creator bless you and keep you through all the days of your life.

> *Thanks be to God!*

[If some participants have brought mementos of former pets, the leader may touch each memento, while speaking these or similar words.]

May God bless the memory of this pet's presence in your life!

> *Thanks be to God!*

---

13 Linda Witte Henke "All Creatures Great and Small" from *Marking Time: Christian Rituals For All Our Days* (Harrisburg, PA: Morehouse Publishing, 2001), 80–82.

Pentecost

Pentecost

[If children have brought stuffed animals to receive a blessing, the leader may touch each toy, while speaking these or similar words.]

May this animal's presence be a source of joy and comfort in this child's life.

Thanks be to God!

May God Almighty, Father, Son, and Holy Spirit, use us as instruments of blessing for all creatures, great and small.

Amen! Thanks be to God!

A Native American Thanksgiving for the Americas and Their People[14]

Columbus Day: October 14

For our ancestors who built nations and cultures; who thrived and prospered long before the coming of strangers; for the forfeit of their lives, their homes, their lands, and their freedoms sacrificed to the rise of new nations and new worlds.

We offer a song of honor and thanks.

For the wealth of our lands; for minerals in the earth; for the plants and waters and animals on the earth; for the birds, the clouds and rain, for the sun and moon in the sky and the gifts they gave to our people that enabled the rise of new world economics.

We offer a song of honor and thanks.

For the many foods coaxed from the heart of Mother Earth; for the skills we were given to develop foods that now belong to the world: potatoes, corn, beans, squash, peanuts, tomatoes, peppers, coffee, cocoa, sugar, and many, many more.

We offer a song of honor and thanks.

For the medicines first discovered by our ancestors and now known to the world: quinine, ipecac, iodine, curare, petroleum jelly, witch hazel, and others; for the healing skills of our people and those who now care for us. For tobacco, sage, sweet grass, and cedar that give spiritual healing by the power of their meaning.

We offer a song of honor and thanks.

For oceans, streams, rivers, lakes, and other waters of our lands that provide bountifully for us; for clams, lobsters, salmon, trout, shrimp, and abalone; for the pathways the waters provide.

We offer a song of honor and thanks.

For the friendship that first welcomed all to our shores; for the courage of those who watched their worlds change and disappear and for those who led in the search for new lives; for our leaders today who fight with courage and great heart for us.

We offer a song of honor and thanks.

For the friends who suffered with us and stand with us today to help bring the promise and the hope that the New World meant to their ancestors.

We offer a song of honor and thanks.

For the strength and beauty of our diverse Native cultures; for the traditions that give structure to our lives, that define who we are; for the skills of our artists and craftspeople and the gifts of their hands.

We offer a song of honor and thanks.

For the spiritualty and vision that gave our people the courage and faith to endure; that brought many to an understanding and acceptance of the love of Christ, our Brother and Savior.

We offer a song of honor and thanks.

Accept, O God, Creator, our honor song, and make our hearts thankful for what we have been given. Make us humble for what we have taken. Make us glad as we return some measure of what we have been given. Strengthen our faith and make us strong in the service of our people, in the name of our Brother and Savior, Jesus Christ, your Son, in the power of the Holy Spirit. *Amen.*

---

14 "1492–1992: A Celebration of Native American Survival. Earth and All the Stars" in *The Wideness in God's Mercy: Litanies to Enlarge Our Prayer* edited by Jeffrey W. Rowthorn (New York: Church Publishing, 2007), 298–299. This litany was prepared for use at a service commemorating the quincentenary of the landing of Christopher Columbus in 1492 with its fateful impact on the Native American peoples, who despite all have survived to this day. The service was held on October 12, 1992 in the National Cathedral in Washington, D.C.

A Litany for Children's Sabbath[15]

October 18

Grant, O God, that all who gather in Christ's name will throw wide our doors and our hearts and lift our hands and voices to proclaim your promise of love and will for justice, especially for those who are young, poor, vulnerable, and oppressed.

Silence

Mighty God, Lover of Justice,

Hear our prayer.

Guide our nation and all of our leaders, that they will champion the cause of the children and families most oppressed and govern with truth, compassion, and justice.

Silence

Mighty God, Lover of Justice,

Hear our prayer.

Bless the families of our world, especially the billion who lack the income, clean water, health care, or education needed to live into the fullness of life.

Silence

Mighty God, Lover of Justice,

Hear our prayer.

Strengthen us to create a nation and world of justice so that every child may live with plenty and not poverty, with peace and not threatened by violence, surrounded by family, not separated, so that all children have lives of hope, not despair.

Silence

Mighty God, Lover of Justice,

Hear our prayer.

Comfort all who suffer, especially those who are hungry, are victims of violence, or struggle without a job or enough income to meet their needs.

Silence

Mighty God, Lover of Justice,

Hear our prayer.

Gather to yourself all who have died, especially those who died from poverty, violence, and other causes we could have prevented.

Silence

Mighty God, Lover of Justice,

Hear our prayer.

Almighty God, Lover of Justice, hear these the prayers of your children and grant them for the sake of your beloved child Jesus Christ our Lord. *Amen.*

An All Hallow's Eve Liturgy[16]

October 31

All Hallow's Eve, later known as Halloween, is celebrated the night before All Saints' Day, November 1. This simple prayer service in conjunction with Halloween festivities to mark the Christian roots of this festival. Begin in partial darkness.

Light and peace, in Jesus Christ our Lord.

Thanks be to God.

If I say, "Surely the darkness will cover me, and the light around me turn to night," darkness is not dark to you, O Lord; the night is as bright as the day; darkness and light to you are both alike (Psalm 139:10–11).

Let us pray. Lord Christ, your saints have been the lights of the world in every generation: Grant that we who follow in their footsteps may be made worthy to enter with them into that heavenly country where you live and reign forever and ever. Amen.

Candles are now lighted as all say recite the *Phos hilaron:*

O gracious Light,
Pure brightness of the everliving Father in heaven,
O Jesus Christ, holy and blessed!

Now as we come to the setting of the sun,
And our eyes behold the vesper light,

15 Children's Defense Fund, *Christian Worship Resources for the Children's Sabbath*, 13. **https://www.childrensdefense.org/wp-content/uploads/2018/09/Sabbath-2018_CHRISTIAN-FINAL.pdf** (accessed February 11, 2019).

16 Anne E. Kitch. *The Anglican Family Prayer Book* (Harrisburg, PA: Morehouse Publishing, 2004), 148–149.

Pentecost

We sing your praises,
O God: Father, Son, and Holy Spirit.

You are worthy at all times to be praised
by happy voices,
O Son of God, O Giver of life,
And to be glorified through all the worlds.

Glory to the Father, and to the Son,
and to the Holy Spirit; as it was in the beginning,
is now, and will be forever. Amen.

Election Day[17]

Tuesday, November 10

Holy God, throughout the ages you have called men and women to serve you in various ways, giving them gifts for the task to which they were called and strengthening and guiding them in the fulfillment of their calling; in this free land you share with us that great responsibility and enable us to choose those who will serve you in positions of leadership in various offices of government.

Help us in so choosing to seek those who have an understanding of your will for us, a commitment to justice, a concern for those in greatest need, a love of truth and a deep humility before you; Send your Spirit among us that we may be guided in the choices we make that so your will may be done on earth as it is in heaven. *Amen.*

A Stewardship Litany[18]

God of life and love: We are quick to accept bounteous gifts from you, but slow to give thanks and to express our gratitude.

We hold too tightly the things of this life,
giving them the allegiance we owe only to you.

Take my life and let it be consecrated,
Lord, to thee.
Take my moments and my days;
let them flow in ceaseless praise,
let them flow in ceaseless praise.

Gracious God, we admit that our lives are too often out of balance; we are more willing to receive than to share, more ready to take than to give.

Created in us grateful and generous hearts,
we pray, and restore us the joy of our salvation.

Take my hands and let them move
at the impulse of thy love.
Take my feet, and let them be swift and
beautiful to thee, swift and beautiful to thee.

Merciful God, form whom comes every good and perfect gift, we praise you for your mercies:

Your goodness that has created us,
your grace that has sustained us,

Your discipline that has corrected us, your patience that has borne with us,

and your love that has redeemed us.

Take my will, and make it thine;
it shall be no longer mine.
Take my heart, it is thine own; it shall be
thy royal throne, it shall be thy royal throne.

Help us to love you, and to be thankful for all your gifts by serving you and delighting to do you will.

Accept now, Gracious God, our offerings,
these our pledges of resources and talents for
your service, and the commitment of our lives,
through Jesus Christ, who gave his all for us.

Take my silver and my gold,
not a mite would I withhold;
take my intellect, and use every power
as thou shalt choose, every power
as thou shalt choose.

Take my love; my Lord,
I pour at thy feet its treasure store,
Take myself, and I will be ever, only,
all for thee, ever, only, all for thee. Amen.

---

17 "Before an Election" by Christopher L. Webber from *An American Prayer Book* edited by Christopher L. Webber (Harrisburg, PA: Morehouse Publishing, 2008), 150.

18 "A Stewardship Litany" by W. Alfred Tisdale, Jr., hymn stanzas by Frances Ridley Havergal from *The Wideness of God's Mercy: Litanies to Enlarge Our Prayer* edited by Jeffery W. Rowthorn (New York: Church Publishing, 2007), 124–125.

The First Sunday after Pentecost: Trinity Sunday

June 7, 2020

The God who creates, redeems, and sanctifies is revealed to us in three persons.

Color   White

Preface   Trinity Sunday

Collect

Almighty and everlasting God, you have given to us your servants grace, by the confession of a true faith, to acknowledge the glory of the eternal Trinity, and in the power of your divine Majesty to worship the Unity: Keep us steadfast in this faith and worship, and bring us at last to see you in your one and eternal glory, O Father; who with the Son and the Holy Spirit live and reign, one God, forever and ever. *Amen.*

Readings and Psalm

Genesis 1:1–2:4a

Our first lesson is **the story of creation.** As this ancient narrative opens, the Spirit of the Lord hovers like a great mother bird over the shapeless world. God then forms the heaven and the earth and all its creatures in six days. The seventh day is set aside as a day of rest. God's ultimate creative act is human life, made in his image, to whom rulership and responsibility over all other life are given.

Psalm 8

The psalmist glorifies the Lord, sovereign of the earth and the magnificent heavens, who has made human life to have mastery over all other earthly creatures.

2 Corinthians 13:11–13

In this passage **Paul closes his painful letter to the Corinthians with final admonitions and words of peace and love.** There have been disagreements between Paul and his new converts. They have shown tendencies to set themselves up as superior in faith and practice to others. But Paul ends on a hopeful note, and his last words have become part of our liturgies—a way of stating the three forms of presence of the divine graciousness.

Matthew 28:16–20

In our gospel reading **Jesus makes his last appearance to his disciples and gives them their mission to baptize and teach through all the world.** These words end Matthew's gospel. His mention of doubt on the part of some of the disciples reminds us that faith has never been an easy matter. But the closing charge is an authoritative commission to bring others to faith in the name of the Father, Son, and Holy Spirit.

Prayers of the People

Let us offer our prayers in the Name of God: Father, Son, and Holy Spirit, responding to each petition, "Hear us, blessed Trinity."

Creator of the universe, and all that dwells in the seas, and skies, and all creatures who inhabit the earth, help us to guard your holy treasures and to delight in all that you have made; let us pray.

Hear us, blessed Trinity.

Word of truth, open our hearts to receive your message as it is revealed through holy scripture, the witness of your Church, and in the minds and hearts of your faithful; let us pray.

Hear us, blessed Trinity.

Spirit of life, strengthen us to reveal the fruits of the kingdom through the actions of our daily lives; let us pray.

Hear us, blessed Trinity.

Architect of all that is, seen and unseen, may we rebuild the world in peace, and give to each other the good gifts which you formed in creation; let us pray.

Hear us, blessed Trinity.

Incarnate One, help us to offer your grace throughout the world, bringing people of every language, nation, and tribe into the baptismal waters of your saving love; let us pray.

Hear us, blessed Trinity.

Wisdom from on high, descend upon your faithful people, that our voices and actions may echo your hope for humanity; let us pray.

Hear us, blessed Trinity.

Gathered on this holy Sabbath, day of rest and praise, joy and worship; we continue our prayers.
(Special intentions of the congregation, the diocese, and the Anglican Communion may be added here or before the formal intercessions.)

The Celebrant adds a concluding Collect.

Images in the Readings

If by Matthew's language of **Father, Son, and Holy Spirit** we imagine two males and a mist, the biblical imagery is failing us. God is beyond all things, dead and alive in Jesus Christ, and experienced in the assembly. Many contemporary hymns add to the doctrinal language other imagery in hopes of opening up the mystery of God. In Genesis 1, God is creator, word, and breath. In Paul, God is love, grace, and communion.

The rhetorically magnificent story of **creation** in Genesis 1 poetically describes the entire universe as originally perfect and formed by God to focus on human need. According to biblical scholars, Genesis 1 was written as praise of the God of Israel, rather than as revealed science, and according to Christian theology, God's creating continues throughout time, rather than being a single prehistoric event. Creation by God through the Word in the Spirit happens today. The post-exilic authors sought also to ground the Jewish Sabbath in God's resting on the seventh day. Christians have moved their holy day from Saturday rest to Sunday assembly so as to meet the Risen Christ on the day of the resurrection.

Ideas for the Day

+ The doctrine of the Trinity is decisive, one of the critical common denominators between Christian churches. However, it is also a sacred mystery that we experience and celebrate but may never be able to contain with the exact right words. This is more frustrating for some than for others, yet we still all belong to God and are welcomed with our questions and doubts. The Trinity offers us a loving relationship instead of fractured arguments, a good example for us to follow. A delighted and powerful intimacy of the Holy Trinity sails through today's lessons. Can this experience of God's dynamism buoy our discipleship with an evermoving and cooperative example of how to live together faithfully?

+ Why didn't we learn this in Sunday School? With a little digging into the Hebrew we find that the sixth word in Genesis might just turn our world upside-down. The word we read as "created" comes from a word in Hebrew that can easily mean "the plural of compassion" or "compassions." This word means womb! So a good translation could be "In the beginning God "wombed" the heavens and the earth. Last I knew, guys don't have wombs! Perhaps this gives us a different insight on the verse, "So God created humankind in God's image, in the image of God, [God] created them, male and female, [God] created them."

+ The relationship of love among the three persons of the Trinity serves as a model for communities of baptized Christians living together in unity. One way this is exemplified is in Rublev's *Icon of the Trinity* (**www.wellsprings.org/uk/rublevs_icon/ rublev.htm**).

Making Connections

God-in-Three-Persons is a mystery, but God's commandment to proclaim the reign of God is clear. Patience, gentleness, and self-control, listed in Galatians as fruits of the Spirit, can be thought of as characteristics of God shaped in each of us. These three characteristics have self-sacrifice in common—of putting the needs of others before self-indulgence. When public discourse on social justice becomes divisive, patience, gentleness, and self-control help us see each other as beloved children of God, created in God's image. True freedom and joy comes from dwelling in God's love, following Jesus before addressing other life demands and duties.

Engaging All Ages

In worship, do you see a cross? One above or on or in front of the altar? Are there crosses on the cloths and the robes; are any etched into wood or marble? Does the priest or anyone else in church make the sign of the cross . . . hand raised to the forehead, down to the center of the chest, then left shoulder, then right shoulder? Have you tried making the sign of the cross? Try it. Think of God to start, then the Holy Spirit coming down, and the spread open arms of Jesus. Each a unique expression but one beautiful gesture.

Hymns for the Day

The Hymnal 1982
All glory be to God on high 421
Ancient of Days, who sittest throned in glory 363
Come, thou almighty King 365
Holy Father, great Creator 368
Holy God, we praise thy Name 366
Holy, holy, holy! Lord God Almighty! 362
How wondrous great, how glorious bright 369
I bind unto myself today 370
O God, we praise thee, and confess 364
O Trinity of blessed light 29, 30
Round the Lord in glory seated 367
Sing praise to our Creator 295
All creatures of our God and King 400
All things bright and beautiful 405

I sing the almighty power of God 398
Immortal, invisible, God only wise 423
Many and great, O God, are thy works 385
Most High, omnipotent, good Lord 406, 407
Most Holy God, the Lord of heaven 31, 32
O all ye works of God now come 428
O blest Creator, source of light (vs. 1–4) 27, 28
The spacious firmament on high 409
The stars declare his glory 431
Thou, whose almighty word 371
Alleluia! sing to Jesus! 460, 461
Lord, you give the great commission 528

Lift Every Voice and Sing II
Oh Lord, how perfect is your name 57
He's got the whole world in his hand 217

Wonder, Love, and Praise
You are the Holy One 745
God the sculptor of the mountains 746, 747
O Trinity of blessed light 744
O threefold God of tender unity 743
O all ye works of God now come 884
Gracious Spirit, give your servants 782
Lord, you give the great commission 780
We all are one in mission 778

Weekday Commemorations

Monday, June 8
The First Book of Common Prayer, 1549
In 1549, the second year of the reign of King Edward VI, the first Book of Common Prayer began its service to Anglicans. Through subsequent editions and revisions, the Book of Common Prayer continues to serve the Anglican Communion. The book was prepared by a commission, comprising learned priests and bishops, but Thomas Cranmer, Archbishop of Canterbury (1533–1556), stamped the book in style, substance, and format. Bishops and priests compiled the book from, among other sources, medieval Latin service books, Greek liturgies, ancient Gallican rites, and vernacular German forms. The English "Great Bible" (authorized by King Henry VII in 1539) supplied the Psalter, and the Litany came from the English form going back to 1544.

Pentecost

Monday, June 8
Melania the Elder, Monastic, 410

Melania (b. 341) was a first-generation Roman aristocrat, who embraced Christianity; she lived to see it become the official religion of the Empire. As a 22-year-old widow, she moved to Alexandria from Rome to spread her wealth among monastics, teachers, and pilgrims. She studied asceticism with the desert mothers and fathers. She arrived in Jerusalem after 372 and founded two monasteries; she underwrote their hospitality for pilgrims seeking holy sites. Despite social mores for rich widows to remain reserved, Melania spoke out for asceticism and learning. She studied, taught, and served as a spiritual director, most notably for Evagrius.

Tuesday, June 9
Columba of Iona, Monastic, 567

Almost immediately upon being ordained a monk, Columba, born in Ireland in 521, set forth on his mission; before being ordained a presbyter in 551, he had founded monasteries at Derry and Durrow. Twelve years later, Columba and a dozen companions journeyed to northern Britain to evangelize among the Picts. Columba was encouraged to preach, convert, and baptize; he was also given the island of Iona, where, according to legend, his small boat had washed ashore. There, he founded the famous monastery. From Iona, for 30 years, Columba founded other monasteries and traveled through the Highlands, thereby establishing Iona as a link between Irish and Pictish Christians. He died while copying the Psalter.

Wednesday, June 10
Ephrem of Nisibis, Deacon and Poet, 373

Ephrem, born in Nisibis in Mesopotamia, spoke Aramaic, the language of Jesus. Edessa, a Syrian city, was the hub of the wheel of Christianity careering throughout the East, long before conversion of the western Roman Empire. His people called him "the harp of the Holy Spirit" for his words, which influenced development of church doctrine; his women-sung hymns, composed to oppose Gnostic hymns, still enrich liturgies of the Syrian Church. After Christians were driven out of Nisibis in 363 by Persians, Ephrem lived abstemiously in a cave above Edessa, where he preached occasionally. During a famine in 372–73, Ephrem fed the hungry and cared for the sick until his own death from exhaustion.

Thursday, June 11
Saint Barnabas the Apostle

Barnabas, born Joseph, was called an apostle, along with the Twelve, for his missions. Like Paul, Barnabas was a Jew of the Dispersion; Barnabas presented Paul to the apostles with the story of Saul's conversion to Paul. Later, Barnabas, having settled in Antioch, sent for Paul to help lead the Christian church there. The two men, sent by the disciples, carried food and relief to the church during a famine in Jerusalem. Afterwards, the church sent out the pair, starting from Cyprus. Their friendship split over Mark, who had left the mission to return to Jerusalem. Barnabas and Mark traveled to Cyprus, where tradition honors Barnabas as the founder of the church and places his martyrdom.

Friday, June 12
Enmegahbowh, Priest and Missionary, 1902

John Johnson Enmegahbowh, an Odawa (Ottawa) Indian from Canada, was raised in the Midewiwin traditional healing way of his grandfather and the Christian religion of his mother. He came to the United States as a Methodist missionary in 1832. Enmegahbowh ("The One who Stands Before his People") is the first recognized Native American priest in the Episcopal Church, ordained deacon by Bishop Kemper in 1859 and priest by Bishop Whipple in the cathedral at Faribault in 1867. His understanding of Native tradition enabled him to enculturate Christianity in the language and traditions of the Ojibway, tirelessly traveling throughout Minnesota and beyond, actively participating in the development of mission strategy and policy for the Episcopal Church.

The Second Sunday after Pentecost: Proper 6

June 14, 2020

God calls a people into intimate covenant relationship.

Color Green

Preface Of the Lord's Day

Collect

Keep, O Lord, your household the Church in your steadfast faith and love, that through your grace we may proclaim your truth with boldness, and minister your justice with compassion; for the sake of our Savior Jesus Christ, who lives and reigns with you and the Holy Spirit, one God, now and forever. *Amen.*

Readings and Psalm

Genesis 18:1–15 (21:1–7)

In our Hebrew scripture story **the Lord appears to Abraham and promises that he and Sarah will have a son.** As often seen in biblical narratives, the Lord's presence is disguised, this time in one of three visitors. Abraham may suspect God's nearness, but he also generously fulfills his duty of hospitality to strangers. Because both of them are well beyond the years of childbearing, Sarah laughs when she overhears the exchange between God and Abraham, but the fulfillment of the Lord's promise will later bring her great joy. Abraham will place his trust in God's power and through this son become the father of a great people.

Psalm 116:1–2, 12–19

An offering of thanksgiving and praise by one who has been rescued from death.

or

Exodus 19:2–8a

In our Hebrew scripture story **the people of Israel arrive at Mount Sinai after being brought out of Egypt. Through Moses the Lord offers to make a covenant with them.** If they will obey God and keep the covenant, they will be to God a special nation. They will become a priestly people, holy and dedicated for God's service.

Psalm 100

A call to praise and to offer thanksgiving to the Lord.

Romans 5:1–8

In this reading **Paul bids the disciples to rejoice in the reconciliation and hope which are theirs because of the sacrifice of Christ on behalf of sinners.** Through faith we have justification; we are given a right relationship with God. Now even our sufferings can lead to endurance, and this to a perseverance which strengthens our hope. God has shown great love for us in that, while we were still God's enemies because of sin, Christ died for us.

Matthew 9:35—10:8 (9–23)

In our gospel reading **Jesus continues his mission of preaching, teaching, and healing, and he commissions his twelve disciples in this ministry with him.** The need for this work is great. The twelve are constituted as a kind of new Israel, and their healing acts and proclamation tell that God's ruling power has drawn near. At first this ministry will be concentrated on the Jewish nation. Later it will reach to all peoples.

When the longer reading is used, the following may be added:

The disciples are to meet every circumstance with confidence and trust in God.

Pentecost

Prayers of the People

Gracious God, give us boldness, justice, and compassion, as we offer our prayers, responding, "Kyrie eleison."

Open our eyes to see the stranger in our midst, offering hospitality and companionship, believing that the Holy Spirit visits us through those we do not know; let us pray.

Kyrie eleison.

Reveal the fruits of suffering to all who are heavy laden with despair, that they may receive your endurance, grow in character, and live in hope; let us pray.

Kyrie eleison.

Strengthen our hands and voices to proclaim the good news of Christ through the daily events of our lives, and to those we encounter in the course of the day; let us pray.

Kyrie eleison.

Increase vocations to the various ministries of our Church, especially our Religious Communities, whose members hold the Church, her mission and peoples, in prayer, and who work for the joy of the gospel; let us pray.

Kyrie eleison.

Bless our nation, our President and members of Congress; give them wisdom in their deliberations, that legislation and programs may serve the best interests of the common good and the needs of the global community; let us pray.

Kyrie eleison.

Hold in your arms of mercy those who are ill, and grant to those who have died a room prepared by your own hands; let us pray.

Kyrie eleison.

Let us endure faithfully in the practice of intercession, as we continue our petitions.
(Special intentions of the congregation, the diocese, and the Anglican Communion may be added here or before the formal intercessions.)

The Celebrant adds a concluding Collect.

Planning for Rites and Rituals: Year A

Images in the Readings

Once the Israelites were settled in Canaan, nomads became famers, and many biblical passages use the image of the **harvest** to connote fulfillment. Some of the Jewish religious festivals that commemorated their past memories were actually reinterpretations of more ancient harvest festivals, Passover at the barley harvest, and Pentecost the end of the wheat harvest and beginning of the grape harvest. Because God is given credit for all growth of life, harvest is an occasion for thanksgiving. Yet God calls us to work the harvest, a task seen in our culture as far too much hard work for its meager pay, a job for other poor people to fill.

The **mother eagle** swoops under the fledglings, her wings outspread to catch them if they falter.

The **Twelve** is the number of completion, from the twelve sons of Jacob to the twelve gates in the city of Jerusalem at the end of time. The two lists of the Twelve cited in the synoptics are not identical. The point is not historical accuracy, but rather the perfection of Jesus' ministry and the church's mission. The apostles replace the twelve tribes of Israel and begin the completion of all things.

Ideas for the Day

- Every age and place has its distractions and demands but like the Desert Fathers and Mothers, following the path of God's steadfast love calls us to "strike out fearlessly into the unknown,"[1] even if that unknown is right around the corner. If someone is comfortable in the country, they may be dismayed by the lifestyle of the city; and the reverse is also true. These lessons move from the negotiations of a nomadic life into the challenges of ancient urban settings: all of which are full of both rebuke and successes. The commission of Jesus is not one of easy relaxation, but of a daring love for all in response to the love of God. Is the Spirit leading your community to "strike out fearlessly" in some new way?

- When we read or hear the ten commandments, they are not usually offered in the context of where they are found in scripture. What we hear today *is* the context. "I bore you on eagles' wings" and "you are my treasured people" and "you shall be for me a priestly Kingdom," is the context of what the famous commandants are about. It is right after this loving declaration

---

1 Thomas Merton, The Wisdom of the Desert.

that the people are consecrated and then that the ten commandments are offered. Here the commandments are not rules handed down but a gift given to God's people. In an interesting way, there are some parallels to what happens when we baptize someone. We declare they are treasured and holy. They are blessed. And then the community affirms to continually offer them the gift of love.

♦ The time we have entered into the Christian calendar is called the "Season after Pentecost." Traditionally it has been called "Ordinary Time." We recognize God in the ordinary moments of our lives as well as in the times of intense revelation and celebration.

Making Connections

To be a disciple of Christ (a Christian) is to realize our call, as the disciple realized their call. Moreover, to be a disciple of Christ is to accept the New Covenant. We open ourselves to the power of the Holy Spirit and live as servants of the Lord. As we do this, we go forth into the world with new authority and a new power. Look over the liturgy of baptism in the prayer book and talk about the kind of commitment that is made in baptism. The Baptismal Covenant is found on pages 304–305 of the Book of Common Prayer.

Engaging All Ages

During worship, you are invited to share the Peace. How do you and your church share the Peace? Do you shake hands? Do you give a gentle hug? Do you flash two fingers at one another? Do you have a quick conversation to catch up? Worship and scripture remind us that we are to be at peace with God, peace with those who we worship with, and peace with neighbors and with strangers. What is one way you can share the Peace with someone outside of your church this week? What might sharing the Peace with them look like?

Hymns for the Day

The Hymnal 1982
Lord, whose love through humble service 610
The God of Abraham praise 401 [SEMI-CONTINUOUS]
All people that on earth do dwell
    377, 378 [GOSPEL-RELATED]
Before the Lord's eternal throne 391 [GR]
Come down, O Love divine 516
Come, thou fount of every blessing 686
Hail, thou once despised Jesus! 495
O love of God, how strong and true 455, 456
Awake, thou Spirit of the watchmen 540
Come, labor on 541
For the fruit of all creation 424
Hope of the word, thou Christ of great
    compassion 472
Lord, you give the great commission 528
My God, thy table now is spread 321
Ye servants of God, your Master proclaim 535

Lift Every Voice and Sing II
Here am I, send me 126

Wonder, Love, and Praise
You who dwell in the shelter of the Lord 810 [GR}
Lord, you give the great commission 780

Weekday Commemorations

Monday, June 15
Evelyn Underhill, Mystic and Writer, 1947
Born December 6, 1875, Underhill was a fine writer whose essays and books appealed to many also drawn by her definitive mysticism. She grew up in London and was confirmed in the Church of England. In the 1890s, she began journeying to Europe, especially Italy, enticed by art and religion. Despite 15 years' wrestling with profound interest in the Roman Catholic Church, she stayed true to her Anglican roots. Although she had little formal religious education, she was curious about religion and spirituality from childhood, when she met Hubert Moore. They married in 1907 and are buried together in London. She believed mysticism belongs not just to a few saints but to any nurturing soul.

Tuesday, June 16
Joseph Butler, Bishop, 1752

Butler, born in 1692, became an Anglican despite having been raised a Presbyterian and educated at Dissenting schools. He was ordained in 1718. He rose to be called "the greatest of all the thinkers of the English Church." His sermons on human nature, preached during his eight years at Rolls Chapel, first brought him to prominence. After a series of rectorships, he was appointed Bishop of Bristol. He declined the primacy of Canterbury and accepted the bishopric of Durham (1750). His fame resides in his profound support for orthodox Christianity against the Deist thinking in England; in 1736, he published *The Analogy of Religion, Natural and Revealed, to the Constitution and Course of Nature.*

Wednesday, June 17
Marina the Monk, Monastic, fifth century

Marina rejected her widowed father's intent to marry her off then retreat to a monastery: "Why would you save your own soul at the cost of destroying mine?" She shaved her hair, donned men's clothes, sold her possessions with his. They proceeded to a monastic settlement in the Qadisha Valley, where he introduced her as his son, Marinos. She lived as a transvestite until death. When a young woman accused "Marinos" of fathering her child, Marina accepted the accusation and the responsibility of raising the boy in the monastery. She is venerated today in Lebanon, Cyprus, and Italy.

Thursday, June 18
Bernard Mizeki, Martyr, 1896

Born about 1861 in Portuguese East Africa (Mozambique), Mizeki escaped to Capetown, South Africa. There, he was harbored by Anglican missionaries and baptized (1886). Five years later, Mizeki voluntarily joined a pioneer mission in Mashonaland as catechist. In 1896, native peoples arose against Europeans and their African allies. Mizeki was targeted, and despite being warned to flee, he would not desert his converts. He was stabbed to death. His body has never been found, nor has his burial site. A shrine at the site of his martyrdom draws pilgrims. The Anglican Churches of Central and South Africa honor Mizeki as their main martyr and witness.

Friday, June 19
Adelaide Teague Case, Educator, 1948

After Case (b. 1887) earned her doctorate from Columbia University, she accepted a custom-created faculty position at Columbia's Teachers' College. As head of the Department of Religious Education, Case advocated a child-centered versus teacher-centered approach: her book *Liberal Christianity and Religious Education* supported children's inquiry into their faith. She was a pacifist who identified with the liberal Catholic tradition in Anglicanism. At the height of her career at Columbia, she was convinced to accept appointment by the Episcopal Theological School in Cambridge as Professor of Christian Education. Case believed that practicing one's Christian faith means making a difference in the world.

The Third Sunday after Pentecost: Proper 7

June 21, 2020

The cost of discipleship.

Color   Green

Preface   Of the Lord's Day

Collect

O Lord, make us have perpetual love and reverence for your holy Name, for you never fail to help and govern those whom you have set upon the sure foundation of your loving-kindness; through Jesus Christ our Lord, who lives and reigns with you and the Holy Spirit, one God, forever and ever. *Amen.*

Readings and Psalm

Genesis 21:8–21

This reading tells of Sarah's jealousy as she fears that Ishmael may supplant her son Isaac in her husband Abraham's affections. As our narrative unfolds, we are reminded that Abraham had grown weary waiting for God to fulfill the promise made and had taken matters into his own hands, having a son through his wife's slave, Hagar the Egyptian. Hagar and Ishmael are driven into the wilderness where, but for God's intervention, they would likely have died. God will provide for Ishmael, and Ishmael will also become the father of a great nation.

Psalm 86:1–10, 16–17

A prayer to the gracious and loving Lord for mercy and guidance.

or

Jeremiah 20:7–13

In our Hebrew scripture lesson **Jeremiah complains to the Lord. He is torn between wanting to give up his mission and his need to speak in God's name and put his trust in God.** Jeremiah has been given a most difficult ministry. In the period shortly before the final defeat of Judah and its time of exile, all he can do is prophesy violence and destruction as God's judgment on the people. Even his so-called friends persecute him. Yet the Lord is on his side.

Psalm 69:7–10 (11–15), 16–18

A psalm of praise to the mighty God who has brought the people out of Egypt and saved Israel from her enemies. God reigns on high.

Romans 6:1b–11

In this reading we learn that, **as Christian disciples have been joined with Christ in his death through baptism, so they are to know a resurrection like his.** In union with Christ we have died to our sinful selves and have begun to experience a new way of life. In one sense, Paul recognizes, our freedom from death still awaits us in the future. Yet, in another sense, we already know what it means to be alive to God in Jesus Christ and to realize the true meaning of life.

Matthew 10:24–39

In our gospel **Jesus warns his disciples of troubles to come, but offers them the assurance of the Father's care and his own readiness to support them before God when they speak up for him.** Because they are Jesus' disciples, people will do to them what they did to him. There will be persecution and divided families, but disciples are not to be afraid. They are to love Jesus more than father or mother, son or daughter, and to be willing to lose their own lives for Christ's sake. Those who live in this way will actually find their true lives, and God will hold them fast.

Prayers of the People

We have been united with Christ in his death, and made one with him in his resurrection. In this newness of life, we raise our hearts in joyful prayer, responding, "Kyrie eleison."

That the Church and her peoples may name the crosses that retard their work and ministry, so that they may focus once again upon the sovereignty of Christ, who is the source of all our blessings; let us pray.

Kyrie eleison.

That we may be softened by the remembrance of personal darkness and despair and give generously to the relief of the hungry and fearful, the sick and those who work multiple jobs and still struggle to provide for the basic necessities of life; let us pray.

Kyrie eleison.

For all who hold positions of public trust and responsibility, that they may serve the common good with integrity and sound moral judgment; let us pray.

Kyrie eleison.

For those who are being cast out of their native land through political chaos, religious persecution, war and famine, natural disasters, and reasons that remain unknown, that they may find receptive countries as they search for a new homeland; let us pray.

Kyrie eleison.

For those who have died, that they may join the community of saints, in whose fellowship we will one day reside; let us pray.

Kyrie eleison.

That the gift of Christ's Body and Blood may sustain and strengthen us as we share the faith of the saints who have come before; let us pray.

Kyrie eleison.

Let us endure faithfully in the practice of intercession, as we continue our petitions.
(Special intentions of the congregation, the diocese, and the Anglican Communion may be added here or before the formal intercessions.)

The Celebrant adds a concluding Collect.

Images in the Readings

God's care for **sparrows** calls us to trust in God, since Matthew states here and in chapter 7 (see Lectionary 8) that humans have more value than birds. Sparrows were among the cheapest birds sold in the markets of Matthew's time. Unfortunately, such biblical passages have been used to devalue God's creation, as if humans are the only creatures to receive divine blessing. Here Matthew states that God does indeed care for the sparrow.

Of course Matthew's description of the natural and married **family** experiencing hatred is disturbing. Matthew even assumes that discipleship will bring about such dissension. Pacifist Christians assert that Matthew's word about the **sword** is only metaphoric, but even as metaphor, it is a harsh word about the difficulties of the Christian life. In Paul's imagery, the Christian life requires our old self to be crucified, as if baptism aims the sword at oneself.

Probing biblical images helps us avoid taming the Bible into Precious Moments™. Matthew's words about a reversal of **slave and master** may sound benign to Americans who believe in equality, but such words would have sounded bizarre—like losing one's life to live—to citizens of a slave culture. Matthew is saying that cultural patterns may be totally inappropriate for those who follow Christ.

Ideas for the Day

♦ Perhaps you have heard the Mexican proverb— "They thought they buried us, but they didn't know we were seeds." Many congregations today may feel down but not out due to forces beyond their control. There is plenty of stumbling and struggle and angst to go around. Daydreams of perfection and easy bounty have eroded, and yet this new perspective is a call not to give up, but to dig deep into the resources of humility and creativity. Tilth can refer to preparing the soil for new growth, but tilth can also refer to spiritual preparation. How can the compost of our wounds and little deaths nurture the growth of fidelity to God's reign and abundant feasts for all?

♦ There was a woman named Helen. Helen radiated the love of God, and shared a sense of peace with whomever she was around. When asked if she knew what opened that door of abundant love and grace within her she said, "There is a lot of death underneath the love. I moved from the pain of death to the joy of love with the help of Jesus." There are many holy people who know this story and have lived it. Who could you name that exemplifies the peace and love of God?

♦ There have been Christian saints and martyrs who have suffered as a result of witnessing to their faith. One who is such an example is Dietrich Bonhoeffer, author of *The Cost of Discipleship*. Formerly a pacifist, he became persuaded of the need for violence against the Nazi regime and joined a group called the *Abwehr*, whose primary mission was to assassinate Hitler. Ultimately, Bonhoeffer was arrested for his involvement in helping Jews flee the country. Still, he continued to teach with the help of guards who smuggled out his writing, until he was transferred to a concentration camp. When his association with other Abwehr agents was discovered, Bonhoeffer was sentenced to death. He was hanged in April 1945, just one month before Germany surrendered. More than seventy years after his death, his life and writings serve as a touchstone for all of us who seek to understand a Christian's responsibility in the face of injustice—and as an encouragement to serve no matter how great the cost.

Making Connections

The sentence the bishop says at the time of confirmation speak of the cost of taking up the role of disciple in the world today: Strengthen, O Lord, your servant N. with your Holy Spirit; empower N. for your service; and sustain N. with your heavenly grace, that N. may continue as yours forever . . . (BCP, 309).

Engaging All Ages

Have you ever seen a butterfly being born? Find a video online. Egg. Caterpillar. Chrysalis. Butterfly. A chrysalis might look like nothing interesting, but on the inside a miracle is happening. See the butterfly wriggle its way out of its old self and into its new self. If baptism is like a dove descending, perhaps this is what dying, being buried, and rising again with Christ, being alive to God, looks like. Being a chrysalis trying to shed your old self isn't the pretty or easy part of life and faith, but it can produce something new and beautiful.

Hymns for the Day

The Hymnal 1982

Praise to the living God! 372
I love thy kingdom, Lord 524 [GR]
Surely it is God who saves me 678, 679 [GR]
All who believe and are baptized 298
Alleluia, alleluia! Give thanks to the risen Lord 178
We know that Christ is raised and dies no more 296
Christ for the world we sing! 537
Day by day 654
He who would valiant be 564, 565
O Jesus, I have promised 655
Praise the Lord through every nation 484, 485
Spread, O spread, thou mighty word 530
Take up your cross, the Savior said 675
They cast their nets in Galilee 661

Lift Every Voice and Sing II

Where He leads me 144
I have decided to follow Jesus 136
He'll understand, and say "well done" 190

Wonder, Love, and Praise

You shall cross the barren desert 811 [SC]
God's Paschal Lamb is sacrificed for us 880
Will you come and follow me 757

Pentecost

Weekday Commemorations

Monday, June 22
Alban, Martyr, c.304

According to tradition, Alban is the first British martyr. He was a Roman soldier, stationed in a city now called St. Alban's, 20 miles northeast of London. He sheltered a Christian priest fleeing from persecution and then dressed as the priest to be tortured and martyred in his place. The site became a shrine soon after the incident: a monastery was established there in 793 and was ranked in the Middle Ages as the premier abbey in England. The Cathedral of St. Alban's, begun in 1077, stands on the site of Alban's martyrdom; it is the second longest church in England. Alban's remains lie in a chapel east of the choir.

Wednesday, June 24
The Nativity of Saint John the Baptist

John was born the son of Elizabeth and Zachariah, who were aged. His birth is celebrated six months before that of Jesus since Elizabeth, Mary's cousin, had become pregnant six months before Mary. John has a role in all four Gospels. His father lost speech when he disbelieved a vision foretelling John's birth, but when his speech was restored, he sang a canticle of praise, the *Benedictus*, now part of the Daily Office. John lived in abstention in the desert, clothed with camel's hair and a belt; he ate locusts and honey. He preached repentance, importuning hearers to prepare for the Kingdom and the Messiah and baptized them to signify new life. He baptized Jesus in the Jordan.

Friday, June 26
Isabel Florence Hapgood, Ecumenist, 1923

Around 1900, Hapgood encouraged ecumenical relations between her Episcopal Church and Russian Orthodoxy in the United States. She excelled as a student, especially with languages—from Latin and French to Church Slavonic and Russian (she translated Dostoyevsky, Tolstoy, Gorky, and Chekov into English). From 1887 to 1889, she traveled throughout Russia, solidifying her love of the language, the culture, and the Russian Orthodox Church. She sought permission of the church hierarchy to translate the rites into English, completing *Service Book of the Holy Orthodox-Catholic Church* in 11 years. Russian Orthodox bishops, particularly Archbishop Tikhon (April 7), supported Hapgood's work.

The Fourth Sunday after Pentecost: Proper 8

June 28, 2020

God has built the church on the foundation of the apostles and prophets with Jesus Christ as the cornerstone.

Color   Green

Preface   Of the Lord's Day

Collect

Almighty God, you have built your Church upon the foundation of the apostles and prophets, Jesus Christ himself being the chief cornerstone: Grant us so to be joined together in unity of spirit by their teaching, that we may be made a holy temple acceptable to you; through Jesus Christ our Lord, who lives and reigns with you and the Holy Spirit, one God, forever and ever. *Amen.*

Readings and Psalm

Genesis 22:1–14

Our Hebrew scripture reading is **the story of Abraham's willingness to sacrifice his only son Isaac in obedience to the Lord's command.** The narrative illustrates Abraham's readiness to abandon all to serve the Lord. Originally it probably also was used as a model story encouraging the substitution of animal for human sacrifices. Ancient Israel was given a better understanding of God's will.

Psalm 13

The psalmist laments the absence of the Lord, but continues to trust in God.

or

Jeremiah 28:5–9

In this lesson **the prophet Jeremiah once again speaks tough and unpopular truths,** now in the temple and before the priests and all the people. Zedekiah king of Judah has joined a rebellion against Babylon, and Jeremiah has predicted that Jerusalem will fall to the Babylonians in consequence, with many taken captive. Another prophet, Hananiah the Gibeonite, offers false and conflicting reassurances of peace. Jeremiah perseveres in his difficult message that comes from God.

Psalm 89:1–4, 15–18

The Lord is praised for faithful love and mighty justice.

Romans 6:12–23

This lesson teaches that **by the grace of God Christians are no longer slaves to sin but are obedient to the service of righteousness.** Paul is concluding his long discussion of the way in which disciples have been given a right relationship with God through faith. They are no longer set on a course that leads through immorality to death. To use a very human analogy, they are now slaves of righteousness and are bound to the service of God, which leads to holiness and eternal life.

Matthew 10:40–42

In our gospel lection **Jesus tells of reward for disciples who find themselves welcomed in his name.** Those who receive Jesus' followers will find they are receiving the Lord himself and God who sent him. Those who do well and help even the least of the disciples will find great reward.

Prayers of the People

We stand before God in awesome fear, as the power of divine grace is revealed through the mystery of word and sacrament. Trusting in his grace, we offer our prayers, responding, "Kyrie eleison."

For those who claim the prophetic voice in our generation, that they may be willing to pay the price of their convictions and, like the prophets of old, have their testimony tried in the fires of eternity; let us pray.

Kyrie eleison.

That we may respond to the needs of others before we are ready, and give of our bounty when we have yet to be generous, that in the companionship of the apostles we will grow in grace and discover our holiness; let us pray.

Kyrie eleison.

For N., our President, that he/she may be given the wisdom to make judicious decisions, seeking the light of the Lord who is the source of all righteousness; let us pray.

Kyrie eleison.

For safety and refreshment for those on vacation, that they may relax from their work and be reunited with those they love; let us pray.

Kyrie eleison.

That those who eat the Bread and drink the Cup of Jesus' holy sacrifice may bear witness to the Paschal mystery in all its fullness; let us pray.

Kyrie eleison.

That the dead may be granted an entrance into the fellowship of the saints; let us pray.

Kyrie eleison.

Enrich our hearts with the gift of hospitality, O God, as we continue our prayers.
(Special intentions of the congregation, the diocese, and the Anglican Communion may be added here or before the formal intercessions.)

The Celebrant adds a concluding Collect.

Images in the Readings

Both of the two primary images in today's readings are somewhat alien to us. In the Bible, a true **prophet** is not a fortune teller or a court appointee, but rather the mouthpiece of God, proclaiming not what will be, but what is. For Christians, the preeminent prophet is Christ, whose words of God are spoken through the scriptures and in the bread and wine. The words are always double-sided, attending to both human sin and divine mercy—what Lutherans have called "law and gospel."

The idea in a **slave** economy is that everyone is born into a lifelong place in a hierarchy in which each obeys those who are above and cares for those who are below. Persons could not choose or alter their place in the hierarchy, and many Christians taught that God was responsible for who was placed where in this ordering of obedience. Despite our resistance to this idea, Paul writes that we are all born slaves of sin. The freedom of our will comes only through baptism, administered in many denominations even to infants, transferring our allegiance over to God and the neighbor. We are enslaved to God—in our culture, not an attractive suggestion.

Ideas for the Day

♦ In two out of the three Episcopal lectionary cycles we can potentially hear the near-sacrifice of Isaac three times a year (and at least two times every year). Again and again, the lesson fosters discomfort and outrage and even heavy doubts. It is an important scene in salvation history that we cannot turn away from, but as people in relationship with each other, God, and the texts, we are also given the freedom to protest. Yet for all our potential outrage, it begs a hard question of us: on what altars of adult needs, vices, and priorities do we sacrifice the well-being of our children? We don't have to have a rock and a knife to be complicit in the terribleness of reliving this scene in our communities.

This is one of the few times when historical context doesn't really matter. We don't know what really caused Abraham to take his son Isaac up to Moriah. The story says that God told him to, but why? Our common experience of God and our common experience of love, mercy, grace, and forgiveness, makes it clear that God would never actually ask or expect that we would kill our child. So the story has to be about something different than the cause of a lot of family therapy. Perhaps we find the reason for the story in the words, "The Lord will provide." And, yes, God does!

Liberation theology focuses on God's liberating action among the oppressed. From this theological perspective, God is always on the side of the exploited. God led the Israelites out of the oppression of Egypt into the Promised Land. God is acting through the persecuted in Central America, Africa, and our own land. The Magnificat or Song of Mary (BCP, 91) says, "He has cast down the mighty from their thrones, and has lifted up the lowly" (Luke 1:52).

Making Connections

We continue to deal with the theme of discipleship in our readings this week. Continue the story, telling about those who have spoken God's word and suffered for their witness. Francis of Assisi rejected his parents' wealth and power to follow Christ. Martin Luther King, Jr. was controversial as he set about to bring liberation to people of color. It cost him his life. Who are some contemporary persons through whom God may be working in our nation and throughout the world? What is their word, and how is it received by the "proud" and by the "humble"? What is our role as disciples and prophets called to speak out in Jesus' name?

Engaging All Ages

In worship, is there someone playing a piano, an organ, or another instrument? Does it sound pretty? Does your church have a choir who use their voices to make a beautiful sound together? Have you ever heard bad music in church? God is like a composer who writes music. People are God's instruments and choir. Each person has a part to play. You can play your part however you want. God hopes you would be an instrument of righteousness doing good, loving people, and bringing harmony into the world. This week, how will you choose to be an instrument of righteousness?

Hymns for the Day

The Hymnal 1982
Christ is made the sure foundation 518
The Church's one foundation 525
O sorrow deep! (vs. 2–4) 173 [SC]
The God of Abraham praise 401 [SC]
Blessed be the God of Israel 444 [GR]
O day of God, draw nigh 600, 601 [GR]
O God of every nation 607 [GR]
Savior, again to thy dear Name we raise 345 [GR]
Creator of the stars of night (vs. 1–4, 6) 60
Crown him with many crowns 494
Here, O my Lord, I see thee face to face 318
Lord Jesus, think on me 641
Now that the daylight fills the sky 3, 4
Wilt thou forgive that sin, where I begun 140, 141
Where cross the crowded ways of life 609

Lift Every Voice and Sing II

Wonder, Love, and Praise
Blessed be the God of Israel 889 [GR]
Lord Jesus, think on me 798
No saint on earth lives life to self alone 776
We are all one in mission 778
Gracious Spirit, give your servants 782

Pentecost

Weekday Commemorations

Monday, June 29
The Apostles Saint Peter and Saint Paul

Peter and Paul, each with his own commemoration as a renowned Church leader, are also remembered together because, by tradition, they were martyred together in Rome under Nero in 64. Paul was a well-educated, urbane Jew of the Dispersion; Peter was an untutored fisher from Galilee. The two disagreed on the issue of mission to the Gentiles in the early years of the Church, but they were committed to Christ and to proclaiming the gospel, which they bore to Rome. According to tradition, Paul was decapitated by sword swipe, as befitted a Roman citizen; Peter suffered death on the cross, it is said, with his head pointed downward.

Wednesday, July 1
Pauli Murray, Priest, 1985

Born in Baltimore in 1910, Murray was raised in Durham, North Carolina, and graduated from Hunter College in 1933. She was denied entry to graduate school at the University of North Carolina in 1938 due to her race; she went on to graduate from Howard University Law School in 1944. While a student at Howard, she participated in sit-in demonstrations that challenged racial segregation in drugstores and cafeterias in Washington, DC. Denied admission to Harvard University for an advanced law degree because of her gender, Murray received her Masters of Law from the University of California, Berkeley, in 1945. In later life, she discerned a call to ordained ministry and began studies at General Theological Seminary in 1973. She was ordained as a deacon in June 1976, and, on January 8, 1977, she was ordained as a priest at Washington National Cathedral. Murray served at Church of the Atonement in Washington, D.C., from 1979 to 1981 and at Holy Nativity Church in Baltimore until her death in 1985.

Thursday, July 2
Moses the Black, Monastic and Martyr, c.400

As a strong, young man in the fourth century, Moses led a marauding band of robbers. Fleeing from authorities, he took shelter with monks. They impressed him with their faithfulness and kindness. Moses chose to be baptized and remain with them in the desert. He lived in a simple cell, eating only 10 ounces of dry bread a day. He set an example during judgment of a brother monk by bearing a basket leaking sand representing his sins. Thus, each monk forgave his errant brother. Moses' mantra was: "Go, sit in your cell, and your cell will teach you everything."

Saturday, July 4
Independence Day (United States of America)

Ten years after July 4, 1776, General Convention called for observance of Independence Day throughout "this Church, on the fourth of July, forever." Proper psalms, lessons, and prayers were appointed for the national recognition of this day; however, they were rescinded in 1789 by General Convention with the intervention of Bishop William White. Although he supported the American Revolution, White revolted against observing the day, given that the majority of the Church's clericals remained loyal to the British government. Not until 1928 was provision made again for the liturgical notice of the day.

The Fifth Sunday after Pentecost: Proper 9

July 5, 2020

God's wisdom, which brings rest and peace, is personified in Jesus.

Color   Green

Preface   Of the Lord's Day

Collect

O God, you have taught us to keep all your commandments by loving you and our neighbor: Grant us the grace of your Holy Spirit, that we may be devoted to you with our whole heart, and united to one another with pure affection; through Jesus Christ our Lord, who lives and reigns with you and the Holy Spirit, one God, forever and ever. *Amen.*

Readings and Psalm

Genesis 24:34–38, 42–49, 58–67

Our Hebrew Bible story is about the arranged marriage between Isaac and his kinswoman Rebekah. Abraham sent his trusted servant to his kinfolk in Haran, as he did not want to select a bride for his son from the Canaanites among whom he dwelt. The providential hand of God is seen in the prosecution and success of this venture.

Psalm 45:10–17

In this psalm for a royal wedding the queen is instructed to leave ancestry behind in preference to loyalty for her king, to whom she goes in procession.

or

Song of Solomon 2:8–13

A woman rejoices in a springtime visit from her beloved.

or

Zechariah 9:9–12

Our opening reading is **a prophecy of great hope and salvation for Jerusalem: her triumphant but humble king comes to rule.** This vision of the victorious yet lowly messiah riding on a young ass derives from ancient rituals in the holy city. Several hundred years before Jesus' time the prophet Zechariah looked forward to a time of restoration for his people and a magnificent new king. His peaceful dominion will reach from the great river (the Euphrates, but mythically the river of paradise) to the ends of the earth.

Psalm 145:8–14

A hymn of praise to the Lord, who is mighty in deeds yet tender and compassionate.

Romans 7:15–25a

In this lesson **Paul continues to wrestle with the question of the role of the law. Although the law is good in principle, without God's saving act in Jesus, it only produces more sinfulness.** Paul feels two strong and opposing tendencies within his being. Without the new relationship of faith through Jesus, the regulations of the law only cause the tendency to break the law to grow stronger. Paul speaks of this as a tendency of his flesh, by which he means all within him that does not seek faithful obedience to God.

Matthew 11:16–19, 25–30

In our gospel lesson **Jesus compares his generation to capricious children, equally displeased by the austere message of John the Baptist and the inviting message of Jesus. Yet God's wisdom will prevail. Jesus bids all to come and find that the yoke of his teaching is easy to bear.** The disclosure of the divine will comes as God's gracious gift, not through human knowledge. Especially intimate is the relationship between the Lord of all life and Jesus—that of Father and Son. Although he is the Son, Jesus is humble of heart and gentle.

Pentecost

Prayers of the People

Let us come before God in a posture of openness, expecting the Holy Spirit to transform our lives and to lead us into the offering of our prayers, as we respond, "Hear us, good Lord."

Free us from the bondage of our sinful ways, our blindness to truth, our stubbornness and lack of discipline, that we may yearn after the fruits of the divine Word and follow its wisdom; let us pray.

Hear us, good Lord.

Strengthen the love and devotion amongst family members, that forgiveness may heal old wounds, and mutual affection pave the way to wholeness; let us pray.

Hear us, good Lord.

Guide the leaders of our Church, that there may be mutual respect across, and a renewed sense of partnership in bringing God's Kingdom into the most troubled corners of our neighborhoods and nations; let us pray.

Hear us, good Lord.

Encourage our civic leaders to modify their convictions with compromise, that there may be a renewal of hope for those who live in poverty, unemployment, and lack of educational opportunities; let us pray.

Hear us, good Lord.

Reveal the unfolding beauty of creation, the uniqueness of seasons, and the joy and wonder of your handicraft, that we may delight in guarding these gifts; let us pray.

Hear us, good Lord.

Receive those who have died into your arms of mercy, that they may sleep in everlasting peace; let us pray.

Hear us, good Lord.

Faithfully seeking the path to new life, let us continue our prayers.
(Special intentions of the congregation, the diocese, and the Anglican Communion may be added here or before the formal intercessions.)

The Celebrant adds a concluding Collect.

Images in the Readings

The **yoke** ties together two beasts of burden. According to this image, Christians do not walk alone, but are tied to Christ and to one another.

In the several centuries before Christ, Jewish poetry developed the image of **wisdom**. Borrowing from neighboring polytheistic religions the picture of the divine consort, the great goddess who personified wisdom, Jews adapted this divine female figure into a way to speak of God's law, a beautiful and powerful aspect of the Almighty, who guided the people into truth. Christians altered the image once again, seeing Christ as this Wisdom, whose words sound like foolishness to the world. In the eighth-century "O" antiphons preceding Christmas and versified in the hymn "O Come, O Come, Emmanuel," Christ is our Wisdom, coming in strength and beauty.

Ideas for the Day

◆ Perhaps you have experienced that moment where you are so caught up in "adulting" that you barely notice something amazing is going on just beyond your attention. And perhaps at that moment, it is a young person who points and says—look! Some of the most popular young adult fiction of the last fifty years have been tales of young people working together to save the adult world from itself and extraordinary evils. More than just entertainment, such stories help prepare us for the moments when we are confronted with real-life disaster and evil. So too, does the regular practice of dwelling with scripture prepare us to pay attention and empower the way of love and dismantle the lies of corruption.

◆ How about we call this Sunday, "Chicken Soup Sunday" or "Valentine's Day Sunday?" The readings are so romantic and so loving: We witness the gentle exposure of a love blooming between Isaac and Rebekah. We are invited to experience the love duet in the Song of Solomon. And don't you think that everyone should simply put to memory, "The Lord is gracious and full of compassion, slow to anger and of great kindness"? Finally, Jesus says it as clearly as can ever be said—if you are tired, come here—if you are burdened then let me take if from you—I will hold you and love you.

◆ Keep the radical words of the previous Sunday gospels in mind as you share today's reading (Matthew 11:25). It would seem that in the Kingdom of God the standards of the world are reversed. The clever and proud are put down, and the lowly and childlike are raised up. The second part of the gospel contains familiar words "Come to me . . ." (Matthew 11:28). The Lord comforts those who experience oppression, sickness, and suffering.

Making Connections

The radical nature of the gospel is the theme carried over from previous weeks. Notice the sense of justice, healing, and love that Jesus offers to those who do come seeking the wholeness that the Lord offers. The proud and powerful miss that strength as they rely on their own power. The church is called to witness to the wisdom of God, which often contradicts the "wisdom" of the culture. The church is to proclaim the way of God's wisdom and peace in every action and word.

Engaging All Ages

Backpacks and bags can get heavy. Heavy from what is needed for day-to-day life. Heavy with things you might find useful in certain circumstances. Heavy with all the stuff picked up along the way. Life gets heavy too. You carry around the needed stuff and potentially useful stuff. There is also the burden of excess baggage that most likely should just be tossed out. Jesus says that he and God are there to help no matter how heavy life gets or the reason for its heaviness. Jesus and God support you as you carry all of your burdens.

Hymns for the Day

The Hymnal 1982

Love divine, all loves excelling 657
Come away to the skies 213 [SC]
God, my King, thy might confessing 414 [GR]
Hail to the Lord's Anointed 616 [GR]
Jesus shall reign where'er the sun 544 [GR]
We will extol you, ever-blessed Lord 404 [GR]
Awake, my soul, and with the sun 11
Hope of the world, thou Christ of great compassion 472
Just as I am, without one plea 693
Blest be the King whose coming 74
Can we by searching find out God 476
Christ the worker 611
Father, we thank thee who hast planted 302, 303
Go forth for God; go to the world in peace 347
How sweet the Name of Jesus sounds 644
I heard the voice of Jesus say 692
Lord of all hopefulness, Lord of all joy 482
O Bread of life, for sinners broken 342

Lift Every Voice and Sing II

Just as I am 137
Come to me 156
Softly and tenderly Jesus is calling 101

Wonder, Love, and Praise

Weekday Commemorations

Monday, July 6
Eva Lee Matthews, Monastic, 1928
Matthews (b. 1862) grew up in Ohio as an active member of her Episcopal Church. Mathews and a coworker, Beatrice Henderson, at Bethany Mission House, created a new religious order to assist Cincinnati's poor, especially the children. As Mother Eva Mary, Matthews led the group as superior until her death. In 1898, the Episcopal Church recognized the women's order, naming it the Community of the Transfiguration. The order relocated to Glendale, Matthews' childhood home, from Cincinnati. By the 1920s, the community had members ministering in two states and China; today it also serves the poor in the Dominican Republic.

Wednesday, July 8
Priscilla and Aquila,
Coworkers of the Apostle Paul
Around the year 50, the apostle Paul went to Corinth where he met Priscilla and Aquila. The married couple, tentmakers, had just arrived from Rome, from which Emperor Claudius had expelled the Jews. The two may have been Christians before meeting Paul or were converted by his preaching. After 18 months, the three traveled to Ephesus, where the couple remained while Paul continued to Antioch. The two were apparently in Rome when Paul wrote to that congregation and in Ephesus when Paul wrote his last letter to Timothy. Clearly dear to Paul, they earnestly and effectively spread the Gospel.

Saturday, July 11
Benedict of Nursia, Monastic, c.543
Benedict is generally accounted the father of western monasticism. He was born about 480, at Nursia in central Italy, and was educated in Rome. Benedict's disapproval of the manners and morals of Rome led him to a vocation of monastic seclusion. He withdrew to a hillside cave above Lake Subiaco where there was already at least one other monk. Gradually, a community grew up around him, and moving with his disciples to Monte Cassino, in about 540 composed his monastic Rule. In the Anglican Communion today, the rules of many religious orders are influenced by Benedict's rule.

Pentecost

The Sixth Sunday after Pentecost: Proper 10

July 12, 2020

God's word is power (The Parable of the Sower).

Pentecost

Color Green

Preface Of the Lord's Day

Collect

O Lord, mercifully receive the prayers of your people who call upon you, and grant that they may know and understand what things they ought to do, and also may have grace and power faithfully to accomplish them; through Jesus Christ our Lord, who lives and reigns with you and the Holy Spirit, one God, now and forever. *Amen.*

Readings and Psalm

Genesis 25:19–34

Esau and Jacob are born to Isaac and Rebekah, but it is the second and younger twin who makes himself first, upsetting the established cultural pattern of primogeniture. God's purposes are fulfilled within the untidy and compromised patterns of human interaction. Jacob deceives his brother Esau, who, driven by his appetites, loses his birthright.

Psalm 119:105–112

Even in times of hardship, the psalmist is committed to following the statutes and precepts of the Lord.

or

Isaiah 55:10–13

In our Hebrew scripture lesson **God's word proceeds purposefully in human affairs and achieves God's intentions** as surely as seed and soil and water combine in the agricultural cycle to produce a good harvest. The people are to take joy in understanding that God's work, though inscrutable at times, is being accomplished in their midst as certainly as it may be seen in the natural world.

Psalm 65:(1–8) 9–13

A psalm of praise and thanksgiving to the savior, the mighty Lord, who creates the earth and causes it to bring forth abundantly.

Romans 8:1–11

In this lesson **Paul draws a sharp contrast between the mind set on the flesh, and the mind set on the Spirit.** The person oriented only toward this temporal world with its rewards and pleasures can neither keep the law nor please God. Only through the grace of God in Christ can a fundamental reorientation toward God's Spirit occur. When God's Spirit quickens faith there is no longer any condemnation, for the Spirit that raised Jesus from the dead now indwells those so animated.

Matthew 13:1–9, 18–23

Our gospel is **Jesus' parable of the sower, together with its interpretation.** The story by itself may once have been used to stress how surprisingly fruitful God's power can be, quite apart from human expectations or control. With its explanation the parable was used as an allegory by early Christians to help them understand the missionary situation of the church. Because of the work of the devil and human weakness and sin, the word they preached did not always produce. But, in the right circumstances, its fruit could be anywhere from substantial to amazing.

Prayers of the People

Mercifully receive our prayers, O God, that we may know your ways and follow where you lead, responding, "Hear us, good Lord."

For those who are seeking a spiritual home, that they may be inspired to visit our churches and to receive a deep sense of God's presence through our worship together and the hospitality we share; let us pray.

Hear us, good Lord.

That we may be set free from the need to claim our worthiness through possessions and position, so that we may discover our true identity in the life and hope of the Holy Spirit; let us pray.

Hear us, good Lord.

That the light of Christ will reveal the path to those for whom the shadows are long, the poor and desperate, the lonely and unemployed, the hungry and fearful, the refugee and homeless, the prisoner and those who live as if in prison, that we may not forget them; let us pray.

Hear us, good Lord.

For our Commander-in-Chief and all who serve in the armed forces, that we may be thankful for their many sacrifices, and honor the service they render to our country and to the security of the world; let us pray.

Hear us, good Lord.

For those who have died, that they may reside in that place where there is no sorrow or pain, but life everlasting; let us pray.

Hear us, good Lord.

For safety for children who are on vacation, that they may have the chance to learn new skills, build healthy bodies, and develop new and lasting friendships; let us pray.

Hear us, good Lord.

With heart and mind turned toward God, we continue our prayers.
(Special intentions of the congregation, the diocese, and the Anglican Communion may be added here or before the formal intercessions.)

The Celebrant adds a concluding Collect.

Images in the Readings

Although seed was valuable, the **sower** strewed the seed widely. In Christian imagination, the sower is Christ, and also the preacher, and also every Christian spreading the Good News to others.

Those who live in the Spirit bear good **fruit**, says Matthew. The imagery of plentiful growth recurs throughout the Bible and can alert us to the beauteous variety of plants and trees we humans can enjoy. In the vision of the heavenly city in The Revelation to John, the Tree of Life can by itself produce twelve different fruits.

The **trees** are clapping their hands. The troublesome thorn is replaced by the medicinally useful evergreen cypress, identified as a tree used in the building of the temple. The briar has been replaced with myrtle, an aromatic evergreen used in the rituals of Sukkoth.

Ideas for the Day

♦ Maybe you have had a bunkmate, sibling, child, neighbor, or coworker with whom there should have been peace, but there was often turmoil—a bit like living with Jacob. He seems to have never come home with a "plays well with others" report card; he is a bit of an antihero. Have you ever imagined this lesson from the perspective of Jacob, who probably doesn't see himself as much of a scoundrel as the holy author seems to? What were his motivations—was it just deceit and money-grabbing or was he well-intentioned in his own mind? Living together is what we are made for, yet it is also our constant trouble because we cannot always know the intentions of people we struggle to love wholeheartedly.

♦ A new person comes to church and then never returns. A new person comes to church and gets so excited they want to join everything. They stay for two months and then never return. A new person drives into the parking lot, pauses, and then decides to go get some coffee instead. And a new person comes to church and fully integrates and there is much joy in the community. It almost comes off like there is only one winner; one good end. But don't you think that God is actively working in all four of the new people? Don't you think that even for the person that drove into the parking lot, even in that ten-second stop, God might have done something wonderful?

♦ In the frustrations we feel in the "seeds" that seem to be dying all around us, the parable of the sower can give us the same encouragement as it did to the disciples who saw so many of Jesus' seeds seemingly fall by the wayside. What is happening in our time in the church? In the world? Where and how do we hear God's word being uttered? Where do the seeds of God's word seem to be falling on hard ground and dying?

Making Connections

Today's focus is the Word of God. Tie it in with John 1, "In the beginning was the Word." The Word of God is not just something we hear; it has a power. It is something we "see" in what is happening around us. The Word is the wisdom that makes sense of creation and puts us in touch with the reality of that sense. Nothing can keep the Word of God from accomplishing its purpose. No matter how discouraging we may feel with the way our history is seemingly working out, God's Word will be accomplished

Engaging All Ages

Consider growing a plant or working in a garden during this time after Pentecost. Identify what plants grow in this season in your environment. Talk about how plants often need to be planted, watered, and fed at the appropriate times for them to grow and blossom fully into what they could become. Wonder if the seeds of your life are being planted and nourished in ways that allow God to help you grow and blossom fully. Even in ordinary times where nothing particularly exciting seems to be happening, we are still growing and that is good.

Hymns for the Day

The Hymnal 1982
Lamp of our feet, whereby we trace 627 [SC]
O Christ, the Word Incarnate 632 [SC]
Surely it is God who saves me 678, 679 [GR]
Eternal Spirit of the living Christ 698
O Spirit of Life, O Spirit of God 505
Almighty God, your word is cast 588, 589
Blessed Jesus, at thy word 440
Father, we thank thee who hast planted 302, 303
God is working his purpose out 534
Lord, make us servants of your peace 593
Spread, O spread, thou mighty word 530

Lift Every Voice and Sing II
Spirit of the living God 115
One bread, one body 151

Wonder, Love, and Praise

Weekday Commemorations

Tuesday, July 14
Argula Von Grumbach,
Scholar and Church Reformer, c. 1554
The brilliant Argula shone gemlike in Germany in her day. She was born in 1492 a noblewoman. Her father gave her a German Bible when she was ten to spur her studies. Her education continued as she served as a lady-in-waiting at the court when reform defined Germany. She married at eighteen and moved to be chatelaine of her household, mother of four, and a theology student. She provided succor for a condemned seminarian, accusing the clerics at the university of "foolish violence against the word of God." She spoke out vociferously, despite being lay and female.

Friday, July 17
William White, Bishop, 1836
The founding of the American Episcopal Church and the United States of America followed many parallel lines, not least of which were drawn by the venerable White. The chief designer of the Church's constitution was born (1747) and educated in Philadelphia. He was ordained a deacon in England in 1770, priest in 1772; returning home, he ministered at Christ and St. Peter's for seven years, whereupon he began a rectorship that continued unto his death. He served as chaplain to the Continental Congress (1777–1789) and of the Senate until 1800. He was Presiding Bishop at the Church's organizing General Convention in 1789, then from 1795 until he died.

The Seventh Sunday after Pentecost: Proper 11

July 19, 2020

God's patience and mercy.

Color   Green

Preface   Of the Lord's Day

Collect

Almighty God, the fountain of all wisdom, you know our necessities before we ask and our ignorance in asking: Have compassion on our weakness, and mercifully give us those things which for our unworthiness we dare not, and for our blindness we cannot ask; through the worthiness of your Son Jesus Christ our Lord, who lives and reigns with you and the Holy Spirit, one God, now and forever. *Amen.*

Readings and Psalm

Genesis 28:10–19a

God comes to Jacob in a dream and, in a vision of a ladder between earth and heaven, renews with Jacob the promise made to his grandfather Abraham. Jacob will become the father of a great nation. Jacob awakes astonished at God's self-revelation and sets up a sacred pillar, calling the place "Bethel," a site which will one day become an important northern shrine city.

Psalm 139:1–12, 23–24

With wonderful wisdom God alone perceives the heights and depths of life.

or

Isaiah 44:6–8

Writing from the Babylonian captivity, **the prophet emphasizes the uniqueness of Yahweh, Israel's Redeemer and King.** There is no other god. The text echoes with remembrance of the promises made to the patriarchs in times past, calling the Hebrew people to act as continuing witnesses of God's faithfulness.

Wisdom of Solomon 12:13, 16–19

God, who is sovereign over all things, is also a God of mercy and forbearance.

or

Psalm 86:11–17

A prayer to the gracious and loving Lord for mercy and guidance.

Romans 8:12–25

In this lesson **Paul teaches that, if we follow our lower nature, we are enslaved and destined to death, but when we are moved by God's Spirit, we become God's children and heirs with Christ.** The Spirit prompts us to call upon God as Father with the same Aramaic word (*Abba*) that Jesus used. Indeed, as heirs with Christ, the whole of creation is now linked with human destiny. As creation shares in the penalty of slavery to mortality and corruption, it will through our freedom as children of God participate in our full redemption. This is our saving hope, greater than any sufferings of this present age, and though still hidden, we now enjoy the first fruits of the Spirit.

Matthew 13:24–30, 36–43

The gospel is **the parable of the wheat and the weeds, for which Jesus then provides an explanation.** The story points to a mystery: why there is both good and evil in life. The parable may at one time have been used to suggest that it is not so easy for humans to know what is good and what is bad from the divine perspective. In a strangely mixed world one must carry on with patience. The allegorical explanation emphasizes the judgment which will take place in the end at the hands of the Son of Man.

Prayers of the People

We lift our prayers to God, who knows our necessities before we ask and rejoices in our asking, as we respond, "Hear us, good Lord."

That judges, attorneys, and juries may be fair and just in their dealings with those who come before them, relying on the law and legal precedence, and weighing their decisions with compassion and forbearance; let us pray.

Hear us, good Lord.

That the Church may welcome young adults into its life, inviting them into positions of responsibility and leadership, listening to their ideas, and joining with them in building for the future; let us pray.

Hear us, good Lord.

That God's will may break through the hardened surfaces of those who release their despair through violence, abuse, gang membership, vengeful societies, and terrorist organizations, so that they may be changed into the architects of a peaceful and prosperous world; let us pray.

Hear us, good Lord.

That the hope of the poor be not in vain, and those with a troubled spirit be not forgotten, but assisted through the generosity of those whose hearts are fertile soil in which the ministry Christ bears much fruit; let us pray.

Hear us, good Lord.

That the leaders of the nations may usher in the peace of God's reign; let us pray.

Hear us, good Lord.

That all who have returned to the dust may be raised to the glory of everlasting life; let us pray.

Hear us, good Lord.

In the light that knows no setting of the sun, let us continue our prayers.
(Special intentions of the congregation, the diocese, and the Anglican Communion may be added here or before the formal intercessions.)

The Celebrant adds a concluding Collect.

Images in the Readings

Contemporary English-language Bibles cleverly translate this parable with nouns that sound nearly identical: wheat and **weeds**. It is easy to think of the other as a weed. Christian theology reminds us that each one of us is both wheat and weed. In Martin Luther's language, we are always both saint and sinner.

Once again this Sunday's readings give us the images of the seed and the harvest. In explicating the allegory, Matthew writes about the furnace of **fire**, where there will be weeping and gnashing of teeth. Scholars suggest that the image of eternal separation from God as fire, Gehenna, recalled the perpetually burning refuse dump that was outside the city walls. Thus God's judgmental fire was about expulsion from the community and destruction of what is worthless. That this fire is an image is made clear in that people are gnashing their teeth; thus they still have bodies that are, however, not being burned up.

We are **children** of God: not natural offspring, but instead adopted, beloved, dependent, obedient.

That the entire universe is **in labor** is a striking image of God's creation that rejects a commonplace Christian notion that God cares only for human beings. According to biblical theology, all God's creation is good; all creation has fallen; all is groaning in pain until God brings about new birth. As in the natural world, so in the human part of it: countless mothers die in childbirth, for new birth is a painful, even dangerous event. The image of all the earth in labor fits well with our scientific knowledge of the earth and its creatures, all of which must continually struggle for life. The natural world is not a benign zoo, but rather billions of life forms created by God that all are headed toward decay.

God is **the first and the last**. Revelation casts this as Alpha and Omega, A and Z. So Christian theology has taught that God was before all things, and when all things come to their end, what will remain is God.

Ideas of the Day

♦ Leaving the scene after "stealing" the birthright, Jacob has this revelatory experience of the borderland between the infinite and the finite. The psalm is an expression of awe and wonder and closeness with God, but perhaps also a hint of God's intentions being at times uncomfortable too. Together the two may recall the scene from the movie *Contact* where the rational Dr. Arroway is overwhelmed by a vision of deepest space and declares, "They should have sent a poet to report the beauty and intimacy of that moment." It is intriguing to imagine Psalm 139 as the inner narrative of Jacob during this revelation.

♦ Don't you love to have God dreams? It has been said that it is a good idea to set a piece of paper and pen next to your bed and try in the moments just before you fall asleep to ask God for a dream. And then the moment you realize your God dream has ended, tell yourself to wake up and write down your dream. After a couple of times doing this, you might actually have something new, something exciting. Jacob found himself in a holy place and was able to hear blessing. Hopefully, we don't need to use a rock as a pillow, but it is during our sleep that we are less likely to try to control God and hear what we actually need to hear.

♦ The gospel reading is a response to the age-old question, "Why does God allow evil to exist?" The evil in the world seems to grow stronger. But God's time is not our time, we hear today. God's patience encompasses eternity, while we live but a moment. What do you think prompted Jesus to tell this parable? What kinds of questions do you think people were asking him?

Making Connections

The reading from Romans is often read at a burial service because it expresses with power the Christian hope. According to the Catechism, the Christian hope is to live with confidence in newness and fullness of life, and to await the coming of Christ in glory, and the completion of God's purpose for the world. How would you describe the Christian hope? What do you believe God's purpose is for the world?

Engaging All Ages

"What is a weed? A plant whose virtues have not yet been discovered." These words are attributed to poet Ralph Waldo Emerson. What do you see when you see a weed? An inconvenient truth to get rid of or virtues undiscovered? Perhaps find a weed and a flower you like and compare them to one another. You are the field that Jesus describes today. But you aren't simply good seed and bad weed. You are complexly, beautifully, and miraculously both seeds. And even weeds at times have their value. Are there weeds growing in you? What are your virtues yet discovered?

Hymns for the Day

The Hymnal 1982

As Jacob with travel was weary one day 453 [SC]
Lord, thou has searched me and dost know 702 [SC]
Eternal light, shine in my heart 465, 466 [GR]
Immortal, invisible, God only wise 423 [GR]
My God, how wonderful thou art 643 [GR]
O day of God, draw nigh 600, 601 [GR]
The Lord will come and not be slow 462 [GR]
Come, thou almighty King 365 [GR]
Praise to the living God 372 [GR]
To God with gladness sing 399 [GR]
All my hope on God is founded 665
Christ is the world's true Light 542
Come with us, O blessed Jesus 336
Creator of the stars of night 60
Almighty God, your word is cast 588, 589
Come, labor on 541
Come, ye thankful people, come (vs. 2–4) 290
Father, we thank thee who hast planted 302, 303
For the fruit of all creation 424

Lift Every Voice and Sing II

We are climbing Jacob's ladder 220 [SC]
One bread, one body 151

Wonder, Love, and Praise

God the sculptor of the mountains 746, 747

Pentecost

Weekday Commemorations

Monday, July 20
Elizabeth Cady Stanton, Amelia Bloomer,
Sojourner Truth, and Harriet Ross Tubman,
Social Reformers

Born on November 12, 1815, into an affluent, strict
Calvinist family in Johnstown, New York, Elizabeth,
as a young woman, took seriously the Presbyterian
doctrines of predestination and human depravity. She
became very depressed, but resolved her mental crises
through action. She dedicated her life to righting the
wrongs perpetrated upon women by the Church and
society. She and four other women organized the first
Women's Rights Convention at Seneca Falls, New
York, July 19–20, 1848.

Amelia Jenks Bloomer, the youngest of six
children, born in New York on May 27, 1818, to a
pious Presbyterian family, early on demonstrated a
kindness of heart and strict regard for truth and right.
As a young woman, she joined in the temperance,
antislavery, and women's rights movements, never
intending to make dress reform a major platform in
women's struggle for justice. But women's fashion of
the day prescribed waist-cinching corsets, even for
pregnant women, resulting in severe health problems.
Faith and fashion collided explosively when she
published in her newspaper, *The Lily,* a picture of
herself in loose-fitting Turkish trousers, and began
wearing them publicly.

Isabella (Sojourner Truth) was the next-to-
youngest child of several born to James and Elizabeth,
slaves owned by a wealthy Dutchman in New York, in
1797 or 1798. For the first 28 years of her life she was
a slave, sold from household to household. During a
women's rights convention in Ohio, Sojourner gave
the speech for which she is best remembered: "Ain't
I a Woman." She had listened for hours to clergy
attack women's rights and abolition, using the Bible
to support their oppressive logic: God had created
women to be weak and blacks to be a subservient race.
In her speech she retorted, "If the first woman God
ever made was strong enough to turn the world upside
down all alone, these women together ought to be able
to turn it back, and get it right side up again! And now
they is asking to do it, the men better let them."

Slave births were recorded under property, not
as persons with names; but we know that Harriet
Ross, born sometime during 1820 on a Maryland
Chesapeake Bay plantation, was the sixth of eleven
children born to Ben Ross and Harriet Green. When
she was about 24, Harriet escaped to Canada, but
could not forget her parents and other slaves she left
behind. Working with the Quakers, she made at least
19 trips back to Maryland between 1851 and 1861,
freeing over 300 people by leading them into Canada.
She was so successful, $40,000 was offered for her
capture. Guided by God through omens, dreams, and
warnings, she claimed her struggle against slavery
had been commanded by God. She foresaw the Civil
War in a vision. When it began, she quickly joined the
Union Army, serving as cook and nurse, caring for
both Confederate and Union soldiers. She served as a
spy and scout. She led 300 black troops on a raid that
freed over 750 slaves, making her the first American
woman to lead troops into military action.

Tuesday, July 21
Maria Skobtsova, Monastic and Martyr, 1945

Divorced from her first husband, suffering the death
of a child, and separated from her second, Skobtsova
(b. 1891) worked with the needy in Paris. In 1932,
she became a nun. When Nazis took Paris in 1940,
she provided a haven for Jews, who sought her help
to prevent deportation through baptismal certificates
provided by her chaplain. Nazis caught her and
imprisoned her in Ravensbrück. Maria defined
Christian asceticism as responses to the needs of others
in creating a better society and defined her fellow
inmates as "the very icon of God incarnate." She died
in a Nazi gas chamber.

Wednesday, July 22
Saint Mary Magdalene

Mary of Magdala, near Capernaum, followed Jesus
and cared for Him-who-healed-her. She appears in
all four Gospels' stories of the crucifixion as witness
to Christ's death. She exemplifies women's faithful
ministry for Jesus, as she and her sisters in faith went
to the tomb to mourn and attend to Jesus' body. That
Jesus revealed himself to her, calling her by name,
makes her the first witness to the risen Lord. She told
the disciples, "I have seen the Lord." According to the
Gospel of Mary, Peter, for one, did not believe that
Jesus would show himself first to a woman. Mary's
reputation, although twisted for centuries, maintains
that she was an apostle.

Thursday, July 23
John Cassian, Monastic and Theologian, 435

John, born in Romania around 365, learned from the desert founders of the ascetic movement in Egypt to rid himself of distractions from loving God. However, he came to this tradition before politics arising from theological controversies forced him out of Egypt about 399. He traveled to Constantinople, then to Gaul. About 415, he founded a monastery in Marseilles and, later, a house for nuns because he thought living in community provided guidance, loving moderation, and companionship. Such was the basis for Benedictine monasticism.

Friday, July 24
Thomas á Kempis, Priest and Mystic, 1471

He was born Thomas Hammerken in the Duchy of Cleves (about 1380) and educated by the Brethren of the Common Life. He joined its order (1399) in Zolle, where he took his vows (1407), was ordained (1415), and made subprior (1425). The order, founded by Gerard Groote, comprised laity and clergy. The Brethren cultivated biblical piety, more practical than speculative, and stressed living the inner life and practicing virtue. The members supported themselves by teaching (Erasmus was a pupil) and copying manuscripts. Thomas is renowned for *The Imitation of Christ*, which Thomas composed, or compiled; the work has been widely translated, nearly as often as the Holy Scriptures.

Saturday, July 25
Saint James the Apostle

James' familiar name, James the Greater, distinguishes the brother of John from the other apostle named James (commemorated with Philip) but also from the other James, "the brother of our Lord." This James was the son of Zebedee, a prosperous Galilean fisher; with his brother John, James left his home and business to follow Christ's call. He seems to have belonged among those chosen for the privilege of witnessing the Transfiguration, the raising of Jairus' daughter, and the agony in the garden. Jesus called the brothers "Sons of Thunder" because of their boiling tempers. James was the first apostle to die for Jesus.

Pentecost

The Eighth Sunday after Pentecost: Proper 12

July 26, 2020

Pentecost

The hidden power of the Kingdom of God.

Color Green

Preface Of the Lord's Day

Collect

O God, the protector of all who trust in you, without whom nothing is strong, nothing is holy: Increase and multiply upon us your mercy; that, with you as our ruler and guide, we may so pass through things temporal, that we lose not the things eternal; through Jesus Christ our Lord, who lives and reigns with you and the Holy Spirit, one God, forever and ever. *Amen.*

Readings and Psalm

Genesis 29:15–28

In our sequential reading from Genesis, **Jacob meets his match in his future father-in-law, the deceptive Laban.** We encounter the cultural power of custom, here applied to women when it is deemed inappropriate to marry off the younger daughter Rachel before the elder daughter Leah. God makes no overt appearance in these events, though God's promise is at work even in the unlikely interactions of an exploitative father-in-law, two competitive sisters, and the compromised patriarch Jacob.

Psalm 105:1–11, 45b

A hymn of praise celebrating God's forming of a people through the generations.

or

Psalm 128

The one who reveres the Lord will be blessed with many children, a long life, and the prosperity of Jerusalem.

or

1 Kings 3:5–12

In the opening lesson **King Solomon pleases the Lord by requesting an understanding mind with which to govern the people.** God appears to Solomon in a dream shortly after he has come to the throne of his father David. Solomon not only wishes the skill to rule but the wisdom to do it justly, distinguishing between good and evil. God grants him this and much more, and Solomon will become famous both for his wisdom and the splendor of his Kingdom.

Psalm 119:129–136

The psalmist continues to praise God's commandments and asks for guidance and the Lord's justice.

Romans 8:26–39

In this lection **Paul expresses his great confidence that God is for us, making love known to humankind through the sacrifice of the Son and the help of the Spirit.** The Spirit pleads with God for us, interceding when words fail. We learn that God works for good with those called according to God's purpose. Nothing, therefore, can separate us from the love of One who did not withhold from us the divine Son. Neither mortal distress nor supernatural power can separate us from such love.

Matthew 13:31–33, 44–52

Our gospel is **five of Jesus' short parables: the mustard seed, the leaven, the hidden treasure, the priceless pearl, and the net.** They suggest how the action of God's reign is realized. What seems insignificant is suddenly of great importance. It is like a marvelous gift which one seizes upon joyfully and for which all else is willingly sacrificed. The Kingdom takes all kinds, and the sorting out must await the end. Wise servants will recognize treasure both old and new.

Prayers of the People

Let us bring before the Lord the prayers that dwell in the heart of our community, responding, "Hear us, good Lord."

Spirit of Wisdom, guide our tongues, that we may speak of your marvelous works and rejoice in your bountiful gifts of forgiveness and new life; let us pray.

Hear us, good Lord.

Righteous Governor, assist our leaders in discerning truth from deception, and good from evil, so that they may exercise their office with integrity and be signs of hope to the people of our country and world; let us pray.

Hear us, good Lord.

Source of strength, be with us in our weakness, and help those who live in the dark corners of hopelessness, so that your love may reveal a greater light and dispel the fears that visit every heart; let us pray.

Hear us, good Lord.

Bearer of our sins, remove the dust that blinds us to our shortcomings, so that in admitting our wayward thoughts and actions we may turn toward your mercy and receive your forgiveness; let us pray.

Hear us, good Lord.

Creator of the universe, who brings us joy in the diversity of all that the eye can behold, make us ever grateful for the splendor of your making, and ever protective of its fruits; let us pray.

Hear us, good Lord.

Son of Righteousness, bring the dead into the brilliance of your light, and make us thankful for the intercession of your saints; let us pray.

Hear us, good Lord.

Bound together in the love of Christ, let us continue our prayers.
(Special intentions of the congregation, the diocese, and the Anglican Communion may be added here or before the formal intercessions.)

The Celebrant adds a concluding Collect.

Images in the Readings

The parables are full of images that raise many questions. The **mustard seed** actually grows into a straggly annual bush, not the monumental Tree of Life (see for example Ezekiel 31:2–9) that is paradoxically evoked in the opening parable. In Jewish religious symbolism, the preferred sex is the man, the holy minister is a priest, and the holy bread is unleavened; yet in the parable the woman adds **leaven** to three measures of flour. The man sells "all that he has" to gain a **treasure**, and we think of Solomon's dream, for whom the preferred treasure was wisdom that comes only from God. The **net** that catches all kinds of fish is a commonplace symbol for the church. Yet by "the Kingdom of heaven" Matthew does not mean merely "the church."

The first reading is one of the several biblical tales about the **wisdom of Solomon,** a phrase come into our language to signify immense and deep understanding. According to the monarchical myths of the ancient Near East, the king was anointed by God, next in power to God, God's servant, even God's son. Yet the later stories in 2 Kings describe Solomon as having been as prone to foolishness and error as any other king, as having given in to many temptations that separated him from the love of God. For Christians, Christ himself is wisdom.

Ideas for the Day

♦ Mustard seeds are not really the smallest of all seeds, and neither do they make champion trees. Most might be referred to as a bush, but hardly a tree. There are varieties that do grow taller, and woodier, but certainly not a tree for climbing or a packed aviary. The parable leans into the outrageous, garners the attention of the hearers who knew the plants well: Why in the world, what, huh? What is Jesus doing with this one? Jesus is illustrating the reign of God and therefore his mission as a tremendous life-hosting tree that is connected to that ancient Tree of Life in the garden of Eden as well as the one of Proverbs 3 saying, "Wisdom, she is a tree of life to those who embrace her."

Pentecost

◆ Here is a different kind of parable. There was a person who wanted to do everything according to the desires of God. This person needed to paint the bedroom, and there were two colors of paint—red and blue. On the first night, the person asked God, what color should I paint my room? There was no answer. On the second night, the person asked God, what color should I paint my room? Again, no answer. On the third night, with a bit of frustration, the person asked God, what color should I paint my room? And on this night God answered, "I don't care, just do something!" In all the parables we hear today, the character began by just doing something.

◆ The thread in today's readings seems to be about trust. Jacob trusts in God (and Laban) that the promise will be fulfilled for him to marry Rachel, even following more years of work than he had anticipated. In Pauls' letter to the Romans, we recognize that God's love and care supports us in our weakness through the Holy Spirit's intercession. We know and trust that Christ is at God's right hand, acting and speaking on behalf of our desires and needs.

Making Connections

What is prayer? It is a gift, often hidden, that can yield more than we can ask or imagine if we put it to use. Like a mustard seed, yeast, hidden treasure, a fine pearl, or a net, we cannot know what can come of it until we tap into its "purpose." Presiding Bishop Michael Curry's call to follow the Way of Love asks us to pray daily. How might we blossom, grow, and be found if we take up the practice to pray every day? How might our lives be changed when we recognize that Jesus is our prayer partner in our conversation with God?

Engaging All Ages

When and how do you pray? People pray in the light of day working in offices, driving here and there, and sitting in class. Prayer happens in the darkest night when fears creep out of the shadows, worries weigh more, and sorrows seem to fill the heart more than blood. Do you always notice when you are praying? For prayers are not only clasped hands, closed eyes, and wishful thinking on Sunday mornings or at bedtime. Prayers are often sighs too deep for words. God hears your sighs. God knows their meaning. God knows every form of prayer.

Hymns for the Day

The Hymnal 1982
If thou but trust in God to guide thee 635
Not here for high and holy things 9 [SC]
Be thou my vision, O Lord of my heart 488 [GR]
Eternal light, shine in my heart 465, 466 [GR]
God, you have given us power to sound 584 [GR]
Open your ears, O faithful people 536 [GR]
Eternal Spirit of the living Christ 698
God moves in a mysterious way 677
God of grace and God of glory 594, 595
Jesus lives! thy terrors now 194, 195
Like the murmur of the dove's song 513
Spread, O spread, thou mighty word 530
The Christ who died but rose again 447
Seek ye first the kingdom of God 711
The Lord will come and not be slow 462
"Thy kingdom come!" on bended knee 615

Lift Every Voice and Sing II
Children of the heavenly father 213

Wonder, Love, and Praise
Even when young, I prayed for wisdom's grace 906 [GR]

Weekday Commemorations

Monday, July 27
William Reed Huntington, Priest, 1909
Born in 1838 in Massachusetts, Huntington served his church not only as ecumenist and statesman but also as a liturgical scholar. When the church faced schism in the late nineteenth century, Huntington encouraged reconciliation from his position as a member of the House of Deputies (1871 to 1907). His passion for unity resulted in *The Church Idea* (1870); the grounds he laid were accepted by the House of Bishops in Chicago in 1886. The sixth rector of Grace Church, New York City, guided with breadth and generosity. He exemplified boldness in 1871, when he moved to support women's roles in the church by reviving the ancient order of deaconesses, which was met with resistance until 1889.

Tuesday, July 28
Johann Sebastian Bach, Composer, 1750
Born in Eisenach, Germany, in 1685, into a family of musicians, Bach achieved an enviable reputation as a composer and performer by early adulthood. In 1708, he became organist and chamber musician for the Duke of Weimar. In 1723, he was appointed cantor of the St. Thomas School in Leipzig and parish musician at both St. Thomas and St. Nicholas churches, a post he held until he died. Bach's music expressed his deep Lutheran faith. He not only interpreted the Bible in his "Passions," but he also wrote music for eucharists, perhaps the most renowned being "Mass in B Minor."

Wednesday, July 29
Mary, Martha, [and Lazarus] of Bethany
According to the Gospels of Luke and John, Jesus loved these sisters and their brother Lazarus. Luke's account tells the story of the sisters' hospitality, styling Martha as active and Mary as contemplative. Such symbolism has caused tension in interpretation through the ages. John's gospel reveals more about the women's characters as juxtaposed against Lazarus' death. Jesus arrives postmortem. Martha meets him, trusting that Jesus will heal their brother, demonstrating her profound faith in Jesus as Messiah. John also describes Mary's anointing Jesus' feet with perfumed salve then wiping them with her tresses, a gesture of love that roused the disciples' criticism. The sisters symbolize faithful friendship.

Thursday, July 30
William Wilberforce, Social Reformer, 1833
Wilberforce dedicated his life to politics and Christianity. Born wealthy on August 14, 1759, he served in the House of Commons (1780–1825). He converted to evangelicalism in 1784. He was convinced by friends not to abandon his outer work in politics for his inner life in religion; however, he refused to accept high office or a peerage. He dedicated himself to promoting overseas missions and popular education and to reforming public manners and morals. He fought unstintingly to abolish slavery (slave traffic ended in 1807); Wilberforce, an eloquent power for good, died a month before Parliament ended slavery in the British dominions. He is buried in Westminster Abbey.

Friday, July 31
Ignatius of Loyola, Priest and Spiritual Writer, 1556
Ignatius was born into a noble Basque family in 1491. In his autobiography, he tells us, "Up to his twenty-sixth year, he was a man given over to the vanities of the world and took special delight in the exercise of arms with a great and vain desire of winning glory." An act of reckless heroism at the Battle of Pamplona in 1521 led to his being seriously wounded. During his convalescence at Loyola, Ignatius experienced a profound spiritual awakening. Following his recovery and an arduous period of retreat, a call to be Christ's knight in the service of God's Kingdom was deepened and confirmed.

The fact that Ignatius was an unschooled layman made him suspect in the eyes of church authorities and led him, at the age of 37, to study theology at the University of Paris in preparation for the priesthood. While there, Ignatius gave the *Exercises* to several of his fellow students, and in 1534, together with six companions, he took vows to live lives of strict poverty and to serve the needs of the poor. Thus, what later came to be known as the Society of Jesus was born.

Saturday, August 1
Joseph of Arimathaea
Little is known of the life of Joseph of Arimathaea beyond the stories of Jesus' burial in the Gospels. John speaks of Joseph as a secret disciple and couples him with Nicodemus, also part of the Jewish Sanhedrin drawn to Jesus. Later legends describe them as leaders in the early church. One of the loveliest legends, which cannot be dated earlier than the 1200s, tells of Joseph's bringing the Holy Grail with him to the ancient Church of Glastonbury in Britain. More concrete, though, is Joseph's boldly stepping forward—unlike the cowering disciples—to do what Jewish piety demanded: to offer his own tomb to prevent further desecration of Jesus' crucified body.

Pentecost

The Ninth Sunday after Pentecost: Proper 13

August 2, 2020

God continues to show steadfast love and compassion. Jesus' compassion for the people leads him to respond with food for mind and body. The feeding of the five thousand expresses the significance of the Holy Eucharist.

Pentecost

Color Green

Preface Of the Lord's Day

Collect

Let your continual mercy, O Lord, cleanse and defend your Church; and, because it cannot continue in safety without your help, protect and govern it always by your goodness; through Jesus Christ our Lord, who lives and reigns with you and the Holy Spirit, one God, forever and ever. *Amen.*

Readings and Psalm

Genesis 32:22–31

Our Hebrew Bible reading tells how **Jacob, on the night before his confrontation with his brother Esau, wrestles all night with a man he comes to recognize as God.** Many years earlier Jacob had tricked Esau and stolen his blessing and birthright. Now Jacob has grown rich in the service of his father-in-law Laban, but he greatly fears his meeting with his brother. Jacob's struggle with God may in part express his guilty conscience and coming to terms with the evil he had done. He has to fight for a blessing and permission to return to his homeland. For his new life he is given a new name, Israel, but is left with an injury as a sign of God's supremacy and a reminder of his wrong.

Psalm 17:1–7, 15

A plea for justice and protection by one who has followed God's ways.

or

Isaiah 55:1–5

In this reading we hear how **the return from exile will be a time of prosperity and abundance when God's covenant will be renewed.** The prophet pictures the great day: for a people who have been near death there will be food and drink without cost. God's covenant with David is to be extended to all Israel, and other nations will come to see her glory.

Psalm 145:8–9, 14–21

A hymn of praise to the Lord, who is mighty in deeds yet tender and compassionate.

Romans 9:1–5

In this reading **Paul expresses his anguish and sorrow that so many of the children of Israel, the people especially favored by God, have not found the Lord's promise.** To them belong the covenants, the law, and so much else. From their nation Christ himself came. Paul would go to great lengths, even see himself an outcast, if such would help Israel to know its salvation. Later in this letter Paul tries to explain how this all may be part of God's plan of redemption, which in the end will include Israel with the Gentiles.

Matthew 14:13–21

Our gospel is **the story of Jesus' feeding of over five thousand persons.** After the death of John the Baptist, Jesus seeks a time of retreat. The crowds, however, follow him, and he has compassion on them. The narrative suggests many levels of meaning. It recalls Old Testament stories, especially God's feeding of the Israelites with manna in the wilderness, and points forward to the legendary banquet at the end of time where Christ the King will preside. The abundant miracle illustrates Jesus' lordship; he is intimate with the powers of creation. Other themes associated with the Eucharist are close at hand.

Prayers of the People

Let us journey to the waters of God's refreshing kindness, offering our prayers and responding, "Hear us, good Lord."

That we may be prepared for the struggles of life, knowing that through suffering we receive grace, and that in the midst of trials Jesus is forming us in love; let us pray.

Hear us, good Lord.

That we may be satisfied beholding the likeness of others, seeing in them the face of Christ, especially through those who are poor and hardworking, homeless and destitute, imprisoned and alone, orphaned and afraid, grieving and lost; let us pray.

Hear us, good Lord.

That we may take responsibility for sharing our ideas and lending our support to those who lead the Church, government, and public institutions, that we may share in the building of the social and spiritual fabric of our society; let us pray.

Hear us, good Lord.

That we may trust the transforming power of Jesus to take even our meager offerings and create the resources that reveal the promises of the kingdom; let us pray.

Hear us, good Lord.

That we may honor the writers of the gospels and epistles, whose unique contributions form our sacred texts, and those in our own day who bring the light of God through books, articles, websites and blogs; let us pray.

Hear us, good Lord.

That light perpetual may shine upon the faithful departed as they come into their true home in the unending joy of the saints; let us pray.

Hear us, good Lord.

In the fellowship of the One who is full of graciousness and compassion, let us continue our prayers.
(Special intentions of the congregation, the diocese, and the Anglican Communion may be added here or before the formal intercessions.)

The Celebrant adds a concluding Collect.

Images in the Readings

The most common biblical image for divine mercy is **food.** In Genesis 1, the plants and trees that God created are given to humans as food. Ancient narratives told of God providing food during famine. The Israelites' memories of their nomadic years recalled a miraculous food, manna, which God sent to keep them alive in the wilderness. Religious rules commanded the faithful to share their food with the hungry and to abstain from eating with the wicked. Disobedience was met with the punishment of deprivation of food. The people of Israel themselves were likened to food that God has planted. Food or no food was central to all the primary religious festivals of the Old Testament. Poems described the law of God as if it is nourishing food. Christ was born in Bethlehem, which means "house of bread." In John's metaphoric theology, Christ says, "I am the bread of life." We need food to live, and Christians have each week served out the word and the sacrament as the food that Christ continues to distribute to those of us who are hungry.

Pentecost

The oracle from Isaiah includes **wine** as one of the foodstuffs that God gives away freely. Wine was not only the safest drink in the ancient world, but it signifies communal celebration, as if the alcohol symbolizes the Spirit that alters the human body into unity with others around the table. However the church has often been stingy with its wine: only the smallest sip is granted, or none at all, and since 1869, when Thomas Welch invented grape juice, wine has sometimes been replaced with a tamer drink. Each congregation may want to think through how the image of wine is conveyed in its communion practice.

Ideas for the Day

♦ God's steadfast love, *hesed* in Hebrew, is one of the most consistent qualities of God in the Hebrew Bible. What does this steadfast love look, feel, and taste like in life? After a long hard day, Jesus' disciples are done. They want to find a rock to lay their head on, so please, close the shop and send the hordes away! Jesus' response is entirely what *hesed* looks, tastes, and feels like. Feeding thousands freely is a revolutionary life-giving act of steadfast love. Jesus breaks the stranglehold of the idols of scarcity and invites us to experience the God of abundance.

♦ The story of Jacob and his wrestling match with God is like a sandwich with two different types of bread. Just before this story is a story of reconciliation between Jacob and Laban, where the harm had been to Jacob. Right after this story is a story of profound reconciliation between Jacob and his brother Esau, where Jacob had originally done the harm. The center of the sandwich is a story of God's promise to be present. In our liturgy, we ask God for forgiveness in the Confession, and then offer forgiveness in the exchange of the Peace. It seems right and a good thing to do to follow these actions by gathering together to receive the bread of life.

♦ Christ has compassion for the people of the Church and the world that hunger for God's Word. When we offer the risen Christ our time, talent, and commitment, he can bring about the Kingdom.

Making Connections

There are Eucharistic overtones to this day's gospel story. Jesus "took bread, blessed the bread, broke it, and distributed it among the people." Notice that Jesus "feeds" the people first with teaching and then with bread. At the Eucharist we first hear the Word and then receive the bread and wine: word and sacrament lie at the heart of Christian life.

Engaging All Ages

Ever have a toy you really loved? So much that you did not want anyone else to play with it? Were you afraid someone else would steal it or break it? Maybe you wanted unfettered access. But you kept it to yourself or cried, "Mine, mine, mine!" One interpretation of today's gospel says the real miracle is not so much that Jesus waved magic hands to produce enough bread for everyone but that everyone chose to share so that each could have some. It does not sound practical, but it is creative. What creative way can you share with others?

Hymns for the Day

The Hymnal 1982
Come, O thou Traveler unknown 638, 639 [SC]
God, my King, thy might confessing 414 [GR]
Surely it is God who saves me 678, 679 [GR]
We will extol you, ever-blessed Lord 404 [GR]
Lord, for ever at thy side 670
O God of Bethel, by whose hand 709
Open your ears, O faithful people 536
Bread of the world, in mercy broken 301
Hope of the world, thou Christ of great compassion 472
I come with joy to meet my Lord 304
My God, thy table now is spread 321
O Food to pilgrims given 308, 309
We the Lord's people, heart and voice uniting 51

Lift Every Voice and Sing II
Break thou the bread of life 146

Wonder, Love, and Praise
With awe approach the mysteries 759 [SC]
The eyes of all wait upon you, O Lord 820 [GR]
All who hunger gather gladly 761
O wheat, whose crushing was for bread 760

Weekday Commemorations

Monday, August 3
Joanna, Mary, and Salome, Myrrh-bearing Women
These three bear the tradition of the women who came to anoint Jesus' body with myrrh after his crucifixion only to find his tomb empty after resurrection. The faithful disciples were known for their unwavering devotion to the Christ in his earthly ministry. Joanna was healed by him, after which she served him loyally. Salome may have been related to Mary, Jesus' mother. Mary Magdalene is often conflated with Mary, the mother of James, and Mary the wife of Cleopas. The Holy Myrrh-bearers are celebrated in the Orthodox Church on the second Sunday after Easter.

Thursday, August 6
The Transfiguration of Our Lord Jesus Christ
God authenticated Jesus as God's Son in a series of supernatural manifestations. The Transfiguration is one in that series and, therefore, not to be taken only as a spiritual experience for Jesus, witnessed by Peter, James, and John. The Transfiguration fits with angels' appearing at Jesus' birth and resurrection and with the Spirit's descent at Jesus' baptism. In the Transfiguration, according to the Gospel of Matthew, the veil is drawn aside, and, again, a few witness Jesus as the earth-born son of Mary and as the eternal Son of God. In Luke's account, a cloud, a sign of divine presence, envelops the disciples, and a heavenly voice proclaims Jesus to be the Son of God.

Friday, August 7
John Mason Neale, Priest and Hymnographer, 1866
Neale, born in London in 1818, is best known as a hymnodist, for a glance to the bottom of many pages of *The Hymnal 1940* and *1982* finds his name as composer or translator. As scholar and poet, Neale composed hymns and transposed Latin and Greek hymns into English spoken syntax in such turns of phrase as "Good Christian men, rejoice" and "Come, ye faithful, raise the strain." He was also a priest of the Oxford Movement, which revived Medieval liturgical forms, and a humanitarian; as such, he founded the Sisterhood of St. Margaret to relieve the suffering of women and girls. A gentle man of good humor and modesty, he lived "unbounded charity."

Saturday, August 8
Dominic, Priest and Friar, 1221
Dominic, who was born in Spain around 1170, founded the Order of Preachers known as the Dominicans. In England, they were the Blackfriars, a reference to the black mantles worn over their white habits. Legend has Dominic, in searching for a life of apostolic poverty, selling all his possessions to help people hungry from the 1191 famine. He was ordained in 1196. In 1203, he began preaching tours in France, and in 1214, he manifested his idea for a preaching order, granted by Honorius III about 1216. The Dominicans' Constitutions, formulated in 1216, set a priority of intellectual rigor: "In the cells, they can write, read, pray . . . and stay awake at night . . . on account of study."

Pentecost

The Tenth Sunday after Pentecost: Proper 14

August 9, 2020

God's infinite mercy far surpasses our understanding. God's power is revealed as Jesus controls the waters.

Color   Green

Preface   Of the Lord's Day

Collect

Grant to us, Lord, we pray, the spirit to think and do always those things that are right, that we, who cannot exist without you, may by you be enabled to live according to your will; through Jesus Christ our Lord, who lives and reigns with you and the Holy Spirit, one God, forever and ever. *Amen.*

Readings and Psalm

Genesis 37:1–4, 12–28

In our Hebrew Bible story, **Israel, once called Jacob, has settled in the land of Canaan. He sends his youngest and favorite son Joseph to assist his older brothers shepherding the flock** in Dothan. Joseph's older brothers despise him out of jealousy and at first conspire to murder him, though in the end they sell Joseph to Midianite traders who carry him off in slavery to Egypt. Joseph will one day see God's providential hand in these actions, and ways in which evil may be turned to good.

Psalm 105:1–6, 16–22, 45b

A hymn of praise celebrating God's forming of a people through the generations.

or

1 Kings 19:9–18

The reading from the Hebrew Bible tells how **God is made known to Elijah—not in wind, earthquake, or fire—but in a still small voice.** In a mood of depression the prophet retreats to Mount Horeb. But the Lord gives him a new mission and a promise that there will be a remnant in Israel who will not worship the false god Baal. Although God is known in a word of revelation rather than in the awesome events of nature, these happenings can also be seen as harbingers of God's presence.

Psalm 85:8–13

The psalmist both celebrates and prays for the Lord's gracious favor, forgiveness, deliverance, and justice.

Romans 10:5–15

In this lesson **Paul teaches that the word of faith is a gift; by it we make our saving confession that Jesus is Lord and that God raised him from the dead.** Without God's grace the way of righteousness would be impossibly distant. But the faith that leads to righteousness is in our hearts and the confession of salvation is on our lips. This is true for all people, no matter what their background, and so it is essential that the Good News be carried far and wide, that all may call upon the name of the Lord.

Matthew 14:22–33

The gospel is the story of **Jesus' walking on the water and his rescue of Peter after his faith fails him.** The narrative has several levels of meaning. In legendary terms Jesus is like the Creator God who strides over the watery chaos monster. Matthew's gospel stresses this revelation of Jesus' close relationship with God, as God's Son, and the importance of faith on the part of the disciples. A church beset by its own problems and lack of faith would be glad to perceive in this story the saving presence of its risen Lord.

Pentecost

Prayers of the People

We glory in God's Name through the offering of our prayers and petitions, responding, "Hear us, good Lord."

For the will to discover God's Word dwelling in our hearts, finding expression through our lips, and revealing hope through our generosity; let us pray.

Hear us, good Lord.

For a renewed commitment to righteousness and peace, that we may join with the leaders of the nations in seeking ways to promote harmony in warring lands, and mutual respect across cultures, races, and languages; let us pray.

Hear us, good Lord.

For creative ways to express the faith, drawing upon the jewels of our tradition, and using our hearts and minds to proclaim Christ's message to those of little faith or who have no faith at all; let us pray.

Hear us, good Lord.

That the summer months may provide opportunities for rest and refreshment, so that we may be rejuvenated for the challenges ahead; let us pray.

Hear us, good Lord.

For medical personnel who volunteer their services in foreign lands and amongst the most needy of the world, that we may lift our voices in praise for the good news they bring to others; let us pray.

Hear us, good Lord.

For those who have died and reside in the tomb of death, that Christ, who broke the chains of death, will bring them to eternal life; let us pray.

Hear us, good Lord.

Ever increasing in faith, we continue our prayers.
(Special intentions of the congregation, the diocese, and the Anglican Communion may be added here or before the formal intercessions.)

The Celebrant adds a concluding Collect.

Images in the Readings

The disciples are nearly drowned by the storm of **wind and waves**. Many poetic passages in the Bible speak of wind and waves as though they are harbingers of death and of a sea monster as embodying chaos. Watch once again the film *Titanic*. In the tale of Jonah, God both sends the storm and calms it. The theophany in Job 38 credits God with having control over the sea, and the authors of Genesis 1, in praising God's creative power, report that God created the sea monsters.

Mount Horeb, where Elijah meets God, is Mount Sinai. According to Exodus, God had appeared in earthquake, wind and fire, but Elijah encounters only **silence**. This story comforts many of the faithful, for whom there seems to be more sheer silence than powerful wind from the Spirit.

Much Christian iconography has drawn the church as the **boat** from which Jesus, the I Am who is God, brings calm to the waters experienced by the faithful. We assemble weekly in the nave—think "navy"—to receive the peace of Christ.

Ideas for the Day

♦ Jealousy and greed are powerful motivators as any two-year-old already knows. In the novel *Sense and Sensibility* by Jane Austen, it is the manipulation of a brother by covetousness and bitterness that sets the downfall of the Dashwood women in motion. Like Joseph, they didn't do anything to garner the ire of their own relations, but the father's extraordinary love for the younger half-siblings was too much to take. Is there a way to restore such terribly fractured family relationships? As people called to act for a healed world, this is a moment to examine where we need to be reconciled and open to new possibilities. We encounter crisis after crisis, and yet, over and over God provides support as we gain perspective and new partners in pursuing the common good.

Pentecost

◆ Do you know that you can sing the words of "Amazing Grace" to the tune of "Gilligan's Island"? Try it up to the line "was blind, but now I see." It might have been a good song for the disciples to be singing; they might not have been so afraid. There are two phrases we might think about today that are often said in the Gospels. The first one is "come" and the second is "do not be afraid." We all know how scary life can be. Sometimes the event is beyond our imagination. But the promise of Jesus is always there, even in the midst of a great storm. Can we listen and hear the invitation to come? Can we listen and hear the comfort of a declaration to not be afraid?

◆ A small boy offers a few loaves and fish to be shared with the crowd. The idea of making an offering of our possessions in faith is conveyed in this story. Often we fail to respond to Christ because we feel that what we have to offer cannot make any difference. "I know world hunger is a problem," we say, "but the problem is so big, what difference is my little sacrifice going to make?" In the hands of Jesus, the small and insignificant offering of the boy became enough to feed the crowd. When we offer the risen Christ our time, talent, and commitment, he can *make* it capable to bring about the Kingdom.

Making Connections

Today is a good time to focus on the Eucharist. As we offer our possessions in faith, we are fed the manna (bread). Even when we turn from God in doubt and fear, God loves us and brings us back as we are fed with the "bread of life," which becomes for us the sign of Christ's presence.

Engaging All Ages

What was the last bit of trivia that you learned and found so fascinating you shared it in as many conversations as possible? Is there a hobby you really enjoy and often share with others by talking to them about it, showing it to them, or teaching them to do it? God's love can be even more fascinating and exciting. Paul's letter to the Romans asks, "And how are they to hear without someone to proclaim him?" So today, how could you tell in word and show in action God's love to someone? And is that fascinating or exciting to you?

Hymns for the Day

The Hymnal 1982

From deepest woe I cry to thee 151 [SC]
Out of the depths I call 666 [SC]
Dear Lord and Father of mankind 652, 653 [GR]
Praise the Spirit in creation 506, 507 [GR]
The Lord will come and not be slow 462 [GR]
At the Name of Jesus 435
In Christ there is no East or West 529
Commit thou all that grieves thee 669
Eternal Father, strong to save 608
Give praise and glory unto God 375
How firm a foundation, ye saints of the Lord 636, 637
I sought the Lord, and afterward I knew 689
Jesus, Lover of my soul 699
Lead us, heavenly Father, lead us 559
O all ye works of God, now come 428
O God, our help in ages past 680
O worship the King, all glorious above 388

Lift Every Voice and Sing II

In Christ there is no East or West 62
Love lifted me 198
Jesus, Lover of my soul 79
Take my hand, precious Lord 106
Stand by me 200

Wonder, Love, and Praise

O all ye works of God, now come 884
Precious Lord, take my hand 800

Weekday Commemorations

Monday, August 10
Laurence, Deacon, and Martyr at Rome, 258
The Emperor Valerian started persecuting upper-class clergy and laity in 257. Properties of the Church were confiscated; Christian worship was forbidden. On August 4, 258, Pope Sixtus II and his seven deacons were apprehended in catacombs and executed, except for the archdeacon, Laurence, who was martyred on August 10, roasted alive on a gridiron. Legend has Laurence presenting the sick and poor to the prefect, who demanded to see the Church's treasures. The Emperor Constantine erected a shrine and basilica over Laurence's tomb. For Laurence, to die for Christ was to live with Christ; a small, round, glass medallion, probably from the fourth century, now in New York's Metropolitan Museum, reads, "Live with Christ and Laurence."

Tuesday, August 11
Clare of Assisi, Monastic, 1253

The daughter of a wealthy family, and a noted beauty, Clare was inspired by Francis' words with the desire to serve God and to give her life to the following of Christ's teachings. She sought out Francis, and begged that she might become a member of his order, placing her jewelry and rich outer garments on the altar as an offering. Francis could not refuse her pleas and placed her in a nearby Benedictine convent. Despite her family's attempts to remove her, she was adamant and other women joined her. She became Mother Superior of the order, which was called the "Poor Ladies of St. Damien," governing and caring for the sisters for forty years.

Wednesday, August 12
Florence Nightingale, Nurse, 1910

Nightingale, born in 1820, was named Florence for the city of her conception. She remained unmarried in order to attack with single-mindedness her calling to the service of the Lord. She manifested that calling from a vision, first, through nursing, considered unseemly for a woman of her class. She showed her mettle as superintendent of a London sanitorium, which was desperate for her organizing skills. Conditions in the military hospitals of the Crimea, where war raged, were just as deplorable; by 1856, Nightingale had set things straight there. Although best known for her role in health care reform, equally important to Nightingale was her commitment to a form of religion that was both personal and mystical.

Thursday, August 13
Jeremy Taylor, Bishop and Theologian, 1667

Taylor, born August 15, 1613, in Cambridge, England, wrote his most influential works, *Holy Living* and *Holy Dying*, in 1651, during days of forced retirement. He had served as chaplain to Charles I, but Oliver Cromwell's minions imprisoned Taylor and reduced him to retirement as a chaplain to a Welsh lord. Another work, *Liberty of Prophesying*, encouraged religious tolerance and appealed for freedom of thought. His work does not appear in the prayer book revision of 1662, but the first American prayer book included one of Taylor's prayers, and another appears in the current Book of Common Prayer. Later, he moved to Ireland, where he ended his days as vice-chancellor of Trinity College.

Friday, August 14
Jonathan Myrick Daniels, Martyr, 1965

Jonathan Myrick Daniels was born in Keene, New Hampshire, in 1939. Like many young adults, from high school in Keene to graduate school at Harvard, Jonathan wrestled with vocation until his discernment was clarified by a profound conversion on Easter Day 1962 and subsequently entered seminary. In March of 1965, the televised appeal of Martin Luther King, Jr. to come to Selma to secure for all citizens the right to vote touched Jonathan's passions for the well-being of others, the Christian witness of the church, and political justice. Going to Selma he found himself in the midst of a time and place where the nation's racism and the Episcopal Church's share in that inheritance were exposed. After seminary he returned to Alabama to resume his efforts assisting those engaged in the integration struggle. Jailed on August 14th for joining a picket line, Jonathan and his companions resolved to remain together until bail could be posted for all of them, as it was six days later. Released and aware that they were in danger, four of them walked to a small store. As sixteen-year-old Ruby Sales reached the top step of the entrance, a man with a shotgun appeared, cursing her. Jonathan pulled her to one side to shield her from the unexpected threats and was killed instantly by the 12-gauge blast.

Saturday, August 15
Saint Mary the Virgin, Mother
of Our Lord Jesus Christ

Mary has been honored as the mother of Jesus Christ since the beginnings of the Church. Two gospels tell the story of Christ's birth to a virgin; Luke's gospel glimpses Christ's childhood in Nazareth under the care of his Mother and earthly father, Joseph. During Jesus' ministry in Galilee, Mary often traveled with the women who followed Jesus, ministering to him; at Calvary, she stood with the women who kept watch at the cross. After the Resurrection, she accompanied the twelve in the upper room. She was the person closest to Jesus, having humbly accepted God's divine will. Later devotions lay many claims for Mary that cannot be proved by Holy Scripture.

Pentecost

The Eleventh Sunday after Pentecost: Proper 15

August 16, 2020

Faith brings salvation to Jews and Gentiles alike.

Pentecost

Color   Green

Preface   Of the Lord's Day

Collect

Almighty God, you have given your only Son to be for us a sacrifice for sin, and also an example of godly life: Give us grace to receive thankfully the fruits of his redeeming work, and to follow daily in the blessed steps of his most holy life; through Jesus Christ your Son our Lord, who lives and reigns with you and the Holy Spirit, one God, now and forever. *Amen.*

Readings and Psalm

Genesis 45:1–15

Our Hebrew scripture lesson relates **a decisive moment in the story of Joseph as he reveals himself to his brothers, who then journey home to tell their father Jacob that his son is still alive.** The brothers are at first overwhelmed by the discovery that the brother they had sold into slavery is now Pharaoh's right-hand man. Joseph tells them not to be upset: this had all been part of God's plan to preserve Israel during the coming time of famine.

Psalm 133

The psalm celebrates the blessing of a harmonious people.

or

Isaiah 56:1, 6–8

In our opening lesson **the Lord exhorts the people to do what is just because the time of righteous salvation is close at hand. The temple will be a house of prayer for all nations.** This vision of hope emphasizes the outgoing aspects of Israel's faith. Historically it deals with the fact that after the exile certain non-Israelites had come to live in Jerusalem and serve in the temple. The passage sets the conditions for their participation, but also looks beyond to a day when many peoples will worship the God of Israel.

Psalm 67

A prayer for God's graciousness and saving power, and a bidding of praise by all people for God's justice and bounty.

Romans 11:1–2a, 29–32

In this reading **Paul sets forth his belief that God plans to bring Jews as well as Gentiles to salvation.** This apostle to the Gentiles continues to wrestle with a difficult question: why is it that so many of Jesus' own people have not accepted him as the Christ? God has not rejected the Jewish people who were foreknown, yet now Jews and Gentiles are equal in that all have been disobedient to God. In the next step the Jewish people will see the mercy shown to the Gentiles and want themselves to share in it in their own way.

Matthew 15:(10–20) 21–28

In our gospel **Jesus teaches that the thoughts and intentions of the human heart are paramount.** Jesus warns against such blind guides preoccupied with externals. He then travels beyond the boundaries of Israel to the territory of Tyre and Sidon and encounters a Canaanite woman who beseeches him to heal her daughter. The first Christians were unsure whether they were to offer the faith to non-Jews, and the give-and-take in this story may reflect that uncertainty. Jesus sees his own mission as confined to Israel, but the woman's faith causes him to give her the bread she asks for. Symbolically it is the saving food of the gospel which heals her daughter.

Prayers of the People

The gift of forgiveness surpasses our understanding; it heals relationships, and mends our wounds. In thanksgiving for God's unfailing love, we offer our prayer, responding, "Lord, hear our prayer."

That the leaders of the nations may maintain justice that leads to peace, and harmony that leads to abundant life for all people; let us pray.

Lord, hear our prayer.

For the humility to receive God's blessings and the willingness to be a blessing to others, especially those who are lost and afraid, ill and without hope for recovery, mentally fragile and without friends; let us pray.

Lord, hear our prayer.

For teachers preparing for the school year that is ahead, that they may be inspired to patiently nurture the minds of those in their charge; let us pray.

Lord, hear our prayer.

That we may be a people of gratitude, giving thanks to God with our whole heart, and soul, and mind; let us pray.

Lord, hear our prayer.

That we may not succumb to the harmful temptations of our culture, the desire to possess things beyond our need, our misuse of intimacy, our reliance on drugs and alcohol to improve our lives, and all things that keep us from trusting the power of the Spirit; let us pray.

Lord, hear our prayer.

That we may set our sight on the new life that awaits all who live in hope; let us pray.

Lord, hear our prayer.

That the dead who have died in the faith of Christ may inherit the kingdom prepared for them, and that those whose faith was known to God alone may receive divine mercy; let us pray.

Lord, hear our prayer.

In the company of all the saints, let us continue our prayers. *(Special intentions of the congregation, the diocese, and the Anglican Communion may be added here or before the formal intercessions.)*

The Celebrant adds a concluding Collect.

Images in the Readings

That Jesus obliquely refers to the Canaanite woman as a **dog** has inspired much creative interpretation over the centuries. Traditionally the sentence was explained away as the technique Jesus employed to test the woman's faith. Some contemporary exegesis reads the exchange seriously and thus credits the woman with instructing Jesus about the breadth of God's mercy. Both of these explanations assume that the story is accurate historical reporting. The story also suggests that if our faith is strong enough, our wishes will be granted. Like the Jesus of Matthew's narrative, we too think of the other as a dog. Like the storyteller, we hope that our faith will bring us instant healing. It is a difficult story to proclaim and expound.

Despite our knowledge of anatomy, the **heart** continues over the millennia to be an image for the source and center of human intention.

Ancient temples were understood to be **houses of the deity**. Architecturally similar to the Lincoln Memorial, an open structure housed a statue of the god or goddess, and sacrifices were offered before the image of the divine. After the exile, strict traditionalists urged hierarchical regulations about how close to the presence of God each type of person could come. But Third Isaiah rejects this understanding of worship, saying the house of God will welcome all peoples. Christians have thought about their churches as in some way houses of God for all peoples. Yet for Christians, God dwells in the community and in word and sacrament, not in a house, and church buildings are less like temples and more like meeting places for the communal prayer of all peoples.

Ideas for the Day

♦ Not everyone receives the chance to be reconciled as Joseph and his brothers are. The lectionary skips how Joseph rises from jail cell to right-hand advisor of the ruler. We know very little of what life was like for his father and brothers and their wives and households. We can only guess that the winds of change were not prosperous. Perhaps you imagine regrets rising up in the brothers, or could they have been haunted but silent about the whole incident? The way of steadfast love is one of seeking the sometimes long slow path to forgiveness and reconciliation. In the life of your community are there stories of fracture and then healing that become a way of good news?

Pentecost

- We are going to have to deal with the reality that even Jesus had to grow in his practice to love, just like each of us have to do the same. Can you think of a time when you really set someone apart, and then for whatever reason were able to see the person (or community) as completely human (created in the image of God)? It was an honest conversation between Jesus and the Canaanite woman that allowed Jesus to expand his notion of love. It was her willingness to speak in powerlessness and his willingness to listen while in power. When this happens, we then find healing surrounding us all.

- Paul speaks as a missionary to the Gentiles, still seeking to save some of his own fellow Jews. If rejection of Jesus Christ meant the reconciliation of the world, their acceptance of him would be like life from the dead. How do we evangelize to those we are alike and in community with as well as those who may be different than us?

Making Connections

The Reconciliation of a Penitent (BCP, 447) is available to all who desire it, but many in our congregations are unaware of the possibility of such a private rite. However, the ministry of reconciliation, which has been committed by Christ to his Church, is exercised through the care each Christian has for others, through the common prayer of Christians assembled for public worship, as well as through the priesthood of the Church and its ministers declaring absolution.

Engaging All Ages

In today's gospel, Jesus talks about defecation—what enters our mouth enters our stomach and then goes out into the sewer. Taro Gomi told people the same thing in the 1970s with *Everyone Poops* (Kane/Miller Book Ltd), a children's book that is still popular (for some) today. Some critics did not like hearing that truth from either Jesus or Taro. Both remind people that what is natural and inherent to being human should not feel shameful. But Jesus says what is wrong is when you allow the nasty and mean parts of being human to have a home in your heart. If you let them grow up and release them into the world, that is when you are truly defiled, defiler, and defiling.

Hymns for the Day

The Hymnal 1982

God moves in a mysterious way 677 [SC]
From all that dwell below the skies 380 [GR]
God of mercy, God of grace 538 [GR]
How wondrous and great thy works,
    God of praise! 532, 533 [GR]
My God, thy table now is spread 321 [GR]
Only-begotten, Word of God eternal 360, 361 [GR]
We the Lord's people, heart and voice uniting 51 [GR]
In your mercy, Lord, you called me 706
Praise, my soul, the King of heaven 410
Sing praise to God who reigns above 408
There's a wideness in God's mercy 469, 470
O Spirit of the living God 531
O Zion, haste, thy mission high fulfilling 539
Thou, whose almighty word 371

Lift Every Voice and Sing II
Pass me not, O gentle Savior 139

Weekday Commemorations

Tuesday, August 18
William Porcher DuBose, Priest, 1918

DuBose spent most of his life as a professor at the University of the South, in Sewanee, Tennessee. He became well known at the age of 56 when he published the first of several books on theology. Fluent in Greek and other languages, doctrine and life were always in close relationship with DuBose, treating them as if they were always in dramatic dialogue, fusing the best contemporary thought and criticism with his own strong inner faith.

Thursday, August 20
Bernard of Clairvaux, Monastic and Theologian, 1153

In 1113, Bernard (born 1090 in Dijon, France) entered the Benedictine Abbey of Citeaux. His family was not best pleased with his monastic choice, but he persuaded four of his brothers and 26 friends to join him in establishing a monastery at Clairvaux in 1115. Bernard fiercely defended the church and preached love for God "without measure." He was absorbed and dedicated to God even to the dismissal of his own health. He refused sleep in order to write. His sermons persuaded the founding of 60 Cistercian abbeys affiliated with Clairvaux. By 1140, his writing made him a profound influence within Christendom. He supported mystery over reason and was canonized in 1174.

The Twelfth Sunday after Pentecost: Proper 16

August 23, 2020

The foundation of faith.

Color Green

Preface Of the Lord's Day

Collect

Grant, O merciful God, that your Church, being gathered together in unity by your Holy Spirit, may show forth your power among all peoples, to the glory of your Name; through Jesus Christ our Lord, who lives and reigns with you and the Holy Spirit, one God, forever and ever. *Amen.*

Readings and Psalm

Exodus 1:8–2:10

A new king arises in Egypt who oppresses the growing population of Israelites and orders all Hebrew boys to be killed at birth. But the infant Moses is set afloat on the Nile in a desperate attempt to preserve his life. Ironically, it is Pharaoh's own daughter who finds and keeps the child, undermining not only her unjust father, but an oppressive future regime.

Psalm 124

A psalm of thanksgiving for deliverance.

or

Isaiah 51:1–6

In our opening lesson **the Lord exhorts the people to do what is just because the time of righteous salvation is close at hand. The temple will be a house of prayer for all nations.** This vision of hope emphasizes the outgoing aspects of Israel's faith. Historically it deals with the fact that after the exile certain non-Israelites had come to live in Jerusalem and serve in the temple. The passage sets the conditions for their participation, but also looks beyond to a day when many peoples will worship the God of Israel.

Psalm 138

A hymn of praise and thanksgiving to the Lord on high, who has saved God's servant and cares for the lowly.

Romans 12:1–8

In this lesson **Paul urges the Christians in Rome to devote themselves to God's service and to recognize that with different functions they are all members of one body.** Instead of dead animals, they are to offer themselves as living sacrifices. Their way of life is to be quite different from worldly standards. So will they know the will of God. All are to live in humility, realizing that they have their various gifts through God's grace.

Matthew 16:13–20

In our gospel **Peter realizes that Jesus is the Christ, and Jesus then sees Peter as the rock foundation for his church and gives to him the keys of the Kingdom.** The passage helps us to recognize that during Jesus' lifetime and afterward there was speculation about his role. Some saw the Son of Man as a kind of reembodiment of John the Baptist or another prophet. Simon is renamed Peter (which means rock), for on him and because of this revelation the church will be built, although Jesus' messiahship must be kept secret for the present. To Peter are given the keys to open or shut the gates of the Kingdom and so to make judgment.

Prayers of the People

Let us lift our voices in prayer, joining with the faithful throughout the world who offer their intercessions this day, responding, "Lord, hear our prayer."

Give your grace to those who care for children in foster homes, sustain them with patience, and encourage them to provide a family of love and respect; let us pray.

Lord, hear our prayer.

Open our eyes to behold your hand in the work of creation, that we may marvel at your intricate craftsmanship and tend the beauty that we behold; let us pray.

Lord, hear our prayer.

Pour your knowledge into the minds of those who are returning to school in the next few weeks, and for those attending for the first time, still their hearts by your loving presence; let us pray.

Lord, hear our prayer.

Grant us the grace to honor the many gifts that you have given, not coveting what our neighbor has received, but grateful for what you have entrusted to our care; let us pray.

Lord, hear our prayer.

Reveal yourself to every nation and people, that we may know you to be the Christ, the Messiah, the one who saves our souls from the pit of darkness, and who comes carrying the lamp of charity that leads us to the divine life; let us pray.

Lord, hear our prayer.

Give life to those in the tomb, opening the gates of heaven to all who desire eternal life; let us pray.

Lord, hear our prayer.

Let us continue our prayers to God, who cares for the lowly and guards us in the midst of trouble.
(Special intentions of the congregation, the diocese, and the Anglican Communion may be added here or before the formal intercessions.)

The Celebrant adds a concluding Collect.

Images in the Readings

Rock is an image for the day. The psalms speak of the safety accorded by the rock; the prophet likens his religious heritage to a rock; Simon gets the name Peter, "Rocky." The Sermon on the Mount speaks of Jesus' teaching as a rock on which we are to build, and Paul writes in 1 Corinthians 4 that the rock from which water flowed was Christ. According to Jewish legend, the miraculous rock followed the Israelites throughout their nomadic decades, perpetually providing water. For Christians, the water of baptism follows the body of Christ, watering us throughout our journey.

According to the worldview of the New Testament, **Hades,** the lowest of the three levels of the universe, housed the dead. Matthew uses the category Hades to indicate the challenge that confronts the Christian community: to fight against the power of death. Eastern Orthodox Christians especially recall this worldview in their beloved icon of the resurrection, in which Christ is standing on the broken doors of Hades and is raising from death into his arms both Adam and Eve.

The Isaiah reading includes the image of the **arm of the** LORD. In the Old Testament, God is described in terms humans know: God has ears, eyes, a mouth, fingers, hands, and strong arms. In the story of Noah's flood, God even smells the pleasant odor of the animal sacrifices. Our task is to ensure that these bodily images do not demote the divine into merely a superman. Christians can apply these very images to **the body** of Christ.

Ideas for the Day

♦ This psalm has a walking rhythm that isn't entirely lost in translation. Could it perhaps be shared by a group of pilgrims, making their way to a festival? Or is there another setting that it calls to mind—a hike or a campout? The imagery certainly suggests Passover and the Exodus: enemies rising, water that could have overwhelmed but did not. It is a shared lyric of reorientation, of having had the experience of being under the thumb of real enemies and knowing real relief. Is there a song that sings to you that we are never left alone by God in pain and fear and panic?

- Do any of us think that Peter responded, "Yay, I get to be the judge for all eternity and decide who is in or out?" Do any of us think that if we were offered control of the keys to the Kingdom of heaven that this would be a good thing? There is a powerful moment in the book *The Shack* by William P. Young (Windblown Media, 2007) where God offers the father, Mack, the ability to be the judge. God says something like, "It makes sense that you should be the judge; you have been practicing pretty much all of your life." Mack was scared to death. The God option, if we are to judge turns out to be love—only love—always love.

- Peter is a symbol of leadership for the Church. What are Peter's qualities that give him this distinction? We are called to build our faith on a solid foundation so we can follow in Christ's footsteps, as well as all those who have come before us in recognizing the true nature of Jesus. Who has also shown the traits that we can model ourselves after (in our world today or in the past)?

Making Connections

The gospel text establishes a sense of authority for the role of the bishop in the church. As Jesus had authority to act for God in the world, so the church has authority to "bind and loose," and its bishops are seen as symbols of that apostolic authority (and succession) in the church today. In the Roman Catholic tradition, the gospel text is cited as the authority for the primacy of the Bishop of Rome (the pope), seated on the "throne" (or see) of St. Peter at the Vatican.

Engaging All Ages

Find some Play-Doh or modeling clay and tools like cookie cutters. What shapes can you make? What are their names? A circle. A heart. Tree. Dinosaur. Imagine something you cannot make with one of your tools. Try making it. Does it look like what you thought it would? Do you prefer the shapes made with tools or those made with your hands? God made you and everyone. And God does not make cookie-cutter people. You are the only you. You have talents and gifts that only you can share with others. Can you name any of your talents and gifts?

Hymns for the Day

The Hymnal 1982

I come with joy to meet my Lord 304
Our Father, by whose Name 587
Praise the Lord, rise up rejoicing 334
Put forth, O God, thy Spirit's might 521
Thou, who at thy first Eucharist didst pray 315
The God of Abraham praise 401 [GR]
To God with gladness sing 399 [GR]
God is Love, and where true love is 576, 577
Holy Spirit, font of light 228
Like the murmur of the dove's song 513
Lord, you give the great commission 528
O Holy Spirit, by whose breath 501, 502
Take my life, and let it be 707
Where charity and love prevail 581
From God Christ's deity came forth 443
Glorious things of thee are spoken 522, 523
The Church's one foundation 525
You are the Christ, O Lord 254

Lift Every Voice and Sing II

Wonder, Love, and Praise

Come now, O Prince of Peace 795
Unidos/Together 796
The desert shall rejoice 722 [GR]
Gracious Spirit, give your servants 782
Lord, you give the great commission 780
Muchos resplandores / Many are the lightbeams 794
Ubi caritas et amor 831

Pentecost

Pentecost

Weekday Commemorations

Monday, August 24
Saint Bartholomew the Apostle

One of the twelve Apostles, he is known to us only by being listed among them in the synoptic Gospels. His name means "Son of Tolmai," and he is often identified with Nathanael, the friend of Philip. Some sources credit Bartholomew with having written a Gospel, whose existence was known to Jerome and Bede, but which is lost today. There is a tradition that he traveled to India, bringing "the Gospel according to Matthew" in Hebrew there.

Tuesday, August 25
Louis, King, 1270

Louis the Ninth of France was canonized by the Church in 1297. A man of unusual purity of life and manners, he was sincerely committed to his faith and to its moral demands. Courageous and fearless in battle, patient and uncomplaining in adversity, he was an impartial, just, and compassionate sovereign. He died while on crusade in Tunis. Because of his determined effort to live a personal life of Franciscan poverty and self-denial in the midst of worldly power and splendor, Louis is honored as a patron saint of the Third Order of St. Francis.

Thursday, August 27
Thomas Gallaudet and Henry Winter Syle, Priests, 1902 and 1890

Gallaudet is called "The Apostle to the Deaf," and Syle was his student. Gallaudet was born June 3, 1822; Syle, November 9, 1846. Gallaudet's mother's speech and hearing were impaired; his father founded a school for the deaf. When Gallaudet wanted to become an Episcopal priest, his father convinced him to teach in a New York school for the deaf instead. Gallaudet was ordained a priest in 1851; he founded St. Ann's Church for Deaf-Mutes, thereby influencing the establishment of deaf missions in many cities. Syle, hearing impaired from scarlet fever, was determined to be educated. Mentored by Gallaudet although opposed by others, Syle was ordained in 1876—the first deaf person to receive Holy Orders.

Friday, August 28
Augustine of Hippo, Bishop and Theologian, 430

Called "the greatest theologian in the history of Western Christianity," Augustine, born in 354 in North Africa, became a Christian in 386 under the guidance of his mother Monnica. He was baptized by Ambrose, Bishop of Milan, in 387. He returned to North Africa in 391, whereupon he was chosen by the people of Hippo to be a presbyter; four years later, he became bishop of Hippo. About 400, he wrote his spiritual autobiography, *The Confessions*; the extended prayer became a classic. Augustine wrote reams of treatises, letters, and sermons, thereby providing a rich source of insights into Christian truth. In 410, he wrote his greatest work, *The City of God*.

Saturday, August 29
The Beheading of Saint John the Baptist

John baptized Jesus. John's preaching foretold Jesus' ministry and his death. All four Gospels describe John the Baptist as the prophet and preacher who created the advent of expectation and who awakened the repentance that leads to baptism. Herod demanded John's beheading out of fear of a leader among the people. Two Sundays in Advent focus on John's preaching; the First Sunday of Epiphany celebrates Jesus' baptism as fulfilling Christ's humanity and revealing his divinity. John's ministry had been integral to the start of Jesus': John's death marked a turning point toward Jerusalem and Jesus' death on a cross.

The cost of discipleship.

Color   Green

Preface   Of the Lord's Day

Collect

Lord of all power and might, the author and giver of all good things: Graft in our hearts the love of your Name; increase in us true religion; nourish us with all goodness; and bring forth in us the fruit of good works; through Jesus Christ our Lord, who lives and reigns with you and the Holy Spirit, one God forever and ever. *Amen.*

Readings and Psalm

Exodus 3:1–15

In our lesson from the Hebrew scripture **Moses is encountered by the Lord in the burning bush. He is called to his mission to lead the people of Israel out of slavery in Egypt, and he asks to know the name of this God of his ancestors.** God's answer to Moses is intriguing and mysterious. The response may indicate a proper name which traditionally has been known as Yahweh. God's answer may, however, suggest a meaning like "The One who causes to be," or "I am who I am," or "I will be what I will be."

Psalm 105:1–6, 23–26, 45c

A hymn of praise celebrating God's forming of a people through the generations.

or

Jeremiah 15:15–21

In this first reading **Jeremiah complains to the Lord about the pain and difficulties of his mission. He then receives God's answer.** The prophet has been called to preach a message of dark judgment to a people who are soon to be sent into exile. Despite persecution, the Lord's words were at first a joy to Jeremiah, but God has become like a treacherous brook—a stream that dried up when its waters were needed. Then the Lord tells Jeremiah that it is he who needs to turn again to God. The Lord will be with him, and he will be a wall of bronze against the people.

Psalm 26:1–8

A plea for justice by one who serves the Lord well.

Romans 12:9–21

In this lesson **Paul exhorts the disciples in Rome to live lives full of Christian dedication and virtue, overcoming evil with good.** One hears strong echoes of Jesus' beatitudes. Also present is Paul's own emphasis on the central role of love together with the importance of a readiness to share in both the joy and sorrow of others. Blended with these teachings are some of the best of both Jewish and pagan ethical counsel. The apostle concludes with the insistence that revenge cannot be a motivation of Christians; final justice must be left to divine retribution.

Matthew 16:21–28

In the gospel reading **Jesus teaches Peter and the other disciples that the way of his ministry and theirs is the way of the cross.** Peter had just confessed Jesus to be the Christ, but now he cannot accept the idea of the Christ being put to death. Jesus calls Peter "Satan" because his words represent a temptation to him. Jesus' way costs no less than everything and leads to the discovery of that which is priceless. In the end the Son of Man will come as judge to repay all people for what they have done.

Pentecost

Prayers of the People

God is the great "I AM" in whose Name we pray, responding, "Lord, hear our prayer."

That we may open our ears to the cries of those who suffer, freeing them from enslavement to poverty, abuse, and lack of opportunity, taking our share in the saving acts of God; let us pray.

Lord, hear our prayer.

That the leaders of the nations may lead their people with integrity, honoring all that is past and moving into the challenges that define a new life; let us pray.

Lord, hear our prayer.

For the courage to lift up our crosses to the light of day, carrying them on our journey of faith, uniting ourselves with the Christ of the passion, so as to share in the glory of his resurrection; let us pray.

Lord, hear our prayer.

That we be given the strength to leave behind the fruits of temptation, turning our gaze upon that which is nourishing and sound, living a life of love, honor, and respect for others, full of rejoicing and thanksgiving; let us pray.

Lord, hear our prayer.

For all laborers, that they may receive a fare wage, a safe working environment, the companionship of fellow workers, and the respect of those who exercise authority over them; let us pray.

Lord, hear our prayer.

For those who have died surrounded by family and friends, and for those who were unloved and unmourned, that all may have a place in God's kingdom; let us pray.

Lord, hear our prayer.

May the Name of God be grafted on our hearts as we continue our prayers.
(Special intentions of the congregation, the diocese, and the Anglican Communion may be added here or before the formal intercessions.)

The Celebrant adds a concluding Collect.

Images in the Readings

That believers are to deny themselves, take up their **cross,** and follow Jesus has been a commonplace message throughout Christian centuries. Care must be taken that more privileged persons do not mouth these words to the less privileged, to those with minimal power to affect their own situation, as if what Jesus meant was to suffer in silence. All the baptized have been marked by the cross, and in the mystery of the resurrection, this cross is the way to life. Perhaps the cross we are called to carry is someone else's, which we willingly help to carry. One possibility is that Matthew was referring to the Tau, the sign of the end time for those who await the return of Christ.

Jesus calls Peter **Satan,** the one who opposes God. Ancient Israel knew no supernatural power of evil. In the Book of Job, the Satan is in God's throne room, goading God and accusing the righteous. By the time of Jesus, largely through influence of their Zoroastrian neighbors, Jews had come to believe in a supernatural being who personified evil and who, like the medieval devil, tempted persons to immoral behavior. Yet Christian theology has always resisted the popular dualist idea that there is a good god and a bad god and that human life is the battlefield between God and the devil. According to the New Testament, evil, although still present, has already been conquered in Christ's resurrection. Satan is behind us. Watch the remarkable film *The Apostle,* in which during the final sermon the Holiness preacher calls out to the devil, "Get behind me! Get behind me!"

The **burning coals** is an image for the shame that evildoers will experience when they encounter Christian forgiveness and generosity. In Romans 12:20, Paul is quoting Proverbs 25:21–22, an example of the degree to which Christian ethics repeats the teachings of the Hebrew Scriptures.

Ideas for the Day

◆ Two crucial skills of servant leadership are being able to listen, and the willingness to trust. To listen with true attentiveness is listening to what is observant and patient and does not jump to conclusions, especially regarding what people are capable of—even ourselves. Moses is invited into so much more than he knew—a deep listening to God's intention and presence. He has to let go and trust God to be with him; he has what is needed in this moment. This is the kind of servant leadership that God sends to interrupt suffering and desperation.

◆ If we read the scripture carefully, we discover that the name of God is I AM and not I AM WHO I AM. When we struggle with trying to figure out who God is and what God is up to, it might be best to simply return to God's name, I AM. At some point, we might actually believe the name. At some point, we might even trust the name; we might even base our faith on the name. God simply IS. On one hand, it is the simplest reality to grasp, and on the other hand, it is the deepest, most mysterious, most profound truth we will ever experience.

◆ People are truly formed as Christians when they are part of a congregation that lives out Paul's words, "Rejoice with those who rejoice, weep with those who weep." How do you invite individuals in the congregation to fully take on this role of hospitality, listening, and walking alongside others in all times and circumstances?

Making Connections

We return this week to the concept of discipleship that was explored earlier this season. We must renounce our own ways and goals in life and accept the will of God. If we attempt to hold on to our lives, we will lose them. As we allow ourselves to be caught up in God's great eternal act of salvation, we will find life at the very moment we think we are losing it. The prayer appointed for Fridays in the liturgy for Morning Prayer expresses this concept: "Almighty God, whose most dear Son went not up to joy but first he suffered pain, and entered not into glory before he was crucified: Mercifully grant that we, walking in the way of the cross, may find it none other than the way of life and peace; through Jesus Christ your Son our Lord" (BCP, 56). What does this say to us who are called to be apostles today?

Engaging All Ages

Do you have enemies? Someone who frustrates and angers you? Your boss who never seems to appreciate your work? A family member who always says something to push your buttons? A bully who makes jokes at your expense? A derisive political figure, a greedy CEO, or an outlandish celebrity? Today, Jesus is talking to you about those people. Jesus claims they can only frustrate and anger you if you allow them. Today, will you choose to be powerful and to be at peace? In what ways can you show kindness to your enemies? And will you?

Hymns for the Day

The Hymnal 1982
Lord, dismiss us with thy blessing 344
We plow the fields, and scatter 291
What wondrous love is this 439 [SC]
The God of Abraham praise 401 [SC]
We sing of God, the mighty source 386, 387 [SC]
When Israel was in Egypt's land 648 [SC]
If thou but trust in God to guide thee 635 [GR]
Surely it is God who saves me 678, 679 [GR]
God is Love, and where true love is 576, 577
Holy Spirit, font of light 228
Like the murmur of the dove's song 513
Lord, whose love through humble service 610
O Holy Spirit, by whose breath 501, 502
Take my life, and let it be 707
Where charity and love prevail 581
Where true charity and love dwell 606
Day by day 654
New every morning is the love 10
Praise the Lord through every nation 484, 485
Take up your cross, the Savior said 675

Lift Every Voice and Sing II
Go down, Moses 228 [SC]
Where He leads me 144
I have decided to follow Jesus 136

Wonder, Love, and Praise
When from bondage we are summoned 753, 754 [SC]
Cuando el pobre nada tiene / When a poor one
     who has nothing 802
Gracious Spirit, give your servants 782
Put peace into each other's hands 790
The church of Christ in every age 779
Ubi caritas et amor 831
Will you come and follow me 757
You laid aside your rightful reputation 734

Pentecost

Pentecost

Weekday Commemorations

Monday, August 31
Aidan, Bishop, 651

After the see-sawing of Christianity and paganism in Northumbria in north England, Oswald regained the throne and restored the Christian mission begun in 627 when his uncle, Edwin, was converted by a mission from Canterbury. During his exile, Oswald had lived at the monastery of Iona, where he had been converted and baptized, so he sent to Iona for missionaries. Gentle Aidan, head of the new mission, set his work on the distant island of Lindisfarne. He and his monks and their trainees restored Christianity in Northumbria, extending the mission through midlands and as far south as London. According to the Venerable Bede, Aidan delighted in giving to the poor whatever kings gave to him.

Tuesday, September 1
David Pendleton Oakerhater, Deacon, 1931

Known as "God's warrior" among the Cheyenne Indians of Oklahoma, Oakerhater was originally a solider who fought against the U.S. government with warriors of other tribes in the disputes over Indian land rights. Upon his capture in 1875, he learned English, gave art and archery lessons to other prisoners in Florida, and had his first encounter with the Christian faith. This led to his call to transform his leadership in war into a lifelong ministry of peace. Baptized in 1878, he was ordained to the diaconate in 1881 and returned to Oklahoma where he was instrumental in founding schools and missions through great personal sacrifice.

Wednesday, September 2
The Martyrs of New Guinea, 1942

Christians began evangelizing on New Guinea in the 1860s and 1870s, to little effect; Anglicans, specifically, began their mission there in 1891. Their first bishop was consecrated in 1898. This mission field still offers challenges because of the difficult terrain on the second largest island in the world and because the indigenes speak some 500 distinct languages. During World War II, missionaries and native peoples were sorely tried. This feast day marks the witness of eight missionaries and two Papuan martyrs, betrayed by non-Christians to the Japanese invaders. The day remembers the faith and devotion of Papuan Christians, who risked their own lives to save the lives of others.

Thursday, September 3
Phoebe, Deacon

According to Paul's letter to the Romans (16:1), Phoebe was a deacon in the church at Cenchreae (near Corinth) and a benefactor to Paul and others. Paul commends her to the Roman church at the end of the epistle, which suggests she was the messenger. That would speak highly of Paul's trust in Phoebe. Perhaps there was more, considering that Paul commands the Christians in Rome to help her however she needs. She exemplifies the many early helpers—women and men—who supported Paul in spreading the gospel, even to personally carrying the message across the Empire.

Friday, September 4
Paul Jones, Bishop, 1941

As Bishop of Utah, Paul Jones (1880–1941), did much to expand the Church's mission stations and to strengthen diocesan institutions. At the same time he spoke openly about his opposition to war. At a meeting of the Fellowship of Reconciliation in 1917, Bishop Jones expressed his belief that "war is unchristian," for which he was attacked with banner headlines in the Utah press. Yielding to pressure, Bishop Jones resigned in spring 1918. In his farewell to the Missionary District of Utah, he said, "Where I serve the Church is of small importance, so long as I can make my life count in the cause of Christ . . . but no expedience can ever justify the degradation of the ideals of the episcopate which these conclusions seem to involve."

Saturday, September 5
Katharina Zell, Church Reformer and Writer, 1562

Zell, a Strasbourg Protestant (b. 1497), chose the holiness of marriage in 1523 over celibacy. Martin Zell was a priest when religion frowned on clergy for marrying. However, his outspoken bride defended the wedding of clergy in a pamphlet explaining to her fellow laity the Biblical basis for marriage and for women to speak out—both acts of love, she claimed. The Zells welcomed 80 Christians driven from their homes for their beliefs; her refugees included John Calvin when he fled France. She also visited those sick with the plague and syphilis. Persistent, her last publication commented on the Psalms.

The Fourteenth Sunday after Pentecost: Proper 18

September 6, 2020

The church is vested with Jesus' authority. Guidelines for discipline and other aspects of church life.

Color   Green

Preface   Of the Lord's Day

Collect

Grant us, O Lord, to trust in you with all our hearts; for, as you always resist the proud who confide in their own strength, so you never forsake those who make their boast of your mercy; through Jesus Christ our Lord, who lives and reigns with you and the Holy Spirit, one God, now and forever. *Amen.*

Readings and Psalm

Exodus 12:1–14

In our Hebrew Bible lesson **instructions are given, and the meaning of the Passover meal is told: it is a remembrance and reenactment of Israel's beginnings as a people when they were saved out of slavery in Egypt.** The details indicate that several different traditions stand behind the Passover memorial. Perhaps it was the Israelites' attempts to keep ancient spring rites, derived from their shepherding and agricultural backgrounds, which caused the Egyptians to persecute them. With these traditions the story of God's judgment on Egypt and victory for the people has become richly entwined.

Psalm 149

A joyful song in which the faithful praise the Lord and anticipate the victory of justice.

or

Ezekiel 33:7–11

In our first lesson **the prophet Ezekiel is like a watchman: it is his responsibility to warn the wicked, but it is the individual's responsibility to stop sinning.** Some people say it is too late to repent—that the burden of past sins is too great to overcome. Ezekiel is to tell them that it is the living God who calls them to cease sinning and find life. These oracles were delivered as Israel's exile was beginning and were meant to instill both a sense of accountability and the hope necessary for repentance.

Psalm 119:33–40

The psalmist asks for the Lord's guidance and promises to keep God's commandments always.

Romans 13:8–14

In this reading **Paul summarizes the heart of the law and urges a way of life in full awareness of the nearness of salvation.** All the commandments and all human responsibility for others are fulfilled by "loving your neighbor as yourself." Disciples must recognize that the nighttime of sinfulness is passing. The daylight, the time for new conduct and the following of Jesus, now comes.

Matthew 18:15–20

Our gospel presents **teaching about how to deal with sin and grievances within the Christian community.** The early churches did not have established codes and regulations and had to fashion their own ways of dealing with such matters. Here every effort is made to bring the sinful member to repentance. Failing this, the individual is to be treated as outside the church. Such decisions are understood to be ratified in heaven and by Christ's presence even in the smallest of Christian gatherings.

Pentecost

Prayers of the People

As the Church, the Body of Christ in this time and place, let us offer our prayers, responding, "Lord, hear our prayer."

That we may love the Lord with our whole heart, and soul, and mind, and our neighbor as our selves, claiming the great commandment as our pathway and destination; let us pray.

Lord, hear our prayer.

That our love may be revealed through our actions, as we commit ourselves to visiting those who are in prison, or confined to their homes, or living in nursing facilities, that in seeing their face we will see the face of Jesus; let us pray.

Lord, hear our prayer.

That peace may flourish wherever there is strife or enmity between peoples, bringing opportunities for improved nutrition, health, and education, revealing God's mantle of light; let us pray.

Lord, hear our prayer.

For the power of the Holy Spirit in guiding us in our discovery of our vocation, our manner of expressing God's indwelling love, so that we may be passionate about our work and ministry; let us pray.

Lord, hear our prayer.

For the grace to turn away from anything that places a barrier between God's love and our actions, so that in turning back to Jesus we may receive mercy for the past and strength for the future; let us pray.

Lord, hear our prayer.

For blessings upon those who have died, that their souls and the souls of all the faithful departed, through the mercy of God may rest in peace; let us pray.

Lord, hear our prayer.

In thanksgiving for the blessings we have received, we continue our prayers.
(Special intentions of the congregation, the diocese, and the Anglican Communion may be added here or before the formal intercessions.)

The Celebrant adds a concluding Collect.

Images in the Readings

We are **bound**, we are **loosed**: these are strong images describing the powers that hold us captive and the gift of God's Spirit that frees us for a life of love. The responsibility for correction, discipline, and forgiveness belongs to the community.

Tax collectors were despised collaborators who were infamous for cheating. Mercifully, Jesus is described as eating with tax collectors. This is good news for all of us.

Ezekiel calls us to be **sentinels**, those assigned to watch from the city walls for both any approaching dangers and any welcome visitors. The life of the Christian is an active life, watching in the world for the bad and the good and reporting to the community what we see.

Paul calls us to wake up; the **day** has come; get dressed, wearing Christ, for today there might be a battle.

In his mixing of metaphors, Paul blends the robe of baptism with the **armor** of a warrior. It's a dangerous world out there, everywhere affected by human sin.

Ideas for the Day

♦ Wicked is the most common English translation of the Heberw *rasha*. However, the likely origin of the word wicked in English is connected to people, usually women, who were accused of witchcraft. While it has come to mean something closer to what the Hebrew word meant—corrupt, profane, wrongful—today we are subject to all sorts of reframing of such judgments. Does the prophetic witness urge us to have more candor about the wickedness: corruption, profanity, and victimization that is laying waste to God's creation and our neighbors?

♦ The Jewish ritual of Passover begins with a loaf of bread that is blessed and shared. The ritual concludes with the final cup of wine that is blessed and also shared by each person. In between the first action and the final action is what the Jewish people know to be the complete story of salvation. On Sundays, when we celebrate the Eucharist, might it be a good practice to be aware of the space found in between the paragraphs during the Words and Institution, and consider *that* space holds the entire story of salvation for us as well? Jesus certainly did.

- We have a responsibility to confront the evil that we see in ourselves, in one another, and in our society. On the other side of confrontation is forgiveness. We do not confront to destroy a person. We confront to lead a person into a deeper relationship with God and with neighbor.

Making Connections

Deliverance from slavery and sin are themes shared between the Old Testament stories and the gospel. Our salvation story is retold each year at the Great Vigil of Easter (BCP, 285–292). Since many in the congregation may not experience or attend the Vigil service, is there a way to help connect this whole sweeping narrative of God's steadfastness and love with today's lectionary readings?

Engaging All Ages

Jesus provides protocols for handling troublesome church members. Interestingly, it is also good instruction on how to be an ally and an advocate for church members. For instance, the care of each child and youth in your church is important. Being the most loving, trusting, and forgiving of God's creations, young people can find themselves used and abused by others. Are there ways you can act as an ally and advocate to prevent such things? What protocols does your church implement to care for young people? In what ways can you talk about this with adults, youth, and children?

Hymns for the Day

The Hymnal 1982
At the Lamb's high feast we sing 174 [SC]
The Lamb's high banquet called to share 202 [SC]
From deepest woe I cry to thee 151 [GR]
Lord Jesus, think on me, and purge away
    my sin 641 [GR]
'Tis the gift to be simple 554 [GR]
Awake, my soul, and with the sun 11
Awake, my soul, stretch every nerve 546
Awake, thou Spirit of the watchmen 540
Eternal Ruler of the ceaseless round 617
For the fruit of all creation 424
Jesu, Jesu, fill us with your love 602
All creatures of our God and King 400
Blessed Jesus, at thy word 440
Christ is made the sure foundation 518
Father, we thank thee who hast planted 302, 303
"Forgive our sins as we forgive" 674
God is love, and where true love is 576, 577
Joyful, joyful, we adore thee 376
Lord, make us servants of your peace 593
Singing songs of expectation 527
Where charity and love prevail 581
Where true charity and love dwell 606

Lift Every Voice and Sing II
Come, ye disconsolate 147 [GR]
Jesu, Jesu 74

Wonder, Love, and Praise
Lord Jesus, think on me, and purge away
    my sin 798 [GR]
Come now, O Prince of Peace 795
Unidos / Together 796
We all are one in mission 778

Pentecost

Pentecost

Weekday Commemorations

Monday, September 7
Kassiani, Poet and Hymnographer, 865

The only woman whose writing appears in official liturgies of the Orthodox Church, Kassiani was born wealthy before 810 and well educated. She entered the monastic life as a nun and exploited her distinct talents for music and literature. She courageously defended veneration of icons and also founded a new convent. Unafraid to enter theological controversies, she declared: "I hate silence when it is time to speak." By 843, she'd built a convent on Xerólophos, the 7th hill of Constantinople, and become its first abbess. Hundreds of her poems are extant; about 50 of her hymns, still sung.

Tuesday, September 8
The Nativity of the Blessed Virgin Mary

Little is known of Jesus' mother—not her home or family. She may have descended from David's line and been brought up in a Jewish family that cherished the hope of Israel for the coming kingdom of God in remembering the promise to Abraham and the forebearers. In the second century, a devout Christian cobbled an account of Mary's birth in an apocryphal gospel, *The Nativity of Mary*. It included legends about Mary's parents, Joachim and Anne, a childless couple rewarded with the birth of a girl. The story goes that they dedicated her life to the service of God.

Wednesday, September 9
Constance, Thecla, Ruth, Frances, Charles Parsons, and Louis Schuyler, Martyrs, 1878

The Sisters of the Community of St. Mary came to Memphis in 1875 in the middle of a yellow fever epidemic; instead of opening a girls' school as planned, the women cared for the sick. When the plague hit again in 1878, many professionals fled. But a few doctors stayed alongside Episcopal and Roman Catholic clerics and nuns, among other religious. Sisters Ruth and Helen came from the Order's Motherhouse. Within three weeks, Sr. Constance died (9/9), followed by Sisters Thecla, Frances, and Ruth, doctors and clerics, and a devoted laywoman, in addition to 12 Roman Catholic clerics and 34 nuns. Many witnesses to the great Physician—winners for their orders of an "imperishable renown"—share burial plots. They have ever since been known as "The Martyrs of Memphis."

Thursday, September 10
Alexander Crummell, Priest, 1898

After receiving a degree from Cambridge, Alexander Crummell went to Liberia as a missionary. The Episcopal Church, with its emphasis on rational and mural discipline, was especially fitted for the moral and spiritual regeneration of Afro-Americans. Euaropean education and technology, combined with traditional African communal culture and undergirded by a national Episcopal Church headed by a black bishop, was the vision espoused by Crummell. Crummell's faith in God, his perseverance, his perceptions that the Church transcended the racism and limited vision of its rulers and his unfailing belief are the legacy of this African American pioneer.

Saturday, September 12
John Henry Hobart, Bishop, 1830

Buried beneath the chancel of Trinity Church in New York City, lies John Henry Hobart, a staunch, devoted, missionary-minded American Churchman of the Episcopal Church. Hobart, born September 14, 1775, graduated from Princeton in 1793, and was ordained a priest in 1801, having become an assistant minister at Trinity the year before. He was consecrated assistant bishop of New York in 1811; five years later, he became diocesan bishop and rector of Trinity. Within his first five years as bishop, Hobart doubled the number of clergy and quadrupled the number of missionaries. He planted a church in almost every major town of New York State and served as missionary among the Oneida Indians. He was a founder of General Theological Seminary.

The Fifteenth Sunday after Pentecost: Proper 19

September 13, 2020

Living in community under God's dominion over evil and sin.

Color Green

Preface Of the Lord's Day

Collect

O God, because without you we are not able to please you, mercifully grant that your Holy Spirit may in all things direct and rule our hearts; through Jesus Christ our Lord, who lives and reigns with you and the Holy Spirit, one God, now and forever. *Amen.*

Readings and Psalm

Proverbs 1:20–33

Our opening lesson is **an instructional poem in which Wisdom is personified as an attribute of God's character and a virtue to be sought and possessed.** Lady Wisdom actively seeks out those as yet unformed in character and strives to gain their attention, for she offers to lead them into the way of life and goodness. Those who scoff or refuse her instruction court calamity, but those who listen will dwell secure.

Psalm 19

A hymn which glorifies the Creator God, with special praise for God's law and a prayer for avoidance of sin.

or

Wisdom of Solomon 7:26–8:1

Wisdom is extolled as an attribute of God of unsurpassed value.

or

Isaiah 50:4–9a

Our first reading tells of **the servant who speaks for the Lord and suffers persecution, but still trusts in God's help and vindication.** This is the third of the "servant songs" which come from a period late in Israel's exile. The servant might be thought to be the faithful of Israel, the prophet himself, or another historical or idealized figure. The people are weary and tired of the Lord's calling, but the servant steadfastly continues. Christians have long perceived in these words a foretelling of Jesus' mission.

Psalm 116:1–9

An offering of thanksgiving and praise by one who has been rescued from death.

James 3:1–12

In this New Testament lesson the community is reminded that one who instructs others will be held to a high standard, and such a position should only be aspired to by those well-formed in faith. **Of particular concern are habits of speech.** The tongue is compared to a small rudder able to control a large ship at sea. There is great danger in an uncontrolled tongue, and many forms of careless speech are enumerated. The Christian must learn self-discipline in order that God may be glorified.

Mark 8:27–38

In the gospel **Peter recognizes that Jesus is the Christ, and Jesus then describes the true nature of the ministry of the Son of Man and what it means to follow in his way.** The passage reminds us that during Jesus' lifetime and afterward there was speculation about his role. Some saw him as a kind of reembodiment of John the Baptist or another prophet. Peter is called "Satan" because his words are a temptation to turn away from the suffering and death which come before resurrection. Disciples must also learn that the true self and true life are found by those who will let themselves be lost for the sake of Jesus and the gospel.

Prayers of the People

Rejoice in the waters of life, those who honor God in all things, and raise your voices in prayer, responding, "Lord, hear our prayer."

In thanksgiving for this holy day where we gather as a household of faith to hear the word of God with open minds and grateful hearts; let us pray.

Lord, hear our prayer.

In thanksgiving for the arms of forgiveness that embrace us in the midst of our sin, leading us to repentance, and filling us with the waters of mercy through which we will forgive others; let us pray.

Lord, hear our prayer.

For honesty in government, and integrity in our dealings with one another, that trust may be restored between people and throughout the institutions of our society; let us pray.

Lord, hear our prayer.

That we may commit ourselves to a life of simplicity, so that we may provide for the needs of the poor and hungry, as Jesus provided nourishment and hope to his followers; let us pray.

Lord, hear our prayer.

That we may share our spiritual doubts with one another, convinced that in our mutual self-disclosure we will be strengthened in faith and grow in the conviction that God's love can forgive all things and transforms all life; let us pray.

Lord, hear our prayer.

In thanksgiving for those who are teachers and catechists in our Church; may they be given the blessing of knowledge and wisdom, as they bear the Christian message to those in their charge; let us pray.

Lord, hear our prayer.

That the dead may be redeemed from the grave, and wear the crown of eternal life; let us pray.

Lord, hear our prayer.

Miriam sang to the Lord for all the glorious gifts her people had received, and so we join with her in continuing our prayers.
(Special intentions of the congregation, the diocese, and the Anglican Communion may be added here or before the formal intercessions.)

The Celebrant adds a concluding Collect.

Images in the Readings

Seventy-seven plays with the ancient idea that seven is the number of fullness and perfection, because seven combines three, a number that suggests divinity, and four, recalling the corners of the flat earth. So with seventy-seven, Jesus multiplies the number of total perfection.

Matthew's allegory utilizes imagery from the economic system of the first century: a **lord** was the owner of land and of all those who work the land, and a **slave** was one perpetually in the service of another. In our English-language Bibles, Hebrew and the Greek words that denote such a masculine societal authority figure are translated as "lord." Christian faith in Christ's resurrection occasions the claim that "Jesus is Lord." "Lord" is the usual circumlocution used in our Bibles to render YHWH, God's first name. That we are slaves of God is New Testament imagery, albeit not a currently popular metaphor.

By the mysterious design of God, **Joseph** brought life to his people. Early Christian preachers saw in the Joseph story a parallel to Jesus, who was first brought low but was then raised to power and authority so as to forgive everyone and to feed the world.

Ideas for the Day

+ The Exodus narrative is a central image of salvation history in the Old Testament. It is used to underscore the witness of real rescue from terrible forces of evil, and it is also a metaphor for liberty from more obscure oppressions. Yet perhaps the words bring you pause, because you or someone near to you has served in the military. Hearing that warriors are being extinguished can be alarming. It is possible to feel both united to the liberation and sympathy for the soldiers who are thrown down. Learning how to be creative and compelling witnesses to the love of God when our feelings are complex is part of the lifelong journey of life together.

◆ We all seem to like winning. We all seem to enjoy the party that often follows. Sometimes there is music, dancing, and cheers. So here is a challenge to us all: We know that God was with the people of Israel on the other side of the Red Sea. But if we believe that God is everywhere, then wouldn't it be true that God might also have been consoling the hearts of the widows, mothers, and daughters of Egypt? Can we imagine that God's love might ever extend beyond the winners? Can we imagine that God's mercy can override the political breaks in our world and in our society? It might be interesting for us to take a look and see what God is doing on the "other" side.

◆ The passing of the Peace is an acting out of a forgiveness principle. God's forgiveness must be passed on to others if it is to be realized in our own lives. So when you are offering your gift at the altar, if you remember that your brother or sister has something against you, leave your gift there before the altar and go; first be reconciled to your brother or sister, and then come and offer your gift (Matthew 5:23–24).

Making Connections

Confession and absolution: we are forgiven over and over. Our liturgy acknowledges that we continually need to seek forgiveness. Each time we come before God and one another with genuine contrition, we receive the healing forgiveness of God made known through the act of the Eucharist. The confession and absolution do not stand on their own, however. They must be preceded or followed by an act of reconciliation to persons hurt by our acts and omissions. It is a model for Christian life—we too, need to forgive each other (our neighbor) week after week as genuine "confession is offered. In the Lord's Prayer were ask to be forgiven only to the extent that we forgive others.

Engaging All Ages

"How often should I forgive?" Peter questions. Jesus says "Seventy-seven times." Seventy-seven does not seem like an excessively large number. But in the culture of the United States, forgiveness can seem for some hard to do and for others in short supply. When you have been hurt again and again, it is difficult to forgive again. Difficult to forgive others. Difficult to forgive yourself. Perhaps it is seventy-seven times because forgiveness takes practice. Today in worship, will you do the practice of Confession? This practice will not make you perfect but it can make you more forgiven and more forgiving.

Hymns for the Day

The Hymnal 1982

Guide me, O thou great Jehovah 690 [SC]
Praise our great and gracious Lord 393 [SC]
Sing now with joy unto the Lord 425 [SC]
When Israel was in Egypt's land 648 [SC]
All my hope on God is founded 665 [GR]
God moves in a mysterious way 677 [GR]
O bless the Lord, my soul 411 [GR]
Praise, my soul, the King of Heaven 410 [GR]
Praise to the Lord, the Almighty, the King of
    creation 390 [GR]
Creator of the stars of night 60
Crown him with many crowns 494
Jesus, our mighty Lord, our strength in sadness 478
All creatures of our God and King 400
"Forgive our sins as we forgive" 674
Go forth for God, go to the world in peace 347
God is Love, and where true love is 576, 577
Joyful, joyful, we adore thee 376
Lord, make us servants of your peace 593
Most High, omnipotent, good Lord 406, 407
Praise the Lord, rise up rejoicing 334
Where charity and love prevail 581
Where true charity and love dwell 606

Lift Every Voice and Sing II

Go down, Moses 228 [SC]

Wonder, Love, and Praise

Wisdom freed a holy people 905 [SC]
Bless the Lord my soul 825 [GR]
No saint on earth lives life to self alone 776
Come now, O Prince of Peace 795

Pentecost

Pentecost

Weekday Commemorations

Monday, September 14
Holy Cross Day

Supervision over the work of erecting a building complex in Jerusalem to mark the site of Christ's resurrection was entrusted to the empress Helena, mother of Emperor Constantine. Under Helena's direction, the excavation discovered a relic, believed to be of the "true cross." Calvary stood outside the city in Jesus' time; when *Aelia Capitolina* succeeded Jerusalem, the hill was buried under construction fill. Constantine's magnificent shrine included two main buildings: a basilica and a round church known as "The Resurrection." The buildings were dedicated on September 14, 335, the seventh month of the Roman calendar; the date was suggested by the account in 2 Corinthians of the dedication of Solomon's temple hundreds of years before.

Tuesday, September 15
Catherine of Genoa, Mystic and Nurse, 1510

Catherine (b. 1447) married at 16 to ward off family feuds. Husband and wife were miserable: he was profligate with sex and money, which depressed her. On March 22, 1473, Catherine had a mystical, life-changing experience of God's overwhelming love. Afterwards, she combined an intense, contemplative life with an active dedication to caring for the sick. Amazingly, her husband joined her in this good work, and the two became close, eventually moving into a large hospital in Genoa to devote themselves as caregivers. There, Catherine dictated works of mystical theology, which were published 40 years after her death.

Wednesday, September 16
Ninian, Bishop, c. 430

The Venerable Bede wrote about Ninian in *Ecclesiastical History*; otherwise, little verifiable information is available. Ninian, a Romanized Briton, was born late in the fourth century in Scotland, and may have been educated and ordained in Rome. He spent much time with and was heavily influenced by Martin of Tours in forming ideals of an episcopal monastic structure for missionary work. Candida Casa, Ninian's base, which is dedicated to Martin, sits in Galloway. Ninian's work may have covered the Solway Plains and the Lake District of England. He serves, with Patrick, as a link between the ancient Roman/British Church and the developing Celtic churches of Scotland and Ireland.

Thursday, September 17
Hildegard of Bingen, Mystic and Scholar, 1179

Hildegard of Bingen, born in 1098, was a mystic, poet, composer, dramatist, doctor, scientist. Her parents' tenth child, she was tithed to the Church and raised by the anchoress Jutta in a cottage near the Benedictine monastery of Disibodenberg. Hildegard lived in a world accustomed to male governance. Yet, within her convents, and to a surprising extent outside them, she exercised a commanding spiritual authority based on confidence in her visions and considerable political astuteness.

Friday, September 18
Edward Bouverie Pusey, Priest, 1882

Pusey led the Oxford Movement, which revived High Church teachings and practices in the Anglican Communion. Pusey, born August 22, 1800, spent his scholarly life at Oxford as professor and as canon of Christ Church. With John Keble and John Henry Newman, he produced Tracts for the Times in 1833 (thus, the movement is also known as Tractarianism). He proved most influential through sermons catholic in content and evangelical in zeal, but dangerously innovative to some (Pusey was suspended from preaching for two years). Pusey influenced many to remain in the Anglican Church after Newman defected to the Church of Rome in 1845. With his money, he built churches for the poor; with his time, he established the first Anglican sisterhood since the Reformation.

Saturday, September 19
Theodore of Tarsus,
Archbishop of Canterbury, 690

Although Theodore was 66 when ordained Archbishop of Canterbury in 668, he provided strong leadership for a generation. He was a learned monk from the East who had been residing in Rome when he began his episcopate. The Church was split between Celtic and Roman customs. When Theodore arrived in England, he set up a school excellent in all disciplines, and he unified Anglo-Saxon Christians, including regularizing Chad's episcopal ordination. He defined boundaries of English dioceses, presided over reforming synods, and laid foundations of parochial organizations. According to Bede, Theodore was the first archbishop whom all English obeyed. He was buried in the monastic Church of Saints Peter and Paul at Canterbury.

The Sixteenth Sunday after Pentecost: Proper 20

September 20, 2020

God's gracious compassion for all people extends beyond human understanding.

Color   Green

Preface   Of the Lord's Day

Collect

Grant us, Lord, not to be anxious about earthly things, but to love things heavenly; and even now, while we are placed among things that are passing away, to hold fast to those that shall endure; through Jesus Christ our Lord, who lives and reigns with you and the Holy Spirit, one God, forever and ever. *Amen.*

Readings and Psalm

Exodus 16:2–15

We hear **the story of God's feeding of the people in the wilderness.** The Israelites are full of complaints and now think they would prefer slavery and death in Egypt to their present difficulties. The Lord appears to them and promises sustenance, but also a test, for they will only be given food on a day-to-day basis. It is possible to explain the food in natural terms: the flock of quail provide flesh and the secretion of insects the bread-like substance. But the point of the narrative is that God provides. The Israelites call the bread *manna* (perhaps from words meaning "What is this?").

Psalm 105:1–6, 37–45

A hymn of praise celebrating God's forming of a people through the generations.

or

Jonah 3:10–4:11

The Lord teaches Jonah a lesson when the prophet is angry because God is merciful to the repentant pagan city that Jonah has gone to great trouble to denounce.

"I knew it," Jonah says, in effect, when the Lord spares Nineveh; "that's why I tried to avoid your mission in the first place, because you are such a gracious God, even toward non-Israelites." The Lord causes a shrub to grow up and provide shade for the prophet. Jonah is again angry when it dies. If Jonah would have mercy for the plant, should God not be gracious toward this whole city?

Psalm 145:1–8

A hymn of praise to the Lord, who is mighty in deeds yet tender and compassionate.

Philippians 1:21–30

In this reading **Paul tells the Philippians that he would prefer to be with Christ beyond death, but he recognizes that he still has good work to do in his earthly life.** The passage suggests that Paul had reason to think his death might be near, perhaps by martyrdom. He looks forward to a closer union with Christ, but believes it more likely that he will be able to visit the Philippians again. Either way, he asks that they live in a manner worthy of the gospel and stand firm in unity with one another.

Matthew 20:1–16

Our gospel **is the story of the laborers in the vineyard, who are all paid the same wage despite their different hours of work.** Like most parables, this story can have many meanings, as have been given to it in the life of the church. On one level it suggests that nobody can presume on God's grace, so often extended to those who may seem the least deserving. The parable deliberately flies in the face of normal human expectations. It offers a clue pointing to God's extraordinary evenhandedness in dealing with people quite apart from human ideas about their merit. Jesus may have told it in defense of his own sharing in the lives of the outcast.

Prayers of the People

Come, all who labor in the vineyard of God's grace, let us join together in the offering of our prayers, saying, "Lord, hear our prayer."

That our commitment to justice may extend to those we employ in our households and businesses, paying a fair and living wage, clarifying expectations, and seeking honest work in return; let us pray.

Lord, hear our prayer.

That we may bridle our tongue against the urge to complain, channeling our energy to generously participate in the building up of the community of faith; let us pray.

Lord, hear our prayer.

That we may receive the sacramental Meal of the Eucharist as a foretaste of God's heavenly banquet, responding to its grace by helping those who are the weakest among us; let us pray.

Lord, hear our prayer.

That our homes may be schools of religious faith, where God's loving presence is revealed through personal sacrifice, ongoing forgiveness, and mutual joy; let us pray.

Lord, hear our prayer.

That we may rejoice in the beauty of the season, and honor the extraordinary diversity of plant and animal life; let us pray.

Lord, hear our prayer.

That those who have died may join in the company of the angels and archangels, all the saints in heaven, and rest in the blessed arms of him who is the first and the last, Jesus our Redeemer; let us pray.

Lord, hear our prayer.

With the steadfast love of God to guide us, we continue our prayers.
(Special intentions of the congregation, the diocese, and the Anglican Communion may be added here or before the formal intercessions.)

The Celebrant adds a concluding Collect.

Images in the Readings

The **vineyard** is a common biblical metaphor that designates the religious community. In biblical times wine was not only usually safer to drink than water, but it also symbolized the shared joy of the community. Its production relies on both the blessing of the Creator and the long-term joint efforts of growers and vintners, and its alcohol transforms our very bodies. Yet many congregations are quite stingy with the cup.

The Jonah story provides many allegorical images: **Nineveh** is the powerful enemy; **Tarshish** is for Jonah the farthest destination in the opposite direction away from Nineveh, across the Mediterranean Sea; the **bush** suggests personal comfort; the **worm** suggests God's correction to our selfishness; the **wind** is the breath of God; **Jonah** himself is a comic depiction of our very selves and of the church when we live out of typical human emotions. We too often do not know our right from our left hand. It is a great story.

The **spirit** of the Risen Christ will bring us into the unity expressive of a mutually forgiving community.

Ideas for the Day

♦ The movie *42* is less interested in baseball and more interested in the relationships of Jackie Robinson and Branch Rickey: two people who were led to prophetic action against the racial divide in professional baseball. Whether it is the historic characters or the screenwriters, there is unavoidable evidence of deep Christian formation in the movie conversations about the choice to step up, stand by, and follow through a difficult witness. As offered in the film, the daring action and the strength to weather the storm is evidence of a people who have a whole lot of gumption and plenty of organized Christian study, conversation, and prayer. These are the practices that can prepare believers to lead lives worthy of the gospel they claim as their own.

• In the second story of creation, God says to Adam and Eve that they are able to enjoy everything found in the garden with the exception of eating of the fruit of the Tree of Knowledge. It turns out that going for the Tree of Knowledge and eating its fruit was the same as attempting to be like God. It can be said that all sin is our attempt to be like God. God says we should stop trying that. Jonah had a hard time learning this lesson because he thought he knew better than God. Do any of us ever believe and act like that as well?

• This Sunday begins a four-week, semicontinuous reading of Philippians. In today's portion, Paul begs them to live worthily of the gospel in unity, harmony, and generosity without grumbling or complaining, keeping always before themselves Jesus Christ as the supreme model for any moral action. How do we stay firm in the faith?

Making Connections

God's merciful forgiveness is a gift to all who reach out for it. This is God's grace freely offered to all. We cannot earn or deserve God's love. God offers it because God loves us. We can identify and sympathize with Jonah (alternative reading) and the laborers in the vineyard who were hired first. Jesus loves the person who has been baptized at age ninety just as much as he loves the one who was baptized as an infant. This theme is expressed in the words of comfort read by the presbyter before the Peace in Rite I of the Eucharist (BCP, 332).

Engaging All Ages

In today's gospel, Jesus talks about money. You should talk about money too. What is your salary or allowance? St. Paul once wrote, "For the love of money is the root of all kinds of evil . . ." The love of it, not the money itself. The way the laborers love money leads them to be offended when all regardless of hours worked are paid the same. Jesus says people can love in a way that the use of money is a manifestation of love. How can you act generously and choose to use your money to show love to someone?

Hymns for the Day

The Hymnal 1982

Glorious things of thee are spoken 522, 523 [SC]
Guide me, O thou great Jehovah 690 [SC]
How sweet the Name of Jesus sounds 644 [SC]
Lamp of our feet, whereby we trace 627 [SC]
Lord, enthroned in heavenly splendor 307 [SC]
O Food to pilgrims given 308, 309 [SC]
Shepherd of souls, refresh and bless 343 [SC]
Give praise and glory unto God 375 [GR]
God, my King, thy might confessing 414 [GR]
O bless the Lord, my soul 411 [GR]
Praise, my soul, the King of heaven 410 [GR]
We will extol you, ever-blessed Lord 404 [GR]
Eternal Ruler of the ceaseless round 617
For thy dear saints, O Lord 279
God be in my head 694
My God, accept my heart this day 697
Singing songs of expectation 527
Christ the worker 611
Come, labor on 541
For the bread which you have broken 340, 341
From glory to glory advancing, we praise thee, O Lord 326
Lord of all hopefulness, Lord of all joy 482
Not here for high and holy things 9
O Jesus, I have promised 655
O Master, let me walk with thee 659, 660
Rise up, ye saints of God 551
Strengthen for service, Lord 312

Lift Every Voice and Sing II

Jesus in the morning 76

Wonder, Love, and Praise

All who hunger gather gladly 761 [SC]
God be with you till we meet again 801 [SC]
We all are one in mission 778

Pentecost

Weekday Commemorations

Monday, September 21
Saint Matthew, Apostle and Evangelist

A disciple of Jesus the Christ, Matthew left everything to follow the Master at his call. Matthew was identified with Levi, a tax collector, when tax collectors were seen as collaborators with the Roman state and, thus, spurned as traitors. Matthew was hardly the sort of person a devout Jew would associate with, yet Jesus noticed Matthew, rather than someone more pious. The disciple himself probably did not write the gospel of his name, given as author in homage. Through this gospel and its parables, Jesus speaks of faith and eternal life; of duty to neighbors, family, and enemies. Matthew is venerated as a martyr although circumstances of his death are unknown.

Tuesday, September 22
Philander Chase, Bishop, 1852

Ordained a deacon in 1798, he began mission work on the northern and western frontiers among the pioneers and the Mohawk and Oneida peoples. At the age of twenty-three he was ordained a priest in 1799 and served as a rector in Poughkeepsie, New York before moving to New Orleans where he established a church, then to Connecticut, followed by Ohio. In 1818 he was elected the first Bishop of Ohio and continued to found new congregations while organizing the diocese. He also established Kenyon College and Bexley Hall Seminary. He served as the Presiding Bishop from 1843 until his death.

Wednesday, September 23
Thecla of Iconium, Proto-Martyr Among Women, c.70

According to tradition, Thecla was a disciple of Paul. After hearing him preach the Gospel, Thecla abandoned marriage plans to follow him. Her legend is found in the second-century *Acts of Paul and Thecla*: Condemned to burn at the stake, she was saved by rain; thrown to beasts in an arena, she was protected by a lioness; baptizing herself in a pool, Thecla saw lightening kill hungry seals therein. Freed by the governor, this Proto-Martyr proceeded to preach the Word and become one of the most popular saints in the early church, exemplifying freedom to teach and baptize.

Thursday, September 24
Anna Ellison Butler Alexander, Deaconess and Teacher, 1947

Alexander (b. 1865) is the only African-American to be consecrated as a deaconess in the Episcopal Church. Her parents had been slaves. Devout Episcopalians, they embued her with a love of learning, and she became a teacher, educating poor African-American children in Georgia. She founded and helped run St. Cyprian's School in Darien; in 1902, she founded a school at Good Shepherd Church in Pennick. She became a deaconess in the troubled times of 1907 when the Diocese of Georgia segregated its congregations. Alexander's loving presence, vested as a deaconess, represented the height of Christian witness.

Friday, September 25
Sergius of Radonezh, Monastic, 1392

Sergius' name is familiar to Anglicans from the Fellowship of St. Alban and St. Sergius, the society dedicated to promoting relationships between Anglican and Russian Churches. To the people of Russia, Sergius serves as their patron saint. Born in 1314, he was 20 when his brother and he secluded themselves in a forest and developed the Monastery of the Holy Trinity, a center for reviving Russian Christianity. There, Sergius remained, a simple servant, mystical in temperament and eager to see his monks serve their neighbors. Sergius' support of Prince Dimitry Donskoi rallied Russians against Tartar overlords, thereby laying a foundation for independence. Pilgrims visit his shrine at the monastery of Zagorsk, which he founded in 1340.

Saturday, September 26
Lancelot Andrewes, Bishop of Winchester, 1626

Andrewes' sermons, witty and grounded, made him King James I's favorite preacher. Andrewes (born 1555 in London) was also a fine biblical scholar, able in Hebrew and Greek, who served as a translator for the Authorized (King James) Version of the Bible. As Dean of Westminster and headmaster of its school, he influenced the education of many churchmen, including poet George Herbert. *Preces Privatae* illustrates his piety. He strongly defended the catholicity of the Church of England against Roman Catholic critics. He was a model bishop, even when bishops were not esteemed. T. S. Eliot was inspired by Andrewes' Epiphany sermon for the opening stanza of "The Journey of the Magi."

The Seventeenth Sunday after Pentecost: Proper 21

September 27, 2020

Society's outcasts are often more righteous before God than those who consider themselves righteous.

Color   Green

Preface   Of the Lord's Day

Collect

O God, you declare your almighty power chiefly in showing mercy and pity: Grant us the fullness of your grace, that we, running to obtain your promises, may become partakers of your heavenly treasure; through Jesus Christ our Lord, who lives and reigns with you and the Holy Spirit, one God, forever and ever. *Amen.*

Readings and Psalm

Exodus 17:1–7

In our Hebrew Bible story **the people are at the point of rebellion because they are without water in the wilderness.** Moses decries their readiness to challenge the Lord through their lack of trust, and he asks God what is to be done. The Lord instructs Moses to strike a rock with his staff so that water will pour from it. This place he named Massah (meaning Challenge) and Meribah (meaning Dispute).

Psalm 78:1–4, 12–16

The psalm recalls Israel's trials and the Lord's sustaining grace in the wilderness after the escape from Egypt.

or

Ezekiel 18:1–4, 25–32

In the Hebrew scripture lesson **the Lord insists that individuals are responsible for their own sins and that the people must now repent, no longer blaming their troubles on the sins of their parents.** So much for the proverb that the fathers have eaten sour grapes and the children's teeth are set on edge! So much for those who say the Lord's ways are not just! These words are intended to bring about a sense of individual responsibility and hope at a time when the nation was gripped by despair because of tribulation and exile. The Lord wants the people to turn away from iniquity and live.

Psalm 25:1–9

A prayer for forgiveness and guidance and an expression of trust in the Lord.

Philippians 2:1–13

In this reading **Paul bids the new disciples to be of one mind in love, knowing how Christ Jesus accepted the condition of a servant and was obedient to the point of death. We now confess him as Lord and are called to an obedient working out of our faith.** Central to this passage is a poem which may have been adapted from the hopes for a savior of a people who did not yet know Jesus. He has fulfilled humanity's dream of one who will share fully in the mortal condition. Now the Lord is known personally—Jesus. His followers must work out their salvation while discovering that God is active in them for his loving purpose.

Matthew 21:23–32

In a response to a question about authority, Jesus tells a parable of two sons who obeyed their father differently, and he indicates that it is the same with those who are apparently obedient and disobedient in this age. Both John the Baptist and Jesus offered their message of repentance and the hope of the kingdom to all. It was the seeming outcasts who most genuinely responded. Then and now it is not a popular idea to suggest that such persons have priority over those who are established in their religion. Action is the test of obedience.

Pentecost

Prayers of the People

In turning to the ways of God our lives are saved from the grip of the Evil One, and the humility of love lightens our path. We offer our prayers, responding, "Lord, hear our prayer."

For the grace to move from grumbling to shared responsibility, from accusation to a search for truth, from humiliation and shame to God's compassion and mercy; let us pray.

Lord, hear our prayer.

That we may bear witness to the wonderful works of God, so that our children and the generations to come may walk in the path of faith and announce the mystery of faith through their lives; let us pray.

Lord, hear our prayer.

That we may bend the knee of our hearts to those who live in despair and great need, knowing that they are Christ to us, a gift of the Holy Spirit who fills us with compassion, and transforms the way we live; let us pray.

Lord, hear our prayer.

For those who work at night, staying awake while others sleep, guarding our streets, and healing the sick, that they may labor in safety and receive the rest that prepares them for another round; let us pray.

Lord, hear our prayer.

For our President, his/her advisors, the members of Congress and the Supreme Court, that they may be honest and vigilant in their duties, knowing that their decisions affect the peoples of our land, and of the nations of the world; let us pray.

Lord, hear our prayer.

For those who have died and now reside on another shore and in a greater light, that their faith may inspire our own, and their generosity encourage the way in which we use our gifts; let us pray.

Lord, hear our prayer.

Let us continue our prayers for all who live in the shadows of life, and those who have commended themselves for our remembrance.
(Special intentions of the congregation, the diocese, and the Anglican Communion may be added here or before the formal intercessions.)

The Celebrant adds a concluding Collect.

Images in the Readings

The parable speaks of a good and a bad **son**. Christianity lauds yet another son, the "only Son," who both answers yes and does the will of God. In the biblical worldview, a son is not understood as an independent agent, but is an extension of the father, owing the father everything. As well, according to the biological understanding of the time, it was the sperm that conveyed full humanity to the fetus. This sense of the child's connection with the parent is evident also in the reading from Ezekiel. Our culture thinks differently.

We are very distant from the first-century's horror at the image of the **cross**. The Roman government reserved this method of death by torture for the lowest criminals, and in Deuteronomy 21, even God is said to curse anyone executed by hanging on a tree. In the fourth century, the emperor Constantine outlawed crucifixion as a mode of execution, and since then jewels and gold, art and design have made of the cross an often beauteous sign of veneration. Some scholars suggest that "even death on a cross" is a Pauline interpolation into the hymn. The Good Friday liturgy invites persons to come forward to a full-sized rough-hewn cross and bend the knee before it in praise of Jesus.

Ideas for the Day

♦ Every congregation is in some sort of transitional time, whether you know it or not, and whether you like it or not. Many are built on memories of a church-going bubble, and now we find ourselves anxious and thirsty for anything except this unsettling experience. We crave the old sense of security, and we wonder how we can dare to live into the mission of Jesus we promised ourselves to. Whether we are like Moses in the desert, Ezekiel in exile, or the Jesus movement of the letters—we are called to unselfish humility and courageous love to meet the difficulties of a transitional time.

♦ Ezekiel offers a pastoral reminder that life toward God is better than life away from God. Again we find ourselves in yet another attempt to be God and attempt to control life for ourselves. Ezekiel is not the nicest prophet, but at least he tries to tell the people the truth. Maybe it is just the way we have translated the words. Ezekiel says "repent," and maybe we should hear "turn around." It certainly is not as judgmental. Consider this, if you will: sometimes the whole world is taking a picture of something very special. Try turning around and then take *that* picture. You might be surprised with the image you capture.

♦ Paul describes the humility of Jesus Christ in the words of an ancient hymn that extols the saving work of Christ. If the hymn is about Christ, it is also about God, making clear the true nature of God. God's true nature is not selfishly to seize but openhandedly to give. Paul is appealing to the Philippians who were acting selfishly, living with a grasping attitude. Paul appeals to them to bring their conduct into harmony with the conduct of Christ. How does this "hymn" from today's epistle speak to us today?

Making Connections

This parable expresses the actions of Jesus after his triumphal entry into Jerusalem (Matthew 21:1–11). His first act was to clean out the Temple (Matthew 21:12–17). He then began to confront the authorities of the Temple with parables that pointed to their unfaithfulness and impending judgement from God. He was there to point to a new Kingdom in which repentant sinners—the tax collectors and prostitutes included—would be invited into covenant with God to replace the unfaithful.

Engaging All Ages

Have you ever promised to do something that you did not do? Why did you not do it? Did anyone find out, and if so, what happened? Has someone ever done this to you? How did you react? Today, Jesus tells a story where this happens. A son promises to do something but never does. But another son who initially refuses to do the work changes his mind and turns a poor choice into a better choice. Today, is there a promise you can fulfill or a poor choice you can turn into a better choice?

Hymns for the Day

The Hymnal 1982

Come, thou fount of every blessing 686 [SC]
Glorious things of thee are spoken 522, 523 [SC]
Guide me, O thou great Jehovah 690 [SC]
O Food to pilgrims given 308, 309 [SC]
O God, unseen yet ever near 332 [SC]
Rock of ages, cleft for me 685 [SC]
Shepherd of souls, refresh and bless 343 [SC]
Surely it is God who saves me 678, 679 [SC]
Before thy throne, O God, we kneel 574, 575 [GR]
'Tis the gift to be simple 554 [GR]
All hail the power of Jesus' Name! 450, 451
All praise to thee, for thou, O King divine 477
At the name of Jesus 435
Morning glory, starlit sky 585
O Spirit of the living God 531
Sing, ye faithful, sing with gladness 492
The head that once was crowned with thorns 483
What wondrous love is this 439
Deck thyself, my soul, with gladness 339
Lord, dismiss us with thy blessing 344
Lord, we have come at your own invitation 348
O day of God, draw nigh 600, 601

Lift Every Voice and Sing II

Come, thou fount of every blessing 111 [SC]
Trust and obey 205

Wonder, Love, and Praise

Gracious Spirit, give your servants 782
You laid aside your rightful reputation 734

Pentecost

Pentecost

Weekday Commemorations

Monday, September 28
Paula and Eustochium of Rome,
Monastics and Scholars, 404 and c. 419

Paula (b. 347) and her daughter Eustochium (b. 386) served as calming companions to the irascible scholar Jerome, whom Paula met in 382. The two women often recalled him to the image of Christ as mild and humble. Eustochium vowed to remain a virgin, instructed by Jerome's *De custodian virginitatis*. The women, fluent in Greek, mastered Hebrew under Jerome's tutelage. They followed him to the Holy Land, where they settled in Bethlehem. There, Paula, a Desert Mother who surrendered her wealth to the service of God, built four monasteries, presiding over them for 20 years, followed by Eustochium.

Tuesday, September 29
St. Michael and All Angels

Of the many angels spoken of in the Bible, only four are called by name: Michael, Gabriel, Uriel, and Raphael. The Archangel Michael is the powerful agent of God who wards off evil from God's people and delivers peace to them at the end of this life's mortal struggle. "Michaelmas," as his feast is called in England, has long been one of the popular celebrations of the Christian Year in many parts of the world. The Archangel Michael is the patron saint of countless churches.

Wednesday, September 30
Jerome, Priest and Scholar, 420

Jerome was the foremost biblical scholar of the ancient Church. His Latin translation of the Bible from the original Hebrew and Greek texts known as the Vulgate version, along with his commentaries and homilies on the biblical books, have made him a major intellectual force in the Western Church.

Thursday, October 1
Remigius of Rheims, Bishop, c. 530

"Remi," born about 438, was but 22 when he became bishop of Rheims. As a patron saint of France, he is most noted for converting and baptizing King Clovis of the Franks on Christmas Day, 496. That changed the religious history of Europe. Most Germans were Arians, but being Christian meant that Clovis could unite the Gallo-Roman population and its Christian leaders and also liberate Gaul from Roman domination. Clovis' conversion eased the Franks' cooperation with Pope Gregory the Great as he evangelized the English. The feast of Remigius is celebrated in Rheims on January 13, thought to be his death day; October 1 marks the translation of his relics to a church in 1049.

Saturday, October 3
John Raleigh Mott, Ecumenist
and Missionary, 1955

Mott connected ecumenism and evangelism, following his mission's motto: "the evangelization of the world in this generation." As a young man (b. 1865, Cornell Class of '88), Mott volunteered in many capacities. He thought Christian communities needed to cooperate in the mission field, and he presided over the broadest gathering of Christian missionaries to that point. He drove the founding of the World Council of Churches. He received the Nobel Peace Prize in 1946 for establishing and strengthening international organizations working for peace. Although Mott was a Methodist, the Episcopal Church made him an honorary canon of the National Cathedral.

The Eighteenth Sunday after Pentecost: Proper 22

October 4, 2020

In the parable of the vineyard, Isaiah and Jesus both warn God's people that they will be held accountable for the fruits of the covenant.

Color   Green

Preface   Of the Lord's Day

Collect

Almighty and everlasting God, you are always more ready to hear than we to pray, and to give more than we either desire or deserve: Pour upon us the abundance of your mercy, forgiving us those things of which our conscience is afraid, and giving us those good things for which we are not worthy to ask, except through the merits and mediation of Jesus Christ our Savior; who lives and reigns with you and the Holy Spirit, one God, forever and ever. *Amen.*

Readings and Psalm

Exodus 20:1–4, 7–9, 12–20

In our first reading **Moses gives the people the ten commandments that God spoke to him on Mount Sinai.** These precepts are at the heart of Israel's law or Torah, and form the basis of the covenant with God established through Moses. The first four commandments prescribe Israel's relationship with God. Those which follow require fundamental responsibilities in human relationships.

Psalm 19

A hymn which glorifies the Creator God, with special praise for God's law and a prayer for avoidance of sin.

or

Isaiah 5:1–7

In our opening lesson **the prophet sings a sad parable about God's vineyard, Israel, and the destruction that must now come upon it.** Despite all God's loving care, this vineyard brought forth only sour grapes. The Lord looked for right judgment and found wrong. God hoped for justice and instead heard cries of distress.

Psalm 80:7–15

A lament and a plea to the Lord, the shepherd of Israel, that the Lord will restore God's ravaged vineyard.

Philippians 3:4b–14

Paul reminds the new Christians at Philippi that **if any have reason to brag because of heritage, lineage, or zeal, it is he. Yet all human achievements are to be counted as rubbish next to the joy and privilege of knowing God in Christ.** Paul does not consider himself complete, but presses forward to learn yet more of the grace of Christ, the power of his resurrection, and the sharing in his sufferings. His goal remains ahead: God's upward call in Christ Jesus.

Matthew 21:33–46

Our gospel is **the story of the wicked and disloyal tenants who are cast out of the vineyard.** The parable is presented to us as an allegory in which the vineyard is Israel and the wicked tenants are its people. The servants sent to them are the prophets, and the son whom they kill is Jesus. To the hearing of the early church the destruction of the vineyard would parallel the destruction of Jerusalem by the Romans in 70 CE, while the heritage of the vineyard is now given to others. There is added an ancient prophecy concerning the stone which was rejected, but which has now become the main cornerstone for the Lord's new work.

Prayers of the People

The ways of God revive the soul, give wisdom to the innocent, and enlighten those of little faith. In thanksgiving we offer our prayers, responding, "Lord, hear our prayer."

In thanksgiving that the forgiving arms of Jesus have embraced us while we were yet sinners, and carried us into the path that leads to eternal hope and heavenly grace; let us pray.

Lord, hear our prayer.

For a heart of abundant generosity, that we may give thanks for all that God has given to us, and share these gifts with all who stand in need, especially the poor and those who live with anxiety and despair; let us pray.

Lord, hear our prayer.

That we may reassess our lifestyles, simplifying the ways in which we live, reducing our consumption, so that we may have more time and treasure to share with others; let us pray.

Lord, hear our prayer.

In thanksgiving for the gifts of liberty and a democratic form of government; may we take our part in its future, and continue to offer prayers for those who exercise leadership in our nation and local cities and towns; let us pray.

Lord, hear our prayer.

For peace throughout the world, beginning within our hearts and families, revealed through our reliance on God's word to lead us into a stable global community; let us pray.

Lord, hear our prayer.

That the faithful departed may rest in peace, and those whose faith remains unknown may receive God's mercy; let us pray.

Lord, hear our prayer.

In the knowledge of the surpassing worth of knowing Jesus Christ, we continue our prayers.
(Special intentions of the congregation, the diocese, and the Anglican Communion may be added here or before the formal intercessions.)

The Celebrant adds a concluding Collect.

Images in the Readings

The importance of wine in the diet of biblical societies is evident in the Bible's continual use of the **vineyard** as an image of the people. Wine, suggesting the goodness of communal participation, serves as a corrective to more recent individualist interpretations of Christian faith. Vineyards grow from age-old roots and require dedicated tending. God owns the vineyard: we are only renters; we need to collaborate with one another to produce good wine.

The passage in the Psalms about the rejected stone becoming the **cornerstone** caught on in Christianity. In Ephesians 2:20 Paul calls Christ Jesus the cornerstone of the household of God; in Acts 4:11 Luke uses cornerstone as a metaphor for Christ, as does the author of 1 Peter in 2:7. It is yet another biblical image about the reversal of values that God intends. The idea is that a huge stone at the foundation is not merely a decorative marker but actually supports the weight of the building above.

Ideas for the Day

♦ Why would someone abandon a vineyard? Even in the biblical era the cost of establishing a vineyard was considerable. There are two primary reasons: disease and changes in water availability. There are some vineyards that once made good wine and no longer do. That is good and healthy to name out loud for any organization. Love and keeping something going forever are not the same thing. Is a healthier, more authentic, and Kingdom-bearing vineyard (and therefore wine) what God is calling us to? If we trust in the steadfast love of God, we must put on the confidence that God is helping us to let go and to plant vineyards that yield fine life-giving fruits.

♦ For many years, the actual tablets from the film, *The Ten Commandments* were in the narthex at St. Stephen's Episcopal Church in Hollywood, California. They were large (and they didn't weight very much). The Ten Commandments seem to be so important to people that they are often found in many other places etched in heavy stone. Rules must be followed. "So let it be written. So let it be done!" How many of us remember that four are on one tablet and six on the other? Jesus knew this. The first tablet shows how we are to love God with all our being. The second tablet shows we might love our neighbor as ourselves. Now where can we hang that?

◆ The concept of stewardship comes out strongly in today's readings. We are stewards, not owners, of the Lord's vineyards. We will be called to an accounting of the stewardship of our resources. Our responsibility to bring justice, to use our resources wisely, and to be concerned for the environment is a part of our stewardship. Stewardship is more than a financial pledge to the church. It is a way of life in which we all recognize our responsibility to be faithful stewards.

Making Connections

The Baptismal Covenant provides a way of assessing the church's stewardship of God's vineyard. The vineyard that we care for is not ours, but God's. What does this say about the way we should take care of our homes, our resources, and one another? How do we share and spread our resources for continuing the apostles' teaching and fellowship, proclaiming the Good News of God in Christ, seeking and serving Christ in all persons, and striving for justice and peace?

Engaging All Ages

Share and tell others about prizes and awards you have won. Sports trophies. Medals from 5Ks and marathons. Certificates from science fairs and trivia games. Stuffed animals and toys won from claw machines. Culturally, in the United States, winning is often prized above all other things. But in Philippians, Paul says the prize is simply the act of participating. To be called by God to godly things is the race you are running and the prize you already have received. Consider what does it look like to run a race you have already won.

Hymns for the Day

The Hymnal 1982
Eternal Spirit of the living Christ 698
Only-begotten, Word of God eternal 360, 361
Help us, O Lord, to learn 628 [SC]
Most High, omnipotent, good Lord 406, 407 [SC]
Praise to the living God 372 [SC]
The stars declare his glory 431 [SC]
Open your ears, O faithful people 536 [GR]
Awake, my soul, stretch every nerve 546
Fight the good fight with
      all thy might (vs. 1–2) 552, 553
Jesus, all my gladness 701
Lo! what a cloud of witnesses 545
Not far beyond the sea, nor high 422
We sing the praise of him who died 471
When I survey the wondrous cross 474
Christ is made the sure foundation 518
Hail, thou once despised Jesus 495
Lord Christ, when first thou cam'st to earth 598
My song is love unknown (vs. 1–2, 5) 458
O love, how deep, how broad, how high 448, 449
The great Creator of the worlds 489
The head that once was crowned with thorns 483

Lift Every Voice and Sing II
Ev'ry time I feel the Spirit 114 [SC]
Leave it there 197
Higher ground 165

Wonder, Love, and Praise
God the sculptor of the mountains 746, 747 [GR]
Ev'ry time I feel the Spirit 751 [SC]
When from bondage we are summoned 753, 754

Pentecost

Pentecost

Weekday Commemorations

Tuesday, October 6
William Tyndale, Priest, 1536

William Tyndale was born about 1495 near the Welsh border. With degrees from Oxford and having studied at Cambridge, he was ordained about 1521 and served as a chaplain and tutor. However, he was a man with a single passion—to translate the Holy Scriptures in English. Lacking official sanction, he went to Germany in 1524 only to have his work strongly opposed by King Henry VIII, Cardinal Wolsey, and others. Betrayed by a friend, Tyndale was strangled and burned at the stake in Brussels. Years later, Miles Coverdale completed the first translation of the whole Bible into English in 1535. Archbishop Thomas Cranmer adopted Coverdale's translation of the Psalter for the Book of Common Prayer 1539.

Wednesday, October 7
Birgitta of Sweden, Mystic, 1373

Birgitta Birgersdotter, born in 1303 to a noble family, discerned a religious vocation early but was married at 13 and had eight children. She practiced asceticism secretly. She had visions as a child, hearing Christ, Mary, and saints' warning voices in Swedish. She was discomfited when the voices became political; still, she criticized the king as a symbol of aristocracy. Birgitta counseled popes, clergy, and rulers, finding fault with their extravagance. She founded the Brigittine order, based on earlier revelations, and worked tirelessly for the pope to return to Rome from Avignon.

Friday, October 9
Robert Grosseteste, Bishop, 1253

Distinguishing himself as a scholar in many disciplines, from law to science and languages, Grosseteste was appointed Master of the Oxford School. He was first teacher of theology to the Franciscans. He translated and commented on Aristotle's works from Greek as well as figuring a scientific method based on Augustine's theories. He influenced both Roger Bacon and John Wycliffe. In 1235, he was consecrated Bishop of Lincoln and executed his office efficiently and conscientiously, traveling to each rural deanery with alacrity to preach, confirm, convene, and answer doctrinal questions. Grosseteste opposed royal abuses of local prerogatives: "As an obedient son, I disobey, I contradict, I rebel . . ."

Saturday, October 10
Vida Dutton Scudder, Educator, 1954

Scudder's love of scholarship was matched by her social conscience and deep spirituality. As a young woman, Scudder founded the College Settlements Association, joined the Society of Christian Socialists, and began her lifelong association with the Society of the Companions of the Holy Cross, a community living in the world and devoted to intercessory prayer.

The Nineteenth Sunday after Pentecost: Proper 23

October 11, 2020

God's coming reign will be like a great banquet (often referred to as the "messianic banquet"), but we must be ready to accept the invitation.

Color   Green

Preface   Of the Lord's Day

Collect

Lord, we pray that your grace may always precede and follow us, that we may continually be given to good works; through Jesus Christ our Lord, who lives and reigns with you and the Holy Spirit, one God, now and forever. *Amen.*

Readings and Psalm

Exodus 32:1–14

In our story from the Hebrew Bible **the people worship an idol, but Moses' prayer saves them from the Lord's punishment.** In one way or another this pattern is repeated throughout Israel's history. The people have just made a solemn covenant with God, but quickly they lose faith and want to put their trust in some more tangible and *useful* religion. In this case the object of their worship is a bull-calf, a divinity among the Canaanites and a symbol of strength and virility. Moses intercedes against God's wrath and reminds the Lord of past help and commitment to the people.

Psalm 106:1–6, 19–23

An affirmation of God's righteousness and favor toward those who love the Lord, and a confession of sins present and sins past.

or

Isaiah 25:1–9

In our Old Testament lesson **the prophet praises the Lord for destroying the cities of the ruthless and for providing a refuge for the poor. Now comes the banquet of the Lord's salvation.** God is the ultimate source of security. The great feast takes place on the mountain of the Lord's temple, Mount Zion, where heaven and earth figuratively meet. The banquet will be for all people, and even the power of death will be overcome.

Psalm 23

The Lord is shepherd and guide. God is present in time of danger and spreads a table for the one who needs comfort.

Philippians 4:1–9

In his letter to the church at Philippi, Paul invites the new disciples to exult in joy in the Lord who is near at hand, and he thanks them for their most recent gift. They need have no anxiety because God's peace, which is beyond human understanding, will keep their hearts and thoughts in Jesus. They should fill their minds with all that is noble and loving, putting these things into practice as Paul has taught them to.

Matthew 22:1–14

Our gospel reading presents **a parable about those who declined invitations to a marriage feast and others who were then invited, followed by the story of a guest who came without wedding clothes.** As the evangelist presents the parable of the feast, it is an allegory about the rejection of the Jews and the acceptance of Gentiles into the Kingdom. At another level, the story suggests that God's Kingdom will become known whether people are prepared for it or not. It is a divine gift. Included will be all kinds of people, many of them not considered worthy by worldly standards. The second parable, originally a separate story, makes the point that one must be ready for the Kingdom at all times; the invitation comes unexpectedly.

Prayers of the People

As Moses interceded with God for the sake of the people, so let us offer our intercessions on behalf of others, responding, "Lord, hear our prayer."

That we may clothe ourselves in garments befitting the faithful: compassion, joy, generosity, gladness of spirit, intentionality of life-style, and dedication to the way of our beloved Jesus; let us pray.

Lord, hear our prayer.

That the Church may be a refuge for the poor and lost, the lonely and those who hunger after righteousness, revealing through fragile human beings the signs of God's glorious kingdom; let us pray.

Lord, hear our prayer.

For peace in our time, that we may not linger in our efforts to secure hope for the peoples of the world, and the prosperity that peace inspires; let us pray.

Lord, hear our prayer.

That we may not make idols out of the many technologies and consumer products that entice our imaginations, but use them as tools for God's mission and glory; let us pray.

Lord, hear our prayer.

That the departed may dwell in the house of the Lord forever; let us pray.

Lord, hear our prayer.

In thanksgiving for the beauty of the earth, the fruits of the sea, the rising and setting of the sun, and all the marvelous gifts of God's creation, that in our wonder we may rededicate ourselves to a stewardship of the environment, so that generations to come may enjoy such pleasure; let us pray.

Lord, hear our prayer.

We continue our prayers in Christ, whose mercy endures forever.
(Special intentions of the congregation, the diocese, and the Anglican Communion may be added here or before the formal intercessions.)

The Celebrant adds a concluding Collect.

Images in the Readings

Here is a listing of only some of this Sunday's images. Matthew's parable merges several biblical images that describe our life with God. The **wedding** suggests lifelong love, commitment to the other, and communal joy in the union as a description of God's choosing and caring for us. Especially in a culture in which food was not plentiful and cheap, the **feast** connotes communal participation and extraordinary fullness. God is likened to a **king**, to whom is due honor and service. We are **guests**: that is, the meal is God's, not ours. The **wedding robe** suggests the white garment of baptism. Since the Bible often describes God as light, **outer darkness** suggests life totally distant and apart from God. Paul calls the somewhat problematic Philippian assembly his **crown**. Another ten images fill the poem from Isaiah. God not only throws out the unprepared guest, God also **shelters** us from storm, removes the **shroud** that finally covers all humans, like some kind of monster **eats up death**, and like a lover or a parent **wipes away our tears**.

Ideas for the Day

- Ancient shepherds lived a difficult, weathered life apart from society as they tended the sheep across the wild landscape. They were often the younger sons of peasants, sons who did not inherit any land. They were the backbone of caring for and moving crucial resources, yet reputationally they were seen as untrustworthy, dirty lowlifes. All of that imagery is startlingly upended in the beloved Psalm 23, which is all about all living together in peace: eating our fill, drinking what we need, and finding security in our divine inheritance. Who are the crucial but maligned people in our neighborhoods that God is calling us to find peaceful union with?
- There are two conflicting realities today in the readings. Midrash suggests that the gold used to create the golden calf came from the spoils collected along the shore of the Red Sea after the Egyptian soldiers had drowned. It certainly is not just the people of Israel who take something they stole from another and make an idol to self-greatness out of it. We might have even done it ourselves. Life is chaotic here. And then Paul shares another truth that leads to something a little more secure. "And the peace of God, which surpasses all understanding." It is good that God always offers a choice.

◆ It is often said that the Holy Eucharist is a foretaste of the "messianic banquet." Jesus may have been referring to this coming banquet when he said, "For I tell you that from now on I will not drink of the fruit of the vine until the Kingdom of God comes" (Luke 22:18). The Eucharist is a dramatization or a living picture of the banquet in Isaiah's poem (25:1–9). We are called to live as if the Kingdom were here, and yet we realize that the struggle still goes on. At the Eucharist we share the Word of God, we pray, we care about each other, we offer ourselves totally to God, and we are fed the "bread of heaven" and "cup of salvation." This is a vision of the heavenly banquet. As we fall short of the vision in our lives, we are called into confrontation as were the Jews of Jesus' time.

Making Connections

A portion of the New Testament reading is found in the final blessings given at the Holy Eucharist, Rite I: "And the peace of God, which surpasses understanding, will guard your hearts and your minds in Christ Jesus" (BCP, 339). How does joining together in worship bless us and send us out into the world to be a blessing to others?

Engaging All Ages

"In everything by prayer and supplication with thanksgiving let your requests be made known to God." In worship today, pay attention to the Prayers of the People. These are your prayers. They are prayers for you, others in your church, and for the world. You ask God for good things and you give thanks for good things. If you can, read a copy of this Sunday's prayers. Is there a prayer you would like to ask to have included in next Sunday's prayers? If so, ask your priest or the person who maintains the prayer list.

Hymns for the Day

The Hymnal 1982

God the Omnipotent! King, who ordainest 569 [SC]
O for a closer walk with God 683, 684 [SC]
Sing praise to God who reigns above 408 [SC]
Glory, love, and praise, and honor 300 [GR]
My God, thy table now is spread 321 [GR]
My Shepherd will supply my need 664 [GR]
The King of love my shepherd is 645, 646 [GR]
The Lord my God my shepherd is 663 [GR]
Christ, whose glory fills the skies 6, 7
Holy Ghost, dispel our sadness 515
Jesus, all my gladness 701
Rejoice, the Lord is King 481
Rejoice, ye pure in heart 556, 557
Savior, again to thy dear Name we raise 345
Come, my Way, my Truth, my Life 487
Deck thyself, my soul, with gladness 339
O Jesus, joy of loving hearts 649, 650
The Lamb's high banquet called to share 202
This is the hour of banquet and of song 316, 317
We the Lord's people 51

Lift Every Voice and Sing II

The Lord is my shepherd 104 [GR]

Wonder, Love, and Praise

As we gather at your Table 763

Weekday Commemorations

Wednesday, October 14
Samuel Isaac Joseph Schereschewsky,
Bishop and Missionary, 1906

When Schereschewsky (born in 1831 in Lithuania) was studying for the rabbinate in Germany, he was enticed toward Christianity through his reading of a Hebrew translation of the New Testament and by missionaries of the London Society for Promoting Christianity Amongst the Jews. In 1854, he immigrated to Pittsburgh to train for ministry in the Presbyterian Church; after two years, he became an Episcopalian. He graduated from General Theological Seminary in 1859, whereupon he emigrated to China, learning to write Chinese enroute. He translated the Bible and parts of the prayer book into Mandarin. He was elected Bishop of Shanghai in 1877; partially paralyzed, he resigned his see in 1883 but continued translating.

Pentecost

Pentecost

Thursday, October 15
Teresa of Avila, Mystic and
Monastic Reformer, 1582

Even as a girl, Teresa studied saints' lives, delighting in contemplation and repeating, "Forever . . . they shall see God." She grew up to be one of two women declared a Doctor of the Church in 1970, primarily because of her two mystical contemplative works, *The Way of Perfection* and *Interior Castle*. To offset girlish worldliness following her mother's death, Teresa's father placed her in an Augustinian convent. After serious sickness ended her studies there, she chose the religious life in a Carmelite convent. She increasingly meditated, and she perceived visions—godly or satanic, she did not know. She traveled for 25 years through Spain, establishing 17 convents of Reformed Carmelites ("discalced," or unshod). Her letters provide insights to her heart.

Friday, October 16
Hugh Latimer and Nicholas Ridley, Bishops
and Martyrs, 1555, and Thomas Cranmer,
Archbishop of Canterbury, 1556

Cranmer (born 1489), the principal figure in the Reformation of the English church, was primarily responsible for the first Book of Common Prayer in 1549. Compromising his political with his reformation ideals led to his death—despite his recanting. Ridley (born 1500) also adhered to reformation ideals as he served as chaplain to King Henry VIII. Unwilling to recant his Protestant theology, Ridley died with Latimer at the stake. Latimer (born about 1490) was installed as Bishop of Worcester in 1535 under Henry VIII; he resigned his see in 1539 and refused to resume it after Edward VI was enthroned. Latimer was imprisoned and burned at the stake with Ridley under the crown of Mary on October 16, 1555.

Saturday, October 17
Ignatius of Antioch, Bishop and Martyr, c.115

Ignatius' seven letters, written to Churches while he sojourned across Asia Minor, offer insight to the early Church. In one, he cautioned against Gnostic teachings that underscored Jesus' divinity over his humanity; in another, he condemned biblical literalism, citing Jesus Christ as "the ancient document." Ignatius held that the Church's unity would rise from its liturgy by which all are initiated into Christ through baptism. Ignatius thought of the Church as God's holy order in the world; he was concerned, therefore, with ordered teaching and worship. In ecstasy, he saw his martyrdom as the just conclusion to a long episcopate as second bishop of Antioch in Syria.

The Twentieth Sunday after Pentecost: Proper 24

October 18, 2020

God's power and will can be revealed even among those considered enemies or aliens. Since God's power extends to everyone, ultimate authority belongs to God.

Color   Green

Preface   Of the Lord's Day

Collect

Almighty and everlasting God, in Christ you have revealed your glory among the nations: Preserve the works of your mercy, that your Church throughout the world may persevere with steadfast faith in the confession of your Name; through Jesus Christ our Lord, who lives and reigns with you and the Holy Spirit, one God, forever and ever. *Amen.*

Readings and Psalm

Exodus 33:12–23

In this lesson **Moses seeks reassurance and to see God's glory. God promises the divine presence and favor.** Although no mortal may see God's face, God's name will be made known through graciousness and mercy.

Psalm 99

The holy and mighty Lord reigns on high. God has spoken to Israel's leaders from a pillar of cloud and has forgiven them their misdeeds.

or

Isaiah 45:1–7

In this Hebrew Bible reading **the Lord anoints Cyrus, King of Persia, to be God's agent in freeing the chosen people from exile.** The time is more than five centuries before the birth of Christ. The prophet perceives that God is working through a foreign king who does not even know the Lord. But God enables Cyrus to conquer Babylonia and then to set Israel free. Boldly the prophet speaks in the Lord's name: the Creator is responsible for everything that happens in the world, whether it seems a blessing or a disaster.

Psalm 96:1–9 (10–13)

A hymn of trust in the Lord. God will guard and deliver the one who loves and seeks refuge with God.

1 Thessalonians 1:1–10

In company with Silvanus and Timothy, Paul greets the new Christians of Thessalonica, giving thanks for their faith and their conversion from idols to the worship of the true and living God. This letter was written not long after Paul's first missionary visit to this city in the country we know today as Greece. Evidently the converts were all former pagans. The apostle refers to the troubles and persecution that are also reported in the Acts of the Apostles. But the gospel, empowered by the activity of the Holy Spirit, has inspired a faith which has become widely known.

Matthew 22:15–22

In our gospel lesson **Jesus answers a question about taxation by teaching that people should pay what belongs to the emperor to the emperor and the things of God to God.** The question was meant as a trap. If Jesus advised the paying of taxes to the occupying Roman powers, many Jews would have considered him a collaborator. Had he counseled nonpayment, the Herodian servants of the Romans could accuse him of sedition. On one level Jesus' answer is a masterstroke of clever ambiguity, but it also causes his hearers to reflect more deeply on their responsibility to God and the state. Perhaps the saying suggests that government has its legitimate yet limited claims. It must not be given the highest allegiance.

Pentecost

Prayers of the People

In the Name of Jesus, let us offer our prayers, responding, "Lord, hear our prayer."

For the desire to reflect God's abundant treasures, freely giving for the mission of the Church in the world, our faithful commitment to the poor and those in need; let us pray.

> *Lord, hear our prayer.*

In thanksgiving for missionaries who serve in foreign lands; may they proclaim the gospel message of hope to those who live in places of instability, and reveal to us at home their extraordinary faith and charity; let us pray.

> *Lord, hear our prayer.*

In thanksgiving for those who serve in our government, especially those unseen workers who toil in federal and state offices, and who attend to the details of daily responsibilities; let us pray.

> *Lord, hear our prayer.*

In thanksgiving for our Creator who formed the darkness and formed the light, leading us through both, so that we may be transformed into a holy people; let us pray.

> *Lord, hear our prayer.*

For all the faithful departed, may they rest in peace through the mercy of God; let us pray.

> *Lord, hear our prayer.*

Continuing in the Holy Name of Jesus, let us add to these prayers.
(Special intentions of the congregation, the diocese, and the Anglican Communion may be added here or before the formal intercessions.)

The Celebrant adds a concluding Collect.

Images in the Readings

Typically, a **coin** is impressed with an image of the authority upon which the coin relies. In the United States, coins and bills bear the picture of presidents who function as model representatives of the sovereign people. In baptism, it is the cross of Christ that has been impressed on our bodies: he is the authority to whom we owe allegiance. As to taxes: Christians in different countries have widely ranging views about how much of our days' wages is rightly owed to the government.

The Isaiah reading plays with the idea of one's **name**. God calls Cyrus by name; God's personal name is YHWH, represented in most English-language Bibles as "the LORD." In his encouragement to the Thessalonians, Paul writes of God the Father, the Lord Jesus Christ, and the Holy Spirit. In baptism, the candidates are first called by their secular name, after which this triune name of God is placed on them. Yet in the second century, Justin Martyr wrote that to imagine that we can know and speak the very name of the almighty God is madness. Perhaps the name of God that we are given in the Bible is like a potholder, a way to hold on to something that is far too hot for bare human hands.

Ideas for the Day

♦ There is an immense difference between knowing about God and knowing God. Moses is giving voice to a broader experience of desiring to feel God's presence and assurance. We want to know for sure that God (or our loved ones) are not going to abandon us. The response of God to Moses' anxiety about God's steadfast presence is gracious, but it is also expected that this intimacy is not a one-way relationship. What people and organizations do we desire the assurance of but regularly manage to be steadfast partners with?

♦ One of the critical points in the Eucharistic celebration is when the Presider takes the host, lifts it high so that the people can see, and then breaks it. God expressed wisdom in not allowing Moses to see the divine face. It would have been too much. So it seems there is also wisdom when we are only allowed to take a *piece* of the consecrated bread each week. A little bit of Jesus might just be what the doctor ordered. It also seems fitting that when we do it in this way, only taking a little bit of Jesus, we are also sharing the love of Jesus with one another.

♦ The church must acknowledge the ultimate allegiance to God. It is important for the congregation to know the stories of those who have witnessed to that ultimate authority with their lives. Dietrich Bonhoeffer, a German theologian (also noted in on Pentecost 3, Proper 7) killed by the Nazi regime, is an example of the witnesses we have in Christian history. Are there other martyrs of modern times that we can speak of today? (See *Lesser Feasts and Fasts*.)

Making Connections

The rubrics for the Prayers of the People specify that the gathered church must pray for "the Nation and all in authority," and "the welfare of the world" at every celebration of the Eucharist (BCP, 383). God uses all kinds of governments and systems for God's purposes. God is concerned about justice and shalom (peace). God used Cyrus the Great, the pagan ruler of the Persian empire, as an instrument to bring about justice. So long as the Romans ruled justly, God would not act to overthrow them. Jesus was not interested in leading an uprising or in protesting against Roman rule. Jesus "simply" challenged the injustices of those systems.

Engaging All Ages

Think and talk about people you look up to, who you consider role models. Who do you look to as examples? Who do you want to imitate? Is it someone you know? A famous person? What makes them a good example? What actions and characteristics do they have that you want to imitate? Why? Today's reading from First Thessalonians describes followers of Jesus as joyful and inspired, as full of conviction, and as examples to all believers and imitators of the Lord. What actions could you take to be an example to all believers and an imitator of the Lord?

Hymns for the Day

The Hymnal 1982

Holy, holy, holy! Lord God Almighty 362 [SC]
Immortal, invisible, God only wise 423 [SC]
Rock of ages, cleft for me 685 [SC]
All people that on earth do dwell 377, 378 [GR]
Before the Lord's eternal throne 391 [GR]
Earth and all stars 412 [GR]
Praise to the living God 372 [GR]
Sing praise to God who reigns above 408 [GR]
I sought the Lord, and afterward I knew 689
In your mercy, Lord, you called me 706
Jesus, our mighty Lord 478
Lord, we have come at your own invitation 348
O for a closer walk with God 683, 684
All my hope on God is founded 665
Father eternal, Ruler of creation 573

God of grace and God of glory 594, 595
Jesus shall reign, where'er the sun 544
Judge eternal, throned in splendor 596
O God of earth and altar 591

Lift Every Voice and Sing II

Wonder, Love, and Praise

Weekday Commemorations

Monday, October 19
Henry Martyn, Priest and Missionary, 1812
Martyn translated the scriptures and Book of Common Prayer into Hindi and Persian and served as an English missionary in India. Born in 1781 and educated at Cambridge, Martyn, influenced by Charles Simeon, Evangelical rector of Holy Trinity/Cambridge, changed his mind about becoming a lawyer and became a missionary. He traveled to India in 1806 as chaplain for the British East India Co. He was there but five years before dying at age 31; however, in that time, he organized private schools and founded churches in addition to translating the Bible. He also translated the New Testament into Persian. He died in Tokat, Turkey, where Armenians honored him by burying him like one of their own bishops.

Friday, October 23
Saint James of Jerusalem, Brother of Our Lord Jesus Christ
Saint James of Jerusalem is called the Lord's brother in the Gospel according to Matthew and the Epistle to the Galatians. However, other writers, following Mark's path, thought James was Jesus' cousin; certain apocryphal writings name him as Joseph's son by his first wife. After Jesus' resurrection, James was converted and eventually became bishop of Jerusalem. Paul's first letter to the Corinthians notes that James beheld a special appearance of the Lord before the ascension; later, James was cordial to Paul at Jerusalem. At the Council of Jerusalem, it was James who would impose "no irksome restrictions" (circumcision) on Gentiles turning to God. His success at converting many to Jesus perturbed factions in Jerusalem, so he was cudgeled to death.

Pentecost

The Twenty-First Sunday after Pentecost: Proper 25

October 25, 2020

To be righteous before God means doing right to the neighbor, the sojourner, and the person in need. To love God is to love the neighbor.

Color　　Green

Preface　　Of the Lord's Day

Collect

Almighty and everlasting God, increase in us the gifts of faith, hope, and charity; and, that we may obtain what you promise, make us love what you command; through Jesus Christ our Lord, who lives and reigns with you and the Holy Spirit, one God, forever and ever. *Amen.*

Readings and Psalm

Deuteronomy 34:1–12

Our Hebrew scripture lection recounts **the death of Moses on the very edge of the promised land.** Moses has fulfilled his purpose as God's faithful servant, the one who led the people from their bondage with many signs, received the law, traversed the wilderness, and knew God intimately. From Mount Nebo, Moses surveys the promised land, and then he dies and is buried in Moab. Joshua, upon whom Moses had laid his hands, succeeds him.

Psalm 90:1–6, 13–17

The psalmist reflects on the passing character of human life in the face of the Lord's wrath, and asks the everlasting God for wisdom to make use of the time.

or

Leviticus 19:1–2, 15–18

In this lesson **the people of Israel are called to lives of justice and love—to be holy because the Lord their God is holy.** The goal for the behavior of God's people is nothing less than the very highest. As God's chosen ones, they are to care for the poor and weak and to avoid any form of oppression. One is to love one's neighbor as oneself.

Psalm 1

The Lord makes fruitful those who choose the way of righteousness.

1 Thessalonians 2:1–8

In this reading **Paul recalls his first visit to the Thessalonians, the troubles he endured, and the straightforward and gentle way in which he presented the gospel.** The opposition that Paul had earlier experienced in Philippi continued in Thessalonica, but, with God's help, Paul preached fearlessly. Unlike certain of the insincere traveling missionaries of the pagan world, Paul acted with integrity and sought in no way to take advantage of his new friends. He and his companions shared not only the gospel but their own selves.

Matthew 22:34–46

In the gospel **Jesus presents the double commandment of love for God and neighbor, and then asks a question concerning whose son the Christ is.** The context of this passage is the effort by certain Jewish officials to test Jesus, hoping to force him to make an unwise or unpopular comment. Jesus first responds by teaching that all the law and the prophetic words depend for their understanding on commandments of love. He then asks his own question. Using an argumentative style of the time, Jesus shows how King David (considered to be the author of the Psalms) called the Christ his Lord. Thus, at the very least, the Christ must be more than the son of David. Christians believe this Christ to be Jesus and trust that through him disciples may learn to love both God and neighbor.

Prayers of the People

As a people entrusted by God with the proclamation of good news, let us offer our prayers and thanksgivings, responding, "Lord, hear our prayer."

That we may love our neighbor as ourselves, sacrificing personal comforts to provide shelter for the poor, sound education for all children, psychiatric care for those suffering from mental illness, living wages to employees, and respite for those who attend to those living with illness; let us pray.

> *Lord, hear our prayer.*

That our personal trials may be seen as pathways to faithfulness, roads upon which we walk in order to gain a deeper understanding of God's enduring love; let us pray.

> *Lord, hear our prayer.*

That peace may reign throughout the world, loosening the chains of incessant poverty, political imprisonment, religious persecution, and the abuse of power that raises a few to prosperity at the expense of the masses; let us pray.

> *Lord, hear our prayer.*

That we may do the work and ministry that reflect God's reign, knowing that we may not see beyond our offerings or the fruit of our labors; let us pray.

> *Lord, hear our prayer.*

For a renewed commitment to righteousness and peace, that we may join with the leaders of the nations in seeking ways to promote harmony in warring lands, and mutual respect across cultures, races, and languages; let us pray.

> *Lord, hear our prayer.*

That we may put aside any vengeance of heart, so that we may offer to one another true forgiveness and amendment of ways; let us pray.

> *Lord, hear our prayer.*

In companionship with those who have died, and with all the saints, let us continue our prayers.
(Special intentions of the congregation, the diocese, and the Anglican Communion may be added here or before the formal intercessions.)

The Celebrant adds a concluding Collect.

Images in the Readings

The term **law** is tricky for us. According to the covenant in the Old Testament, the law was graciously given by God to delineate the way toward communal happiness. However, Paul uses the term critically, teaching that keeping these 613 commands will not bring us to God. Luther uses the term far more broadly to refer to everything in the Bible that preaches our sin and announces our death. For many contemporary hearers, the term means governmental regulations. Our task is to make sure that the meaning of any particular use of the term is clear. Psychologists suggest, in accord with Luther, that confronting the truth of the human condition is, although sad, finally welcomed, but then as Christians we gladly take refuge in the gospel of God's love in Christ Jesus.

Probably in 1 Thessalonians 2:7 Paul is suggesting that evangelists are like a **nursing mother**, since the children are her own. So Paul offers a balance to Matthew's image of the late-first-century church leader as an exegetical authority. Both are helpful images.

Pentecost

Psalm 110, cited in Matthew 22, pictures the Messiah sitting at the **right hand** of God. In ancient Near Eastern courts, the prince or a kind of prime minister sat on the right side of the monarch. From the psalm the phrase made it all the way into our creeds. In the fifteenth century, the mystic Julian reminds us that the phrase is a metaphor: "But it is not meant that the Son sits on the right hand as one man sits by another in this life, for there is no such sitting, as to my sight, in the Trinity." She suggests that the metaphor means that Son is "right in the highest nobility of the Father's joy."

Ideas for the Day

♦ There is a part of "happy" that is utter joy, warm-cookies delight. But there is also a side of how we use the word "happy" that is saccharine, shallow, and vapid. "Happy" can also be an unattainable goal that shames our doldrums and griefs and steals the good and the holy from the daily reality of life. What is translated in the prayer book as "happy" is elsewhere sometimes translated as "blessed." It is that wish or prayer for well-being we utter when we say "bless you." It is the naming of the glowing centeredness and glad purpose with which we desire we leave the Eucharistic liturgy with. How is holy happiness or blessing experienced by the people in your life?

♦ A blessing is best defined as the willingness to name how one sees God working in and through another person at that very moment. Can you imagine a world where we did this more than degrading the humanity of one another? Joshua was most likely already filled with the spirit of wisdom, but it was the laying on of hands and the naming by Moses that allowed Joshua to know his truth. He was affirmed, and he was loved. Chances are that you might know someone who is broken, who needs to hear that you see God working through them.

♦ Our response to God comes as we respond in justice and love to one another. The one cannot be separated from the other. For a different perspective, see 1 John 4:20–21 for the negative way of stating this.

Making Connections

The Baptismal Covenant repeats the commandments to love God and neighbor. To embody the covenant means responding to God in praise, seeking and serving Christ in others, striving for justice and peace (BCP, 305).

Engaging All Ages

The Ten Commandments are a set of guidelines from God that was given so that people could be better and treat other people better. Where else do you find guidelines and rules? At home? No dessert before eating your vegetables. Going to bed at a certain time. At school or the office? Types of clothes you can and cannot wear in those places? Discuss all these rules and why you think they were made. Think how these rules demonstrate love for God and love for others. If they do not, could you suggest ways to change them so that they do?

Hymns for the Day

The Hymnal 1982

O God, our help in ages past 680 [SC]
Praise to the living God 372 [SC]
Before thy throne, O God, we kneel 574, 575 [GR]
Father all-loving, who rulest in majesty 568 [GR]
Give praise and glory unto God 375 [GR]
Thy strong word did cleave the darkness 381 [GR]
God of mercy, God of grace 538
Lord, make us servants of your peace 593
O Spirit of the living God 531
Take my life, and let it be 707
All hail the power of Jesus' Name! 450, 451
Come with us, O blessed Jesus 336
Jesu, Jesu, fill us with your love 602
Lord, whose love through humble service 610
O Spirit of Life, O Spirit of God 505
Rise up, ye saints of God 551
Where charity and love prevail 581

Lift Every Voice and Sing II
Jesu, Jesu 74

Wonder, Love, and Praise
Jesus said: The first commandment is this 815

Weekday Commemorations

Monday, October 26
Alfred, King, 899

Alfred, born in 849, one of five sons of King Aethelwulf, lived during a time of murder as Vikings invaded and settled in Britain. At four, he was blessed by Pope Leo IV on a trip to Rome. Alfred became king in 871. He halted the invasions through heroic battles and stratagems, thus securing control of southern and parts of midland England. He persuaded his foe, the Dane Guthrum, to accept baptism after Alfred won the battle of Edington in 878. He sought to repair damage wrought by the Viking invasions, especially on culture and clergy. Because of his courage and virtue, Alfred is the only English ruler to be called "great."

Wednesday, October 28
Saint Simon and Saint Jude, Apostles

Little is known of either Simon or Jude. The gospels name Simon as one of the disciples, the "Zealot," but that adjective may refer to his enthusiasm as much as to his membership in the "Zelotes" faction. John mentions him as being at the Last Supper. The Epistle of Jude may have been written by the disciple Jude, who is mentioned by John as brother to James the Greater. By tradition, the two are associated with Persia; some stories characterize them as martyrs. Jude may be confused with another Jude, who was surnamed Thaddeus; still, he is prayed to as the patron of Lost Causes. More questions than answers ensnare these two.

Thursday, October 29
James Hannington, Bishop, and his Companions, Martyrs, 1885

Born in Sussex (1847), educated at Temple School, Hannington worked with his father in the family warehouse, and with his family joined the Church of England in 1867. He was ordained at Exeter. In 1882, he presented himself as a missionary to the Church Missionary Society for its mission in Victoria, Nyanza, Africa. He went home after an illness but returned to Africa in 1884 as Bishop of Eastern Equatorial Africa. From his mission field on the shores of Lake Victoria, Hannington and his party ventured toward Uganda; they were stopped by emissaries of King Mwanga, tortured, and martyred. His last words were: "I have purchased the road to Uganda with my blood."

Pentecost

All Saints' Day

November 1, 2020

We remember the saints of God—all faithful and believers; we are surrounded by a great cloud of witnesses.

Color   White

Preface   All Saints

Collect

Almighty God, you have knit together your elect in one communion and fellowship in the mystical body of your Son Christ our Lord: Give us grace so to follow your blessed saints in all virtuous and godly living, that we may come to those ineffable joys that you have prepared for those who truly love you; through Jesus Christ our Lord, who with you and the Holy Spirit lives and reigns, one God, in glory everlasting. *Amen.*

Readings and Psalm

Revelation 7:9–17

This lesson presents a **vision of those who have survived great tribulation and now worship before the throne of God and the Lamb.** These myriad saints come from all over the world and have been purified through their own sufferings in association with the sacrifice of the Lamb. But now the Lamb (which is a figure for Jesus) will be their shepherd, and they will suffer no longer. Such a vision would be a great consolation to those undergoing persecution.

Psalm 34:1–10, 22

A hymn of blessing and praise to the Lord for deliverance.

1 John 3:1–3

In this lesson we learn that **through God's love, disciples are now children of God; their destiny is to be like Christ.** Those who did not recognize Jesus will not recognize his disciples either. Though the mystery of what those disciples are to become has not been fully revealed, Christians know that a dramatic change has taken place in their lives; an earnest of the transformation underway. Those who stand in this hope will purify themselves as Christ is pure.

Matthew 5:1–12

The gospel is **the opening sayings of the Sermon on the Mount, words of both comfort and challenge.** The values of the kingdom are quite different from worldly standards. Those who are to find blessing will know want and thirst, if not because of their own circumstances, then for the sake of others. Those who hunger for righteousness will find fulfillment, but first they must suffer persecution.

Prayers of the People

With clean hearts and a pure faith, let us ascend the hill of the Lord, offering our prayers and thanksgivings to the one who hears our petitions and answers our call, responding, "Hear us, O Host of Heaven."

In thanksgiving for many peoples, languages, tribes and nations, whose diversity of thought and action become blessings to all who seek the fullness of God's presence in the midst of daily life; let us pray to the Lord.

Hear us, O Host of Heaven.

In thanksgiving for the Eucharistic Meal in which we are fed by Christ, who reveals his goodness and invites us to trust in his love with our whole heart, and soul, and mind; let us pray to the Lord.

Hear us, O Host of Heaven.

For the commitment and strength to share God's blessings throughout the world, honoring those who hunger and thirst, who mourn, and who live in fear and anxiety, giving out of our weaknesses to fill the hopes of others; let us pray to the Lord.

Hear us, O Host of Heaven.

For the peacemakers who proclaim justice in the marketplace, and petition prime ministers, presidents and legislators, to turn the ways of war into the dividends of peace; let us pray to the Lord.

Hear us, O Host of Heaven.

For those who volunteer their time to enlighten the lives of others, especially those who work in our schools, recreational centers, and wherever young people seek enrichment and encouragement; let us pray to the Lord.

Hear us, O Host of Heaven.

For holy women and men who have died in the light of Christ, and whose righteousness inspired the faithful of every generation; may their souls and the souls of unsung heroes in every age enter the gates of paradise; let us pray to the Lord.

Hear us, O Host of Heaven.

In companionship with the Blessed Virgin Mary, (blessed _____,) and all the saints, we continue the offering of our prayers.
(Special intentions of the congregation, the diocese, and the Anglican Communion may be added here or before the formal intercessions.)

The Celebrant adds a concluding Collect.

Images in the Readings

The main image in the gospel reading is **the Kingdom of heaven**. The image of Kingdom stresses a communal and social reality, not an individual psychic experience. This image has been so narrowed by especially nineteenth-century artists into a kind of summer camp in the skies that it is not easy to see in the image God's transforming rule of righteousness. In Revelation, the Kingdom is imagined with all the angels and saints gathered around God's throne, a depiction common in medieval art but itself distant from our understanding of the universe.

The reading from Revelation resembles a concordance of biblical imagery, each of which connects with numerous biblical passages: **every nation, throne, Lamb, palm branches, angels, the four living creatures, washed, blood, hunger, thirst, the sun's heat, shepherd, springs of the water of life.** That the saints are **robed in white** suggests early Christian baptismal garb, and the word "alb" refers to these white robes that clothe the baptized. In true metaphoric fashion, in which words assert the opposite of a literal meaning, the robes are made white by being washed in blood.

Ideas for the Day

+ Here in this sermon on the plain, Jesus is speaking to the people in the scene, but he is also speaking to us. He makes his mission and our duties in the company of the saints simply: lift, tell, feed, heal. God's path, shape, and redemptive work will be recognized in its fullness from the underside and its living witness, not affirming statements and gilded eggs. When we spiritualize Jesus' demands, the poorer in spirit we become. We may dwell in sad darkness, but God demands that we never ignore that we have neighbors whose darkness may be worse. There is hardship and bloodshed in the company of the faithful. Facing our challenges head on is taking our place within the sacred circle of saints.

+ The image is simple, profound, and true. When we get to the place in the Eucharistic Prayer that says "with Angels and Archangels and with all the company of heaven" (BCP, 362), we should probably look around and bathe ourselves in the glory of creation. We will know what it was like to be a shepherd and see the heavenly host and hear their singing. We will feel the light of the presence of Jesus in each saint, each soul. It might be a good time to light our own candle to reflect Jesus in our life as well.

+ All Saints' Day is one of the most important celebrations of the church year. Surprisingly, it is also the ideal time to expose children and adults to the important subject of death. God's creation is present as much in death and dying as in birth and growth. If death is seen as a part of life in a natural yearly cycle of proclaimed truth, the reality of death will not be so forbidding when it comes into every person's life. We cannot be fully alive until we have faced the reality of our aging and death.

Making Connections

When we learn of a death, we say "Rest in peace." We write obituaries and eulogies that celebrate the life of the deceased. We think "May your memories bless you." We tend to think of saints as those who have already departed this life. Every day we encounter saints who offer a smile, a kind word, a helping hand, and solidarity with our human condition. Share a compliment, thank a store employee, give a big grin to a parent shopping with children to spread the cheer and encourage another person. Be the saint that blesses others with your gift of human solidarity.

Engaging All Ages

All Saints' Day as well as the commemoration of All Faithful Departed or All Souls' Day is a good time to examine how world cultures experience life and death. *Dia de Los Muertos* (Day of the Dead), which is a Mexican tradition, is happening around this same time. The United States just celebrated Halloween. Halloween is a scary time filled with frightening ghosts. But All Saints' Day does not lift up the dark and ugly truth of death as much as celebrates the joy of life. You honor saints in heaven by acknowledging that you are a saint on earth and eternally connected.

Hymns for the Day

The Hymnal 1982
Christ the Victorious, give to your servants 358
For all the saints, who from their labors rest 287
For the bread which you have broken 340, 341
For thy dear saints, O Lord 279
From glory to glory advancing, we praise thee,
     O Lord 326
Give rest, O Christ 355
Jerusalem, my happy home 620
Let saints on earth in concert sing 526
All glory be to God on high 421
By all your saints still striving (All Saints' Day) 231, 232
Give us the wings of faith to rise 253
Glorious things of thee are spoken 522, 523

Hark! The sound of holy voices 275
Hearken to the anthem glorious 240, 241
Holy God, we praise thy Name 366
Jerusalem the golden 624
My God, how wonderful thou art 643
Nature with open volume stands 434
O God, we praise thee, and confess 364
Sing alleluia forth in duteous praise 619
Who are these like stars appearing 286
Ye holy angels bright 625
Ye servants of God, your Master proclaim 535
Ye watchers and ye holy ones 618
Ancient of Days, who sittest throned in glory 363
Jesus, the very thought of thee 642
Blessed Jesus, at thy word 440
Blest are the pure in heart 656
Lord, make us servants of your peace 593
Rejoice, ye pure in heart 556, 557
Remember your servants, Lord 560
Tis the gift to be simple 554
All who believe and are baptized 298
Baptized in water 294
Come away to the skies 213

Lift Every Voice and Sing II
Taste and see 154
We shall overcome 227
We'll understand it better by and by 207
Children of the heavenly Father 213
Baptized in water 121

Wonder, Love, and Praise
All who hunger gather gladly 761
Give thanks for life 775
No saint on earth lives life to self alone 776
I will bless the Lord at all times 764
Sing alleluia forth in duteous praise 777
Beati 828
Gracious Spirit, give your servants 782
You shall cross the barren desert 811
Baptized in water 767
I believe in God Almighty 768, 769
You're called by name, forever loved 766

Weekday Commemorations

Monday, November 2
All Souls/All the Faithful Departed

The New Testament uses the word "saints" to describe all members of the Christian community; in the Collect for All Saints' Day, the word "elect" is used similarly. From very early times, however, the word "saint" was applied primarily to people of heroic sanctity, their deeds recalled gratefully by succeeding generations. Beginning in the tenth century, the custom began to set aside another day on which the Church recognized the whole body of the faithful, unknown to the wide fellowship of the Church, a day to remember family and friends who have died. During the Reformation, observance of this day was abolished, but Episcopalians, redefining its meaning, include it as optional observance on their calendar.

Tuesday, November 3
Richard Hooker, Priest and Theologian, 1600

Born in 1553 near Exeter, he was admitted in 1567 to Corpus Christi College, Oxford of which he became a Fellow ten years later. Ordained in 1581, he served in a number of parishes but is noted for his comprehensive defense of the Reformation settlement under Queen Elizabeth I. His masterpiece, Laws of Ecclesiastical Polity, states that all positive laws of Church and State are grounded from Scripture revelation, ancient tradition, reason, and experience. Book Five of the Laws is a massive defense of the Book of Common Prayer, directed primarily at Puritan detractors.

Friday, November 6
William Temple, Archbishop of Canterbury, 1944

As bishop and later as archbishop, William Temple committed himself to seeking "the things which pertain to the Kingdom of God." He understood the Incarnation as giving worth and meaning not only to individuals but to all of life. A prolific writer on theological, ecumenical, and social topics, his two-volume *Readings in St. John's Gospel*, written in the early days of the war, became a spiritual classic. Temple was appointed Archbishop of Canterbury in 1942 and reached an even wider audience through his wartime radio addresses and newspaper articles.

Saturday, November 7
Willibrord, Bishop and Missionary, 739

While studying in Ireland for a dozen years (678–690), Willibrord heard a call to missionary work. Born in Northumbria (about 658), he was educated at Bishop Wilfrid's monastery at Ripon. In 690, he set out with 12 companions for Frisia (Holland); the area, though pagan, was increasingly being dominated by Christian Franks. Bishop Wilfrid and a few English people had delved in this mission field unsuccessfully, but, aided by the Frankish rulers, Willibrord established a base at Utrecht. Thus, Willibrord prepared the way for Boniface's greater achievements. Pope Sergius ordained him a bishop in 695. Three years later, Willibrord founded the monastery of Echternach, near Trier, where he died.

Pentecost

The Twenty-Third Sunday after Pentecost: Proper 27

November 8, 2020

Being ready for judgment means striving for justice and righteousness.

Color   Green

Preface   Of the Lord's Day

Collect

O God, whose blessed Son came into the world that he might destroy the works of the devil and make us children of God and heirs of eternal life: Grant that, having this hope, we may purify ourselves as he is pure; that, when he comes again with power and great glory, we may be made like him in his eternal and glorious kingdom; where he lives and reigns with you and the Holy Spirit, one God, forever and ever. *Amen.*

Readings and Psalm

Joshua 24:1–3a, 14–25

In our Hebrew scripture lesson, **Joshua, like Moses before him, acts as a mediator between the people of Israel and God at Shechem.** He calls them to reaffirm their covenant with the Lord. It was at Shechem that God first spoke to Abraham in Canaan, and at Shechem that Jacob abjured his family to "put away the foreign gods among you." Joshua recalls the Lord's faithfulness through history and his consistent benevolence toward Israel. The choice is stark, for the Lord demands entire devotion; all other deities must be shunned and put away. In language reminiscent of treaty documents of the period, the people swear their loyalty to God.

Psalm 78:1–7

The psalm recalls Israel's trials and the Lord's sustaining grace in the wilderness after the escape from Egypt.

or

Wisdom of Solomon 6:12–16

Our first lesson portrays Wisdom as a radiant and virtuous woman who should be wholeheartedly pursued. Those who seek for Wisdom will find her; she will meet them in their every thought. This book emerges from Hellenized Judaism in the first century before Christ. It is attributed to Solomon because of its deep concern for the pursuit of understanding and wisdom among those striving to be faithful to God.

or

Amos 5:18–24

In this Hebrew Bible lesson **the prophet proclaims that the day of the Lord will be a day of deep gloom. God despises the ceremonies of his people and calls for a continuous stream of justice and righteousness.** In this era people looked forward to "the day of the Lord" as an annual time of festival and also a symbol of the great final day when God would make all things well. How wrong they are! It will be a day of darkness, not light. No matter where a man turns, disaster awaits him. The Lord is done with rites without righteousness, and religiosity as a substitute for equity.

Wisdom of Solomon 6:17–20

A yearning after wisdom prepares the soul for eternal life.

or

Psalm 70

A prayer for help and vindication.

1 Thessalonians 4:13–18

In this reading **Paul offers a vision of how the dead in Christ will rise and then, together with those who are alive, be caught up to meet the Lord in the sky.** Apparently some members of the Thessalonian church had died, and there was this concern: would they miss the Lord's coming? First, Paul reminds them that the Christian hope is rooted in the God who raised Jesus. He then describes the day of the Lord's appearing and the raising up of the dead and the living, using highly poetic imagery conditioned by the worldview of his time. The essential meaning is clear: we shall be with the Lord.

Matthew 25:1–13

Our gospel is **the parable of the wise and foolish maidens—those prepared and unprepared for the bridegroom's coming.** In several ways the details of the story may strike us as odd and even a little unfair, but such a concern misses the main point, which has much in common with other of Jesus' parables. One must at all times be ready with repentance and decision for the kingdom's coming. In a later period this story was read with allegorical overtones. Jesus is the bridegroom whose return is delayed. Some in the church are falling asleep while others remain expectant.

Prayers of the People

We offer our prayers in the presence of Wisdom, who makes herself known to all who seek her gifts, responding, "Lord, hear our prayer."

In thanksgiving for our church school teachers, who awaken in their students the mystery of faith: Yaweh's great acts of deliverance, Christ's victory of life over death, and the eternal light that breaks through every darkness; let us pray.

Lord, hear our prayer.

Keep us ever watchful for your face shining through the faces of the poor and downtrodden, the wait staff and the salesperson, the toll collector and the crossing guard, lest that in missing them we may not see you; let us pray.

Lord, hear our prayer.

Place your wisdom in the heart and mind of our President and Governor, that the decisions they make this year may bring righteousness and justice to all peoples everywhere; let us pray.

Lord, hear our prayer.

Inspire us with a sense of urgency, that we may relate to others the joy of a Christ-centered life, welcoming others into our fold, and showing increase in the household of faith; let us pray.

Lord, hear our prayer.

In thanksgiving for those who have served in the armed forces, defending our country in times of war, and ensuring peace in places where there is instability; let us pray.

Lord, hear our prayer.

In thanksgiving for those who have died, especially during military service, may they and all the faithful departed live with the Lord forever; let us pray.

Lord, hear our prayer.

As we await the coming of the Bridegroom, let us be attentive through the continuation of our prayers. *(Special intentions of the congregation, the diocese, and the Anglican Communion may be added here or before the formal intercessions.)*

The Celebrant adds a concluding Collect.

Images in the Readings

The **wedding feast** is a biblical image for our life with God, and Christians have used the image as one way to describe holy communion. Philipp Nicolai's hymn "'Sleepers, wake!' A voice astounds us" (Hymnal 82, 61 and 62), is a fine example of the use of marriage imagery. In biblical times, a wedding was not about personal choice and lavish expense but about the communal celebration of the promise of new life and commitment.

Christians have used the **lamp** as an image for the word of God, with which we see God's way. Many Christians use oil as part of the ritual of baptism.

Pentecost

When Amos writes of the **waters** and "ever-flowing stream," Christians think of the water of baptism, which means to carry us, in the ship of the church, into a life of justice and righteousness.

Many Christians have literalized Paul's eschatological imagery of Christ's **appearance** in the skies, an **archangel**, a **trumpet**, and **clouds**. Recall that for Paul, this picture fit scientifically with his understanding of the universe. For us it does not, and to be Christian does not mean to hide in archaic thinking. Thus we need use care when citing this first-century picture of the end of all things. We repeat Martin Luther: "What is this? What does this mean?"

Ideas for the Day

♦ How do you travel? Do you bring along everything you could possibly need? Or do you make do, getting what you need along the route? The reason to practice exercises of fellowship, study, prayer, and sacrament regularly (in smooth and easy times) are so we are prepared with the skills of faithfulness when the going gets rough. Our lessons are leaning into the eschatological—the last things—to prepare (if asked) to whom and what is our allegiance. Are you prepared to follow Jesus with light into the darkness? Perhaps the advice from this gospel lesson is to not only pack light, but to bring a light.

♦ The parable of the bridesmaids and their lamps is difficult because it seems to support the notion that it is okay to be selfish. The parable seems to say that some are in and some are out. And finally, the parable seems to suggest that Jesus will forget your name and not even know who you are. What we do know is that being selfish is not appropriate. We know that with the love of Jesus, all are welcomed and included. And we are aware that Jesus knows the name of even the lost sheep. As we come to shorter days and longer nights, perhaps the message is simple: Pay attention. Be aware, for miracles happen even in the dark.

♦ All three readings focus on the coming of light out of darkness, the coming of Christ in glory, and on the last judgment. We live in the light of the resurrection and the final judgment. Hope and judgment characterize the outlook of the church as it proclaims Christ to the world.

Making Connections

The Apostles' Creed and the Nicene Creed affirm the resurrection of the dead and the final judgment: "He will come again in glory to judge the living and the dead, and his Kingdom will have no end" (BCP, 359). The joy of the resurrection is also reflected in the traditions of Christian burial. See the rubric that begins, "The liturgy of the dead is an Easter liturgy. It finds all its meaning in the resurrection. Because Jesus was raised from the dead, we, too, shall be raised" (BCP, 507).

Engaging All Ages

"We do not want you be uninformed . . . about those who have died, so that you may not grieve as others do who have no hope." All Saints' Day, All the Faithful Departed or All Souls' Day were recent dates on the church calendar. Maybe you thought about loved ones who have died. It often happens during those times. Perhaps now is a good time to have an open conversation about death, especially if you have any young people in your life unaccustomed to death. Inform them of death's reality. Help them to hope in a God who promises more than death.

Hymns for the Day

The Hymnal 1982
O heavenly Word, eternal Light 63, 64
Guide me, O thou great Jehovah 690 [SC]
O God of Bethel, by whose hand 709 [SC]
Praise our great and gracious Lord 393 [SC]
Before thy throne, O God, we kneel 574, 575 [GR]
Judge eternal, throned in splendor 596 [GR]
The Lord will come and not be slow 462 [GR]
Jerusalem, my happy home 620
Jesus came, adored by angels 454
Jesus lives! thy terrors now 194, 195
Let all mortal flesh keep silence 324
Lo, he comes with clouds descending 57, 58
Rejoice, the Lord is King! 481
Lift up your heads, ye mighty gates 436
Once he came in blessing 53
Rejoice! rejoice, believers 68
"Sleepers, wake!" A voice astounds us 61, 62

Lift Every Voice and Sing II

Wonder, Love, and Praise
Even when young, I prayed for wisdom's grace 906 [GR]
Signs of ending all around us 721 [GR]

Weekday Commemorations

Monday, November 9
Richard Rolle 1349, Walter Hilton 1396, and
Margery Kempe c. 1440, Mystics

Rolle, Hilton, and Kempe developed the English mysticism that influenced Anglican spirituality. Rolle (b. 1290), a hermit and spiritual director, wrote widely and was read widely on theology and spirituality. Hilton (b. 1340) was a hermit then an Augustinian canon at a Nottinghamshire priory; in his great work, *The Scale of Perfection*, he addressed the "luminous darkness" between loving oneself and God. Kempe (b. 1373), an illiterate mother of probably 14 with her husband John, dictated *The Book of Margery Kempe*, which explored her mystic visions as well as her pilgrimages (Canterbury, Santiago de Compostela), and her compassion for sinners.

Tuesday, November 10
Leo of Rome, Bishop, 461

Unanimously elected Pope in 440, Leo's ability to preach is shown clearly in the 96 sermons that exist to this day in which he expounds doctrine, encourages almsgiving, and deals with various heresies, including the Pelagian and Manichean systems. His letter to the Council of Chalcedon in 451 dealt effectively with the doctrine of the human and divine natures of the One Person of Christ. With similar strength of spirit and wisdom, Leo negotiated with Attila when the Huns were about to sack Rome, as well as other barbarians who sought to pillage and burn this city.

Wednesday, November 11
Martin of Tours, Bishop, 397

Martin, a patron saint of France, was born (about 330) in Hungary; he grew up in Italy, where he served in the army. He finally settled in Poitiers because he admired Hilary, the bishop. Hilary ordained Martin to the presbyterate about 350. Inspired by the monastic movement stemming from Egypt, Martin established a hermitage near Ligugé. Elected Bishop of Tours (372), he agreed to serve only if allowed to retain his asceticism. His monastery at Marmoutier, near Tours, influenced the development of Celtic monasticism in Britain. Martin was not popular among his fellow bishops partially because he opposed their violent repression of heresy. His shrine at Tours became a secure sanctuary for seekers of protection.

Thursday, November 12
Charles Simeon, Priest, 1836

Simeon's influence on Christian life was greater "than any primate," according to historian Thomas Macaulay. Simeon converted in 1779 while a student. His first communion depressed him, based as it was on a devotional tract, "The Whole Duty of Man." While preparing for communion before Easter, he read Bishop Thomas Wilson's *Instructions for the Lord's Supper*, wherein he recognized a truth: the law cannot make one righteous; only faith can enable a worthy communication. He experienced communion as the marriage of peace and exhilaration. That led to his becoming leader of the evangelical movement in the Church of England and his founding of the Church Missionary Society. His sermons were consistently biblical, simple, and passionate.

Saturday, November 14
The Consecration of Samuel Seabury, 1784

Seabury could not—would not—swear allegiance to the English crown. He had sailed for England in 1783 after the American Revolution to seek episcopal consecration in England, but as an American citizen, he refused to swear. He turned to the Non-Juring bishops of the Episcopal Church in Scotland: he was consecrated on Nov. 14, 1784, as the first American bishop of the Episcopal Church. When he returned to these shores, he was recognized as Bishop of Connecticut, and with Bishop William White, he helped organize the Episcopal Church at the General Convention of 1789. He kept his promise to persuade the American church to adopt the Scottish form for the celebration of Holy Eucharist.

Pentecost

The Twenty-Fourth Sunday after Pentecost: Proper 28

November 15, 2020

Being ready for the final judgment.

Color   Green

Preface   Of the Lord's Day

Collect

Blessed Lord, who caused all holy Scriptures to be written for our learning: Grant us so to hear them, read, mark, learn, and inwardly digest them, that we may embrace and ever hold fast the blessed hope of everlasting life, which you have given us in our Savior Jesus Christ; who lives and reigns with you and the Holy Spirit, one God, forever and ever. *Amen.*

Readings and Psalm

Judges 4:1–7

In this lesson from the Hebrew Bible **the Israelites prove unfaithful to the Lord, going after foreign gods and doing what is evil in God's sight.** In consequence, they fall under the oppression of the Canaanite King Jabin and the commander of his army, Sisera. The Lord raises up for the Hebrew people Deborah, a prophetess, to arbitrate for justice among them. Deborah, a gifted leader, is inspired to liberate the Israelites from their Canaanite overlords and summons the warrior Barak. Deborah commands Barak in the name of the Lord to gather warriors against the superior chariots and troops of Sisera, confident that God will grant the Israelites success.

Psalm 123

Those who are lowly and scorned place their trust in the merciful Lord.

or

Zephaniah 1:7, 12–18

In this opening lesson **the prophet proclaims the hastening approach of the day of the Lord, a day of judgment and fearful distress.** Zephaniah calls for silence as the Lord prepares what will be a sacrifice of terror. Everywhere in Judah there is corruption. People are drunk with wine and say that the Lord will do nothing, either good or bad. But they will never enjoy their wealth, nor will their silver or gold be of any use. The portrayal of the end is vivid and terrifying.

Psalm 90:1–8 (9–11), 12

The psalmist reflects on the passing character of human life in the face of the Lord's wrath, and asks the everlasting God for wisdom to make use of the time.

1 Thessalonians 5:1–11

In this reading **Paul counsels the new disciples to be alert as in the daylight, for the day of the Lord will come swiftly and unexpectedly, although at a time unknown to mortals.** Many early Christians believed that the course of world history would soon come to an end. Paul urges the Thessalonians not to live like people of the night, but soberly and expectantly. Whether they first die or remain alive they may look forward, not to God's wrath, but to a salvation that has been gained through Jesus. Paul's central point remains valid for us: we do not know when the consummation of history will take place, but are to live always prepared for judgment.

Matthew 25:14–30

Our gospel is **the parable of the servants who made different uses of the money entrusted to them.** The evangelist intends the story to be instructive to Christian disciples. The master Jesus is now away. When he returns, he will expect his followers to have made diligent use of the faith he has left in their charge. If it has not grown, then it has been without value and will be taken away. One also recognizes how immense are the sums left with the servants. The parable warns against the false security of only guarding the traditions and not investing them in life and in others.

Prayers of the People

Let us rise from our spiritual complacency and offer our prayers to God, responding, "Lord, hear our prayer."

That our local and federal judges may have the wisdom of the prophet Deborah, whose strength was revealed in passing judgment for condemnation when necessary and for growth when warranted; let us pray.

Lord, hear our prayer.

That we may clothe each other with faith and love, hope and salvation, encouraging one another in discipleship and building up one another for the growth of Christ's Body, the Church; let us pray.

Lord, hear our prayer.

That we may expose our gifts to the light of day, using them as instruments of salvation for those who live on the margins of society, and for those who though rich, have an emptiness too painful to expose; let us pray.

Lord, hear our prayer.

That our treasures of time and money may be used wisely, to our personal benefit and for the betterment of our Church and society; let us pray.

Lord, hear our prayer.

That we may humbly open our hands to receive the Bread of Life, and joyfully drink the Cup of Salvation, becoming one with Christ in his death and risen life; let us pray.

Lord, hear our prayer.

That all who have died may come to the glory of that place where the noise of daily life has given way to the peace of eternal rest; let us pray.

Lord, hear our prayer.

Trusting in the One who sweeps away our sins and invites us to begin again, let us continue our prayers. *(Special intentions of the congregation, the diocese, and the Anglican Communion may be added here or before the formal intercessions.)*

The Celebrant adds a concluding Collect.

Images in the Readings

It is interesting that our English word **talent,** meaning ability, comes from interpretations of this parable. Christians believe that God's creation is ongoing, that every human capability is a gift from the Creator, and that we are called to use all of God's creation wisely.

Zephaniah's litany describing **a day of wrath** continues in our time especially in popular disaster movies. Humans continue to be fearful of an unknown future. When Christians gather on Sunday before an image of the crucified Christ, we acknowledge our fears, and protecting ourselves with the breastplate and helmet of the faith, we join together hoping for God's mercy.

Paul likens the coming of the end to **labor pains.** With the pregnant woman, we hope that the pains will lead to life. The infant will come into the light.

Ideas for the Day

♦ There are formal church seasons, like Advent and Easter. They get colors and festivals. Then there are the informal church seasons, like fall. During this "ordinary time" we typically hear lessons about property and stewardship, lessons about what we own and what owns us. This parable ask questions: What are you going to do? What are you going to trust, when everything else is pushed out of view? It seem judgmental, but this is a Kingdom parable, a reign of God parable, a radical invitation to live into the last things which is going to demand some deciding. God wants to know our passion for God's estate, our generosity to God's creation, and wants to know of our love and trust in the Owner in the testimony of how we lived.

◆ At one time you may have tried to read the Bible from beginning to end. Certainly the first two books are a fairly easy read. We know the stories, and we have seen the movies. Then it gets somewhat boring (for many). There are a lot of lists and a lot of laws. And then we get to the book of Judges. We find a lot of fighting and a lot of what is called unfaithfulness. Then we come to chapter 4 and the women, Deborah and Jael, are introduced. For two whole chapters we are shown the power of two women (not men) who are intentional about doing what is right. We need to pay attention to the final verse at the end of chapter 5 where it says "and the land had rest for forty years."

◆ We have the responsibility to use our talents to mirror God's creative action in the world. What we do shows forth the glory of God, no matter how insignificant we think our actions might be. We must face the consequences of our failure to mirror God's creation, whether through our fear or rebellion. We face these consequences individually and as a nation and society.

Making Connections

Today's Collect addresses how God continues to speak to us through the Bible. In "An Outline of the Faith" (The Catechism, BCP, 853), we have the church's explanation of what we believe the Bible to be—the Word of God.

Engaging All Ages

"Blessed Lord, who caused all holy Scriptures to be written for our learning: Grant us so to hear them, read, mark, learn and inwardly digest them…" Did you hear this prayer in church today? For the next several worship services bring a Bible, notebook, and pen or pencil. During readings, open the Bible and follow along. You can find the chapter and verse in your bulletin most likely. Take notes. What words or phrases stand out to you? Write down any questions or thoughts you have. Keep and return to chew over these notes throughout the days and weeks ahead.

Hymns for the Day

The Hymnal 1982
O Christ, the Word Incarnate 632
Word of God, come down on earth 633
Open your ears, O faithful people 536 [SC]
Before thy throne, O God, we kneel 574, 575 [GR]
O God, our help in ages past 680 [GR]
The Lord will come and not be slow 462 [GR]
Awake, O sleeper, rise from death 547
Eternal Ruler of the ceaseless round 617
Hark! a thrilling voice is sounding 59
I want to walk as a child of the light 490
From glory to glory advancing, we praise thee,
    O Lord 326
Lord Christ, when first thou cam'st to earth 598
Not here for high and holy things 9
O Jesus, I have promised 655
Once he came in blessing 53
Rise up, ye saints of God 551
Strengthen for service, Lord 312

Lift Every Voice and Sing II

Wonder, Love, and Praise
With awe approach the mysteries 759 [SC]
Signs of ending all around us 721 [GR]

Weekday Commemorations

Monday, November 16
Margaret of Scotland, Queen, 1093
Scotland's most beloved saint was an English princess when King Malcolm married her about 1070. She devoted her queenly life to country, Church, and family (this conscientious wife bore eight children). She considered practices among Scottish clergy to be old-fashioned and sloppy: Lent should start on Ash Wednesday not on the following Monday; the Lord's Day was for applying "ourselves only to prayers." She encouraged the founding of schools, hospitals, and orphanages, and she provided opportunity for her servants to worship. She influenced Malcolm, who trusted her political judgment, to reach out to isolated clans, although she was not successful in ending their bloody warfare. Malcom and Margaret rebuilt the monastery of Iona.

Tuesday, November 17
Hugh of Lincoln, Bishop, 1200

Born into a noble family at Avalon in Burgundy (France), Hugh become a canon regular at Villard-Benoit near Grenoble. About 1160 he joined the Carthusians, the strictest contemplative order of the Church and later became their procurator. Reluctantly, he accepted the invitation of King Henry II to come to England as prior of a new Carthusian foundation, and later reluctantly accepted the King Henry's appointment to the See of London in 1186. Respected for his humility and tact, his total lack of self-regard, and his cheerful disposition, he was loved for his constant championship of the poor, the oppressed, and outcasts, especially lepers and Jews.

Wednesday, November 18
Hilda of Whitby, Monastic, 680

Born in 614, Hilda lived chaste and respected for 20 years at the court of her great-uncle, King Edwin. Bishop Aidan was so impressed with her holiness of life that he recalled her to her home country in East Anglia and the next year appointed her Abbess of Hartlepool. There, Hilda established the rule she had been taught by Paulinus, a companion of Augustine of Canterbury, and by Aidan. She became renowned for her wisdom, eagerness to learn, and devotion to serving God. Later, she founded the abbey at Whitby for nuns and monks to live by her strict rule. Hilda was sought by royalty and public servants for her advice and counsel.

Thursday, November 19
Elizabeth of Hungary, Princess, 1231

Born in 1207 in Bratislava, the daughter of King Andrew II of Hungary married Louis IV in 1221, then bore three children. Elizabeth, who had always been concerned with the poor and ill, was attracted to the Franciscans, who arrived in the Wartburg in 1223 and directed her spiritually. Louis allowed her to spend her dowry for almsgiving. In 1226, during a famine and epidemic, she sold her jewels to establish a hospital, which she supplied by opening the royal granaries. When Louis died in 1227, the court opposed her "extravagances," forcing her to leave. She eventually donned the habit of the Franciscans. With Louis of France, she shares the title of patron of the Third Order of St. Francis.

Friday, November 20
Edmund, King, 870

At 15, Edmund ascended the throne of East Anglia and ruled as a Christian for 15 years before Danish armies invaded England in 870. The Danes burned monasteries and churches, among other murdeous atrocities. The leaders confronted Edmund and demanded he acknowledge their supremacy and forbid the practice of Christianity. Edmund refused. His army fought bravely against the Danes, but King Edmund was eventually captured; according to the account by Dunstan, Archbishop of Canterbury 90 years later, Edmund was tortured, beaten, shot with arrows, and beheaded. His remains were enshrined in a Benedictine monastery now called Bury St. Edmunds; this place of pilgrimage honors a saint steadfast in faith and to his people.

Saturday, November 21
Mechthilde of Hackeborn and Gertrude the Great, Mystics and Theologians, 1298 and 1302

This pair of Benedictine nuns lived at St. Mary's Monastery in Helfta, known for encouraging the sisters' knowledge. Mechthilde (b. 1240) grew up pious and noble in Germany. Impressed with her abbess sister's convent library, Mechthilde refused to return home. She was well educated there and came to direct the choir and the library, illuminate manuscripts, and write (*Book of Special Grace*). Gertrude was given as a child to Mechthilde to raise at Helfta. Gertrude's writing, including *The Herald of Divine Love*, manifests her education with fluent Latin and extensive familiarity with Scriptures and Christian authorities.

Pentecost

The Last Sunday after Pentecost: Christ the King

November 22, 2020

This day is often referred to as the Sunday of Christ the King, or The Reign of Christ, meaning that Jesus stands above all earthly power and authority.

Color   White

Preface   Of the Lord's Day

Collect

Almighty and everlasting God, whose will it is to restore all things in your well-beloved Son, the King of kings and Lord of lords: Mercifully grant that the peoples of the earth, divided and enslaved by sin, may be freed and brought together under his most gracious rule; who lives and reigns with you and the Holy Spirit, one God, now and forever. *Amen.*

Readings and Psalm

Ezekiel 34:11–16, 20–24

In our opening reading **the Lord promises to be the shepherd of the people.** God will bring them home and heal them. God will feed and protect them. The exile of Israel is coming to an end. Ezekiel has prophesied against the false shepherds, the rulers who only fed off the flock. Now God will tend the sheep who have been dispersed and preyed upon, but the overfed will be judged.

Psalm 100

A call to praise and to offer thanksgiving to the Lord.

or

Psalm 95:1–7a

A call to worship the Lord our God.

Ephesians 1:15–23

In this lesson **Paul gives thanks for the faith and love of the Ephesians and prays that they may see with their inward eyes the power of God, who has raised and enthroned Jesus far above all earthly and heavenly dominions.** How vast is the treasure that God offers to those who trust in the Lord! The Lord Christ now reigns as head of the church, which is his body and which experiences the fullness of his love.

Matthew 25:31–46

Our gospel presents **a picture of the universal judgment when the Son of Man, acting as judge and king, will separate humankind into two groups: those who have cared for the Lord in the needy, the stranger, and prisoners—and those who have not.** On one level the evangelist intends those in need to be understood as Christian disciples. But the bringing of all peoples into judgment has caused Christians to realize that the Christ is to be recognized in every individual. Beneath this awareness lies a profound theological mystery: the likeness of God, which has been decisively revealed in the human person of Jesus, may be perceived in each human being.

Prayers of the People

Jesus the Christ, you reign in glory as our King, and to you we lift our voices in prayer, saying, "Lord, hear our prayer."

That we may serve God with gladness and generosity, discovering his likeness in those who hunger and thirst, in those who are threadbare and in prison, and in those who are sick, lonely, depressed, sorrowful, and rejected; let us pray.

Lord, hear our prayer.

For the forgiveness of our sins, the times when we were blind to the needs of others, and deaf to their shout for assistance, that we may move beyond our selfish greed and love with the measure that Jesus loves humanity; let us pray.

Lord, hear our prayer.

That the leaders of our Church may receive the immeasurable greatness of God, seeking the holy way with every step they take, guiding the faithful and those who have strayed into the glorious dwelling place of divine love; let us pray.

Lord, hear our prayer.

For the sea and the dry land, molded by the Creator's imagination, that we may cherish the gifts they bring forth, and be good stewards of their fragile ecosystems; let us pray.

Lord, hear our prayer.

That the sin of division may be lifted from family life, and from wherever it fractures the bonds of affection or movements toward peace, that forgiving what is past and trusting in God's future, we may work to reveal the kingdom in our time; let us pray.

Lord, hear our prayer.

That the righteous dead may live into eternal life, and that those who have gone astray may receive the mercy of the Maker; let us pray.

Lord, hear our prayer.

Rejoicing in the reign of Christ over all creation, let us continue our prayers. *(Special intentions of the congregation, the diocese, and the Anglican Communion may be added here or before the formal intercessions.)*

The Celebrant adds a concluding Collect.

Images in the Readings

Calling this Sunday Christ the **King** may elevate that image above all others. Currently on the world scene some nations have rejected monarchies, some maintain figurehead monarchs, and some, while not using the term king, maintain heads of state with absolute, even ruthless, power over the people. The Bible promises that God's power and majesty differ radically from the reign of most human monarchs. Thus we need to use the image of King as correcting the image of king. Several hymns do a splendid job of playing the image against itself. As an example of how God's reign differs from that of human monarchs, the baptized saints receive riches and power from God. Some churches prefer the phrase "the Reign of Christ" as stressing the activity, rather than the status; unfortunately English has the problem of the homonym "rain."

In the Bible, written within a culture that treasured its pastoral past, **sheep and goats** are images of the life God gives to the people. Like sheep and goats, we are created by God to live together and offer ourselves for others. It is an urban prejudice to defame sheep as dirty and stupid.

Matthew's parable was depicted in sculptures over the main doorway and in wall paintings over the chancel of countless Christian churches, and one can imagine the fun that artists had in shaping the monsters on the left side of Christ the **judge**. As this imagery becomes less important for some Christians, it is important not to lose the biblical call that we saints are to live out the justice that God intends, serving each needy person who is Christ-for-us.

As the first-century decades progressed, **saints** became an increasingly common term for the baptized people of God. The usual English translation of "being personally holy," the word "saint" is used differently by the several Christian branches. In Ephesians, everyone who is enlightened is called saint, the meaning most Protestants have retained.

Pentecost

Pentecost

Ideas for the Day

♦ It isn't simple to follow the lead of God, to acknowledge our relatedness and reliance as well as our dependence. Especially for people who enjoy the blessings of the status quo, it may be slow to relinquish one's self-determination. However it is this letting go that prepares us for the season that comes next, that expectant desire for Jesus' full and glorious incarnation. Giving our allegiance over to the reign of Christ is being in solidarity with the weak, exiled, persecuted, and challengers of evil across time and place. It is putting our heart, soul, and faith in solidarity with God's ways and prerogatives rather than our own.

♦ We have spent a little more than six months making our way through Matthew's Gospel. We discovered a lot of teaching, some parables, and conflicts with authority. The twenty-fifth chapter of Matthew is the cornerstone for many as what a life with Jesus is all about. We can say that we are followers of Jesus, but unless we are actually reaching out and naming the humanity of *every* human being, we have simply missed the point. We don't have to like everyone, but we do need to love them. The journey is about figuring out the infinite number of ways to love.

♦ The earliest Christian creed, "Jesus is Lord," means that Jesus stands above all other earthly power and authority. All through history and into the present moment, choosing God above earthly authority has caused persecution and conflict in the life of the church. The congregation and wider church must witness always to the authority of Jesus Christ, realizing that there will be times when conflict will be the direct result of such a witness.

Making Connections

Some of the traditions in the Episcopal Church have their origins in the royal court. For example, purple—the color for Advent and Lent—was the color associated with royalty and became linked to the coming of Christ as king. We seek the Kingdom of God, where we will feast at the banquet table of the Lord. In the age to come, Christ will reign, and God's will will "be done on earth as it is in heaven."

Engaging All Ages

Today is the feast of Christ the King. Talk about kings you know of from history or kings/queens alive today. Discuss what it means to be a good king. Was Jesus a good king? This is the last Sunday in the liturgical year, but hold on to this image of Jesus Christ the King. As a new year begins and you start moving from Advent toward Bethlehem, baby Jesus being born, and then moving toward and passed Lent and Easter, death and resurrection, and all the other events, try to keep in mind throughout the year the full story.

Hymns for the Day

The Hymnal 1982
Alleluia, sing to Jesus (vs. 1, 3–5) 460, 461
All praise to thee, for thou, O King divine 477
At the Name of Jesus 435
Hail to the Lord's Anointed 616
Jesus shall reign where'er the sun 544
King of glory, King of peace 382
Lead on, O King eternal 555
Let all mortal flesh keep silence 324
Ye servants of God, your Master proclaim 535
All people that on earth do dwell 377, 378
Before the Lord's eternal throne 391
Jesus, our mighty Lord 478
To God with gladness sing 399
All hail the power of Jesus' Name 450, 451
Crown him with many crowns 494
Hail, thou once despised Jesus 495
Lord, enthroned in heavenly splendor 307
Rejoice, the Lord is King 481
Christ is the King! O friends upraise 614
Father eternal, Ruler of creation 573
Lord, whose love through humble service 610
Praise the Lord through every nation 484, 485
Where cross the crowded ways of life 609

Lift Every Voice and Sing II
Soon and very soon 14
He is King of kings 96

Wonder, Love, and Praise
Cuando el pobre nada tiene / When a poor one who as nothing 802

Weekday Commemorations

Monday, November 23
Clement of Rome, Bishop, c.100

Little is known of the life of Clement, and what is known is contested. He is said to be the third bishop of Rome, after Peter and Linus, or the fourth, after Jerome. Clement, it is also said, was consecrated by Peter himself. Clement governed from 88 to about 100. As a disciple of the Apostles, he was active in the early church. He is generally regarded as having written a letter about 96 from the Church in Rome to the Church in Corinth. A younger group at Corinth had deposed the elder clergy, jeopardizing the Church. In response, Clement organized a hierarchical structure of Church authority, interchanging the terms "bishop" and "presbyter." This letter was rediscovered in 1628.

Tuesday, November 24
Catherine of Alexandria, Barbara of Nicomedia, and Margaret of Antioch, Martyrs, c. 300

Popular as Catholic saints, Catherine, Barbara, and Margaret attracted even Anglican devotion after the Reformation. The waxing and waning of their popularity parallel interest in female martyrdom, including recasting trauma so devotees may *want* to remember them. Catherine, a young scholar who rebuked the emperor for cruelty, was tortured on a spiked wheel that broke so was beheaded. Beautiful Barbara, locked in a tower, was available only to her pagan tutors so was educated; when she confessed to being Christian, she was executed. Margaret embraced Christianity at her nurse's breast; for her faith, Margaret was sorely persecuted and eventually executed.

Wednesday, November 25
James Otis Sargent Huntington, Monastic and Priest, 1935

Huntington, committed to active ministry based in the spiritual life, founded the first permanent Episcopal monastic community for men in the United States on those commissions. He was born in Boston (1854), graduated from Harvard, and studied theology in Syracuse, New York. He was ordained deacon and priest by his father, the first bishop of Central New York. Upon receiving a call to religious life, he resolved to found an indigenous American community. Beginning his common life at Holy Cross Mission on New York's Lower East Side, Huntington made his life vow on November 25, 1884. He increased his social witness to the Church by working with immigrants and for the single-tax and labor union movements.

Saturday, November 28
Kamehameha and Emma, King and Queen of Hawai'i, 1864, 1885

Within a year of ascending the throne in 1855, King Kamehameha IV and Queen Emma (each 20 years old) solicited funds to build a hospital in response to a smallpox epidemic. The people of Hawai'i, more accustomed to pomp than to humility in royalty, came to revere Emma and Kamehameha. In 1860, the king and queen petitioned the Bishop of Oxford to send missionaries to establish the Anglican Church in Hawai'i; the priests arrived in 1862 to confirm the queen and king. Kamehameha translated the Book of Common Prayer and the Hymnal. He died a year after his little boy. Emma declined to rule alone but chose to end her days in a life of good works.

Pentecost

Thanksgiving Day

November 26, 2020

The church recognizes the traditional Thanksgiving holiday as a holy day for our land, life, and heritage.

Pentecost

Color   White

Preface   Of Trinity Sunday

Collect

Almighty and gracious Father, we give you thanks for the fruits of the earth in their season and for the labors of those who harvest them. Make us, we pray, faithful stewards of your great bounty, for the provision of our necessities and the relief of all who are in need, to the glory of your Name; through Jesus Christ our Lord, who lives and reigns with you and the Holy Spirit, one God, now and forever. *Amen.*

Readings and Psalm

Deuteronomy 8:7–18

In the lesson from the Hebrew Bible **Moses addresses the people as they prepare to enter Canaan,** a productive and rich land where they will lack for nothing. As the people experience abundance they must not forget God, who has given them all things, nor imagine that it is only by their own strength that they prosper. The people must recall the lessons of the past, the commandments of the Lord, and the covenant they have sworn.

Psalm 65

A psalm of praise and thanksgiving to the savior, the mighty Lord, who creates the earth and causes it to bring forth abundantly.

2 Corinthians 9:6–15

In this epistle lesson **Paul encourages believers at Corinth to be generous in giving toward a collection that he is gathering for the relief of the church in Jerusalem,** mindful of how God has provided for the physical and spiritual needs of the Corinthians. A farmer who is stingy in sowing seed does not see great yield, but one who scatters seed freely enjoys a large harvest. In the same way free and joyful giving will bring reward. This summons to ministry is a test of their confidence in God, who will supply all things.

Luke 17:11–19

In the gospel story **Jesus' command brings about the cleansing of ten lepers, but only one, a Samaritan, returns to give thanks.** Jesus is on the way to his destiny in Jerusalem. The narrative illustrates the power of the reign of God to give a new lease on life. The lepers, who were formerly outcasts, would not be allowed to return home. Only a despised Samaritan recognizes that a life of gratitude and faith is now possible. Physical healing is but a first step. He becomes whole and finds salvation.

Prayers of the People

A Litany of Thanksgiving

Let us give thanks to God our Father for all his gifts so freely bestowed upon us.

For the beauty and wonder of your creation, in earth and sky and sea,

> *We thank you, Lord.*

For all that is gracious in the lives of men and women, revealing the image of Christ,

> *We thank you, Lord.*

For our daily food and drink, our homes and families, and our friends,

We thank you, Lord.

For minds to think, and hearts to love, and hands to serve,

We thank you, Lord.

For health and strength to work, and leisure to rest and play,

We thank you, Lord.

For the brave and courageous, who are patient in suffering and faithful in adversity,

We thank you, Lord.

For all valiant seekers after truth, liberty, and justice,

We thank you, Lord.

For the communion of saints, in all times and places,

We thank you, Lord.

Above all, we give you thanks for the great mercies and promises given to us in Christ Jesus our Lord;

To him be praise and glory, with you, O Father, and the Holy Spirit, now and for ever. Amen.

Images in the Readings

We are **lepers**; this is true: our very bodies are dying, little by little. Most of us are also **Samaritans**; this is true: we are seen by at least some others as not religiously pure enough. So in this worship service and with our entire lives, we are to praise God with a loud voice.

Paul's use here of the image of the **seed** can be applied to the New Testament's metaphor of the Word of God as seed. God provides the seed in the hearts of the baptized, and that seed grows in order for its fruit to be shared with others.

The **good land**, as the Deuteronomy passage calls the Promised Land, has been interpreted in the church as our life together in the faith. The land with the flowing streams, vines, and wheat: these can have not only literal reference to a contemporary life of plenty, but to the gifts of God that are realized in faith. But millions of people in the world, including many Christians and perhaps some worshippers present, are not eating their fill (Deut. 8:10).

Ideas for the Day

♦ All the lessons push into our lives with the Word of God and ask revealing questions. Have we lived as if we know that all is God's and all goes back to God? The fall decor and game times only sort of block the darker truths that also come to our tables: truths about our lack of generosity and unforgiveness and the terror of religious dissenters who risked the wild unknown rather than stay at home and the trauma that caused for indigenous peoples. What is it about the holidays that are supposed to be beautiful but somehow seem to bring out the broken in us?

♦ Thank you. Gracias. Grazie. It is easier in Spanish or Italian to see the word "grace" in the word for "thank you." The Eucharistic Prayer is a Prayer of Thanksgiving. Every time we express our thanks to God, we start the glorious cycle of a holy conversation and dance with God. We say thank you, and we see grace. If we do it enough, it turns out it can be the same thing, the same action.

Making Connections

A young child, before the advent of language skills, squeals her gratitude with delight and joy while eating a ripe fruit, its juices flowing down her chin and hands, wonderful physical sensations and emotional satiety filling her up. A parent and child leap with joy and excitement to greet a military spouse returning from a long deployment. Gratitude is more than just an attitude of thanksgiving for all the blessings we enjoy. Gratitude is ultimately an acknowledgment of God's desire that everyone come to the knowledge of the truth that God intends the goodness of Creation for the enjoyment of all humankind. We are created for community.

Engaging All Ages

God gives abundantly. This is the theme in all the scriptures today. It is Thanksgiving after all. A holiday when people gather with their families. There is often a moment when you are told, "Say something you are thankful for." The response may come easy, or it may come with a groan. Sometimes overflowing and sometimes a quick one-word answer. In the United States, it is really a holiday that seems to celebrate the success of the American Dream. But are there things in your life you can only attribute to God's blessing? Name them.

Pentecost

Hymns of the Day

The Hymnal 1982

All people that on earth do dwell 377, 378
As those of old their first fruits brought 705
Come, ye thankful people, come 290
For the beauty of the earth 416
From all that dwell below the skies 380
Glory, love, and praise, and honor 300
Now thank we all our God 396, 397
Praise to God, immortal praise 288
We gather together to ask the Lord's blessing 433
We plow the fields, and scatter 291
When all thy mercies, O my God 415
For the fruit of all creation 424
I sing the almighty power of God 398
Let us, with a gladsome mind 389
O all ye works of God, now come 428
Seek ye first the kingdom of God 711
Sometimes a light surprises 667
Holy Father, great Creator 368
To God with gladness sing 399
By gracious powers so wonderfully sheltered 695, 696
Commit thou all that grieves thee 669
Jesus, all my gladness 701
Joyful, joyful, we adore thee 376

Lift Every Voice and Sing II

Give thanks to the Lord for he is good 93
God is so good 214

Wonder, Love, and Praise

Let all creation bless the Lord 885
O all ye works of God, now come 884

INDEX OF SEASONAL RITES

Index of Seasonal Rites

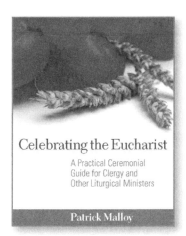